Liberty and Reformation

in the Puritan Revolution

Liberty and Reformation

in the Puritan Revolution

WILLIAM HALLER

PROFESSOR EMERITUS OF ENGLISH IN BARNARD COLLEGE

COLUMBIA UNIVERSITY

FELLOW OF THE FOLGER SHAKESPEARE LIBRARY

IN LITTERIS LIBERTAS

1754·1893

COLUMBIA UNIVERSITY PRESS

New York and London

To

THE MASTER AND FELLOWS

OF EMMANUEL COLLEGE

'*In piam memoriam fundatoris nostri*'

Acknowledgments

THE account of Puritanism here presented is based directly upon my reading of the printed tracts, sermons, and other literature of the period, as I have indicated in the notes. The notes are intended to give a fair sampling of the material I have examined but not a complete record. I have worked from the published catalogues of the Thomason Collection in the British Museum and the McAlpin Collection in the Union Theological Seminary. Most of my reading has been done in the British Museum, the Library of the Union Theological Seminary, the Huntington Library, and the Folger Shakespeare Library. To the officials and attendants of these institutions I am indebted for many services and courtesies. The John Simon Guggenheim Foundation and the Folger Shakespeare Library have helped me to find leisure to complete the writing of this book. To the numerous scholars and critics who have written about Milton and the Puritan Revolution I owe more than I have been able to acknowledge in detail. For the general outline of events I have depended mainly upon S. R. Gardiner, whose work, when all necessary allowance is made for changes in interest and point of view since the nineteenth century, still commands confidence and admiration. For biographical information I have turned often to the *Dictionary of National Biography*, most often and with greatest profit to articles signed with the initials of C. H. Firth. For information about Milton I have made use of Masson's *Life* with the necessary reservations and corrections. I am grateful to the many friends who have so encouragingly read what I have written or listened while I talked about the subject of this book. I am especially grateful to Kathrine Kollar, Leonard P. Trinterud, and Willson H. Coates for many valuable suggestions. My debt to Louis B. Wright and to Godfrey Davies for wise counsel on all these and many other matters is great and of long standing. Malleville Haller has as always been my most constant critic and assistant.

WILLIAM HALLER

The Folger Shakespeare Library
August, 1953

Contents

Foreword

FROM its beginning in the early days of Elizabeth the Puritan movement had two distinct though closely related objectives. The Puritans sought to push reform of government, worship, and discipline in the English church beyond the limits fixed by the Elizabethan settlement. In this purpose they failed, and if this had been all, Puritanism would never have become the revolutionary force it proved to be in the life of the English people and of people within the English tradition throughout the world. But though the hope of the Puritans was to reconstitute the ecclesiastical organization of society, their overriding endeavor at all times was as they said to preach the Word, and this they were never effectually or completely kept from doing. Hence the Puritan movement developed down to the outbreak of revolution in 1640 not only as a campaign for reorganizing the institutional structure of the church but also as a concerted and sustained enterprise of preachers for setting forth in the pulpit and the press a conception of spiritual life and moral behavior. Puritanism in this sense was not incompatible with any given ecclesiastical system, episcopalian, presbyterian, or congregational, so long as its promoters were left free to preach. It was in fact nothing but English Protestantism in its most dynamic form, and before it had run its course, it had transfused in large measure the whole of English life.

In *The Rise of Puritanism* in 1938 I gave an account of the writings and ideas of Puritan preachers and their adherents from the time of the Elizabethan settlement to the breakdown of episcopal authority in the early days of the Long Parliament. My intention was to continue the account in another volume down to the climax of the revolutionary movement in 1649. The present work, delayed and otherwise affected by the revolutionary disturbances of our own time, may be taken as the fulfillment of that intention. The scope and aim of the work should be clearly understood. It is not to rehearse again the story of the struggle between the king and parliament or of the accompanying controversy over church government. But against the background of these events, my purpose is to present the history of the discussion which ensued when in November, 1640, all restraints on pulpit and press came suddenly to an end and preachers found themselves free as they had never been before to expound the Word in confident expectation that the long-awaited reformation of the English church was at last to be accomplished and that reformation in England would lead to the reformation of the church throughout the world and so to the final redemption of mankind.

To understand the history of ideas it is not sufficient, however, merely to trace the passage of certain general notions from mind to mind or from printed page to printed page. It is also necessary to take account of the interplay of ideas and experience, more often than not of old ideas and new experience, in the lives of the people concerned. If men may be said to find meaning in experience by the help of ideas, they may also be said to discover meaning, often new and surprising meaning, in ideas by the light of experience. The liberty which came so suddenly to the Puritan preachers in 1640 was full of implications they had not anticipated. The perfect reformation for which they had so long been striving, though seemingly within their grasp, had still to be achieved. But freedom, which was to have been the fruit of reformation, was now the condition under which reformation had to be accomplished if at all. For the light of the Word was not to be reserved to the preaching order alone. The Word as given had become accessible to all who could read, and all were in effect free to make of it what they would according to their own notions of truth and for their own ends. And to the Word was added the illumination which came from many other books now also in English print. The argument initiated by the preachers was at once taken up by all sorts and conditions of men in churches and conventicles, in streets, shops, taverns, law-courts, and jails, in parliament, the assembly of divines, and the army. Most important, it was carried on more and more by all parties in the press, which no power in church or state, try as it might, was able to deny to anyone really determined to make use of it. There had been revolutions in England before this but never one in which the press had been at so many men's command. And never one in which so many men found themselves so full of ideas concerning the nature of man and the structure of human society.

The purpose of the narrative presented in these pages is to follow the argument thus induced as it proceeded from situation to situation, crisis to crisis, in the revolution which began with the convening of parliament in 1640 and came to its climax with the fall of the monarchy and the disruption of the church in 1649. The story opens after its Scottish prelude with the Puritan preachers calling upon parliament to cast off the authority of bishops and erect a godly preaching ministry throughout the realm. Parliament responded as civil war got under way by calling upon the preachers and their Scottish brethren to draft the long-looked-for scheme of reformation by the process of free discussion by the light of scripture. But free discussion in the assembly of divines soon led to disagreement concerning the nature and extent of the reformation intended, and disagreement grew more acute and profound the longer discussion continued. Some were for setting strict bounds to liberty in order to secure order and unity. Others were for running all the risks of difference and disunion in order to preserve and extend freedom. But the dispute was such as no assemblage of churchmen could any longer keep to themselves. Discussion spread to the press and the public. Men of varying interests and tempers, such as John Goodwin, Roger Williams, Henry Robinson, William Walwyn, Richard Overton, and John Milton were soon raising questions as to the scope and function of liberty within the framework of society which went far beyond the expectations of the original champions of reform—liberty of conscience, of thought and expression, of preaching and the press, of religious and political association, of legal status, of economic enterprise and social opportunity. The effect was to set Puritans of all sorts at odds among themselves, to put the central corps of ministers on the defensive, and in the end to discredit them and their cause. As the arena of discussion shifted and spread, spiritual leadership passed to men of bolder temper. In London it was taken up by unorthodox preachers like John Goodwin and his disciples and by popular agitators and party organizers like Lilburne and Walwyn. In the army it was seized by visionaries and enthusiasts such as Saltmarsh and Dell or by such pragmatic executive saints as Cromwell, Ireton, and Peters. The question was no longer how to reform the church under the conditions brought about by revolution but how, under those conditions and with the church disrupted, to establish and maintain some sort of spiritual unity and constitutional order in the community. This was the issue at stake in the final contention between the victorious army on the one hand and king, parliament, and the Presbyterians on the other. It was still the issue in the debate between the army commanders led by Cromwell and Ireton and the levellers and agitators led by Lilburne and Wildman. And when all argument was brought to a halt by the army in January, 1649, the issue was still unsettled.

The excesses of the Puritan spirit, especially in its later manifestations, have given Puritanism a bad name even among the legitimate heirs of the Puritan movement. I have not thought it necessary in these pages to reassure myself or my readers of the correctness of familiar traditional judgments on these battles long ago. It has seemed to me more useful to treat revolutionary Puritanism not as a great madness or a great wickedness, which it may have been, but as a great dynamic force, which it certainly was, in the corporate life of the English people. It was, if I may say so, such a cyclonic shattering storm of the spirit as that by which we have been beset in our own time. I have tried to address myself to the question, how did the Puritan Revolution come to pass? What induced these men to think as they did? What in intelligible human terms did they suppose they were trying to accomplish? How does it happen that, in spite of everything about them which repels us, they still retain their hold upon imagination and belief? I cannot pretend to have answered these questions once for all. I have, however, tried to describe Puritanism as Puritans themselves conceived and expressed it, to bring them credibly before the reader, to suggest something of the color and drive of their thinking and of their characters, to present them in their human predicaments without sentimentality or condescension.

I have given particular attention to Milton's part in all this. It is true, as we shall see, that his tracts had little immediate effect, and that he and his ideas were little regarded until he came forward in 1649 as the assailant of royalism on behalf of the Commonwealth. Nevertheless his participation in the argument for liberty and reformation was a fact of quite extraordinary significance in the history of that argument. He brought the highest intellectual and literary culture of Renaissance and Reformation to the support of the Puritan cause. In greatness of spirit his only peer among immediate contemporaries was Cromwell; in vigor and originality of mind his only peer was Hobbes; as a writer he was without equal. When the other advocates of revolution were silent in the grave, his writings carried the enduring ideas of Puritanism to later generations. He transmuted its human meaning, its noblest ardors and its most tragic flaws, into great and enduring poetry.

It seems best to conclude this foreword on a note of caution. The participants in the argument which is my subject were occupied with many matters which still deeply concern us, and they said much that seems apposite to our own problems. We must not, however, make the laboring disputants of the Puritan Revolution out to be more consistent speculative thinkers than they probably were or than men in such situations commonly are. They thought of many things which still give us reason to ponder, but they did not necessarily think them through to the conclusions which seem obvious to us. They were men pleading and arguing often at cross purposes concerning issues the implications of which they did not wholly understand, certainly did not understand alike, and in conclusion they found themselves still at odds. Having sought liberty, expecting reformation, they found that they had achieved not reformation but only liberty, without which, however, no reformation was possible at all. This was not the New Jerusalem but something like the modern English state.

Liberty and Reformation
in the Puritan Revolution

I

A Godly Preaching Ministry

1638-1641

i. KIRK AND COVENANT

THE story of the argument concerning liberty and reformation in the Puritan Revolution begins with the Scots.[1] No Tudor had sprung up in Scotland to organize the state, reduce the feudal nobility to order, rally the gentry and the middle class about the crown, attach the church to the monarchy, and assert national independence. The crown had fallen in 1542 to a child and a woman, a Catholic, reared in France, and married to the heir to the French throne. Control over the authority of the state became under successive regencies a prize for the contention of rapacious vassals and venal churchmen with parliament serving whatever faction of lords and prelates happened to be in the saddle at the moment. Hence, while the English were learning to look to the throne for security, the people of Scotland continued the victims of feudal anarchy.

The leaders of the movement which brought these conditions to an end were the reformers who came back to their native land at the time of the accession of Elizabeth to the English crown. Like English reformers of the same date, they are commonly referred to as Calvinists, but they must be thought of as Calvinists with a difference Calvin himself might not have approved. Protestantism in England and Scotland had roots which reached back into the native past beyond Luther and Calvin. Protestant exiles from both countries found refuge in various places besides Geneva and came under various influences besides that of Calvin. In any case our concern in these pages will be not with the sources whence ideas may have been drawn but with the ideas themselves and the meaning they came to have in the circumstances of men's lives. To reformers both Scots and English the ideas of greatest importance were, to begin with, those they held in common with one another and with Protestants in general. They believed that the scriptures contained a perfect rule of life for all to follow in family, church, and state, a rule to be comprehended by the exercise of reason in the spirit of faith and to be made known through the arts of discourse. They believed in the spiritual equality of all men before God and in the possibility of a spiritual election transcending all other distinctions between man and man. They tended to conceive of the visible church less as a hierarchy descending from the apostles than as a communion of the elect coming together in mutual understanding and agreement. They inclined more and more to the idea that the church is an independent domain of the spirit to which rulers as well as other men, elect and reprobate, are subject and which the magistrate is bound to respect and support. Its sovereign, they held, was Christ, and Christ's people, sharing equally in his grace, had authority to choose whom they would to teach, care for, and govern the church in his name. Upon his second coming, which they believed to be certain and perhaps imminent, the saints were destined with him to rule the earth, the earth to be redeemed, and the power of Antichrist to be overthrown.

Yet how far, how fast, and with what effect upon society in general Protestant reformers were able to apply these ideas to the reorganization of the actual church depended everywhere upon circumstances which were nowhere the same. In England Elizabeth took the Protestant side but kept control of the church in her own hands and made the crown the symbol and instrument of national unity and independence. In Scotland Mary followed a course which subordinated Scottish to foreign interests and kept her people in turmoil. Reformers in England, soon to be called Puritans, were prevented from taking over the government of the church but were not persecuted or denied opportunity to preach so long as they refrained from challenging the authority of the queen and her bishops. Reformers in Scotland on the other hand had from the start to face the danger of repression and persecution by the crown. The outcome in England was that the main body of Puritans put aside their hopes of immediately reforming church government and devoted themselves over the years to preaching and to building up a powerful if unacknowledged preaching order within the church. But the outcome in Scotland was that the reform clergy entered at once upon a long struggle with Mary and her successors for control of the church and the nation which led finally to the discomfiture of Charles by his Scottish subjects in 1638.

English sympathy for the Scots on that occasion did not arise from much knowledge or approval of the work of Scottish reformers in reorganizing the structure of the church or the mode of worship. It was due to the resounding effect with which the leaders of the kirk, from Knox to Henderson, had voiced a conception of the responsibility of rulers which the English now found supremely apposite to their own situation. Knox, from demanding instant reformation of the church, had gone directly on to claim for the church and of course its ministers authority to call rulers to account under the law of God on the people's behalf. According to his own report, he told Queen Mary in 1561 that 'Subjects, having power, may resist their Princes,' whenever princes command that which God forbids. For it is with princes, he said, as it is with parents who would slay their own children. They are as though mad, 'and therefore to take the sword from them, to binde their hands, and to cast them into prison . . . is no disobedience against Princes, but just obedience, because that it agreeth with the Word of God.' The astonished queen replied, 'Well, then I perceive that my subjects shall onely obey you, and not me; And shall do what they list, and not what I command, and so must I bee subject unto them, and not they to me.' Knox replied, 'My travell is, That both Princes and subjects obey God.' [2] The well-known but disputed principle thus dramatically stated, which the champions of Mary's own church also put forward against her great rival in England, had been presented by the Scottish humanist, poet, and historian, George Buchanan, in the form of a classical tragedy on John the Baptist, written while the author was in exile at Bordeaux in 1539–1542 and published in 1578–1579. It was presented again but more explicitly in Buchanan's dialogue published in the same year, *De jure regni apud Scotos*, and it was illustrated at appropriate points in his *Rerum scoticorum historia* (1582) as well as in Knox's own *Historie of the Reformation* (1587).

In 1567 Mary was declared to have forfeited her throne and was succeeded by her infant son. There followed another of those periods of inner contention which had for generations plagued the Scottish people, one turbulent faction of nobility ranged against another, the French interest against the English, Catholic against Protestant. But in the course of this struggle the reformers steadily extended their hold upon the church and the church's hold upon the people. In the Second Book of Discipline, approved by the General Assembly of the church in 1581 under the leadership of Andrew Melville, the reform party worked out a comprehensive scheme of church government which became the prime instrument for bringing unity and discipline to a people who had had their fill of rapine and disorder. But the struggle was not yet over. James, coming to manhood with his eye constantly on the English crown, naturally regarded presbyterianism with its conception of the church as an independent spiritual power with authority to hold kings to account before God as a challenge to royal supremacy. He had been exposed to the tutelage of Buchanan and the admonitions of Melville, but he liked the instruction he received from those worthies no better than his mother had done that of Knox. Growing up to be a scholar and a theologian in his own right, he argued that kings owed their authority only to God and were responsible to no other power. Growing up also to be a master of intrigue under the hard conditions of Scottish politics, he determined to get the better of the ministers and impose his own will upon the church. In 1592 he was compelled to approve an act of the Scottish parliament ratifying presbyterianism, but in the years succeeding he labored to undo that decision, and in 1616 he came back from England to force a General Assembly at Perth to reinstitute bishops and follow modes of worship conforming to English use. But the ministers had done their work too well. Neither James nor his successor was able really to alter the character which the kirk had imposed upon Scottish life. Bishops or no bishops, the hold of the ministers upon their people remained substantially undiminished, and the presbyterian system remained sufficiently intact to be used by them in the direction and expression of the popular will. To what purpose and with what effect, Charles and his subjects south of the border were now to learn.

In England, by the beginning of 1638, Charles had apparently succeeded in reducing both church and state to his personal rule. He had checked the gentry who opposed him in parliament; he had repressed the preachers who refused to yield to Laud in the pulpit;

he had punished the pamphleteers who assailed the policies he approved; he had apparently made good his claim in the ship-money case to raise money without parliament's consent. Meanwhile he had alienated the Scottish nobility by seeking to recapture ecclesiastical lands which had been expropriated to their advantage, and his final move was to impose a version of the English prayer book upon the kirk, thus at one stroke overriding religious conviction, economic interest, and established legal procedure. The result was rioting in Edinburgh and a general outcry for recall of the new prayer book. The king's refusal to heed this demand at once provoked nobles, gentry, commoners, and ministers to bind themselves by a National Covenant to defend each other and the 'true religion, liberties and laws of the kingdom . . . against all sorts of persons whatsoever.' [3] Charles thereupon reluctantly consented to the calling of a general assembly of the kirk at Glasgow in November. This body immediately struck at the bishops as agents and creatures of royal authority in the church and was at once ordered by the king's commissioner to dissolve. Alexander Henderson as moderator, however, declared that, although they acknowledged 'the power of christian kings for convening assemblies, and their power in them, yet that must not derogate from Christ's right, for he hath given warrant to convocate assemblies whether magistrates consent or not.' [4] With that, in defiance of the king's commands, the assembly voted to abolish prayer book and prelacy, to expel from the kirk all who refused to swear to the National Covenant, and to call for a parliament to ratify these acts. Finally, asserting the authority of the kirk to convene a general assembly once a year or oftener, it summoned another meeting to be held at Edinburgh in the following July.

The defiance of his commands by the Glasgow Assembly provoked Charles to march a half-hearted army to the border in the spring of 1639 only to encounter a Scottish host arrayed against him. The result was an uneasy truce at Berwick in June and the king's return to London seeking expedients to undo the reverse he had suffered. He called parliament (April 13, 1640) but almost as soon dismissed it (May 5), and in August marched another army north only to be again repulsed. This time, however, the Scots crossed over to English ground and refused to go home until their expenses were paid. 'Now,'

Milton says, 'finding the whole English nation enraged, and justly, to the last degree against him,' [5] Charles summoned another parliament —the Long Parliament—which convened on November 3, 1640.

The meaning of the Scottish revolt to Milton and his countrymen at this stage of affairs should not be misunderstood. In Scotland the imperative need had been to secure the freedom and therefore the solidarity of the church as the effective organ of spiritual life within an unstable social and political order. The need was not, as it became in England, to gain freedom and security for men of divers minds and divergent interests within a national order which as yet no one thought of questioning or disturbing. In the hard conditions of Scottish existence, presbyterianism with its close-knit theocracy seemed the answer to Scottish needs. But what won English attention and approval at the outset of the Puritan Revolution was not presbyterianism as such but the effective resistance which, under presbyterian leadership, the Scots had been able to put up against arbitrary authority, the vigor and clarity with which they asserted the historic and timely doctrine of the responsibility of rulers. The spirit, ideas, and even the phrases of Knox and the sixteenth-century reformers resounded in the declarations of Alexander Henderson at the Glasgow Assembly and in the manifestoes and pamphlets which he and his associates issued during the succeeding months in the hope of winning the support of the king's English subjects to their cause. Again secular authority had to hear it said that magistrates were made by the people, not the people by the magistrates, that although the people were bound to obey their rulers, they were bound first to obey God, that rulers were bound to obey the ten commandments and the laws of the realm, and that if they did not do so, the people were required in the nature of things to defend themselves as best they could. Private persons might not rebel, but if a whole people took up arms to preserve justice and religion, that was not disobedience but true obedience. [6]

Clarendon testified years later to the effect of such arguments in England in 1639. [7] Their purport was as obvious to Charles as it had been to his grandmother. 'The aim of these men,' said a royal proclamation in February, 1639, 'is not Religion . . . but it is to shake all Monarchical Government.' The question, it was said, was not whether the prayer book was to be admitted or the church to be governed by bishops or presbyters, 'but whether We are their King or not.' The Scots were, moreover, accused of striking at 'the very Root of Kingly Government' by defying the royal prerogative over the press. 'For whereas the Print is the King's in all Kingdoms, these seditious Men have taken upon them to print what they please, though we forbid it; and to prohibit what they dislike, though We command it.' [8]

There were other features of the Scottish system which many besides Charles were certain to dislike when they became better acquainted with it. Milton, for one, still had much to learn about 'new Presbyter' and 'Scotch what d'ye call.' In a few years he would be rebuking the Scots for their unwillingness to follow their own principles clear through to the conclusion reached in 1649, principles, he was to remind them, which at the beginning of the common struggle had been set out by 'Scotchmen of best repute . . . as if they labour to inform us what wee were to doe, and what they intended upon the like occasion.' [9] But at the beginning he endorsed their position in the quarrel with the king, and he praised his own countrymen for scorning Charles's poor attempt 'to make a *Nationall Warre* of a *Surplice Brabble, a Tippet-scuffle,*' or to engage them in so unworthy a purpose 'as to force upon their *Fellow-Subjects,* that which themselves are weary of, the *Skeleton* of a *Masse-Booke.*' For Milton at this stage, as for the Scots, the problem of the church came first, that is to say, the problem of delimiting and coordinating the civil and spiritual authorities in the nation. The worst effect of royal tyranny in suppressing parliament had, in his opinion, been the subjection and corruption of the church, and the necessary first step toward reform of both state and church was the liberation of the church. In this the Scots seemed to be pointing the way, and he exhorted the two nations to go forward together—'the *Praise* and *Heroick Song* of all Posterity'—united not by military conquest but by the settling of 'the *pure worship* of God in his Church, and *justice* in the State.' [10]

ii. THE ENGLISH CHURCH AND THE PURITAN BROTHERHOOD

Parliament convened on November 3, 1640, in order to receive the king's request for money to pay off the Scots and send them home. But Charles was allowed to escape from his difficulty only by plunging into still greater ones. He came back from the border to face the gentry who, with their kinsmen and allies the lawyers and merchants, had been growing rich, numerous, and bold under his father and the Tudors. Entrenched in parliament they now took advantage of his predicament in order to attack the authority of the crown itself and assert the supremacy of parliament in the government of both state and church. Before they would settle with the Scots, they sent one of his chief ministers to the block, the other to the Tower charged with treason. They forced him to approve an act for triennial parliaments and another forbidding the dissolution of the present parliament without its own consent. They compelled the abolition of the courts of Star Chamber and High Commission. They made clear their determination to reduce if not to abolish both the civil and ecclesiastical power of bishops, named by the crown. They also made clear their unwillingness to entrust him with independent command of money or an army. Consequently by the end of 1641 Charles had to choose either to surrender ancient prerogatives of the crown or to resort to the use of force.

But just as the crisis had been brought to a head by Scottish resistance to royal authority in the kirk, so the great dispute that followed between Charles and the English parliament centered finally upon the question of the church, how it should be governed, by whom, and to what end. The conception of the church which filled the minds of the English Puritans at the opening of the Long Parliament was not the same as that which moved the Scottish Presbyterians at the Glasgow Assembly. It drew from some of the same sources, but the Reformation in England had developed differently. English reformers at the accession of Elizabeth had not been permitted to gain control of the church or make over its government. Elizabeth, by maintaining the hierarchy, kept control of the ecclesiastical state in her own hands, and the authority of the church extended far. The bishops ordained the clergy and issued or withheld license to preach. The Archbishop of Canterbury and the Bishop of London were entrusted with authority over the press, and Laud took a prominent part in the Court of Star Chamber, which had the duty of enforcing that authority. The church in Convocation, meeting concurrently with parliament, had power to make decrees binding the clergy and to enforce them through the Court of High Commission. The church through its courts exercised jurisdiction over marriage and inheritance. It directed education. All these functions and the functionaries involved were supported independently of parliament from endowments and fees, and although many parish livings were impoverished, the great sees and cathedral establishments still commanded substantial wealth. The bishops, finally, as spiritual peers, made up about a third of the membership of the house of lords and so were in a position to exercise a check upon the action of parliament.

Thus control of church government as established under Elizabeth remained firmly in the power of the crown. Yet, though English reformers were prevented from instituting presbyterianism, they were far from being completely suppressed. They were not permitted to rule, but neither were they ruthlessly driven out or totally silenced, and so long as they refrained from opposing the government by law established, they enjoyed a wide if undetermined degree of freedom to edify the spirits of men in their own way. A few, growing impatient for perfect reformation in their own time, now and then broke away from the church and in one way or another suffered the fate of reformers who will not tarry for the magistrate. Yet notwithstanding the fame that overtook them in later times, they did not become numerous or important until after 1640. Up to that time, the main body of Puritans kept within the church, or thought of themselves as seeking to do so, content to move as circumstances permitted toward the fulfillment of their hopes. In the meantime, under Elizabeth and James and even in some measure under Charles and Laud, they were able to preach the Word, that is, to set forth in pulpit and press, not to be sure their notions for reforming church government, but their conception of spiritual life and the code of behavior that best expressed it.

By 1632 the Puritans had succeeded in establishing within the church a veritable though unacknowledged and unauthorized order or brotherhood of preachers, working in large measure independently of, though not in direct conflict with, constituted authority. Its members were linked together by ties of youthful association, kindred, friendship, and marriage as well as by conviction and interest. They looked mainly to Cambridge as their seminary and training-ground. They had the countenance and support of many of the peers and gentry, merchants and lawyers, of East Anglia, the midlands, London, and the home counties. They did not in most instances go directly from the university to undertake the cure of souls in the ordinary parish livings but, perhaps after an interval as chaplains or tutors in the households of sympathetic patrons, they commonly took up posts as 'lecturers,' that is to say, as preachers especially engaged to expound the scriptures to congregations served as to the ordinary offices by incumbents designated in the customary way. A lecturer might owe his appointment to the people of the parish, the corporation of the town, a self-appointed committee, or a patron. He had, of course, to be licensed to preach by the bishop of the diocese and so might have to submit to restrictions and harassments. But he was often able by the help of influential friends to circumvent such interference, and he was generally better paid for his services than the incumbent. He often fell heir in due course to the benefice. In any case his livelihood and success depended upon his ability to gain the approval and support of the people who paid him to dispense the Word in the pulpit. Bishop Montagu testified that 'the first, most hugged, followed, admired and maintained' sort of preacher was 'a super-inducted Lecturer in another mans cure and pastorall charge.' [11] Selden is reported to have said that 'Lecturers do in a Parish Church what the Fryers did heretofore, get away not only the Affections, but the Bounty that should be bestow'd on the Minister.' They 'preach the People tame,' he said, '[as a man watches a Hawk] and then they do what they list with them.' [12]

Such was the order which had sprung up in the church under the politic, unacknowledged, variable tolerance practiced by Elizabeth and not actually abrogated by her successor. James talked about harrying the Puritans out of the land but did them less harm by his fitful persecution than he did service by exacerbating Protestant sentiment in general. It remained for Charles to essay what his father never really attempted. The fact was that, if the Puritans had been allowed to continue their activities in the church, they might in a few years have commanded influence and resources greater than those of the establishment itself. By the time Laud came to power the London preachers and their supporters had organized a body, well supplied with funds but presently adjudged to be an illicit corporation, for the purpose of buying up impropriated tithes, not that they might be restored to the parish livings whence they were derived but that they might be used to provide lecturers wherever the Puritan leaders might determine. Charles was, consequently, compelled to take action against the Puritans if he was to maintain effective control of the church by the crown. The 'Feoffees for impropriated tithes' were suppressed. The universities were subjected to Laud's power of visitation. Lectureships and chaplaincies were forbidden. The writers of illicit pamphlets were prosecuted. Preaching in general was put under restraint. Convocation, finally, which met as usual at the same time as parliament in April, 1640, issued canons asserting the duty of absolute obedience to the crown and requiring 'all Bachelors or Doctors in Divinity,' together with certain other persons of formal education, to swear that they approved 'the Doctrine and Discipline or Government established in the Church of England' and that they would never 'consent to alter the Government of this Church, by Archbishops, Bishops, Deans, and Archdeacons, &c.' Continuing to sit, by royal command though contrary to custom, after the dissolution of parliament, Convocation also voted a subsidy or benevolence as support for the king in his contention with the Scots.[13]

The subsidy was, however, worth nothing without the concurrence of parliament, and the 'Et cetera Oath,' as it was called, was no effective counterstroke against the Scottish covenant. The failure of Charles's second attempt to reduce the Scots to obedience meant the defeat of his efforts to regain control of the church in either kingdom. But it brought the end of much besides. By January, 1642, the Long Parliament had demolished the main fabric of Tudor-Stuart monarchical authority and had laid the foundation for the parliamentary state of the future. To nineteenth-century historians this seemed the great positive accomplishment of the Puritan Revolution. 'Whatever had been done so far,' Gardiner wrote, 'stood the test of time'; whatever was attempted after 1641 to remold the institutions of national life fell into nothingness, and the rock of offense was the problem of the church.[14] Yet to repine, as Gardiner does, at the fact that the Long Parliament was not able to anticipate the Toleration Act of 1689 does not help us to understand the issues which divided men in 1641. Toleration, when it came, did not solve the problem of the church which troubled the Long Parliament; it merely enabled a later generation to get around a difficulty for which no remedy had been found. It did not reunite the people in the church; it merely set bounds to religious strife, and so released men's energies for other things. But in 1641 not many foresaw that the disruption they were witnessing in the historic ecclesiastical framework of society was to prove irreparable. Not many were prepared to think that the reconstitution of the state was of greater importance than the reform of the church or that the state's responsibility for religion would for the future be fulfilled when it had simply policed the anarchy into which the church had fallen.

The convening of a new parliament as the result of the king's failure to impose his will upon the church in Scotland was the signal for a popular demand for the reduction or abolition of prelacy in England. Since Elizabethan times prelacy had been the representative of royal authority in the church. Under Charles it had been used more and more as an instrument to advance the interest of the crown as opposed to that of the men who now controlled parliament, and bishops as spiritual peers were still able to impede parliamentary action hostile to the crown. The king's opponents were by no means all of them extreme Puritans, but when they came back to Westminster in November, 1640, they were determined to assert the power of their class and the authority of parliament in both church and state. Hence, without intending the destruction of episcopacy as an institution, they were nevertheless quite ready to take advantage of the outcry against the bishops in the expectation of wringing concessions from Charles in their struggle for power and position in the state and the community at large. What to do with the church, however, once the bishops had been rendered helpless in parliament, was a matter involving much more than the question of the clergy's position in the civil state, much more than the question whether the church should be governed by bishops approved by the crown or presbyters chosen by the people. The real problem was to determine how, by whom, and to what ends the spiritual life of the community in all its aspects was henceforth to be constituted and directed. On that problem the influence of the pulpit in the early years of the revolutionary crisis was of primary importance, and about that matter the writings, above all the sermons, of the Puritan preachers tell us more than the reports of speeches and debates in the house of commons.

The experience of the Puritan leaders, since the early days of the Elizabethan settlement, had brought them to a position as paradoxical as it was important in its effects. That spiritual life could exist on earth except as organized under a single comprehensive church was to most of the brotherhood still inconceivable. If their conscious expectations could have been fulfilled, the church, far from being disrupted by dissent or attenuated by toleration, would under their direction have been restored and strengthened, and its authority extended into the life of every individual. The disruption they promoted was the last thing they intended. Yet, while asserting nothing more earnestly than the necessity for government and the duty of obedience, they had been able to advance their cause only by acting independently of the government by law established in the church, circumventing it when possible and defying it when nothing else would serve. This they did in order that they might preach a doctrine and way of life calculated to invigorate an active independent religious faith in their followers. The result was that the Puritan preachers developed not into experienced ecclesiastical statesmen but into the evangels of a dynamic minority, a minority which tended, the more devotedly its leaders applied themselves to their task, to generate still other minorities within itself, up to the ultimate minority of one. They were in a word preachers, mendicant preachers at that, depending each man on his skill and address in the pulpit.

Laud's attempt to stamp out Puritanism by forbidding lectureships, by suppressing the scheme for supporting lecturers out of impropriated tithes, and by punishing critics who assailed his authority in the press merely served to spread the fire. One group of preachers led an exodus to New England and others betook themselves to the continent. The majority, too well entrenched to be easily uprooted, stayed more or less quietly at home, ready to resume activities in full whenever opportunity should afford. With the convening of parliament and the collapse of Star Chamber and High Commission, all restraints were suddenly removed, and the London preachers, their ranks increased by others coming back from abroad or up from the country to get themselves pulpits within earshot of Westminster, at once embarked upon a concerted effort to make permanent and secure the freedom which had been so providentially restored to them. For advancing their cause among the people their prime instrument was the pulpit. For controverting their opponents they made use of the press and of a style of discourse very different from that of the sermon. For bringing pressure to bear upon parliament, they resorted to the mass-petition, drafted and promoted by a self-constituted committee, subscribed by as many hands as could be got to sign, brought to the doors of parliament by noisy and sometimes riotous deputations of citizens, supported by seconding petitions from localities outside of London, and in most cases freely and promptly circulated in print. Such was the apparatus of propaganda available to the Puritans upon the convening of parliament and the break-down of control over pulpit and press.

The liberation of the pulpit, however, was parliament's first concern, and the sermons preached in and about London and Westminster, if we take pains to unravel their mystery, are the best clue to the understanding of much that was to follow as the revolution proceeded. Petitions to parliament were the fruit of preaching; pamphlets were at first mainly an auxiliary aid. The earliest recorded resolution of the house of commons in the Long Parliament called for a day of fasting, prayer, and preaching. November 17 was set as the date for this observance, and Cornelius Burges and Stephen Marshall were appointed to preach to the members at St. Margaret's, Westminster. The house also arranged to sit one afternoon a week as a committee for religion and another for the consideration of grievances. The business of both committees had chiefly to do, as was said, with driving dumb dogs out of the church and filling the pulpits with a godly preaching ministry. The day after that first of many fast days, Robert Baillie, newly arrived from Scotland, wrote to his wife a letter full of astonished delight. He appears to have thought that something like the Scottish National Covenant was about to be enacted before his eyes in England. He was soon to learn better, but the English were nevertheless going about their own affair in their own English way. 'The Toun of London,' he wrote, 'and a world of men, minds to present a petition, which I have seen, for the abolition of Bishops, Deanes, and all their aperteanances . . . Hudge things are here in working.' [15]

The First and Large Petition of the Citie of London and other Inhabitants thereabouts: For a Reformation in Church-government, as also for the abolishment of Episcopacie was presented to parliament by

Alderman Pennington and a company of fifteen hundred citizens on December 11. According to most reports, fifteen thousand names were attached to it, and the text was soon circulating in print in spite of the fact that the house ordered that only members were to have copies. It was quickly followed by a series of similar petitions from neighboring localities. Nor was this all. The preachers also circulated a number of petitions, apparently somewhat more moderate in terms but similar in substance, for signature among members of their own order, and at a meeting in London of perhaps eighty or a hundred of their number, they drew up a final version of their demands, including a remonstrance, and transferred to it the signatures they had collected. The honesty of these proceedings was questioned in the house, but spokesmen for the group made no concealment of what had been done, and there can be no doubt that the document in its final form, which we are told filled twenty sheets of paper, represented faithfully enough the desires of the group as a whole. It has not come down to us in print, but its tenor can be inferred from the debate which followed in the house and from another petition which the same men presented later in the year. With the names of nearly a thousand ministers attached to it, the petition of January 23 was presented to the house by Sir Robert Harley, attended by a number of 'the eldest and gravest' of the ministers, such men as Marshall and Calamy.[16]

The 'root-and-branch' petition of December 11 touched off the train of events which led finally to the disruption of church government, the confusion of civil war, and the attempt of one faction of the brotherhood of preachers to replace prelacy by an English version of presbyterianism. But these consequences of the preachers' activities were not among their conscious or expressed purposes at the beginning. They took the principal hand in initiating and fomenting the campaign against the bishops which began as soon as parliament assembled. And yet, finding themselves suddenly free to speak without restraint, the thought uppermost in their minds was to make certain not of ultimate command but of present freedom, not how to reconstruct and control the ecclesiastical state but how to promote preaching and protect and advance the preaching order. The appetite for power came to them naturally enough as events moved on. But up to this time, the function allowed them had been to preach, not to govern, and all they asked for at the moment was liberty to go on preaching. The mere power of God's Word in the pulpit, it seemed to them, had brought them to their present triumph. They asked for nothing more to overthrow the kingdom of Antichrist once and for all in England and if in England then surely in all the world.

Cornelius Burges and Stephen Marshall in their sermons on that first fast day of the Long Parliament spoke for the brotherhood of preachers but, more than that, for the English Protestant movement from the beginning.[17] Burges opened in the morning with Jeremiah's prophecy (Jer. 50; 5) that Babylon would fall when a nation out of the north had made her desolate and the people had turned back toward Zion, saying, 'let us joyne our selves unto the Lord in an everlasting Covenant.' The prophet goes on, as everybody knew, to lament that the people have been as lost sheep whom their shepherds had led astray. Marshall followed in the afternoon with the words of Azariah to Asa the king when the latter had destroyed the abominations of Rehoboam and overthrown Zerah the Ethiopian (2 Chron. 15: 2, 12): 'the Lord is with you, while yee bee with him, . . . but if yee forsake him, he will forsake you.' Again the preacher's hearers would have known that Israel had for a long season been without a teaching priest and without law but that now, the scriptures said, 'they entred into a covenant to seeke the Lord God of their fathers.' [18]

The word covenant bore a very special meaning of which no one in St. Margaret's church on that day was likely to be ignorant. It stood for an idea which had often been advanced in the pulpit in mitigation of the stark determinism of the pure doctrine of predestination but not of the responsibility placed upon the elect by the gifts and opportunities granted to them. True, God out of his free grace alone chose whomsoever he would to be saved, and no wish or merit in sinful man could affect divine judgment. Yet though the elect did not merit and could not earn or buy salvation, they were bound to work for it nonetheless, and their work was not unavailing. If they failed to strive for the redemption they believed was assured to them, they could be certain it was not to be theirs. If they did strive for it, they could be certain the Lord had it in store for them, and if it seemed slow and difficult of attainment, that was merely a sign that they must strive all the harder. For the elect were in covenant with the Lord and must beyond peradventure keep their part of the bargain if they expected him to keep his, as he would surely do if they never failed him even in the greatest trials.

Burges and Marshall left no room for doubt as to the relevance of this familiar doctrine to the situation in which members of parliament now found themselves. They were called by the Lord, they were in covenant, to rebuild Zion and overthrow false gods and their priests, assured that the Lord would bring to success the work he had appointed to be done whether they acted their part like the faithful servant in the parable or not. They might fail but not he. The covenant was, moreover, national as well as personal, binding them as Englishmen as well as saints. Burges and Marshall made much of the fact that the day of this the first fast day of the new parliament fell—they were certain by God's providence—on the anniversary of Queen Elizabeth's accession. The coincidence gave them their cue for calling up the legend of England's destiny, which, since Elizabethan days, Protestant Englishmen had been told was historic fact. All history, according to Foxe's *Actes and Monuments,* centered in the agelong struggle of Christ and Antichrist; the pope was Antichrist; and England, the elect champion of the true faith, was his chosen enemy, especially called by God to be the agent of his predestined overthrow. Henry VIII drove him out; Edward reformed the church; Mary brought popery back; Elizabeth 'that glorious Deborah' overcame the hydra of stout popelings at home and their supporters abroad. So in spite of all that Antichrist could do, the Lord, having delivered England out of Babylon, had then preserved her from Spanish invasion, gunpowder treason, and many other perils.[19] 'All the Nations in *Christendome,*' Marshall could say, 'have been in grievous perplexities many yeers round about us: we have bin hitherto kept as another Land of *Goshen,* where light hath still shined, when all others have been in darkness.' Yet God's favor to his elect people brought responsibility not to be forgotten. 'All your counsels and advising will bee nothing, if God say, *I will stay no longer in England,*' [20] and this he will surely do if parliament now fails to keep covenant with him and, in Burges's words, 'cast out all idle, unsound, unprofitable, and scandalous Ministers; and provide a sound, godly, profitable and setled Preaching Ministry in every Congregation through the Land.' [21] 'The preaching of the Word,' Marshall declared, 'is the *Scepter* of Christ's Kingdome, the *glory* of a Nation, the *Chariot* upon which life & salvation comes riding . . . if all the good Lawes in the world were made, without this, they would come to nothing; order what you can, leave this undone, you will never doe the thing you aime at.' [22] Whatever parliament may attempt for the people's good, the preaching of the Word must come first.

The 'root-and-branch' petition of December 11, to which the sermons of Burges and Marshall served as prelude, was already in circulation when these words were spoken at St. Margaret's. Its preamble begged that the government of the church as then constituted, 'with all its dependencies, rootes and branches,' might be abolished and 'the government, according to Gods word' established in its place. But how government according to God's Word was to be constituted, the petitioners did not specify. They recounted instead the 'many foule evils, pressures and grievances' in the church to which they had recently been subjected, the ignorance, corruption, and avarice of the prelatical clergy, the overinsistence on forms and ceremonies, the usurpation of secular authority, and the betrayal of the church to papists and to popish ways. The prelates were also blamed for patents and monopolies, for the increase of customs and taxes, for ship-money and 'many other great burthens upon the *Common-wealth.*' But the most numerous and significant complaints were directed at the restraint of 'Godly and able Men from the Ministry,' the hindering of godly books from being printed, and the suppression of the 'godly Design' for maintaining lecturers out of impropriated tithes. Finally came long and bitter protest, surely the work of some clerical pen, against the all-too-familiar apparatus of spiritual and intellectual tyranny, the 'reaching even to mens thoughts,' the 'suspending and depriving of Ministers,' the 'breaking up of Mens Houses and Studies,' the 'taking away Mens Books, Letters, and other Writings,' the 'separating between them and their Wives against both their Wills,' all 'to the utter infringing of the Laws of the Realm and the Subjects Liberties.' [23]

Nothing, however, in the petition of December 11 or in the supporting petitions that followed showed that its authors had as yet addressed themselves to the problem that must be faced once archbishops, bishops, deans, and archdeacons, with all their courts and canons, were swept out of the way of the brotherhood of preachers.

The Puritans proposed that the church should be reformed according to God's Word, and by that they no doubt meant that it should be governed by elders chosen by or in some fashion representing the people, but they were still a long way from any clear or workable plan for administering the ecclesiastical state. They had still to learn, if indeed they ever did learn, to think first of the church as a whole going concern rather than first or solely—as indeed they had been compelled to think—of themselves, of their own position in the church, of their order, of their converts and congregations, of the Word and that preached by one man in a pulpit. The Puritan brotherhood was the fruit of that liberty which had been tacitly allowed within limits under the Elizabethan compromise. It had grown up under conditions which allowed a man to take his own line in association with others like himself so long as he let the things of government alone. And so long as he was left free to edify the church invisible of the saints, what signified the church visible? Hence liberty, which the preachers had learned so well to take advantage of, was still first in their thoughts when government, having in the meantime reversed itself and grown oppressive, suddenly fell to pieces.

Few in the audience which heard Marshall and Burges on November 17, 1640, would have questioned the supreme need to promote preaching, and most would have agreed that the pretensions of bishops should be cut down. But parliament, though it set the pulpits free, could hardly take the single-minded view that that was all the situation required. The campaign for liberating the pulpit from prelatical control raised the whole question of government in the church, and to this question the brotherhood of the pulpit had no clear constructive answer. To be sure, the Scottish commissioners took pains to explain their system to the English in the press, and Baillie wrote home that everybody in London was 'for the erecting of a kind of Presbyteries.' [24] Moreover, Digby in the house likened the London petition to a comet with a terrible tail pointing toward the north. [25] But of the actual working of presbyterianism in Scotland neither parliament, if we may judge from the record of its debates, nor the preachers, if we may judge from their sermons and pamphlets, had any complete or detailed understanding. The preachers, as we have seen, were taken up with preaching. The leaders of parliament were bent upon pressing its claims against the crown, and though they were willing to take advantage of attacks on the bishops, they were not ready to sweep away the existing system of church government without knowing how, by whom, and in whose interest the ecclesiastical state would then come to be administered. They had little love for bishops and no violent objection on principle to presbyterianism, but they did have an apprehension of anarchy and a determination that control over the establishment should neither be allowed to lapse nor be entrusted to any power they could not themselves control. First of all, it must not be left to Charles, and hence the clergy must be stripped of temporal authority. But though presbyterianism in some form was the commonly accepted alternative to prelacy, not even the prelates' worst enemies in the house of commons were inclined to hand over to an irresponsible theocracy the authority they had just struck from the hands of a hierarchy responsible only to the crown. Digby expressed what was in many minds when he said that 'instead of every Bishop wee put down in a Diocesse, wee shall set up a Pope in every Parish.' [26] Whatever form of government for the church might finally come to be agreed upon, parliament was determined not to relinquish its own ultimate control. Hence the question of church government could never be settled until the question of government in the state was settled, and every attempt to force the issue led that much nearer to the final break between the king and parliament.

The break came with the Grand Remonstrance at the close of 1641, and with it the climax to the first stage in the struggle of the Puritan brotherhood to establish its ascendancy in the church. In August Charles had gone off to Edinburgh to try his fortune once more with the Scots, and he had dispatched thence a defiant communication in support of episcopacy. Then on November 1 news reached London of rebellion in Ireland and alleged massacre of Protestants, accompanied by rumors of army plots against parliament. Thereupon Charles's opponents, countering what they believed to be a threat of violence, forced through the house of commons a petition and remonstrance addressed to the king but directed in fact at his subjects (December 1). The Grand Remonstrance charged that all the mischief that had been done had sprung from the design of papists, corrupt bishops and clergy,

and self-seeking courtiers and councillors to subvert religion and
justice. In a long catalogue of grievances and demands, it begged the
king to concur in depriving the bishops of their votes in parliament
and in 'abridging their immoderate power usurped over the Clergy.'
It denied, however, that parliament intended to abolish church government and 'leave every man to his own fancy for the service and worship of God.' Rather, it claimed, 'there should be throughout the
whole realm a conformity to that order which the laws enjoin according
to the Word of God.' But as for defining that order, the Grand Remonstrance got little farther than the London petition a year earlier.
That is, it merely proposed that a synod of divines be called, 'with
some of foreign parts,' to consider 'all things necessary for the peace
and good government of the Church' and to submit the results of its
deliberations to parliament 'to be there allowed of and confirmed.'
The authors of the Grand Remonstrance were not ready to settle the
question of the church themselves or to let it be settled by others. They
were not ready to commit themselves to presbyterianism. All they
proposed was that 'grave, pious, learned and judicious divines' should
come together and consider the matter.[27]

Events moved swiftly from this point toward irretrievable conflict,
and as they did so the brotherhood of preachers took a more and more
important role in promoting the spirit of resistance in parliament.
On December 10 Charles responded to the Grand Remonstrance
by a blunt proclamation demanding obedience to established laws
governing the church.[28] The next day a deputation of citizens appeared
at the bar of the house bearing a petition with 15,000 names and
offering to procure more if that were not enough. They praised parliament for all that it had done, expressed alarm at events in Ireland,
and urged the expulsion of popish lords and bishops from the upper
house.[29] On December 20 the ministers, with Cornelius Burges
as their spokesman, followed with a petition of their own. Parliament,
they declared, had done well in freeing godly ministers from prison
and exile, in countenancing the sacred order of preaching, and in re-
moving the tyranny of High Commission and other ecclesiastical
courts. It had united England and Scotland in 'a firm and Religious
Peace.' But the ministers were by now aware that, notwithstanding

all they had so far gained, their position was not yet secure, and they made two recommendations which revealed as clearly what they had not been able to accomplish as what they had.

Realizing that prelacy had not yet been uprooted, that church government had not yet been reorganized, and that they themselves had not yet come to agreement as to how that government should henceforth be constituted, the ministers, following the cue given by the Grand Remonstrance, proposed that in place of Convocation there be called together 'a free Synod, of Grave, Learned, and Judicious Divines . . . , for the more through and fruitful Debate of the Premisses, to expedite a full Reformation, by the High Court of Parliament, for the setling of a Godly and Religious Order and Government in this Church, as your Wisdom shall find convenient.' [30] That is to say, the whole problem of church government was to be referred under the authority of parliament to an assembly of divines with full freedom of debate.

In their other proposal, the ministers were upon more familiar if not surer ground. They reminded parliament that at its very first sitting it had called for a public fast, and this, they said, 'hath prevented many Mischiefs, and drawn down many Blessings upon the Kingdom ever since.' Though there had been no regularly appointed fast days in the meantime, parliament had proclaimed a day of thanksgiving for conclusion of peace with the Scots in August and there had been plenty of preaching besides. There had in fact sprung up an anomalous but effective procedure for filling pulpits in spite of the almost complete suspension of the ordinary administrative machinery of the church. Parliament from the beginning assumed authority to make or sanction from day to day the decisions and arrangements found necessary if the church was to function at all. But since the most important function of the church was now believed to be preaching, parliament had especially to take up the duty of approving the appointment of preachers and of enforcing disciplinary measures against incumbent but recalcitrant clergy. For months through its committees it dealt with such cases one by one as they arose, and then in September the house of commons voted general permission to the people of any parish to 'set up a Lecture' and maintain a preacher at their own charge 'to preach every Lords Day, where there is no Preaching; and to preach One [week-]Day in every Week, where there is no weekly Lecture.' [31] Thus, without as yet actually abrogating the old establishment, the house sanctioned the setting up of a new establishment of 'lecturers' derived from the Puritan brotherhood. And now three months later the brotherhood proposed that the recognition of their function and authority in the church be carried an important step farther.

They asked, that is, 'that a publick Fast may be Commanded, and Religiously observed throughout the Kingdom, once in every Month, during your sitting in Parliament.' Everyone understood, of course, that fasting could not go on without a great deal of praying and preaching. It was also understood that parliament itself would participate with special solemnity in these observances.

Three days after the ministers presented this request, 'divers young men' appeared at Westminster with still another petition, 'made up into a grat Roll of paper with about 30000 hands to it' [32] and addressed to king and parliament 'in the Name of the Apprentices, and others whose Times are lately expired in and about the City of *London*.' [33] This was the voice of the Puritan populace, with John Lilburne in their midst, also demanding the extirpation of bishops. Clarendon said that at this point 'the Commons liked well the visitation of their neighbours; so that the people assembled in greater numbers than before about the House of Peers, calling still out with one voice, *"No bishops, no popish lords."* ' [34] Milton presently commended parliament for its considerate reception on the same occasion of the petitions even of its humblest citizens.[35] Twelve of the bishops, however, claimed that they were kept by violence from taking their seats and that parliament had no authority to act in their absence. The house of commons impeached them for treason, and the lords sent them to the Tower. Thus the prelates were in effect at last removed. Meanwhile the mob scuffled with the swordmen that Charles had posted about Westminster, and blood was shed. Report places Lilburne, as we should expect, in this fracas, among the wounded.[36] On January 4, with armed men at his back, Charles marched into the house of commons in the vain hope of arresting the leaders of the party who opposed him.

Meanwhile a few days after the citizens' petition of December 11, the house of commons, spurred by the excitement caused by the Irish rebellion, sent up to the lords a request that they join in petitioning the king to declare a public fast throughout the nation for the relief of distressed Protestants in Ireland. The king consented, and December 22 was fixed as the day for London. The house reserved St. Margaret's church for its own use and invited Stephen Marshall and Edmund Calamy to preach to the members. The day after the service, it voted that the two men be thanked, that they be requested to print their sermons, and that each should have a piece of plate of twenty pounds.

Hundreds of sermons had by this time been preached in and about London and Westminster for every one that found its way into print, but enough were published to enable us to understand what the preachers were in their own idiom saying to the people and to parliament. Experience had taught them to believe that anything was possible for them and their order if they continued free to preach. To confirm themselves in their new-found freedom was therefore still their prime, even their desperate, objective. They may not all of them have been opposed to the principle of hierarchy in church government, but if bishops opposed preaching, then as preachers they must take their stand against bishops, and along with bishops against any power of state which upheld bishops in opposition to God's Word. Obedience to God's Word, whether in print or on the lips of his prophets, might thus come to require disobedience not only to bishops but to princes and magistrates. All this the preachers in their pulpits did not need to say explicitly and directly. They could say it with greater authority of a sort by making use of the special body of knowledge and technique of discourse which were the mystery to which they were bred and which their audiences expected of them. In the Old Testament they had a store of pregnant narratives concerning an elect people, now faithful, now unfaithful; now betrayed by corrupt rulers and misled by false priests and prophets; now redeemed by virtuous kings and enlightened by men who walked with God; now downtrodden, oppressed, driven out, and their city laid waste; now redeemed, restored, and their city rebuilt in glory. Here was the perfect typological mirror in which to make their hearers see themselves and the crises and predicaments through which they were themselves passing. The effect was strengthened by the fact that the stuff the people got from the pulpit was the very stuff of the imagination clothed in what they were assured was not fable but truth and irrefutable logic.

Though fewer sermons found their way into print before the open break with the king early in 1642 than after that event, enough have come down to us to allow us to measure their quality and effect. On Sunday April 4, 1641, Thomas Wilson and Samuel Fairclough preached 'before sundry of the Honourable House of Commons' at St. Margaret's, Westminster. The trial of Strafford had been going on for two weeks and Pym had just exposed a plot to bring the army up to London to overawe parliament. Wilson's sermon, *Davids Zeale for Zion,* was on Psalms 69: 9, 'the zeale of thy house hath eaten me up.' Parliament's duty was to be eaten up by zeal for God's house; the business of God's house was the preaching of his Word; parliament must bend every effort to raise up preachers and destroy their enemies. Fairclough's sermon, *The Troublers Troubled, or Acan Condemned, and Executed,* was on Joshua 7: 25. His hearers did not need to be told how Achan had brought the anger of the Lord upon Israel by disobeying Joshua or how Israel, heeding Joshua, took Achan and all his people and stoned them in the vale of Ancor. Fairclough told his hearers that they too were in covenant with the Lord to destroy every troubler of God's people. 'Up, for the matter belongs to you, wee also will be with you; wee, even all the godly Ministers of the Countrey as *Aaron* and *Hur* with *Moses* and *Joshua.*' [37]

The peace treaty with the Scots, confirmed on August 10, provided that both nations should hold a day of public thanksgiving on September 7. Parliament accordingly ordered that there should be prayers and preaching on that day in all churches. The house of commons ordered a special service for its members in Lincoln's Inn Chapel and desired Stephen Marshall and Jeremiah Burroughs to address them from the pulpit. Both expressed the almost bewildered exultancy of the Puritan brotherhood at the great reversal of their position which had taken place since the convening of parliament. Marshall in his sermon called *A Peace-Offering to God* took his theme from the fifteen short psalms (120–134) in which David rejoices at the escape of the people from their enemies. Whether the psalmist spoke historically or prophetically, the preacher said, does not matter. The spirit of God intended his words 'to *suite* the like condition of the Church in all ages: so that even we enjoying the same mercie, and called to performe the same duty, may say for *our sakes* no doubt this Psalme was written.' We may learn that the Lord does not give his own, though they may seem few and weak, to be a prey to the teeth of their enemies. Yet the triumph of the saints is their trial for the time to come. They may rejoice at the wonders, 'I had almost said the *miracles,*' God has wrought through and for them, and yet there is much still to be done. 'The Ministery is not purged . . . great Cities and Towns, and many thousand other places in the kingdome want bread for their souls. . . . Now you have built your own house, and procured Civill Liberties, should you let Gods house lie waste[?]' [38]

Burroughs began his sermon, *Sions Joy,* with lyric elaboration on Isaiah 66: 10, 'Rejoyce yee with Jerusalem, and be glad with her, all yee that love her, rejoice for joy with her, all yee that mourne for her.' He goes on from that point in much the same way as Marshall had done but with a note of greater personal urgency. Burroughs had himself been suspended from preaching by Wren of Norwich and had fled to Rotterdam. If none had been willing, he told the members of the house, to suffer by denying illegal taxations or refusing superstitious innovations, what had become of them all? 'Therefore these who have born the brunt . . . These, I say, ought now to be comforted by you.' [39]

Stephen Marshall and Edmund Calamy preached to the house of commons at St. Margaret's on December 22, the fast day for the Irish rebellion. What effect their words had on men who had just forced the Grand Remonstrance through the house and into print and who a few days later were to defy Charles on the floor of the house itself, there is of course no telling. But the Puritan preachers had not been setting forth the epic of spiritual war for three generations for nothing. They held that the most important means of grace next to the scriptures was the preaching of God's Word. By that they meant the story as they had been telling it of the fall and redemption of man, of the calling of God's predestined saints, of the consequent struggle in the breasts of the elect between the old Adam and the new and of both with the evil one, and of the foreordained triumph of the elect with Christ in this world and the next. Salvation came through faith, and faith was manifested by deeds. The afflictions of the saints were mercies bestowed to make them strong to endure and achieve. They must struggle unceasingly because their efforts were essential not to the fulfillment of God's purposes but to the saints' own realization of his grace in themselves. These doctrines, with which the Puritan brotherhood had long been edifying private hearts, now began to be urged at St. Margaret's and in a hundred pulpits besides as incentives to public action. The campaign against the bishops became another engagement of the saints against Antichrist. The struggle with Charles, first in its political and then in its military phase, was shown as the projection of that spiritual war which every saint kept up in his own members. Advantages won were calls to keep on fighting, reverses were warnings to fight harder, and though all men were required to obey the authorities set over them in church and state, they were bound first to save their own souls, obey the Lord, and heed his prophets.

Calamy entitled his sermon on December 22 *Englands Looking-Glasse*. The particular portion of the scriptural mirror for magistrates which he held up before parliament was Jeremiah 18:7–10, and the lesson his audience was to read there was that the grace of God moved in the same way to the regeneration of an entire people as of a single soul. What ruins kingdoms—the traitor within who opens the gates to the enemy, weakens the hands of defenders, and makes them unapt to fight—is sin. What upholds and repairs nations, 'their Munition, Armour, and Wall of Brasse,' is repentance and reformation. Divine power to build and to destroy is declared to be unlimited, but the doctrine of the covenant is again brought in to temper that of God's absolute sovereignty. God admits a 'mercifull qualification' in the exercise of his will. He 'indents and covenants' with every people that, if they repent, he will repent. He does not, of course, repent the way a man repents, but though he never changes his will, he does sometimes will a change, and when nations repent, he turns his judgments into mercies. 'But the change is in the Nation, not in God.' [40] Thus parliament learned that repentance was above everything a militant virtue which need not go unrewarded.

'I rejoyce,' Stephen Marshall said when it came his turn to speak, 'that you had these things set so home in the morning.' He turned in *Reformation and Desolation* to another text (2 Kings 23:26) once more to impress upon his hearers the doctrines of calling and covenant as applied to men in their position. The Lord withheld his hand from Judah for a time because of Josiah, though not even Josiah's virtues could in the end abate divine anger for the sins of Manasses. The wrath of God, says the preacher, like a great bell long rising, is not easily aroused, 'but when it is once up, makes such a dreadfull sound, as no tongue can expresse.' Nevertheless, the example of Josiah—breaking the idols, laying waste the high places, driving out the priests of Baal —is to be followed, whatever the sequel may be. Those who do the thing God raised them up to do may be sure they will be never a whit less regarded or rewarded of the Lord, whatever their success among men. For 'the Lord hath tied himselfe in his covenant to reward every man according to his owne worke, and not according to the worke of another.' He does not require that ministers save souls or that magistrates preserve nations. That is the Lord's own business. He requires only that his servants obey his will; 'wherein if they be faith- full, they shall not misse of their reward.' The application of this lesson to the predicament in which parliament found itself at the close of 1641 hardly needed to be stated.

You (Right honourable and beloved) are employed in great services, God hath raised you up to attempt glorious things for his name, for the purging of his house, and the establishing of this great people in the peace of the *Gospel:* how farre God will use any of you, I cannot tell; and how farre this unworthy Nation will acknowledge your indefatigable paines, I cannot tell; . . . But however goe on, yee Worthies of the Lord, with sincere hearts to doe what God requires at your hands; and whether this Nation be gathered or not, you shall be *glorious in the eyes of God, and the Lord will be your strength.*[41]

Simeon Ashe preached the same doctrine with even more open reference to contemporary events on January 4, 1642, the day of the king's attempt on the five members. In a sermon called *A Support for the sinking Heart in times of distresse . . . January 4th. Which was a day of great trouble and deepe danger in the City*, he construed the story of the sacrifice of Isaac to mean that 'whatsoever Promise is registered in the book of God . . . Jehovah will set all his attributes on work, for the full and seasonable accomplishment thereof unto his own people by special covenant.' [42] The preacher unfolded this doctrine with the help of a series of scriptural illustrations such as Daniel in the lions' den, David pursued by Saul, Paul at Jerusalem, Peter beset by Herod, Israel escaping from Egypt, and Shadrach, Meshach, and Abednego in the fiery furnace.

II

Reformation in England

1638-1642

THUS all through 1641 the preachers called upon parliament to keep
covenant with the Lord by consummating the reformation of the
church, and by reformation they meant first of all the erection everywhere, as they said, of a godly preaching ministry free from prelatical
control. But along with the pulpit the press was now also free, and the
press was at the disposal not only of the preachers but also of their
critics and opponents from whatever quarter. Control of the press had
always been the prerogative of the crown, but until Charles came to
the throne censorship had been exercised with a varying but genuine
degree of politic restraint. At the same time the number and variety
of printed publications, the number of printers and booksellers, the
use and sale of printed matter, steadily increased. Hence Laud's
attempt to use the authority of the crown over printing for the purpose
of suppressing opposition to his policy in the church exacerbated in the
public a sense of grievance at the sudden denial of an assumed customary right, though a right that few even among Laud's critics may
previously have thought much about or would themselves have
granted. Leighton in 1628 and a few years later Prynne, Bastwick, and
Burton had got into print, no matter what was done to prevent them,
and their publications continued to circulate. Nothing Laud was able
to do altogether sufficed to stop Prynne and Lilburne, even in prison,
from getting their diatribes printed and passed about, and once
parliament had come together the former victims of censorship were
immediately released. Prynne, Bastwick, and Burton came back to
London in triumph, welcomed by great crowds of people with sprigs
of rosemary in their hands. Their cases were promptly aired in

parliamentary committees and in the press. Lilburne, humbler in station but not in spirit, was released upon Cromwell's motion in the house of commons,[1] and he too at once went about reprinting his story. Nothing gave more resounding emphasis to the overthrow of Laud's power in the state than the collapse of his power over the press. The crowning irony came when the work of prosecuting him for what he had done was entrusted to Prynne, his most notorious victim.

But there was irony also in the fact that the press, which they had formerly denied to their now triumphing opponents, was soon the principal means left open to the bishops themselves for defending their interests before parliament and the public. They could not directly attack the preachers, and for preaching in their own behalf they had neither opportunity nor perhaps much heart. But thanks to their own defeat, the press was now more than ever a weapon that anyone could lay hold of at little risk. They had for spokesman Joseph Hall, Bishop of Norwich, a seasoned and prolific writer, well known as a poet, man of letters, moralist, and apologist for the established order since Elizabeth's days. In 1640, under Laud's direction, he had argued for prelacy against the Scots in *Episcopacy by Divine Right*. He now resumed the argument more briefly and circumspectly in *An Humble Remonstrance to the High Court of Parliament, by A dutifull Sonne of the Church*, published in January, 1641 shortly after the 'root-and-branch' petition and just at the time when the ministers' first petition was being submitted to parliament. Without referring explicitly to the latter document, Hall assured parliament that he too could have got 'Millions of hands' to subscribe his plea 'if that tumultuary, and under-hand way of procured subscriptions could have reason to hope for favour in your eyes.' He published his appeal 'lest the world should think the Presse had of late forgot to speake any language other then Libellous.' His argument, directed as much against the Scots as against the English Puritans, is a defense of liturgy and of the historical continuity of episcopacy from the apostles to the present bishops of the English church, the commonplaces of episcopal apologetics on the issue of the Bible vs. tradition, the pulpit vs. the prayer book. But Hall also points out that the Puritans were agreed upon nothing except the destruction of the only authority which held the church together. He had supposed that there was only one church in England. If there are now to be two, what is the other to be called? The 'Church Antiprelaticall'—but that would not do. The Puritans would have to make other distinctions besides, since some were for presbyteries and synods and some for parochial independence.

> Yes, and of these, there will be a division, in *semper divisibilia;* till they come to very Atomes: for to which of those scores of separated Congregations, knowne to be within and about these walls will they be joyned? and how long without a further scissure? [2]

Although Hall's defense of liturgy and episcopacy could have made small headway against the tide of exhortation rising in the London pulpits, echoes of his arguments were heard in the debate on the ministers' petition in the house of commons on February 8–9, and rejoinders were presently made ready for the press both by the sponsors of that document and by the Scottish commissioners. The Scots were the first to reply, but they were full of Scottish needs and notions and only dimly grasped the complexities of the English situation. For the Puritan brotherhood the task of preparing a suitable rebuttal was taken in hand by a committee of preachers, consisting of Stephen Marshall and Edmund Calamy, who had been active in promoting the ministers' petition; Thomas Young, who had recently covered the whole ground of the argument in his *Dies Dominica* (1639); and two younger men, Matthew Newcomen and William Spurstowe. The five called themselves Smectymnuus, an anagram composed of their initials, not calculated or intended to conceal their identity. The fruit of their collaboration was *An Answer to a Book Entituled, An Humble Remonstrance,* published in February, 1641.[3]

The authors professed diffidence at entering the lists against so famous and learned an antagonist, but they could hardly have believed that five preachers were required to cope with one bishop. They put their names together in print as spokesmen for the hundreds of their associates who subscribed the recent petition to parliament. Their joint tract was of the nature of a party brief or textbook, a quasi-official rebuttal of the arguments currently raised against their party's proposals. In their preface they allowed themselves some asperities in rejoinder, not surprisingly since Hall's plea for moderation and Christian charity sat ill with men who had recently smarted under prelatical intolerance. The main body of their discourse, however, kept strictly to point-for-point refutation of their adversary's case according to the rules for disputation they had learned in the schools of the universities. This method, which now seems so arid, futile, and absurd, was the basic convention of all such controversy in the period, though its ineffectiveness when applied to revolutionary debate in the press soon became apparent.

The Smectymnuans' *Answer* to Hall's *Remonstrance* derived its principal importance at the time of its publication from the position and influence of its authors and the body of men they represented. Marshall and his associates were known as leading members of the resurgent brotherhood of Puritan preachers, each in his own way being typical of his order. Young, as will be seen, though a Scot by birth, was no exception. At fifty-four he was the oldest of the five; Marshall was about forty-eight, Calamy forty-one, Newcomen thirty-one, and Spurstowe thirty-six. All except Young were Cambridge men, Marshall and Spurstowe from Emmanuel, Calamy from Pembroke, Newcomen from St. John's. In 1638 Spurstowe became rector of Great Hampden, Buckinghamshire, and in 1642 chaplain of his patron John Hampden's regiment. Marshall, Calamy, and Newcomen were among the considerable group of Puritan preachers who enjoyed the protection of Robert Rich, the great Puritan Earl of Warwick, Lord-Lieutenant of Essex. In 1618 Marshall succeeded Richard Rogers, one of the patriarchs of the Puritan brotherhood, as lecturer at Wethersfield and later became vicar of Finchingfield. Calamy in 1626 was lecturer at Bury St. Edmunds but was driven out by Bishop Wren. In 1640, through Warwick's favor, he took up a preaching post in Rochford. Newcomen was lecturer at Colchester in 1636, and there is record of his having preached on one occasion in Young's pulpit at Stowmarket. Marshall and Calamy, we have seen, were in the group which managed the ministers' petition of January 23. After the break with the king in 1642, these two frequently and the others occasionally were called on to preach before one or both houses of parliament. Each of the Smectymnuans was appointed to the Westminster Assembly. When Manchester was made chancellor of the University of Cambridge in 1644, he appointed Young to be master of Jesus College and Spurstowe of Catharine Hall. Marshall, Newcomen, and Calamy were recommended by Baillie in 1646 as fit persons to be spiritual directors of the king's children. Marshall, dying in 1655, was buried in Westminster Abbey. Calamy, Newcomen and Spurstowe survived to become leading nonconformist divines after the fall of the Commonwealth.

Stephen Marshall was by far the most important person in the Smectymnuus group, the most famous and probably the most admired preacher of the Puritan brotherhood. He was described to Laud in 1637 as 'a dangerous person, but exceeding cunning,' a man with the art of keeping up appearances with an 'inconformable heart.' It was said, 'he governeth the consciences of all the rich Puritans' in his neighborhood and 'in many places far remote' and that he had himself grown rich.[4] Fuller said, 'He was of so *supple* a *soul* that he *brake not a joint*, yea, *sprained not a Sinew*, in all the alteration of times.'[5] The Short Parliament invited him to preach on a fast day for both houses but that plan was frustrated by the dissolution of May 5. When the Long Parliament convened in November, he was, as we have seen, summoned with Cornelius Burges to preach at the first parliamentary fast day. Clarendon says bitterly, 'the archbishop of Canterbury had never so great an influence upon the counsels at Court as Dr. Burgess and Mr. Marshall had then upon the Houses.'[6] According to Fuller, no man stood higher in the members' graces. 'He was their *Trumpet*, by whom they *sounded* their solemn *Fasts*, preaching more *publick Sermons* on that occasion, than any *foure* of his Function. In their *Sickness* he was their *Confessor* in their *Assembly* their *Councellour*, in their *Treaties* their *Chaplain*, in their *Disputations* their *Champion*.'[7] He and Burges were at Edgehill with Essex's own regiment.[8] In 1643 he was sent to Edinburgh with Sir Henry Vane and Philip Nye to open negotiations for the Solemn League and Covenant. Baillie at that time found him 'a notable man' and heard him preach 'with great contentment,' but was much disappointed later when, in the Westminster Assembly, Marshall worked with St. John and Vane for a compromise between Presbyterians and Independents.[9] In 1648 he was among the divines sent with the parliamentary commissioners to treat with the king at Newport and was also among the ministers who attended Charles from that point on.[10] The Westminster Assembly named him as chairman of the committee to confer with the

Scots commissioners in preparing the Directory of Worship and designated him specially to have charge of the section on preaching. Unlike the other Smectymnuans, he adhered to the Commonwealth in 1649 and supported Cromwell's effort to restore order in the church while accommodating tender consciences.

Marshall was the greatest master of that rhetoric of godliness which he and most of his fellows had learned at Cambridge in the great days of John Preston. Calamy, his colleague in the pulpit on several occasions, was, perhaps, among all the preachers, the next greatest favorite with parliament. The third member of Smectymnuus, Thomas Young, played a somewhat different role. He was a Scot, born in Perthshire in 1587 and educated at St. Andrews, but he was plainly the kind of Scot who quickly takes on the color of a new and more generous environment. He attached himself as assistant or disciple to Thomas Gataker, who was intimately associated with William Bradshaw, Richard Stock, Simeon Ashe, and others prominent in the Puritan brotherhood. After leaving Cambridge, Gataker had lived in the household of a wealthy patron in London, served for a time as lecturer at Lincoln's Inn, and then in 1611 at Stock's persuasion became rector of Rotherhithe in Surrey, where he remained until his death in 1654. He was one of the most learned of Puritan divines and one of the most prolific with his pen. Like other members of the brotherhood, he maintained a kind of private academy or school of the prophets. His friend Simeon Ashe tells us that 'his house was a private semminary for divers young Gentlemen of this Nation, and more forreigners did resort to him and sojourn with him, to receive from him advice and advancement in their studies.' The same authority lists Young among the 'Persons of note that had been his Assistants.' [11] Certainly such a connection helps to explain Young's advancement from this point. In 1618 he became tutor to the son of the scrivener Milton, one of Richard Stock's parishioners, who lived in the same street with the church of Allhallows. About 1620 he went to Hamburg as chaplain to the English merchants at that place.[12] Early in 1628 he returned to England to become vicar of Stowmarket, Suffolk. In July of that year his former pupil wrote from Cambridge accepting an invitation to visit him.[13] Thus firmly planted in an East Anglian living, Young found himself at the very center of the Puritan movement, and in 1639, just as the king was getting disastrously involved with the Scots, he issued a work in Latin for the instruction of his fellow-preachers which in fact laid the basis for the brotherhood's *Answer* to Hall's *Humble Remonstrance*.

This was called *Dies Dominica*, translated in 1672 under the direction of Richard Baxter as *The Lords-Day. Or, A Succinct Narration Compiled out of the Testimonies of H. Scripture, and the Reverend Ancient Fathers.* Baxter says, 'the Author was a man eminent in his time, for great Learning, Judgment, Piety, Humility; but especially for his acquaintance with the Writings of the Antient Teachers of the Churches, and the Doctrine and Practise of former ages.' But *Dies Dominica* was something more than a treatise for the learned on the sabbath. Behind his Latin erudition and his elaborate pseudonym, the author took advantage of his party's resentment at royal encouragement of Sunday sports in order to put forth a reasoned statement of the Puritan conception of the church. He begins, as we should expect, with preaching rather than with government. 'For,' he declares in his preface, 'so long as a door is open to hear Gods Word,' godliness will flourish, faith abound, and charity not wax cold. The serpent knows, even while he is being cast out of heaven by the power of preaching, that he must employ all his strength to impede the gospel. But Young does not stop at that point. By the time he gets to Book II, he declares that the title of bishop in the ancient church comprehended both bishops and presbyters and that the principal office of both was to preach. Indeed, 'the Bishops work was especially to interpret the Holy Scriptures, when the Church was gathered together.' [14] So he goes on to present a Puritan statement, well buttressed by ancient learning, of the general Protestant view of the history of the church and of the relation of the church, the church fathers, councils, and historians, to the scriptures.

The purpose of *Dies Dominica* was in effect to refute the doctrine of the church, its history and function, which was being set forth in the same year on behalf of Laud and his party by Bishop Hall in *Episcopacy by Divine Right*. The purpose of the five Smectymnuans' *Answer* to Hall's *Humble Remonstrance* in February, 1641, was the same.[15] The Puritan attack on prelacy was now fully launched, and if anyone demanded a clear statement of the preachers' conception of the church with an outline of the standing arguments for its acceptance, based upon scripture and recorded history, here it was. And having done their party that service, the writers turned back to their pulpits, where, they believed, their really important work was to be done. Yet the issues before them were not so simple as they thought, and the implications of the Puritan case, whether argued in the peculiar dialectic of a pamphlet or expounded in the special idiom of the pulpit, were more far-reaching than most preachers were ready to conceive. What those implications might be, what belief in the sole sufficiency of the scriptures, read by reason in the light of history, might lead to, what practical deductions might be drawn from the doctrine of calling and covenant—these things were at once plainly indicated in the extraordinary pamphlets put forth in the Smectymnuans' support by Thomas Young's friend and former pupil, John Milton.

Bishop Hall for his part quickly made ready *A Defence of the Humble Remonstrance, Against the frivolous and false exceptions of Smectymnuus* (April, 1641).[16] On May 1, 1641, the king's opponents introduced a bill in parliament for the exclusion of bishops from the house of lords and on May 27 another for the extirpation of prelacy 'root and branch.' Toward the end of June Smectymnuus countered Hall's new attack with *A Vindication of the Answer to the Humble Remonstrance* [17] in which the preachers repaid in kind the aspersions the bishop had directed against them. In June Milton entered the dispute with an anonymous tract, *Of Reformation touching Church-Discipline in England: and the Causes that hitherto have hindred it.*[18] Meanwhile, someone hopeful of preserving at least the principle of hierarchy in the church issued a small tract of sixteen pages with the title *The Judgement of Doctor Rainoldes touching the Originall of Episcopacy. More largely confirmed out of Antiquity by James Archbishop of Armagh* (1641). The names of Reynolds, an Elizabethan Puritan, and of Archbishop Ussher carried weight for godliness and learning, and Milton lost little time in putting forth a brief reply, entitled *Of Prelatical Episcopacy, and Whether it may be deduc'd from the Apostolical times by vertue of those Testimonies which are alledg'd to that purpose in some late Treatises: One whereof goes under the Name of James Arch-bishop of Armagh.*[19] Milton was, however, by no means through with Bishop Hall. Sometime during the summer he replied to the latter's strictures upon his ministerial friends in *Animadversions upon the Remonstrants Defence, against Smectymnuus,*[20] while Hall issued a second rejoinder to his opponents, entitled *A Short Answer to the Tedious Vindication of Smectymnuus.*[21] Stung by Milton's *Animadversions,* the bishop or his son early in 1642 attacked its author in *A Modest Confutation of a Slanderous and Scurrilous Libell, entituled, Animadversions upon the Remonstrants Defence against Smectymnuus.*[22] To this Milton replied a few months later in *An Apology Against a Pamphlet call'd A Modest Confutation of the Animadversions upon the Remonstrant against Smectymnuus.*[23]

Both parties to this dispute observed the unmannerly conventions of scholastic disputation rather than the amenities of debate among gentlemen approved by later generations. Milton was a man of ardent temper with an ability to strike harder with words than most men. Hall was an elderly dignitary making haste at the eleventh hour to counsel moderation and compromise. His provocation, however, for doing all he could to defend himself and his order was great. In December, he was in his place in the house of lords when the populace came in thousands to Westminster, shouting 'No bishops, no bishops,' and he was one of the twelve of his order who were charged with treason for protesting too pointedly against the danger with which they were threatened. *A Modest Confutation* was written in fear of the mob, and by the time it appeared in print, its author was in the Tower.[24] Meanwhile Milton, early in 1642, followed up his first brief reply to the argument for a limited episcopacy with *The Reason of Church-Government Urg'd against Prelaty,* the longest, most deeply considered and important discussion of the subject he had yet put forth and the first of his pamphlets which he acknowledged by setting his name on the title page. It was probably written during the excitement over the Grand Remonstrance (November 22) and it may have been going through the press during the petitions and riots which then ensued.

ii. MILTON: THE ANTI-PRELATICAL TRACTS

Milton's tracts against the bishops revealed more clearly than any-thing else written at the time some of the deepest roots and much of the ultimate meaning of the Puritan revolutionary movement. Their author's relationship to the Puritan brotherhood of the pulpit was from the beginning close but exceptional. He had spent the usual seven years at Cambridge, and in the ordinary course of things should have gone on to a fellowship and so to ordination and a pulpit. But this course he chose not to take, and one reason doubtless was, as he said, that he felt church-outed by the prelates. Yet this was not the only reason. He had been taught to believe that the power of discourse, truly mastered and faithfully exercised, was the power to win men and nations to their salvation. He had also learned that, of all the forms of discourse, poetry was the noblest and the most effective, surpassing the pulpit but not differing essentially in its purpose. He discovered at the same time that he could write, that he had it in him to be a poet if he would. This discovery—the discovery of poetry, of his own ability in this the highest of the arts, and of the responsibility which the gift brought with it—here was the determining experience of Milton's youth and the principal theme of everything he had written up to this point.

But if he was to 'leave something so written to aftertimes, as they should not willingly let it die,' if he was to write with regard only to 'Gods glory by the honour and instruction of my country,' he must choose as his portion in this life 'labour and intense study.' [25] Leaving Cambridge in 1632, he settled down in his father's house in the country to a program of private reading designed to prepare him for the composition of heroic poetry, English in subject, Protestant in spirit, fit to compare with Homer, Virgil, and Tasso. He should master the timeless laws of his art as laid down by the best authorities and ex-emplified in the scriptures and the classics. He must study the history of mankind—the relations of church and state through the ages; the dealings of kings and emperors with priests, prelates, and popes; Eng-land and the reformation of the church. After spending six years on such pursuits, he undertook a journey to Italy which, as he tells the story in 1654, had about it something of the spirit of a pilgrimage but something also of a voyage of discovery. He had thought of Italy as the spot on earth where the beautiful ordered realm which humanist imagination created for itself out of the literature of the ancient world came nearest to actuality, and he found a welcome, to be sure, among the young men of the academies in Florence and with Tasso's friend and patron, Manso, in Naples. But he also encountered the Italy of the Counter-Reformation, and while in Naples he received news of the outbreak of the struggle against oppression at home. The effect was to bring him back to England feeling more English and more Protestant than ever, though still determined to outdo Virgil and Tasso. He reached home in August, 1639, just as the king was endeavoring to retrieve his first discomfiture at the hands of the Scots. By November, 1640, when Charles faced parliament again, Milton had settled in a house of his own in London and had resumed his old association with Thomas Young.

For a picture of the way of life he undertook for himself on his return from Italy, we have but to turn to his description of that ideal academy in which he would have had noble and generous youths learn prentice-fashion from their teacher. The end of learning was 'to repair the ruines of our first Parents by regaining to know God aright,' and the way to that end was to study God's creation, though not of course neglecting his Word. Milton had in mind nothing like Bacon's new instrument. The study of creation meant for him the study of humanity. It required one to read the best authors in every language on every subject concerning the life of man. One began with natural philosophy but went on to the nature of man and society and concluded with 'those organic arts which inable men to discourse and write perspicuously, elegantly, and according to the fitted style of lofty, mean, or lowly,' namely logic, rhetoric, and poetry. Having thus learned 'what religious, what glorious and magnificent use might be made of Poetry both in divine and humane things,' and having gained 'an universal insight into things,' Milton and his noble youths were prepared to become 'able Writers and Composers in every excellent matter.' 'Or whether they be to speak in Parliament or Counsel, honour and attention would be waiting on their lips.'

Or, he might have added, if they were to dispute with learned bishops in the press. But what he did say was that, if men were trained thus, 'there would then also appear in Pulpits other Visages, other gestures, and stuff otherwise wrought then what we now sit under.' [26] These scornful words were written when their author was smarting under the disapproval of his pulpit friends for having carried principles he shared with them to lengths they were unwilling to go. The program he outlined in *Of Education* he similarly pressed beyond the compass of ordinary mortals. Yet the fact was that the discipline there prescribed was no more than an idealized version of that in which both the preachers and he had alike been schooled. All had alike been grounded in the discipline of languages, of the classics and the scriptures, and of the arts of discourse. All could and upon occasion did quote philosophers, poets, orators, and historians for their purpose as well as the Bible. All believed that, knowing these things and commanding these arts, they held the key to salvation hereafter and to power here and now in church and state. The difference, all the difference, was that the extraordinary coadjutor who came to the Smectymnuans' aid in the pamphlet war against the bishops was not a preacher but a poet with an impassioned view of their common enterprise, not an evangelical mendicant 'lecturer' of the Puritan brotherhood, but a towering idealist and incorrigible individualist with a private income, a mind that moved swiftly to extreme conclusions, and an incomparable gift of expression. Probably little in the struggle to come would have turned out differently if Milton had taken no part in the attack on prelacy.

Yet little in the development of Puritan revolutionary ideas, little that is fundamental in Milton's own thought, failed somehow to find expression in these tracts. They started from the same conception of the church which had been set forth in Thomas Young's *Dies Dominica* and Smectymnuus' *Answer*. Both the form of church government and the method of enforcement and discipline that went with it were, these men held, prescribed by Christ and the apostles and set down in the New Testament. Everything prior to that was superseded, everything contrary corrupt, everything added inessential and suspect. All ministers of the gospel, since the apostles, owe their authority to the people to whom they minister, the communion of saints liberated by grace from condemnation under the law. Bishops and presbyters are equal in rank and have the same primary function, namely to preach the Word. The saints are to maintain unity among themselves and peace with the state by taking counsel with one another in consistories, synods, and assemblies. The lessons of the gospel are to be enforced by discipline, by admonition, censure, and casting out. But excommunication must be from the body of the elect by that body, with no compulsion, interference, or mitigation by outside authority. Such in principle was the basis of presbyterian church government, and in 1642 Milton's acceptance of the principle appeared complete. But in practice there was more to presbyterianism than the theory that Christ's sovereignty rests in his people, and Milton had little or no experience with any attempt to apply presbyterian principle to church government on a national scale. He had no inkling as yet of the practical difficulty, under any system based upon freedom and equality, of keeping the servants of the people from becoming their masters. He did not apprehend as yet the rise of a pope in every parish or a priest in every presbyter. Above all neither he nor anybody else foresaw the full effect upon all plans for the reorganization of church government of the popular acceptance of the Bible.

None of the teachings of the pulpit was fraught with graver consequences than the doctrine that the will of God is revealed in his printed Word for all men to comprehend. For the Bible was not mainly a book of law and precept but of tale, prophecy, and vision, a picture of human life of incomparable intensity, a mirror in which men and women might see the reflection of their own souls. To declare that they should look in the Bible for guidance was as if to tell them to look in life itself, and both they and their teachers were now to learn that such a book though sweet in the mouth might prove bitter in the belly. The doctrine of the sole sufficiency of the scriptures for salvation, pressed just far enough, upheld and strengthened the authority of the pulpit. Pressed farther, it led men to question any authority beyond their own judgments. In the end it even prompted some to question the peculiar authority of the scriptures themselves. It prompted men at any rate to ask, what actually had the Holy Spirit written? What were God's words as distinguished from his Word? In what language, text, or translation were they most certainly to be found? Above all, What did the Spirit mean by them? Who should say and how was one to know?

Milton committed himself with characteristic verve and abandon to the dogma of scriptural infallibility, but then, just as unhesitatingly, he entered upon the line of deduction and qualification in the application of that principle which rational consistency seemed to require. Let who will, he declared, appeal to custom, prerogative, acts and statutes in defense of prelacy; he will tell them of scripture, and still of scripture. He will hold the gospel ever in their faces like a mirror of diamond, maintaining its sufficiency and inviolability. God's Word alone 'hath within it selfe the promise of eternall life, the end of all our wearisome labours, and all our sustaining hopes.' [27] But having taken that position so unequivocally, he did not blink the difficulties that followed. He was aware of the philological and textual problems it involved. More important still, he recognized that the scriptures were at best not always either clear or consistent in what they purported to reveal for man's guidance, and this brought him to the age-old question, where to look for an authority by which to determine finally what the Holy Spirit intended, on any doubtful point, to be understood for truth. The answer could not lie in unconsidered tradition or in current opinion: It depended on what he believed to be the nature of truth itself and the way of knowing truth. The full import of Milton's ideas on this subject would not be apparent until he had launched upon his campaign for the reform of marriage, but all the essential points were already present in the tracts against the bishops.

True, he concedes, the scriptures are in some places difficult and obscure. But 'the very essence of Truth is plainnesse, and brightnes,' and 'the *wisdome* of God created *understanding*, fit and proportionable to Truth the object, and end of it, as the eye to the thing visible.' Hence it follows that whatever in the scriptures is 'most necessary to be known is most easie; and that which is most difficult, so farre expounds it selfe ever, as to tell us how little it imports our *saving knowledge*.' [28] The principles of church government may not seem to be 'formally, and profestly set downe' in scripture; nevertheless, 'to him that heeds attentively the drift and scope of Christian profession, they easily imply themselves.' [29] For the Bible, like every rule and instrument of knowledge, 'ought to be so in proportion as may bee weilded and manag'd by the life of man without penning him up from the duties of humane society,' and it is in fact 'the just and adequate measure of truth, fitted, and proportion'd to the diligent study, memory, and use of every faithful man.' [30] Truth is single, clear, and bright—'the darkness and crookednesse is our own.' Every man has fallen from grace, but any man may rise again through knowledge of the truth.

If we will but purge with sovrain eyesalve that intellectual ray which *God* hath planted in us, then we would beleeve the Scriptures protesting their own plainnes, and perspicuity, calling to them to be instructed, not only the *wise*, and *learned*, but the *simple*, the *poor*, the *babes*, foretelling an extraordinary effusion of *Gods* Spirit upon every age, and sexe, attributing to all men, and requiring from them the ability of searching, trying, examining all things, and by the Spirit discerning that which is good.[31]

This principle was to carry Milton, as it was at the moment carrying Lord Brooke and other converts of the Puritan pulpit, far beyond the limits set by the pulpit itself.

They were not satisfied, however, merely with proving that the scriptures supplied no warrant for the bishops' claims. More was involved in the dispute than what seems the fruitless question whether the apostles agreed in the matter of church government with Hall and Ussher or with Milton and Smectymnuus. Puritan apologists held the New Testament to be both God's revealed word and a valid historical record, a body of constitutional precedents, by which the acts and decisions of the church in later times were to be determined. But the same men were consequently bound to assert that tradition, the fathers, councils, and church historians, rightly weighed, must agree with scripture or be without avail. And they had finally to explain how and why the church as seen in the New Testament so quickly fell away from its original purity and remained so long in corruption and under affliction. For answer to that question they constructed out of the same evidence of fathers, councils, and historians, with resort also to secular and profane authorities, their own account of what had happened in the church from the beginning to their own day. The true church, they said, had been betrayed when priests, prelates, and popes conspired with rulers to persecute the saints, suppress the gospel and promote idolatry, ignorance, and superstition for the purpose of deceiving the people and enriching themselves.

This was of course the common Protestant view of church history, but since the accession of Elizabeth, it had flourished nowhere more vigorously than in England, where it was given a special English character and application. 'God is English,' Bishop Aylmer declared in 1559; out of England came Wycliffe 'who begate Husse, who begate Luther, who begat truth.' [32] Thus, he says, Christ was pleased to be born again, as it were, of England among Englishmen. The full authoritative documented explication of this idea was provided by John Foxe, Aylmer's fellow-exile of Marian days, in *Actes and Monuments of Matters Most Speciall and Memorable, Happenyng in the Church, with an Universall History of the Same,* commonly known as 'The Book of Martyrs' and long since assigned a place, in many churches, beside the Bible. The first English version of this work appeared in 1563, the eighth edition in 1641 during the Puritan attack on prelacy. It was much more than a Protestant martyrology. Foxe served both Protestant piety and English patriotism by presenting a view of universal history centering upon England and the English church. All history, he held, was occupied with the struggle of Christ and Antichrist for the souls of men, particularly of Englishmen. The climax of that struggle began with the Reformation and is destined to end in Christ's approaching final triumph in England. To the question, Where was your church before Luther? Protestants in general were taught to reply, With the apostles, with the martyrs under the heathen emperors, at Rome with Peter and Paul and their successors until Antichrist usurped the chair of Peter and the dragon drove the true church into the wilderness. And English Protestants were taught by Foxe to answer that the true church since apostolic times had always been present in some guise in England, that in England, though continually beset, it had never been overwhelmed, that in England with Wycliffe the Reformation had begun and spread thence to all the world, and that in England, if Englishmen did their part, it was destined to be consummated and Antichrist brought to his final doom.[33]

Here was the conception of universal history and of England's peculiar place and responsibility in history instilled in the English mind by Foxe's tremendous folio in the generations after the accession of Elizabeth. Here for English Protestants was the explanation of everything that had happened to England since that time. Here for Puritans, any time after Laud's rise to power, was justification for their attacks upon prelacy. In 1628 Alexander Leighton, to his cost, had elevated English prelates to the bad eminence assigned to papists, foreign or homebred.[34] Prynne turned the same legend against Laud in the series of tracts which finally in 1634 and again in 1637 landed him in the pillory. 'There is,' we read in the anonymous *Looking-Glasse for all Lordly prelates* of 1636, probably from his pen,

and hath been from the fall of *Adam*, to this present, a bitter, perpetuall, implacable enmity and warre, betweene the old Serpent (the divell) and his seed, and Christ the seede of the Woman, his Church, and her seed, the elect and regenerate Saints of God: Genes. 3.15. So hath there beene betweene the Lordly Prelates, their officers, spawne, and generation, and Christ and his true spirituall seede and faithfull members, even from their first originall, till this present; witnesse the desperate enmity, the implacable malice, and horrid cruelty of the ancient Lordly *Arrian* Court-Bishops towards the orthodox Christians of old; Of the Popes, and popish Prelates to the true Ministers, Professors of the Gospell, and Protestants; and of the ceremonious[,] pompous, Lordly English Lord Prelates towardes the Puritans, and Precisions (as they nickname them) the powerfull, painefull, zealous, godly Preachers, Ministers, and Christians since; Of all which, our Bookes of Martyrs, with other Ecclesiasticall Histories, and late Treatises give ample testimony, which present experience cannot but subscribe to.[35]

But as time was framed in eternity, so history must square with scripture. The world, having begun, must come to an end, and the key to the whole mystery of past, present, and future was to be looked for in the prophecy of Daniel and the Apocalypse of St. John. These strange writings bred notions in certain minds which eventually made wild work of Puritan plans, but they were also used by the most sober and eminent divines to bring the all-important authority of scripture to support their reading of history and their understanding of the contemporary crisis. The book of Revelation, they were certain, was nothing less than a symbolic prophetic account of the struggle through the ages to the end of time of Christ's church with the church of

Antichrist, of the true church with the church of Rome. Thomas Brightman set forth such an interpretation in *Apocalypsis apocalypseos* in 1609, issued in English in 1611, 1615, and 1644. But a clearer, more influential presentation of the subject was Joseph Mede's *Clavis Apocalyptica*, published in Latin in 1627 and again in 1632. Mede, an Essex man, had gone to school at Wethersfield in the days when Richard Rogers preached and taught at that place. Daniel Rogers, the son of Richard, was his tutor at Christ's College, Cambridge. He himself became a fellow of Christ's in 1613 and continued in that post for the rest of his life. Milton, though not among his pupils, could hardly have escaped the influence of his personality and reputation in the university. He was a teacher and a scholar, not a reformer, but he was also a conscientious Protestant with personal connections among the East Anglian squirearchy. He was a student of history, and he kept himself informed of public events by frequent visits to London and through an active regular correspondence. He had no sympathy for trouble-makers like Leighton and Prynne, but on the other hand he shared and vividly reported the popular enthusiasm for the Petition of Right and the general hatred of Buckingham. He also shared the growing apprehension at Laud's encroachments in the church and the university. In temper and outlook, but from the Puritan side, his position was not unlike that of John Hales. The first question he propounded to his pupils, we are told, was always '*Quid dubitas?* . . . (For he supposed that *To doubt nothing* and *To understand nothing* were verifiable alike.)' [36]

'A well-furnish'd Divine,' Mede's biographer said, must study histories of all sorts, 'General, National, Ancient and Modern, Sacred and Secular,' [37] and *Clavis Apocalyptica* was the final fruit of Mede's historical learning. It consisted of an ingenious analysis of the complex symbolisms and 'synchronisms' of St. John's vision with an explanation of the reference of each detail to historical events, namely, the rise of the church, its degeneracy after Constantine, the recovery of the gospel at the Reformation, and the proximate dawn of the millennium. The last-named event, Mede declared, would occur on the day of the seventh of the seven trumpets, comprised within the seventh of the seven seals of the great book which John beheld, signifying the seven epochs of the history of the world since the proclaiming of the gospel.

The seventh trumpet would blow when the seventh and last vial of the wrath of God was poured out on the head of the beast who fornicates with the great whore on the hills of Rome. Then 'the nations of them which are saved' would dwell at peace in the light of the New Jerusalem until the advent of Christ, the Last Judgment, the casting out of the wicked into the lake of fire, the paradise of the just. And to Mede as to most English Protestants the first of the nations to be saved was surely England, where the recovery of the church after its long night of wandering in the wilderness had first begun.

The Smectymnuan preachers in their pamphlets controverting Bishop Hall hewed closely to the usual method and style of scholastic argument, reserving apocalyptic exhortation for the pulpit. Milton, with no pulpit to thunder in, lavished his eloquence on their common theme in the pamphlets he wrote to support their cause. In a form he would not have chosen and in a style that was hardly prose and not quite English, he brought the force of his rhetoric and the weight of his erudition to setting forth that almost mystical view of history and of England's special role in history on which the Puritans grounded their case for the complete liberation of the church from the authority of bishops and the exaltation of the preaching order. He would make parliament see the crisis of the moment as nothing less than the grand decisive engagement in that long struggle of Christ with Antichrist in which England by God's appointment bore so momentous a responsibility.

Hence in *Of Reformation* he began by telling the familiar story of decline and fall from the pure dawn of the gospel, of the long night of corruption, ignorance, and superstition, of the reawakening of the true church at the Reformation, and of present anticipation of new heaven and new earth. He gave also the familiar account of the special glory reserved by providence for England in the church's recovery. England, he says, had been the first to blow the '*Evangelick Trumpet* to the *Nations.*' At Wycliffe's preaching the other reformers had lit their tapers. In England, in Wycliffe's time, the Bible had first been 'sought out of the dusty corners where prophane Falshood and Neglect had throwne it, the *Schooles* opened, *Divine* and *Humane Learning* rak't out of the *embers* of *forgotten Tongues,* the *Princes* and *Cities* trooping apace to the new erected Banner of *Salvation.*' In England the martyrs had first shaken the powers of darkness, 'scorning the *fiery rage* of the old *red Dragon.*' [38] Popes and prelates, to be sure, had labored ever since to stifle truth in England; nowhere had Antichrist resisted the gospel more fiercely or deviously; nowhere had reformation suffered more setbacks and delays. Yet like the preachers Milton was the more certain on that account that God, having all the world to choose from, 'hath yet ever had this Iland under the speciall indulgent eye of his providence,' and that Englishmen by God's favor might now look forward to finishing the work which Wycliffe began. So he concludes his account of the church in *Of Reformation* with a vision of his countrymen being received at last as 'the *soberest, wisest,* and *most Christian People*' before the throne of the Lamb in Zion while the enemies of reformation are consigned to be 'the trample and spurne of all the other *Damned*' forever.[39]

But the doctrine of sole reliance upon scripture led Milton as it did other Protestants to still another position of far-reaching implications. The scriptures, granted that they contained the only acceptable rule for the church, necessarily provided a rule for criticizing as well all received accounts of the church and indeed every professed authority whatever, and such criticism, depending upon the capacity and temper of the critic, might range far and arrive soon at unexpected conclusions. How far and how quickly should have been apparent to anyone who observed Milton's handling of historical evidence and authority. By 1641 he had read the church fathers—Clement, Cyprian, Ignatius, Justin Martyr, Lactantius, and others—and the ecclesiastical historians after Constantine, especially Eusebius, Socrates Scholasticus, and Evagrius. The councils, he admitted, he had read only here and there, regarding them as a waste of time, though he was ready to make himself expert in them in three months if sufficiently provoked.[40] He also drew, needless to say, upon classical historians, orators, and poets and in English history upon such writers as Bede, William of Malmesbury, Holinshed, Stow, Speed, Sir Thomas Smith, and Camden. He did not hesitate to cite Dante, Petrarch, Ariosto, Chaucer, Gower, and Spenser as witnesses against churchmen in high places.

All this erudition, we must still note, even to the poets, differed from that of the ministerial champions of reform less in kind than extent, especially the extent to which it was displayed, and above all in the lengths to which Milton was prepared to go in developing the common point of view of his party. Polemic strategy required Puritan apologists to scan the sources and channels of prelatical tradition in the light of scripture. A learned man, Milton said, should read the fathers and early church historians not 'to controule, and new fangle the Scripture' but 'to stop the mouthes of our adversaries, and to bridle them with their own curb.' Yet he also said that the Bible as an instrument of knowledge must be such as can be 'weilded and manag'd by the life of man,' and what was true of the Bible must be true of all instruments of knowledge secondary to the Bible.[41] In saying that every authority must accord with the scriptures, he meant the scriptures understood according to his humanist conception of reason and truth.

This conception he now brought to the consideration of the sources upon which the defenders of the traditional authority of the bishops drew for their justification. His method is clear, critical, and scornful. He endeavors to judge each writer according to his agreement with scripture but also according to his setting in time, the evidence of personal interest and motive, the condition of his text, the inherent human credibility of what he says. He would scrutinize his author's words, analyse his grammar, and compare his statements one with another. A man was not to be believed simply because he suffered martyrdom; 'he is not therfore above all possibility of erring, because hee burnes for some Points of Truth.' Nor because he wrote a long time ago. To hold truth in low esteem 'unlesse shee can bring a Ticket from *Cranmer, Latimer,* and *Ridley;* or prove her selfe a retainer to *Constantine*' is absurd.[42] What Milton thought of Thomas Fuller, who disapproved of his irreverence toward the English martyrs, we are not told, but he probably thought as he did of Camden, who, he said, loved bishops as he did old coins. The church fathers, taken as a whole, he deemed quite unreliable. 'Whatsoever time, or the heedlesse hand of blind chance, hath drawne down from of old to this present, in her huge dragnet, whether Fish, or Sea-weed, Shells, or Shrubbs, unpickt, unchosen, those are the Fathers.'[43] The oldest of them were most credible because they lived nearer gospel times; the best of them agreed most closely with the scriptures upon which they depended. But Milton does not begin to feel himself upon firm ground until he comes to Eusebius and the historians who report the circumstances which seemed to him to account for the corruption of the church, the degeneracy of the ministry, and the rise of prelacy after Constantine. Constantine was a figure concerning whom Puritans did not always agree. He could be held up as the nursing father of the church, type of the Christian magistrate who brings the authority of the state to the support of the church. To Milton he stood for secular tyranny corrupting the clergy by the gift of worldly power in order to enslave the people by promoting ignorance and superstition and suppressing the gospel. If the later fathers extolled Constantine, it was because he extolled them. 'If he had curb'd the growing Pride, Avarice, and Luxury of the *Clergie,* then every Page of his Story should have swel'd with his Faults.' No man had ever 'set open a dore to more mischiefe in Christendome.' [44]

But again Milton went beyond any limit the Puritan brotherhood was prepared to set in reforming the ecclesiastical state. Many preachers had not themselves, of course, for a long time enjoyed any part of the gift the church owed to Constantine. They derived their main strength from the voluntary support of their adherents, and their initial demand was in effect for the extension of that system. They had not yet as a body faced the question as to how far they would go in relinquishing the tangible power of the ecclesiastical establishment once that power was put within their own grasp. But the Smec-tymnuans must have read with misgivings the pamphlets Milton wrote in their support, if they read them at all. For antiprelatism in his case was the next thing to out-and-out anticlericalism. The argument for the equality of bishops and presbyters, as he presented it, based as it was upon the doctrine of the equality of all believers, came near to overriding all distinction between lay and cleric. The argument for stripping the prelatical church of power in the state became with him an argument for stripping the church of every means of enforcing its rule except persuasion and its ministers of any support they could not win for themselves directly from the people.

There could be no mistaking the direction of his reasoning upon this point. Truth as revealed in scripture was one and the same, intelligible and without mystery, for all who would read. The only thing that could obscure knowledge was sin and the ignorance bred by the deceit and violence practiced by the sinful. The overt effects of sin it was the duty of the magistrate to repress, but the most he could hope to accomplish was to punish crime and maintain civil peace. He could not hope to eradicate sin itself, which was a malady of the spirit no law or power of state could touch. Power to oppose sin and liberate the soul was granted not to or by the state but by the grace of God to the church alone. That is to say, to the faithful, and if ever the church or its ministers sought to lay hands on any power save the pure spiritual power of God's Word, they betrayed themselves and the people to the devil.

> The Churchmans office is only to teach men the Christian Faith, to exhort all, to incourage the good, to admonish the bad, privately the lesse offender, publickly the scandalous and stubborn; to censure, and separate from the communion of *Christs* flock, the contagious, and incorrigible, to receive with joy, and fatherly compassion the penitent, all this must be don, and more then this is beyond any Church autority.[45]

The final extreme statement of this devolution of all ecclesiastical authority to the congregation and of ministerial function to the body of the elect was reached by Milton in the second part of *The Reason of Church-government*. God, he there says, governs the church no longer as a judge or a schoolmaster but as the father of a family of sons. He has committed the cure of souls to 'his spiritual deputy the minister of each Congregation,' but to the minister he has joined the people. The people are not set apart as laic and unclean. They are admitted into the tabernacle, 'a chosen generation, a royal Priesthood.' 'All Christians ought to know,' Milton insists, 'that the title of Clergy S. *Peter* gave to all Gods people.'

Hence it followed that discipline in the church was to depend first of all on the people's respect for the judgment of elders, brothers, and friends, as Hector remained on the field 'lest the Trojan Knights and Dames should think he did ignobly.' But beyond that, it was to depend on 'pious and just honouring of our selves.' 'He that holds himself in reverence and due esteem, both for the dignity of Gods image upon him, and for the price of his redemption, which he thinks is visibly markt upon his forehead, accounts himselfe . . . a fit person to do the noblest and godliest deeds.' These things, strictly speaking, were put forward by Milton in defense of the presbyterian institution of lay or ruling elders, but few members of the ministerial order,

certainly few Presbyterians, would have approved the further conclusions he now drew from the principle of the priesthood of all
believers. When every good Christian, he goes on to say, having
been made acquainted with the 'glorious privileges of sanctification
and adoption which render him more sacred then any dedicated altar
or element,' has been restored to his right, he will no longer be afraid
of profaning 'some outward holy thing in religion' by his lay touch or
presence. He will fear only 'lest something unholy from within his
own heart should dishonour and profane in himselfe that Priestly
unction and Clergy-right whereto Christ hath entitl'd him.' Let the
people be thus liberated from within from such fear, and 'then would
the congregation of the Lord soone recover the true likenesse and
visage of what she is indeed, a holy generation, a royall Priesthood, a
Saintly communion, the household and City of God.' [46]

Secure in his inheritance from his scrivener-father, Milton went on
to make some practical applications of his idealistic conception of the
church which should have given pause to his ministerial friends. From
assailing the corruption of prelates by worldly power, he went on to
assail the corruption of the clergy in general and finally to argue that
the special mark of the true pastor was that for all his labors and merits
he required 'either nothing, if he could so subsist, or a very common
and reasonable supply of humane necessaries.' There need be no endowments, no tithes, no fat livings and prebends, no hireling clergy.
God 'can easily send labourers into his Harvest, that shall not cry,
Give, give, but be contented with a moderate and beseeming allowance,' freely bestowed by the people themselves.[47] Moreover, even
'the meanest Christians,' having read the scriptures and heard sermons
and lectures all their lives, should be able to judge for themselves of
the abilities of ministers and of the truth of their teachings.[48] As for
the training of ministers, God 'can stirre up rich Fathers to bestow
exquisite education upon their Children, and so dedicate them to the
service of the Gospell.' Certainly there is no need for the kind of
education bestowed at the universities and no need to provide for
the kind of men who flock thither; 'a plaine unlearned man that lives
well by that light which he has, is better, and wiser, and edifies others
more towards a godly and happy life.' [49] Thus Milton renews the
attack he had begun in his own academic exercises on the scholastic
curriculum, assailing the manners, morals, and minds of university

students and ridiculing the learned fools and hypocrites turned loose by the universities to prey upon the people.

These attacks were aimed immediately at the prelatical clergy, but they laid Milton open to the charge leveled against all his party of promoting schism and the multiplication of sects. His rejoinder, up to a point, was the usual one. The means to end the present troubles of the church was not to repress knowing and zealous Christians but to call a council or series of councils with each parish consistory or little synod 'moving upon her own basis in an even and firme progression, as those smaller squares in battell unite in one great cube, the main phalanx, an embleme of truth and stedfastnesse.' [50] But this was merely a Miltonic way of stating a theory of church government Milton actually knew little about and would be one of the first to reject in practice. He was, for him, on surer ground in declaring that 'the timeliest prevention of schisme is to preach the Gospell abundantly and powerfully throughout all the land.' And he was upon grounds of deep personal conviction in declaring, on the authority of St. Paul, that 'there must be sects for the manifesting of those that are sound hearted.' 'For if there were no opposition where were the triall of an unfained goodnesse and magnanimity? vertue that wavers is not vertue, but vice revolted from itselfe, and after a while returning.' There can be no change or accomplishment, 'without the struggle of contrarieties . . . No Marble statue can be politely carv'd, no fair edifice built without almost as much rubbish and sweeping.' Even rebellion in Ireland should be no hindrance to reformation but a spur; the lack of reformation has been the cause of rebellion. To clinch the argument he quotes the same words of Azariah to King Asa which had served Stephen Marshall in his first sermon to the Long Parliament, 'Now for a long season . . . Israel hath beene without the true God, and without a teaching Priest, and without law.' [51]

iii. MILTON: THE ANTI-PRELATICAL TRACTS; THE PAMPHLETEER AS POET-PROPHET

As the expression of an extraordinary mind in an extraordinary crisis, Milton's tracts against prelacy are now of the most absorbing interest. As revolutionary manifestoes designed to have an immediate effect upon the public for which they were intended, they were patently unsuccessful, and of this fact their author, as he went on, became increasingly, unhappily, and confessedly aware. Indeed, from the beginning, a certain vacillation in method, tone, and style, not to say confusion in form, indicates that Milton quickly became conscious that in attempting to write pamphlets he was at a disadvantage, writing as he said with his left hand. The preachers were never in such doubt about themselves. They had the well-understood conventions of the sermon to depend on in the pulpit and the methods of scholastic disputation to fall back on when they controverted opponents in the press. Milton, unpulpited, could not avail himself of the sermon and, though he had learned to dispute with the best, he did so with ill-concealed disdain. We see him, therefore, constantly shifting or trying to shift now to one now to another more congenial mode of discourse. He lays aside the debater in order to 'soare a while as the Poets use' or let himself go in such a 'hymne in prose' [52] as the invocation and imprecation which conclude *Of Reformation* or as the prayer for the advent of the redeemer in *Animadversions*. Or he digresses into oratory, strictly observing the classical rules, either invective against churchmen or eulogy of parliament, or into personal apologetic in the convention of classical rhetoric and of spiritual autobiography. The anti-prelatical tracts have indeed been best remembered not for their formal argument but for their digressions addressed to the reader on matters of vital concern to the writer in the course of a rebuttal directed with avowed distaste at an antagonist. They made little impression on parliament or public in 1641–1642, but they tell us much about Milton and, taken as a whole, they reveal some of the most far-reaching energies of the Puritan movement.

What impression Milton's version of the case against prelacy made upon his ministerial friends, what he thought of their actions and demands as the situation developed, we are left to infer. He could not have failed to note that, as compared with the sermons of such men as Marshall and Calamy, pamphlets, at any rate his pamphlets, made little stir and were of small effect. And he must before long have begun to be aware that beyond a certain point he and Smectymnuus were not at one in their conception of the church and its ministry. He was perhaps not ready for a complete break with his old associates, but better acquaintance with them in their prosperity surely did not make it easier for him to go on pamphleteering in their behalf or to endure patiently the return of clericalism in Puritan guise. In this, his first engagement in the spiritual war to recover the lost Jerusalem, he had in a sense misjudged his party, his aim, and his weapon, and as he went on in his tracts against the bishops, he attempted none too successfully to retrieve his mistake and strike out by other means more effectively for his own purposes.

In his first three tracts, digressions aside, he kept in the main to his brief against prelacy and for unfettered preaching, though he could not forbear giving assurance that at the right moment he would take up his harp and sing 'an elaborate Song to Generations.'[53] While he was writing his next tract, *The Reason of Church-government,* during the excitement following the Irish rebellion and the Grand Remonstrance, parliament was voting to hold a fast day with prayer and preaching every month, and about the time, February 23, that the first of these observances was being held, he was probably seeing his work through the press. Stephen Marshall said in his famous sermon on this occasion, called *Meroz Cursed:*

It hath been a custome almost amongst all Nations, after any notable Victory, to have their "ἐπινίκια, their Triumphant Songs. . . . The *Romans* had their *Salii* Priests, who after any victory went dancing through the City, singing their *Hymnes,* and *Paeans* to *Mars,* and the rest of the favourable Gods. . . . Thus *Moses* and *Aaron* sang unto the Lord, when he *triumphed gloriously over Pharaoh and all his Host.*[54]

The preacher of course supposed that the epinikia of the Long Parliament were to be the sermons that he and his brethren would preach as the war against Charles and Antichrist proceeded. He was not thinking of the hymns and paeans which Thomas Young's friend was proposing to write when the people should have got over the Red Sea that still lay before them in the early months of 1642. But Milton at the same moment had reached the point of declaring that poets had power 'beside the office of a pulpit'[55] to do all the things, treat all the subjects, which the preachers were in fact busying themselves about. Whether or not he was as yet convinced that they were betraying the cause of reform, he was having to recognize that they were out-rivaling him in pleading for it, and he was taking thought how to make his own special abilities count more effectively in the situation immediately before him.

To that problem he addressed himself especially in the often-quoted digression with which he opened the second part of *The Reason of Church-government*. So far he had been loyally arguing that the surest way to reform and to Christian unity was to preach the gospel and establish church government on presbyterian principles. Now, however, he boldly asserts the equal responsibility of all who have knowledge to teach and of all who have the gift of utterance to speak. He himself, gifted with the ability and the training to 'leave something so written to aftertimes, as they should not willingly let it die,' has been unable to keep silence. Thus he excuses himself to himself for having again postponed his grand poetic plans in order to embark upon these hoarse disputes, and perhaps because of some misgiving lest he may after all have been wasting his time, he tells us something more definite concerning those plans. He intends to write an epic after Homer, Virgil, and Tasso or the Book of Job, a drama after Euripides and Sophocles or the Song of Solomon and the Apocalypse of St. John, or odes and hymns like those of Pindar and Callimachus or 'those frequent songs throughout the law and prophets.' [56]

Milton speaks here as though questioning which of these forms would be most 'doctrinal and exemplary,' but concerned as he was at this time with the problem of reaching his public directly through his art, he was, it seems clear, thinking most immediately of some form of drama. In a note in his *Commonplace Book* he had dismissed the scruples of Tertullian, Cyprian, and Lactantius against the theater on the ground that nothing in philosophy was 'more impressive, purer, or more uplifting than a noble tragedy.' [57] More to the point is the proposal he now makes after reiterating the classical doctrine of the moral function of poetry and deploring its betrayal by 'libidinous and ignorant Poetasters.' It would be well, he says, for the rulers of the commonwealth to arrange public sports and pastimes for the encouragement of war-like skill among the people, to set up academies for improving their minds, and to procure 'wise and artfull recitations sweetned with eloquent . . . inticements to the love and practice of justice, temperance and fortitude.' He would have the rulers of the state consider "Whether this may not be not only in Pulpits, but after another persuasive method, at set and solemn Paneguries, in Theaters, porches, or what other place, or way may win most upon the people to receiv at once both recreation, & instruction." [58]

Milton recollects at this point that he is still writing as a pamphleteer, not as poet. So, begging his reader to take the poems on trust for a while longer, he returns to the distasteful task of clubbing quotations with his opponents. Yet the suggestion that parliament set up a sort of Attic theater for the edification of the populace was seriously meant. At any rate, he did actually about this time draw up a list of about a hundred subjects for tragedies,[59] several of which he took the trouble to outline in some detail. These subjects, especially those that deal with Adam and with Samson, have often been considered in their bearing upon the great poems published in later years. At the moment when Milton devised and set them down, however, he was absorbed in the events and anticipations of 1642, and they reflect the hope that in the regenerated commonwealth now to be looked for poets might have opportunity to match the sermons of preachers with poetic dramas *ad populum*. But if he had had a pulpit to speak from, he would have chosen no different themes or doctrines. The audience in his theater would have witnessed the same texts dealt with on the stage which it had often heard expounded in church. It would have brought to the consideration of what it saw and heard a familiarity not simply with the Biblical story but also, thanks largely to the pulpit, with a code of meaning and store of association which the modern reader knows little of. The audience would probably, if it thought about the matter at all, have accepted without question the idea, assumed by Milton as self-evident, that the scriptures exemplified the classical forms of discourse as perfectly as anything in the classics themselves.

One third of the subjects on Milton's list are drawn from the English chronicles, but these are only briefly set down. The scriptures were more to his purpose, and the subject he worked out most carefully was, as we should expect, the fall of man, that great aetiological fable which served as starting point both for the Puritan legend of the church and for parliament's defense against the king. Of the remaining subjects, over half were taken from the Old Testament and of these all but four from the chronicles of the chosen people. They begin with 'the golden calfe or the massacre in Horeb' and conclude with the fall of Jerusalem. The majority come from the two books of Kings. A few—'Sodom Burning,' 'Moabitides Num. 25,' 'Abias Thersaeus 1 Reg. 14'—are outlined in some detail. The egregious classicism which disguises such a subject as the sons of Ahab devoured by dogs under the title 'Achabaei Cunoboroomeni' does not conceal Milton's intent. He chose his subjects as the preachers did their texts to teach the same lessons to the same public. Indeed he chose many of the same texts—Achan, Phineas, Ahab, Joshua, Josiah, Hezekiah, Samson—to set forth similar ideas concerning the relations of people, prophets, and rulers to God and to one another. At the same time his variations upon the common practice of the pulpit, if indeed they may be called such, reveal his interest in a subject which was soon to become of the greatest importance in all his thinking. Coming to the New Testament, he let his thoughts dwell briefly on 'Christus patiens' but less briefly on the suffering of John the Baptist under a uxorious tyrant. In 'Theristria, a Pastoral out of Ruth,' he would doubtless have treated one of the favorite questions in Puritan love casuistry, that of the virtuous woman seeking out the husband providentially designed for her. In the 'Sheepshearers in Carmel a Pastoral. 1 Sam. 25' he would probably have dealt with another, that of the wise and gracious woman married to a churl. We may regret that Milton was not led to dwell longer with Abigail, that woman of good understanding and charming countenance. What aspect of the same general subject he would have treated in 'Salomon Gynaecocratomenus' is perhaps all too apparent.

What if any progress Milton made in 1642 toward the accomplishment of any of these dramatic plans, we cannot tell. Now may have been the time when, as Phillips tells us, he began the composition of *Paradise Lost* in the form of a tragedy. Not impossibly he may also at this time have made some beginnings toward a drama on Samson or some other figure included in his list of subjects. Nothing immediate, however, came of all his projects for making poetry serve the cause of reform and revolution. Parliament in February instituted not poetic dramas but monthly fast days and in August took steps to put down stage plays. In the meantime the poet went back to pamphleteering in order to defend himself against the charges which Hall or someone writing on his behalf had directed against him in *A Modest*

Confutation. Milton had previously said that 'when God commands to take the trumpet and blow a dolorous or a jarring blast, it lies not in mans will what he shall say or what he shall conceal.' [60] The chariot of zeal, we are now told, is drawn by two meteors, 'the one visag'd like a Lion to expresse power, high autority and indignation, the other of count'nance like a man to cast derision and scorne upon perverse and fraudulent seducers.' [61] But Milton's *Apology* was not all satire and polemic. When he had refuted eight of the twelve sections of *A Modest Confutation*, he paused in avowed disgust in order to relieve himself and his reader, he said, with something more entertaining. The method of point-for-point disputation to which he felt himself committed as a pamphleteer was proving, as others besides himself were discovering, not only distasteful but ineffective. But what form should he adopt instead? Convention forbade his writing a sermon, even if he had wished to do so; it did not forbid him to address the house of commons, after the manner of Isocrates, in a written oration. At any rate, he now tried his hand, 'although it be a digression,' at a brief formal eulogy of the Long Parliament, constructed strictly according to the rules of classical rhetoric.

The men of parliament, he declares, in spite of the hindrances which high birth and riches put in the way of virtue and notwithstanding the misinstruction to which they were subjected at the universities, have in a brief time done more to recover liberty and religion than their ancestors in many ages. These two things are inseparable and any who would corrupt the one would enthrall the other. The men of parliament, after regaining 'our lost liberties and Charters,' have gone on to subdue 'the second life of tyranny,' superstition and 'miter'd hypocrisie.' Their achievement is beyond comparison with exploits even 'of highest fame in Poems and *Panegyricks* of old.' The ancient worthies delivered men from outward tyranny; parliament 'by this only repulse of an unholy *hierarchy* almost in a moment replenisht with saving knowledge their countrey nigh famisht for want of that which should feed their souls.' Rumors, threats, and plots have not weakened their resolution. Their reward is 'to be saluted the Fathers of their countrey; and sit as gods among daily Petitions and publick thanks flowing in upon them.' [62]

Which doth so little yet exalt them in their own thoughts, that with all gentle affability and curteous acceptance they both receave and returne that tribute of thanks which is tender'd them; testifying their zeale and desire to spend themselves as it were peice-meale upon the grievances and wrongs of their distressed Nation. Insomuch that the meanest artizans and labourers, at other times also women, and often the younger sort of servants assembling with their complaints, and that sometimes in a lesse humble guise then for petitioners, have gone with confidence, that neither their meannesse would be rejected, nor their simplicity contemn'd, nor yet their urgency distasted either by the dignity, wisdome, or moderation of that supreme Senate; nor did they depart unsatisfi'd. And indeed, if we consider the generall concourse of suppliants, the free and ready admittance, the willing and speedy redresse in what is possible, it will not seeme much otherwise, then as if some divine commission from heav'n were descended to take into hearing and commiseration the long remedilesse afflictions of this kingdome.[63]

At the conclusion of this interjected address, Milton resumes the debater and goes about disposing of the remaining sections of his adversary's case. The eulogy of parliament, however, was the true climax of his argument against prelacy, and his argument against prelacy, little regarded at the time, gave a true forecast of what was now to be made of the ideas which the Puritan brotherhood had set going in men's minds. The main body of preachers, for whom Smectymnuus spoke, expected an order to be presently set up in church and state which would render the preaching of the Word as they understood it secure and free. But the Word meant many things to many men, and freedom came while the preachers were still only on their way toward Zion and before the expected new order could be got under way. Freedom, in fact, with its multifarious complications and difficulties was what unimpeded preaching was bringing about, freedom and more freedom, not the godly community of the preachers' hopes. All this was clearly enough indicated in Milton's tracts if one were able and willing to follow the course of his thinking in the torrent of his rhetoric. He had come to Smectymnuus' support, believing that reform of the church was the necessary first step toward any general reform whatever. He also assumed that reform of the church, if it was to follow the scriptural model, required that prelatical be replaced by presbyterian government. But the basic principle of presbyterianism, as he understood it, was the priesthood of all believers. This conception accorded with his belief in the capacity of the human spirit to receive the progressive enlightenment of truth through the Word and his conviction that the preaching of the Word was the one essential function of the church. Yet the ministry of the Word, for the humanist poet-scholar, was not to be confined to the pulpit or the clerical caste. It was for all to follow who believed in the Word and had any gift whatever for making it known.

III

The Consent of the Governed

1642-1644

THE Grand Remonstrance at the close of November, 1641, the petitions of citizens, ministers, and apprentices with the riots that attended them, the fast day sermons of Marshall and Calamy on December 22, and finally the king's intrusion into the house of commons on January 4 marked the opening of the next stage of debate in the Puritan Revolution. The lords at last adopted and the king approved the bill excluding bishops from parliament, but although Charles thus in effect surrendered his control over the church, parliament was still unwilling to yield him command over the armed forces to be raised for subduing the Irish rebellion. He withdrew from Whitehall to Hampton Court and Windsor soon after his attempt to arrest the five members, and early in March he set out for the north while parliament voted to put the kingdom in a state of defense. In April he was denied access to the magazine at Hull, and in August he raised his standard at Nottingham and gathered an armed force. A few weeks later a parliamentary army with the Earl of Essex at its head marched out of London to oppose him.

The king and his party, not without reason though not with entire justice, attributed to the preachers an evil priority in fomenting what they naturally regarded as rebellion. In a manifesto directed to the house of lords at the time of his repulse at Hull, Charles complained of a notion 'grown into frequent Discourse, and vented in some Pulpits (by those desperate turbulent Preachers, who are the great Promoters of the Distempers of this time) *That humane Laws do not bind the Conscience.*' [1] In his 'Declaration,' issued in August, 'concerning the proceedings of this present Parliament,' he asserted that 'the preaching of the Word of God, is turned into a Licence of libelling, and reviling both Church and State, and venting such seditious positions, as by the Laws of the Land are no lesse then Treason.' [2] Clarendon tells us that the 'wild-fire' which now spread among the people was kindled not so much by parliament itself as by the clergy, 'who both administered fuel and blowed the coals in the Houses too.' As war began, he says, they raised their voices against the king himself, applying to him whatever God or the prophets declared against wicked rulers. The evidence of their wresting of the scriptures, he assures us, is preserved 'in the seditious sermons at that time printed, and in the memories of men of others not printed.' [3] Charles himself observed to his wife a few years later, 'if the pulpits teach not obedience, . . . the king will have but small comfort of the militia.' [4] The preachers might have replied that they were merely heeding for the benefit of the king's subjects the advice his father had given to his other son. 'Would ye see how good men are rewarded, and wicked punished?' James asked of Prince Henry in his book on kingship. Then, he said, read the law of Moses as interpreted and applied by the prophets and as illustrated in the historical books of the Old Testament, especially the books of Kings and Chronicles. 'For there yee shall see your selfe, as in a myrrour, in the catalogue either of the good or the evill Kings.' [5]

All that parliament had done about the church by the time fighting began was to make certain that the Word should be preached and that the Puritan brotherhood should be free to preach it as they saw fit. On December 24, two days after Calamy and Marshall addressed the members from the pulpit of St. Margaret's, the house of commons approved the ministers' request for a regular fast day every month while still withholding approval for their other request for a free synod to debate church government. The lords at once concurred in recommending to the king 'that a monthly Fast may be kept and observed by both Houses of Parliament, and the whole Kingdom, while the troubles continue in Ireland.' [6] Charles, to his later regret, approved the proposal and issued the necessary proclamation on January 8. When in August fighting became imminent parliament issued an order requiring everyone to observe the public fast days by abstinence from food and attendance upon prayers and preaching. Nothing was to be sold, eaten, or drunk, no tool was to be lifted or wheel to turn on those days, until the preachers had done their work.[7] In February, 1643, faced by the prospect of another year of war, parliament issued still another ordinance, imposing a general confession of national and personal sins to be read in churches every month.[8] In October of that year Charles revoked his original proclamation of a monthly fast, seeing 'what Ill use hath been made of those publick Meetings, under the pretence of Religion, in Pulpits, and Prayers, and Sermons of many Seditious Lecturers, to stir up and continue the Rebellion raised against us.'[9] Yet at the same time he proclaimed a rival fast day to be held on the second Friday of each month.

Thus the Haggais and Zechariahs of the Puritan brotherhood gained acknowledgment of the need for their services from the Nehemiahs and Zerubbabels of the Long Parliament. The first of the long series of parliamentary fast days on the last Wednesday of each month was held in St. Margaret's Church on February 23, 1642,[10] with Marshall and Calamy again in the pulpit. The next day the house ordered that the two preachers be thanked for their pains and that they be requested to print their sermons, which other persons were forbidden to publish for two months. A few days later the house ordered that Simeon Ashe and Cornelius Burges be invited to preach at the next fast day, March 30. From now on such was to be the regular procedure. The members gathered on these occasions, morning and afternoon, at St. Margaret's, being required to attend on pain of being fined for absence or lateness. Other persons were excluded. The house of lords, which was by this time much less numerous, usually met separately. The services over, members returned to their usual meeting places to resume their usual business. But this was not all. Special days of fasting or thanksgiving continued to be proclaimed from time to time. The lord mayor, aldermen, and common council also called for edification from the pulpit as need arose, and on very special occasions both houses, the city fathers, and later the assembly of divines came together, usually at Christ Church in Newgate Street, for the same purpose. In addition to instituting monthly observances for its own members, parliament also recommended to the people of the parish of St. Margaret's that they appoint Stephen Marshall to be their ordinary lecturer, and the house rejected a petition from the patron and parishioners of Finchingfield that Marshall return to his normal duties as pastor and incumbent at that place.[11] Later the house directed that the use of the pulpit in the abbey be allowed every Sunday afternoon to preachers nominated by itself [12] and a little later still that an 'exercise,' ending at eight o'clock, be kept in the same place for half an hour every morning by seven designated preachers, including Stephen Marshall, taking turns.[13] The lord mayor and aldermen were directed to see that orthodox ministers were engaged to preach regularly at St. Paul's, the Spittle, and other places in the city.[14] Sermons preached under official auspices were usually published not long after delivery, with a dedicatory epistle, perhaps some revisions and additions, and the authorization of the inviting body conspicuously displayed. Booksellers from time to time issued complete lists of all parliamentary sermons from the beginning.[15] The more noteworthy sermons were occasionally republished. And besides all this setting forth of the orthodox Word, there were the outpourings of the pulpit's illegitimate offspring, the conventicle and the tub, which were also served by that common maid-of-all-work, the press.

The fixing of the custom of regular fast days, with special services at St. Margaret's for the house of commons, gave the preachers recognition and responsibility such as they had never known. They now found themselves the prime exponents of the religious and moral sanctions of a revolution moving forward at a quickening pace to conclusions they had not foreseen and were not likely to approve. Their chief object to begin with had been to liberate the pulpit, and to that end they had soon found it necessary to demand the removal of prelacy. But Charles clung to prelacy with a conviction as stubborn as their devotion to preaching, and hence in their holy war against Antichrist, they were constrained to preach war also against the head of the state. Calamy and Marshall in their sermons before parliament on December 22 had denounced woe on those who do the work of the Lord negligently, especially after such evidences of his favor as England had just received. What work he expected Englishmen to do next, the same men in their sermons on February 23 left no manner of doubt. Calamy told his hearers, 'I have chosen this Text,' namely Ezekiel 36: 32, 'to help you in the work of this day.' The text was drawn from the chapter in which the Lord declares through his prophet that he will surely beat down the heathen, give a new heart to Israel, and cause the people to walk in his statutes and keep his judgments—'and ye shall be my people, and I will be your God.' The Lord will do this, not for their sakes—'be ashamed and confounded for your owne waies, O house of Israel'—but out of his own free grace. The mercies of the last two years had come to England, Calamy said, not because England deserved them but because God had determined that England should be saved. So the men of parliament should know that what the Lord intended them as agents to do next would surely come about, not if they chose but because God willed.

Calamy's sermon was entitled *Gods free Mercy to England. Presented as a Pretious, and Powerfull motive to Humiliation.* What humiliation might mean in the mouths of men who thus identified their own purposes with the will of God was made clear in Stephen Marshall's sermon on the same day, called *Meroz Cursed.* The text came from the song of Deborah, Judges 5:23, a text and a theme, the preacher said, exceeding seasonable at such a time 'when abundance of mighty enemies rise up against the Lord, and against his Church.' It should seem most of all seasonable for the assembly which heard him, 'who should all be as the Lord: *their Horses as his Horses, their Chariots as his Chariots,* they being all called to bee Leaders and Captaines of the Lords Host.' For as Marshall's audience knew, the angel of the Lord cursed Meroz because '*they came not to the helpe of the Lord, . . . against the Mighty,*' and Meroz, the preacher made plain, comprised all those '*neuters*' who now failed to bring their gifts to the service of parliament and the Puritan brotherhood. The mighty, of course, comprised all those possessed of authority, wealth, parts, and learning who opposed parliament and made war upon the church as the preachers conceived the church. This bold and eloquent attempt, fortified as it was with citations from classical historians, to make men see the lamb of God in the Puritan brotherhood and Sisera in King Charles was bitterly condemned and long remembered by outraged royalists.[16]

ii. THE LAWYERS AND THE LAW OF REASON

Marshall and Calamy set the example for a succession of preachers who took their monthly turns at persuading parliament and people that religious duty required that they defend themselves and the church against the king and the prelates. None denied that civil obedience was expected of every man but, said the preachers, when rulers attempt to invade the spiritual freedom vouchsafed to believers under the gospel, then obedience to rulers must give way to obedience to God and to conscience. This doctrine was well calculated to appeal to the king's parliamentary opponents. The preachers asserted a right grounded upon the law of God revealed in conscience and the scriptures, a law which, they claimed, took precedence over all other commands. The lawyers and gentry of the house of commons, in the course of their long contention with Charles and his father before him, had committed themselves to a conception of the state which also put law above the will of kings and on the side of the subjects' inherent rights as represented by parliament. The basis of this conception was the doctrine of the common law as set forth by Sir Edward Coke, but in the dispute which now ensued over sovereignty and obedience, the defenders of parliament supplemented and extended their argument with momentous if confusing results by appealing also to the doctrine of equity or natural law as expounded to English lawyers by Christopher St. German. Thus the preachers of the Puritan brotherhood and the lawyers and gentry of parliament were able to join forces against the king in 1642 in the name of conscience, law, and equity combined.

Coke, from the death of Elizabeth to his own death in 1634, had been the champion, recorder, and expounder of the common law as opposed to the prerogative and of the common law courts as opposed to the courts directly depending upon the crown. He contended that the essence of law is not power of state but reason revealing itself continuously in the whole life of a people. Law was not something invented upon occasion and imposed by fiat but a vital principle which judges had but to observe and declare. Coke countered the claims of the crown by appealing to practice and precedent and the decisions of judges in former times. He thought of the law much as Protestant reformers thought of the church. First came its pure apostolic age, represented for later times in the laws of the Saxons. Corruption set in when the Norman Conqueror overrode the courts of law or turned their decisions to the aggrandizement of power at the expense of justice. Recovery began with Magna Charta. Since that time the maintenance of the law in its purity has depended immediately upon the fidelity of judges, ultimately upon parliament, which was its embodiment and representative in the state. The soundness of Coke's legal and historical scholarship does not concern us. His stubborn incorruptible resistance to James brought about his dismissal in 1616 as chief justice of the king's bench, and this event was followed by his election to the parliaments of 1621, 1624, and 1628. There he became one of the leaders of opposition to the crown and one of the chief authors and promoters of the Petition of Right. This was the climax of his career but not of his fame and influence. By 1628 he had completed three parts of his *Institutes of the Laws of England*, of which only the first part was published at that time. The king, hearing that Coke had written a book prejudicial to the crown, forbade the appearance of the rest of the work and upon the author's death seized his papers.[17] They were, however, not forgotten. In December, 1640, parliament gave orders for their recovery and publication. The second part of the *Institutes*, consisting of the text of Magna Charta and related statutes, with Coke's characteristic commentary, made its appearance in June, 1642, just in time to supply what seemed incontrovertible proof that the laws to which parliament appealed sprang from the mind of God revealed in the life and history of men.

But the champions of parliament as the embodiment of law in the state now found themselves in a predicament which the king's advocates exploited to the best of their ability. The crux of the dispute was control of the armed forces to be raised for service in Ireland. Command of such forces, according to custom and expectation, belonged to the king, and his consent was necessary to any act of parliament relating to the matter. But parliament was unwilling to entrust an army to Charles, and Charles was unwilling to relinquish his prerogative. The outcome was that in March, 1642, parliament gave orders without the king's approval for raising a militia subject to its own control, independently of the crown. It declared, moreover, that in view of Charles's refusal and the public danger, 'the Ordinance agreed on by both Houses . . . doth oblige the People, and ought to be obeyed by the fundamental Laws of this Kingdom.'[18] Parliament was declared to have supreme authority to determine the law of the land, and anyone who disputed that authority or commanded that it be disobeyed was guilty of a high breach of the privilege of parliament.[19] The king's declaration of May 19 made the unanswerable retort that this was to subject the known law of the land to the will of a majority of the men then assembled at Westminster.[20]

Thus the professed champions of law laid themselves open to the charge of setting themselves above law and usurping the sovereignty of the state. Parliament had either to abandon its role as the embodiment of law and historic practice or find some plea that should serve in lieu of strict legality to justify a course of action obviously unprecedented and unconstitutional. Its apologists found what was needed, not now in Coke and the common law, but in the theory and practice of equity derived from canon law by way of the court of chancery. The principle of a law of nature, revealed by reason and imposed by conscience, superior to all positive and customary laws whatever, had been set forth in the first book of Hooker's *Of the Laws of Ecclesiastical Polity*, but the exposition of the subject of greatest influence upon lawyers and students of law was Christopher St. German's *Dialogue in English, betweene a Doctor of Divinitie, and a Student in the Lawes of England*, commonly known as *The Doctor and Student*. The courts of the church, by setting up rules of equity based upon universal reason and conscience, had endeavored to supply inadequacies and correct injustices arising under the laws of states. Upon the advent of lay chancellors in England in the sixteenth century, St. German undertook to expound these rules for the guidance of English lawyers trained in English law. From him they learned that God has imprinted the law of nature in every man, 'teaching him what is to bee done, and what is to be fled.' This law must be obeyed upon peril of one's soul, and it cannot be contravened by human custom, enactment, or decree. In ordinary legal practice, of course, what the law of reason and conscience might require in any given case was for the lord chancellor to determine. Now, however, in the predicament created by the king's intransigence over the militia bill, the defenders of parliament seized upon the principle of natural law to justify parliament's extraordinary action against the crown, and the arbiter they set up to decide what reason and conscience required was parliament itself. If there appeared any inconsistency in the theory that parliament was the embodiment both of the law and of the equity which supervenes law, this did not concern the king's opponents in 1642. Neither were they concerned at this stage with the confusion that presently arose in many minds between the liberty all men may claim as children of nature, the liberty Englishmen are entitled to under the laws of England, and the liberty enjoyed only by the children of grace.

Charles and his friends had blamed the disaffection of his subjects first of all on the preachers, and there can be no question as to the continuing influence of the pulpit on revolutionary opinion. But as legal and political questions grew more and more acute, lawyers found as much to say as preachers. The open break between Charles and parliament evoked an interchange of declarations, manifestoes, and pamphlets in addition to sermons on the great issues of law and liberty, sovereignty and obedience. Just at the moment when Charles was being denied access to the munitions of war stored at Hull, the case for parliament was put into print in a broadside with the heading, 'A Question answered: How Laws are to be understood, and obedience yeelded.' The answer was that 'there is in Laws an equitable, and a litteral sence.' Command of the militia may be entrusted by law to the king for the public good, to serve which is the reason and equity of law. But when any commander whatever acts contrary to the public good, then he himself 'gives liberty to the Commanded to refuse *obedience* to the Letter. . . . Nor need this *equity* be expressed in the Law, being so naturally implyed and supposed in all Laws.' Parliament cannot be required to vote its own destruction. A general may not turn his guns on his own men. Were he to do so, he would '*ipso facto* estate' them 'in a right of disobedience, except we thinke that obedience binds Men to cut their owne throats.' [21]

The chief exponent in the press of this point of view was the lawyer, Henry Parker. As St. John told parliament in January, 1641, the issue in the ship-money case had been whether the king should be sole judge of the danger of the kingdom and of the means to be taken for its prevention.[22] Immediately upon the convening of parliament in 1640 Parker had taken up the argument on that point in *The Case of Shipmony briefly discoursed,* and he carried it forward in a number of additional pamphlets, the most noteworthy being *Observations upon some of his Majesties late Answers and Expresses,* a copy of which Thomason entered in his collection on July 2, 1642. Parker offered the clearest assertion which had yet appeared in print of the dependence of government upon the consent of the governed. The sole end and purpose of the state, he held, is the safety of the people, without distinction between man and man. Since every man bears a command within himself to defend himself, the people are required in the nature of things to determine wherein their safety consists. This is the voice of reason and conscience, which no man may disobey without enslaving himself to the will of others. This is the law of nature, the basis for all law in the state, and England is fortunate among nations in having found means by which the people may give or withhold consent to the laws which rulers seek to impose upon them. That is, parliament, being in essence the people, is the supreme judicature of the realm, and from its decisions there can in the nature of things be no appeal. For the king is bound by conscience and the terms of his office to obey the will of the people, thus embodied and expressed, with or without the agreement and consent of his private conscience and opinion.

Parker's *Observations* set off a long dispute in the press which culminated, so far as he was concerned, with the publication of his *Jus Populi* in October, 1644.[23] The question, he there concludes, is not whether the power of kings is derived from God but whether it may be exercised without the subject's consent, a question which in the seventeenth century could not be discussed without reference to Adam and the fall of man. Before the fall, Parker reasons, man lived without government but under a manifest order to which he freely consented, an order 'such as nature in its greatest purity did own.'[24] Government became necessary only because man rejected and disobeyed the order of his being. It was the means granted to the sons of Adam for relieving themselves of some of the worst consequences of Adam's sin and recovering some measure of the natural order disrupted by his disobedience.

The royalist rejoinder to this notion was that, since the fall, men are bound by the law of God to obey their princes absolutely as wives are bound to obey their husbands and children their parents. But Parker rejected both the argument and the analogy, holding that marriage itself rests upon the free consent of both parties, that neither the woman nor the man is put under absolute subjection. The wife may claim a kind of parity in the disparity of the matrimonial bond. The husband, for whose sake she was created, may not turn wedlock to her disadvantage, which is in truth to say to his own. A similar rule holds for parents and children and for rulers and people, as Parker seeks to demonstrate by a long series of instances drawn from history and scripture. All types of government, he holds, monarchy, aristocracy, and democracy in their several mixtures, depend upon agreement for the satisfaction of natural need, and no interest in the state must be permitted to obscure or impede that principle. 'When wee are treating of worldly affaires, wee ought to bee very tender how we seek to reconcile that to Gods law, which we cannot reconcile to mens equity: or how we make God the author of that constitution which man reaps inconvenience from.' [25]

Thus to the incitements of the pulpit against the king the lawyers, with Parker for their spokesman in the press, added arguments drawn from the doctrine of equity and natural law. And the liberty all men were alleged to possess as children of nature was also appealed to in further support of the claims the preachers put forward for the liberty of the elect as children of grace. When the Earl of Essex, with his coffin, winding-sheet, and scutcheon, ready at need for his funeral, arrived at Northampton on September 10 to take command of the parliamentary army, he found 'an abundance of famous, excellent divines' on the spot before him, beating the drum ecclesiastic. Stephen Marshall and Cornelius Burges were the chaplains of his own regiment. In the campaign that ensued the preachers were said to have 'subdued and satisfied more malignant spirits . . . than a thousand armed men could have done.' They were described at Edgehill on October 23, riding up and down the lines, 'exhorting and encouraging the Souldiers to fight valiantly, and not to flye, but now if ever to stand to it, and to fight for their Religion, Lawes, and Christian liberties.' [26]

Edgehill, however, decided nothing. Charles advanced to the outskirts of London and then withdrew to Oxford. A winter of futile negotiations followed while the champions of king and parliament in pulpit and press kept up the argument concerning sovereignty and obedience. Stephen Marshall, turning pamphleteer in self-defense against *Mercurius Aulicus* of February 17, reiterated Parker's contentions in *A Plea for Defensive Armes*. Francis Cheynell in a sermon before the house of commons on May 31 declared that the church was to be protected from her enemies in the name of natural law as well as Christian liberty.[27] Andrew Perne, preaching at St. Margaret's on the same day, declared that, 'if a Nation consent together, and chuse a King to Reign over them,' the people will fight for him so long as he keeps the agreement between them.' But God is above kings and religion above civil laws. Nature requires all people to be 'peremptory' in defense of their beliefs, whatever their beliefs may be, and the law of nations forbids the repression of the godly.[28]

But the most peremptory defense of parliament at this stage of affairs came from John Goodwin, vicar of St. Stephen's, Coleman Street. He had incurred disapproval for the notions concerning justification expressed in his *Imputatio Fidei* in January, 1642, and he was not one of the inner circle of the Puritan brotherhood, but he was nevertheless one of the most influential and sought-after preachers in London. No one represented more clearly the influence of Christian humanism in its Protestant phase upon the Puritan revolutionary movement. From that point of view, he rejected royalist talk of divine right and passive obedience and embraced Parker's conception of natural law in relation to the state. Shortly before Edgehill in October he published *Anti-Cavalierisme, or Truth Pleading As well the Necessity, as the Lawfullness of this present War*,[29] and as the king's forces were approaching the city after that engagement, he issued *The Butchers Blessing, or the Bloody Intentions of Romish Cavaliers against the City of London above other places.*[30] Both pamphlets were based upon sermons intended to arouse popular feeling for the support of parliament and the City in the face of what seemed imminent actual danger.

Oh let it be as abomination unto us, as the very shadow of death, to every man, woman, and child of us, not to be active, not to lie out and straine our selves to the utmost of our strength and power in every kinde, as far as the Law of God and Nature will suffer us, to resist that high hand of iniquity and blood that is stretched out against us; to make our lives, and our liberties, and our Religion good against that accursed Generation that now magnifieth themselves, to make a prey and spoyle of them, to make havock and desolation of them all at once, if the Lord shall yet please to deliver us out of their hands.[31]

But Goodwin was not simply a religious demagogue turning to his own purposes the legal-political formulas and slogans which Parker made current. In the pulpit he was the voice of the same idealism, drawn from the same sources, which Lord Brooke and Milton in their several roles also expressed. He believed that salvation depends upon faith, but that the effect of faith is to prompt ceaseless search for truth, revealed not in its entirety once for all to any man, class, or profession but continuously step by step to all who are moved by faith to seek it out. To that end they must be left free to search the scriptures, preach the Word, and debate, as long as need be, every point of truth, near-truth, seeming truth, or error. The state is necessary for the maintenance of civil peace, but in matters of belief government itself must proceed by the method of inquiry and discussion. Any government which does otherwise thereby claims to be infallible. Any king who pretends to rule by divine right sets himself up as God. To obey such and not to resist by every means in one's power is to deny truth.

Thus pamphleteers and preachers, lawyers and divines, accommodated the notion of a law of nature governing all men to a belief on the one hand in a law of grace vouchsafed to the elect and on the other to the doctrine of a common law of the state which Englishmen had enjoyed since time immemorial. And running through all these arguments, there was the recurring irrepressible presumption of the existence of truth to be found out through observation, discourse, and progressive discovery. But preachers, pamphleteers, and lawyers had done another thing too. By clothing their ideas in the scriptural legend of man's fall and redemption, they had at the same time gained force for their argument and lent new meaning and vitality to the Puritan version of the Christian epic. The law of nature was said to consist of all those divine decrees which called creation into being and by which it moves. It is a law evident to reason, which is itself a work of God, and this law, though transcended, is by no means invalidated by grace. Laws of man's making must conform to the law of nature or be of no force. No state may contravene it. To disobey it is to seek death. Yet disobedience and death come about through no failure in nature itself, which would argue imperfection in the divine being who is its author, but through the corruption of nature, first of all of human nature, caused by man. So long as Adam obeyed the natural laws of his being, he enjoyed the bliss of paradise. When he disobeyed, through no compulsion but by his own choice, he lost his power to follow nature perfectly, and nature lost its perfect efficacy in him to life and happiness. Sin and death came into the world. The hand of every son of Adam was raised against his brother, and all would have perished but that nature itself forbade. God's command, still speaking in their corrupted hearts, drove men to forfend death as best they could by setting bounds to the war by which they destroyed each other. They were driven to agree to obey not each his own depraved will but everyone the will of one chosen by all and bound by his own word to protect all from attack from any quarter. On such terms and such terms only, it was said, did rulers hold authority over subjects, husbands over wives, parents over children. And since rulers and subjects, husbands and wives, parents and children, being all children of Adam, were equal in sin, it followed that neither authority nor obedience held any longer than it served the divine purpose for which in the nature of things it was intended. That God intended nothing but the good of man, however that good might be defined, was an axiom not to be questioned.

iii. MILTON AND THE LAW OF MARRIAGE

The principles and policies urged by the Puritan preachers, full of their need to make secure their freedom in the pulpit, soon led to conclusions they had not foreseen and were not ready to admit or approve. Their first thought from the beginning had been to preach the Word, but the more freely they preached the Word as they conceived it, the nearer they drew to the point at which control of any sort over the spiritual life of the people would become impossible. The more unreservedly they justified disobedience to royal authority on grounds of reason and conscience, the nearer they drew to the time when any constituted authority whatever in state or church might expect to be challenged on the same grounds. In *The Reason of Church-government* Milton had clearly pointed to such a conclusion as the logical consequence of the campaign against prelacy. He did not, however, as might have been expected, next join the preachers and the lawyers in defending parliament against the king. He turned instead, still on the basis of the same principles though on the level of his own lofty idiosyncrasy, to urging revolutionary reform in another but parallel direction.

Whatever misgivings concerning his ministerial associates he may have begun to feel, he still believed, as he said in 1654, that, 'if discipline originating in religion continued its course to the morals and institutions of the commonwealth,' the result would surely be 'the deliverance of the whole life of mortal man from slavery.' He also appears to have assumed that the final removal of the bishops from the house of lords in February, 1642, cleared the way for reformation of church government, liberation of pulpit and press, and consequent unimpeded advance toward the New Jerusalem. He tells us that, since religious liberty seemed now to be assured and parliament to be diligently occupied in defending civil liberty, he for his part undertook to write on behalf of what he calls domestic liberty, the liberty, that is, to marry, to learn, and to think and speak according to reason and conscience for the satisfaction of imperative need arising in nature.[32]

First as it happened came liberty to marry, and the occasion which prompted Milton to choose that subject at this point was his own marital misadventure. In May, 1642, having completed the last of his antiprelatical tracts, he married the daughter of an Oxfordshire squire of royalist sympathies.[33] After a few weeks the young wife returned to her own people in the country and, as the civil war began, presently refused to return to her husband. A year later, about the first of August, 1643, Milton published a tract of forty-eight pages, entitled *The Doctrine and Discipline of Divorce Restor'd to the Good of both Sexes*. Six months later he issued a second edition, almost twice the length of the first, followed in July, 1644, by *The Judgement of Martin Bucer concerning Divorce*, and in March, 1645, *Tetrachordon* and *Colasterion*. Few episodes in the lives of poets have provoked more speculation upon the part of biographers and critics. What happened in that household, supposing it were possible to know, is, however, not necessary for our purposes in these pages to inquire. Our concern is rather to understand what Milton, no doubt moved by unfortunate personal experience, actually said about the subject of divorce, which is to say about love, marriage, and the family. It is also to note the relation of his ideas regarding those important matters to the general movement of his party and his age for liberty and reform in church and state.

He was quite alone in raising any such question at this particular time. Yet his doing so as well as the tenor of his argument was entirely consistent with Puritan teaching, the campaign against prelacy, and the current challenge to the authority of the crown. Milton was occupied in his tracts on divorce with the predicament of one who, under existing laws, finds himself bound without hope of redress to an uncongenial unresponsive mate. But the existing laws governing marriage had been established by the church without reference to the civil state, and though prelacy had now been cast off, the authority of the church to enforce such laws still remained unquestioned.[34] Milton's proposals for reform were of far-reaching and to his contemporaries startling significance. The marital relationship was commonly understood to be the seed and mirror of every other relationship, and any consideration of the origin, purpose, and structure of this institution in the general scheme of things necessarily involved consideration of the conditions underlying every other. Milton's argument concerning marriage and divorce proceeded from the same premises as Parker's argument concerning liberty and obedience in the state and arrived by parallel reasoning at a similar conclusion.

The basis of Milton's thinking was of course Christian morality intermingled with Renaissance idealism, the traditional set of reasons and rules for marrying, for loving, and at the same time for avoiding confusion to the soul. There is no subject harder to write about without misunderstanding and misjudgment. When Paul told women to submit to their husbands, he was stating the patriarchal conception of the family which prevailed in the ancient world. The ancients did not regard the association of a particular kind of mental excitement with the desire for procreation as necessary to marriage. Plato analyzed and described such excitement as a profound reorganization and reorientation of consciousness and called it love, but he left to later generations the association of what he called love with the specific attraction exercised by persons of opposite sex upon each other. Paul underwent the same kind of experience, but again the love which made him into a new man was not the love of woman. Under his influence, the church, while admitting sex as the natural basis for marriage, rejected it as the appointed sphere for a transforming spiritual experience. Marriage was sacred, passion profane. Moreover, in providing sanction, status, and function for the married, the church did not fail to provide also for the unmarried. Matrimony with the family for its organ was one way of life; celibacy organized in monasticism was another. Having approved marriage for the relief of concupiscence, the church offered religious celibacy as an alternative to marriage. Not the least important effect of the decline and final destruction of monasticism was the cutting off of that alternative. For as celibacy lost its recognized place and function and fell into disrepute, marriage came to be regarded as the one way of life instituted by God and required by nature for every normal person, and the state of the unmarried became something to be ridiculed, pitied, and scorned. Hence Milton, who in another age might have lived all his life in the condition of Petrarch or Erasmus, and who did live half a busy and productive lifetime without woman, decided at the age of thirty-four that he must take a wife.

In making that decision, he expected to find himself in love, that is, to enter upon the enjoyment of a very special state of spiritual intimacy with the woman he had chosen. We must not suppose, because men in ancient and medieval life did not think it necessary to fall in love in order to get married, that they did no falling in love. They learned from Plato how the soul may be transformed by desiring beauty upon beauty and discovering good upon good. They read in Paul and Augustine how the soul might be transformed by discovering God. But from Ovid they learned, if only to pretend, that the attraction exercised by a woman might also do something quite exciting to the soul. They learned to play that falling in love was like being reborn in spirit, as though the woman were divinity and her beauty the fair face of the good enlightening the heart of the sinner who adored her, in short as though courting a lady were like worshiping God. In medieval life, this lady worship had nothing necessarily to do with marriage. Marriage was a serious affair involving the church, property, and the family. Love was a game, sometimes an art, for those to play at who could afford it, and when game led to earnest, as of course it often did, it did not necessarily lead to wedlock. Guinevere and Iseult never thought of divorcing their husbands in order to marry their lovers. But love might also lead, as Petrarch showed, to a life of fascinating introspection, a life spent in the enjoyment not of the lady but of the emotions the lady aroused, not in actually making love but in thinking and writing about loving. Or, as in the case of Dante or in the manner described by Castiglione, love might in truth lead a man to heaven, though still not to marriage.

The Renaissance literature of lady-worship was taken up in England in Tudor times for the entertainment of courtiers but quickly spread beyond the aristocratic coterie for which it was designed. Through the press and the theater it reached the great popular audience which had come into being in the sixteenth century, and in passing from court to city it underwent a change in accordance with the taste, the moral sentiments, the religious convictions of the new public. Exactly when this transition from the *amour courtois* to the *amour bourgeois* was complete would be difficult and is not important to say. For there was another influence at work, modifying that of lady-worship but conducing also in its own way to a more idealistic or at any rate to a heightened emotional attitude toward woman. That was the influence of Puritanism, which is to say of the pattern of feeling and code of behavior set forth in pulpit and press by the brotherhood of preachers. Earlier in the history of the church, the members of such an order would have dedicated themselves to chastity and the celibate life. These men did not, in deference to Paul, actually condemn celibacy but, depending upon Paul, they insisted that the power to abstain from woman was a gift of God proper to few and no more proper to themselves than to other men. On the contrary, since all men were equally sinful in the eyes of God, preachers were as liable to the burning of the flesh as others. If anything they were more liable since they were Satan's special targets. Consequently, seeing that marriage was the appointed remedy for concupiscence, they married, almost to a man, remarried whenever mortality gave occasion, and begot children without restraint. This dedication of Puritan churchmen to conjugal life as to a holy rule was no less important in its effect than that of courtly poets to the worship of feminine beauty. The Puritans were committed to the belief that the sphere of religious experience was the individual soul, and that the decisive event in the life of the soul was the experience of being transformed by faith, of being reborn precisely as Paul had been, and, they might have observed, in a manner not altogether unlike that which Plato had analyzed and described. The truth of this belief was set down for all to read in the scriptures and for each to confirm in the experience of his own heart. The preachers' special calling was to observe, understand, and report what happened within themselves, and then in sermons, commentaries, journals, and biographies to teach others that by the grace of God the same might happen to them. The primary means by which God called upon the soul was, of course, his own Word in scripture, brought home by words from the pulpit, but the whole of experience resounded with vocation to the soul. Everything that happened to a man provoked the old man in him to die again and the new to be reborn in the faith that follows upon calling and in the assurance, ever to be renewed, of salvation that follows upon faith. Nor did the preachers content themselves with merely explaining and proving this doctrine; they went on to tell what emotions men and women might expect to observe within their breasts, supposing them to be truly called, and how, granting them to be of the elect, they should endeavor to behave.

But few occasions could call upon the soul more compellingly than love and marriage, and therefore a most important question requiring to be answered for the edification of saints was how to feel and act in those relationships. Consequently there flowed from the Puritan preachers a steady stream of instruction on love, marriage, and family life. There was William Perkins' *Christian Oeconomie*, translated into English in 1609 from the Latin of 1590; Henry Smith's *Preparative to Marriage*, 1591; John Dod and Robert Cleaver's *Godlie Forme of Householde Government*, 1598; William Whately's *Bridebush*, 1617, and *Care-cloth*, 1624; William Gouge's *Domesticall Duties*, 1622; Daniel Rogers' *Matrimoniall Honour*, 1642; not to mention other books on the art of loving and living with a woman and at the same time of keeping up the eternal warfare of the soul against the devil.

This literature was not directed at change of existing laws concerning marriage and divorce. There had been agitation of that sort in England under Henry VIII and Edward VI as there had been among Protestants on the continent, but after the Elizabethan settlement the unexpressed condition under which the Puritans were allowed to continue preaching was submission to established law and authority. Hence the early agitation for reform of the marriage law died down, not to be revived in any important way until Milton took it up; the preachers devoted themselves instead to teaching people how to suffuse relations between the sexes with religious emotion. Their teaching has been much misunderstood. It had, of course, to be based upon scripture, and if scripture made anything clear, it was, in the words of Paul, that the husband is the head of the wife, that the wife should submit to the husband as the husband to the Lord, but that husbands ought to love their wives even as Christ loves his church. Now the scriptures, taken by and large, are far from squeamish concerning the intercourse of the sexes, and Paul himself adjured husbands and wives to render due benevolence to each other, by which was commonly understood just one thing. It seemed then natural and right to marry but, though it was obvious that according to the law of God wives should submit to their husbands, it was essential that husbands and wives should love each other. Loving each other, due benevolence and all, was like nothing less than the love of Christ and the church. Long before Milton Puritan writers had much to say on the theme 'he for God only she for God in him' but mostly to emphasize not how far he was above her but how closely she might approach his level by yielding for love of him the submission which he for love of her chose not to exact. Another doctrine, also well buttressed in Paul, taught them that, though differing in gifts and authority, they were equal in their claims upon God's grace.

In less rarefied language, all this meant that Puritan preachers, being for the most part men of sensitive feeling and lively imagination, discovered matrimony to be much more endurable when they had the good luck or the good judgment to marry congenial women and when they relied most upon affection, sympathy, and understanding as the means to domestic harmony. That at any rate was the aspect of the matter which they chiefly dwelt upon in their books. After all, few men needed to be told to marry and to govern their wives. What they needed was to learn how to marry in the spirit of godliness. So the preachers taught that a wife should be treated not as a servant or simply a bedfellow but as a spiritual equal and companion. They gave instruction in the difficult art of finding a woman suitable for such a role. They enjoined young people in choosing their mates to obey their parents and to exercise all prudence, but they exhorted parents not to interfere with the choices their children made within the dictates of godliness. They dilated upon the joys of spiritual love, sealing and sanctifying the union of the flesh, and upon the miseries of those who, coupled in body, were divided in soul. Some like William Whately or Daniel Rogers went so far as to suggest that husband and wife in their spiritual communing with one another might attain communion with God himself. One step, however, they drew back from taking. They warned the godly against the danger of marrying the wrong woman, but if by chance spiritual union did not come off, there was nothing the saint could do about it except pray for patience to endure the worst trials of unhappy wedlock. Whately in a moment of unguarded zeal proposed to relax the law that forbade divorce, but prodded by the Court of High Commission he quickly found reason to recant. It remained for a more resolute mind to carry Puritan insistence upon the spiritual character of marriage to its logical conclusion.

Such was the conception of the part of marriage in the life of man which had been set forth time and again by members of the ministerial caste to which Milton had himself aspired, and it was to be set forth again in his own writings. Yet Milton, and the same is to some extent true of the Puritan preachers, did not look only to St. Paul, St. Augustine, and the Protestant reformers for instruction concerning love. When the apologist for Bishop Hall accused Milton of frequenting bordellos, he refuted the charge in an extraordinary burst of self-revelation. He owned that in truth he knew about love, but what he knew he had learned not in bordellos but from the best authors. As a boy at school he had read 'the smooth Elegiack Poets,' meaning chiefly Ovid, and had enjoyed them, he confessed, better than the orators and historians he had also been caused to read. He had enjoyed both their art and their subject matter, 'which what it is, there be few who know not.' They wrote, of course, about love, but he observed that under the names of the ladies they celebrated they thought it their chief glory to judge, to praise and to love certain 'high perfections.' What they could do he could do. If indeed he wished to show what 'judgement, wit, or elegance' had fallen to his share, he must show 'how much more wisely and with more love of vertue' he chose '(let rude eares be absent) the object of not unlike praises.' For 'not to be sensible, when good and faire in one person meet, argues both a grosse and shallow judgement, and withall an ungentle, and swainish brest.' When, moreover, he found his authors speaking unworthily of themselves or unchastely of their ladies, he still applauded their art but deplored the use they made of it. 'And above them all,' he concludes, he preferred 'the two famous renowners of *Beatrice* and *Laura* who never write but honour of them to whom they devote their verse, displaying sublime and pure thoughts, without transgression.' Next, he tells us as we should expect, his young feet wandered 'among the lofty Fables and Romances, which recount in solemne canto's the deeds of Knighthood founded by our victorious Kings,' by which he surely meant Spenser's *Faerie Queene*, though he may also have had in mind the poets, especially Ariosto and Tasso, from whom Spenser had drawn so much of his inspiration and material. In those writers he read that every knight was bound to defend the honor and chastity of woman, adding, however, his personal conclusion that 'every free and gentle spirit' without oath or spur or touch of sword was bound to do the same 'both by his counsell'—a true Miltonic note—'and his arme.'

So much the poets taught him about love, and then, he adds, 'riper yeares, and the ceaseless round of study and reading' led him to the philosophers and 'chiefly to the divine volumes of *Plato* and his equall *Xenophon*.' What he learned about love from this source, mainly, that is, from Plato, what he learned about true love, 'whose charming cup is only vertue' and is bestowed only on the worthy, while a 'certaine Sorceresse, the abuser of loves name' cheats others with 'a thick intoxicating potion,' how he learned that 'the first and chiefest office of love, begins and ends in the soule, producing those happy twins . . . knowledge and vertue,'—all this, he somewhat abruptly concludes, it might sometime be worth his readers' hearing about. Thus Ovid, Dante, Petrarch, Ariosto, Tasso, Spenser, and finally Plato helped to teach not only Bishop Hall's assailant but also the husband of Mary Powell and the author of the divorce tracts what to look for in a wife. Even if he had not been carefully trained in the precepts of religion, even if 'Christianity had bin but slightly taught me'—and we have seen what it taught about love when voiced to Puritan youth by Puritan preachers—he was still confident that 'a certain reserv'dnesse of naturall disposition, and morall discipline learnt out of the noblest Philosophy was anough to keep me in disdain of farre lesse incontinences then this of the Burdello.' [35]

So when Milton read what was revealed in scripture about the love of woman, he knew that it meant something very like what the poets and philosophers meant. What the lover honored in the lady was what the apostle called the glory of man which is in the woman, the reflection in woman of the glory of God which is in the man. He should honor chastity in woman because he should honor in her whatever was most to be honored in himself, but he should honor it in himself even more than in her. Milton adds that he has not slumbered over the place in St. John's vision where it is said the redeemed, 'those,' he notes, 'who were not defil'd with women,' heard and understood the song which was sung before the mystical lamb. St. John says the blessed were not defiled 'for they are virgins,' but Milton, perhaps nodding over that word, explains that 'defil'd' 'doubtlesse meanes fornication: For mariage must not be call'd a defilement.' [36] Those who in his vision bore the Father's name on their foreheads were married, and they loved their wives because they saw in them not only what St. Paul but also what Ovid, Dante, Petrarch, Spenser, and Plato taught them to expect.

'The first and chiefest office of love, begins and ends in the soule.' So much Milton could have learned from Plato, Dante, and Petrarch, but not that the office of love which begins and ends in the soul must be sought only in marriage. For teaching that lesson the one poet was Spenser. At the time Milton wrote *Comus*, he was captivated by Britomart as the image of spiritual self-sufficiency, and he took no notice, as was natural, of the fact that what made her so perfectly self-sufficient was married love. But to suppose that he stopped at that point in his reading of a poet so full of ideas which, in however different a guise, were to reappear so often in his own writings is hardly possible. That part of *The Faerie Queene* in which Britomart is concerned deals ostensibly with virtues called chastity and friendship, actually with married love as the very apex and type of all true amity of souls. The poem at this point becomes a fabric of interlacing tales of unmatched or mismatched lovers, sorting themselves out, finding each his or her own proper mate and spiritual counterpart. The base souls, though they may begin in seeming love and harmony, end in strife and hatred. The nobler spirits, however they begin, all end in love and peace, signified but for one exception by marriage. As the characters intermingle in their encounters and adventures, their souls are discovered to one another; like joins with like, and true and false fly asunder. The key figures are five women, expressing as many variants of the poet's conception of the ideal relation between man and woman. Belphoebe, in compliment to Queen Elizabeth, is the inconclusive attempt of a Renaissance Protestant mind to imagine woman not unloved though unmarried. Radigund is woman in unnatural rebellion against man. Florimell is the woman who is afraid of men until she runs into the arms of the man who is afraid of women, whereupon each becomes the other's remedy, and they love, marry, and fear no more. The union of Amoret and Scudamour, children of nature, is endangered by the false love which masquerades in the artificial forms of the *amour courtois*. It is saved by Britomart—until Spenser remembers he must not let her steal the show from Arthur—and Britomart is married love. She has seen her husband and her children's father in the mirror of her soul and has come forth, secure in the rectitude of her intentions, to find him. Nothing can harm or frighten such a woman, and nothing can withstand her. She finally meets her beloved in battle, and when he beholds her, beautiful though a little sweaty, he can only make religion of his wonder and she can only yield to the beauty which she sees in him, 'tempered with sternesse and stout majestie.'

Such briefly was the conception of wifehood which Milton found in those 'solemne canto's' which formed so important a part of his education in the philosophy of love and beauty. Not without reason was he to praise their author in *Areopagitica* as a better teacher than Scotus or Aquinas. That he expected to find a Britomart in the child he married, one would not dare to say, but clearly the predicament from which his divorce argument starts is that of the man who, expecting much of marriage, wakes to find himself joined to an 'uncomplying discord of nature, . . . an image of earth and fleam,' 'a loyal and individual vexation,' a creature who supplies him with little more than 'a displeasing and forc't remedy against the sting of a bruit desire.' Men of loose lives, who have, so to speak, gone through many divorces, learn from experience to avoid error such as sober, chaste men easily fall into through their little practice in these affairs. The honorable lover may discern too late 'the unliveliness and naturall sloth' which often hides under 'the bashfull mutenes of a virgin.' He is permitted no free access to the woman before marriage. 'Acquaintance,' her friends persuade him, 'as it increases, will amend all.' Hence it happens that the sober man, respecting modesty and hoping for the best, often meets, 'if not with a body impenetrable, yet often with a mind to all other due conversation inaccessible, and to all the more estimable and superior purposes of matrimony uselesse and almost liveles.' [37]

Nothing, it seemed to Milton, could be easier or less blamable than to be mistaken in choosing a wife. Yet as the law stood, 'one moment after those mighty syllables pronounc't which take upon them to joyn heaven and hell together unpardnably till death pardon,' and all the promised blessings of matrimony might vanish. Against this danger, against all the miseries of unhappy wedlock, the people had often enough been forewarned by their preachers, but Milton set himself the task of persuading parliament and assembly to adopt what seemed to him the obvious remedy and 'with one gentle stroking to wipe away ten thousand teares out of the life of man.' The reform of the law of marriage was to his mind the logical consequence of the abolition of prelacy and the projected reform of the church.[38]

In course of time the church had brought marriage under its authority and had finally declared it to be a sacrament, a mystical union not to be dissolved this side the grave. But the church also provided legal means for permitting the parties in certain cases to separate or for nullifying such unions as might be determined never to have taken place in the sight of God. This conception of marriage and the abuses which grew up in the administration of these laws were the object of frequent attack by Protestants. Starting with Luther, the reformers denied the sacramental character of marriage, granted some control to the civil magistrate, and permitted remarriage under certain conditions of separation. This was the historical beginning of what has come to be called divorce as distinguished from simple separation from bed and board and from annulment under canon law. The first condition for divorce set up by the reformers, in accordance with Matthew 5: 32 and 19: 9, was adultery, but to this on the authority of I Corinthians 7: 10 was frequently added desertion, more or less broadly defined. These changes were accompanied by no little discussion, in England especially after the separation of Henry VIII from his first wife and of the church from Rome. The German reformers, Fagius and Bucer, who were brought over to Cambridge under Edward VI, both advocated, as Milton was happy to discover, the adoption of Protestant principles of marriage in England. The English church, however, adhered to canon law right down to Milton's time. Under Laud it continued to grant separation on the ground of adultery but not the right of remarriage. When remarriage occurred, as it frequently did, the parties merely assumed a privilege which strictly speaking the law did not grant.

If, then, Milton had desired strictly to obey the law and yet to marry again after his wife left him, he might have applied to the church courts to have the union annulled on any of a number of recognized grounds. But he had been seeking the overthrow of prelacy and with prelacy the authority of canon law and of the courts by which it was administered. In the circumstances, consistently with Protestant principles, he might have disregarded canon law and taken his freedom on the ground of desertion, especially if, as there is no evidence for believing, his marriage had failed of consummation. He did not, however, do this, and what he said in his argument for divorce was that an errant or even a faithless wife could be forgiven and taken back. The unforgivable thing was 'indisposition, unfitnes, or contrariety of mind.' This was 'a greater reason of divorce than naturall frigidity, especially if there be no children, and that there be mutuall consent.' Marriage was no sacrament or mystical union but a simple compact made by two human beings for their own good, and as they consented to come together, they might consent to part. The only power with any shadow of right to compel or forbid was that which resided in their own breasts. The woman's right, we must note, though not her authority or her responsibility, was the same as the man's. She too must consent; she too was entitled to demand 'solace and peace'; and if she failed to get them, she was entitled to the same redress. Authority naturally rested with the husband except under one condition. It normally rested with him because, according to the law set down in scripture and made plain in nature, man is normally the superior. But whenever the woman happens, as she may, to 'exceed her husband in prudence and dexterity, and he contentedly yeeld, . . . then a superior and more naturall law comes in, that the wiser should govern the lesse wise, whether male or female.' [39]

The merits of these theories and proposals concern us less than their significance in the general development of their author's ideas. He had, it is evident, read and thought upon the subject before 1643, but there is nothing in the first divorce tract to show that Milton had by that time informed himself at all extensively concerning the teachings of Protestant reformers on such matters. He himself roundly asserted that when he first wrote about the subject, he owed nothing to any authority but scripture and that as he wrote he felt himself to be 'no other then a passive instrument under some power and counsel higher and better then can be human.' [40] This statement is somewhat misleading. Milton owed little perhaps to previous writers on divorce, but he had read the Bible with the eyes of a man whose hopes in matrimony had been formed by much reading in other sources on the subject of love. The point was that, wherever he may have got his ideas, he had to satisfy himself that they were to be found in scripture too. Consequently in *Tetrachordon* he set out to demonstrate that Genesis 1: 27, 28 and 2: 18, 23, 24; Deuteronomy 24: 1, 2; Matthew 5: 31, 32 and 19: 3–11, and I Corinthians 7: 10–16 squared exactly with each other and with his own ideas. The account in Genesis of the creation of woman and the institution of matrimony, involved as it was in the account of creation and the fall, presented little difficulty. The problem was to reconcile with the law of Moses the injunction given by Christ to the Pharisees and reiterated by Paul to the Corinthians, and the crux was that the law granted a liberty which the gospel seemed to take away. Moses ruled that, when a woman lost favor or was found unclean, her husband should write her a bill of divorcement, and she might go and be another man's wife. Christ ruled that a wife might be put away only for adultery and that she might not then be married again. Milton had to find arguments to convince himself that by adultery at this point Christ did not mean what was commonly supposed but what Milton designated as spiritual fornication.

There is no need to debate whether Milton's method of interpreting scripture was correct or his idea of the relation of the sexes right.

Quoting scripture, as obviously everyone else did, for his own purposes, he thought about marriage precisely as, up to a certain point,
most English Protestants thought about it. The divorce tracts are a
part of that literature of edification concerning marriage which
Puritan churchmen had been turning out ever since the sixteenth
century, and Milton's arguments spring directly from the doctrine
and code set forth by such men as Perkins, Smith, Whately, and
Gouge. The basis and the end of marriage, they all held, was spiritual.
It was, Milton said, 'a divine institution joyning man and woman in
a love fitly dispos'd to the helps and comforts of domestic life.' 'The
internal *Form* and soul of this relation, is conjugal love arising from
a mutual fitness to the final causes of wedlock, help and society in
Religious, Civil and Domestic conversation, which includes as an in-
ferior end the fulfilling of natural desire, and specifical increase.' First
comes 'the apt and cheerfull conversation of man with woman, to comfort and refresh him against the evill of solitary life,' and then, 'a
secondary end in dignity, though not in necessity,' 'the purpose of
generation.' It is a greater blessing, more worthy of man, more
honorable and sanctifying to marriage, 'whenas the solace and satisfaction of the mind is regarded and provided for before the sensitive
pleasing of the body.' When Paul said it was better to marry than to
burn, Milton could not understand him to mean mere carnal burning
—'God does not principally take care for such cattell.' That kind of
burning can be allayed by 'strict life and labour, with the abatement of
a full diet.' The apostle meant the 'more inbred desire' of joining to
one's self 'in conjugall fellowship a fit conversing soul.' This is that
desire stronger than death which is properly called love, 'that rationall
burning that mariage is to remedy,' that 'intelligible flame, not in
paradice to be resisted.' [41]

All this is the stereotype of Puritan edification, but the happiness
which Milton proposed to himself in marriage was not suggested by
the scriptures alone. The preachers referred often enough to Rebecca
and Ruth and the Shulamite but seldom, owing to the conventions of
the pulpit, to teachers of the art of love outside the scriptures with
whom they as well as Milton must surely have been acquainted.
Milton, however, was free to be more explicit. The poet who moves
through the divorce tracts hand in hand with the dialectician is a

Renaissance poet of humanistic learning who calls upon the *Symposium* and the *Phaedrus* to help him understand Genesis and the epistles of St. Paul. For example, what Socrates tells of love, 'the sonne of *Penury*, begot of *Plenty* in the garden of *Jupiter*,' makes clear to Milton what Moses means when he reveals 'that *Love* was the son of *Loneliness*, begot in Paradise by that sociable and helpfull aptitude which God implanted between man and woman to each other.' It is the same love which in all circumstances 'still burnes' for Milton 'in the proper meaning of *S. Paul*,' the same 'matrimoniall love' which, waxing or waning as it meets or misses its true conversing counterpart —'reflection of a coequal & *homogeneal* fire'—is likened by the ancient sages, Milton says, meaning of course chiefly Plato, to Eros and Anteros, 'no meer amatorious novel' but 'a deep and serious verity.' Again it is Plato and Spenser, surely, who help him to quote Solomon for his purpose, to frame a sort of spiritual epithalamium out of the eighth chapter of Proverbs and the Song of Songs. Sometimes, he says, a man must slacken the cords of thought and labor. 'God himself conceals us not his own recreations before the world was built.' He delights in his own wisdom which plays daily before him. For to God wisdom is 'a high towr of pleasure, but to us a steep hill, and we toyling ever about the bottom.' That is to say, men grow weary even in worthy enterprises, cannot 'always be contemplative, or pragmaticall abroad, but have need of som delightfull intermissions, wherein the enlarg'd soul may leav off a while her severe schooling; and like a glad youth in wandring vacancy, may keep her hollidaies to joy and harmles pastime: which as she cannot well doe without company, so in no company so well as where the different sexe in most resembling unlikenes, and most unlike resemblance cannot but please best ánd be pleas'd in the aptitude of that variety.' God, we are to understand if we read the scriptures aright, gave man to delight in woman as it were himself delighting in that reflection of himself which is the eternal wisdom.[42]

'Part of my Soul, I seek thee,' Adam says upon his first beholding Eve in paradise, 'and thee claim my other half,' thus echoing another of the images of the *Symposium*. Marriage, whatever it might comprehend, was essentially a marriage of true minds. And yet God in giving man a wife was no such unbounteous giver as Jupiter when, instead of Juno, he gave Ixion a cloud to embrace. Communion with no other soul can take the place of that which a husband may enjoy with his wife. Milton scorns Augustine's 'crabbed opinion' that it would have been more becoming for Adam to have found solace in the friendship of another man rather than 'spend so many secret years in an empty world with one woman.' Adam had the company of God himself; he had the angels to converse with and the creatures to delight him; he could have had 'a thousand friends and brother Adams' created out of the same mold as himself. Nevertheless, the text 'it is not good for man to be alone' means nothing but 'alone without woman.' 'Till Eve was giv'n him, God reckn'd him to be alone.' No creature but woman in no relationship but wedlock could satisfy that 'rational burning,' that solitariness of the soul, which was the first thing in this world 'which Gods eye nam'd not good.' Milton goes even farther. Not only is marriage essential for the solace of man's loneliness of spirit, but the ministering to that loneliness is the essential function of marriage from which all its other uses directly flow. The coupling of bodies may be accomplished without joining of souls, but the mere traffic of male and female is not marriage, nor even can it make one flesh. Nothing can make man and wife truly one 'but likenes, but fitnes of mind and disposition, which may breed the Spirit of concord, and union between them.' Where that is absent ' 'tis not to say they shall be one flesh, for they cannot be one flesh.' Indeed, those who are truly united in spirit, 'where the mind and person pleases aptly,' can in case of need more readily forego the body 'then when the mind hangs off . . . for there all corporall delight will soon become unsavoury and contemptible.' [43]

From all this it follows that marriage is the natural and holy way of life. There is no other relief for man's acutest need. There is no other function for woman. Milton admits that God grants to some the ability to remain as Paul was, but he does so very rarely. For anyone to abstain from marriage 'who hath not receiv'd the continence' is inexpedient, is plainly wicked. One who does abstain, 'not being supernaturally gifted,' is 'in a diabolicall sin, equall to that of Antichrist who forbids to marry.' There was still another conclusion to such reasoning which Milton did not hesitate to make. Up to this point he had brought the authority of his learning and his gift of utterance to the reiteration of familiar Protestant doctrine. Many a preacher had taught that the spiritual end in marriage took precedence over the physical, but even the Puritans in England, adhering strictly to scripture, had been loth to allow divorce for any cause but adultery. For betrayal of the spiritual obligations of marriage they proposed only spiritual remedies, patience, resignation, prayer. For Milton these were not enough unless one were willing to let the spirit and its needs wait upon the body. 'Mariage is a human Society,' he declared, 'and . . . all human society must proceed from the mind rather then the body . . . if the mind therefore cannot have that due company by mariage, that it may reasonably and humanly desire, that mariage can be no human society.' To provide for man's worthiest part is most worthy God's care; to set the body above the mind is contrary to nature. A marriage in which the mind is denied contentment 'is not of God's institution, and therefore no mariage.' [44]

When he reached this point, Milton had come full circle in the philosophy of love. Plato and the poets had taught him that the office of love begins and ends in the soul. He concludes that where love cannot exercise its office 'there can be left of wedlock nothing, but the empty husk of an outside matrimony.' There can be no marriage without the marriage of true minds. Any other union is sin, and any law which would compel men to sin is not law but tyranny. Thus the reasoning which led from the idealization of love and beauty to the idealization of marriage led Milton to the argument for divorce. 'As no man apprehends what vice is, so well as he who is truly vertuous, [as] no man knows hel like him who converses most in heav'n, so there is none that can estimate the evil and the affliction of a naturall hatred in matrimony, unlesse he have a soul gentle anough, and spacious anough to contemplate what is true love.' [45] When it comes about that, in order to save his soul, he who loves must marry and he who is married must love, it follows that, in order to love, marry, and save his soul, a man may have to divorce. For, as the need for marriage is rooted in the nature of man, so the need for divorce results inevitably from the fall of man which resulted from the freedom imposed upon man in the beginning and renewed in Christ as the condition for all attainment and enjoyment of good. In order to clinch the argument for divorce, Milton found himself under the necessity of justifying the ways of God, of providing scriptural and theological support for the

belief already set forth in his poems and tracts that through knowledge
and discourse men could progress in the apprehension of truth to the
command of destiny. Marriage must surely be marriage of minds because its creator reveals himself to us in scripture and in nature as an
intelligible being, justifiable to reason in everything we need to understand.

Thus in the divorce tracts, particularly *Tetrachordon*, and in *Areopagitica* Milton found himself embarked upon the theme of *Paradise
Lost*. His dialectical difficulty in this matter of marriage was to reconcile
the relevant texts in Matthew and I Corinthians with those in Deuteronomy. His manner of dealing with the problem followed the pattern
of most thinking on such problems in his age. He fastened upon
Biblical myth for aetiological proof that matrimony as God designed
it was everything that could be called for of rational and humane.
Nothing commanded later in law or gospel could possibly bear a
contrary interpretation. To be sure, God had a secret as well as a
revealed will; providence had also hidden ways; but these we should
adore and search not. All that is necessary to be known concerning
God's secret will is that it conflicts in no way with his revealed law.
Nothing mysterious or supernatural may be supposed to set aside the
natural and the intelligible. God in his revealed will 'appears to us as
it were in human shape, enters into cov'nant with us, swears to keep it,
binds himself like a just lawgiver to his own prescriptions, gives himself to be understood by men, judges and is judg'd, measures and is
commensurat to right reason.'

Here was the fundamental tenet of Milton's faith. He is speaking at
this point of the law as revealed through Moses, but the same is true
of the law revealed in Christ. Christ does not abrogate the law of
Moses, much less introduce new severities; he grants us freedom to
obey or not obey its strict injunctions in the light of the higher law
which he has imprinted in our hearts. 'Our Saviours doctrine is, that
the end, and the fulfilling of every command is charity; no faith
without it, . . . no worship, no workes pleasing to God.' That is to
say, 'the great and almost only commandment of the Gospel, is to
command nothing against the good of man,' and how to determine
wherein the good of man consists is no mystery. We are required to
obey law 'not otherwise then to the law of nature and of equity im-

printed in us seems correspondent.' The laws of God are to be extolled not merely because they are God's, 'not onely as they are his,' but because they seem right, 'as they are just and good to every wise and sober understanding.' [46]

Milton's argument for divorce, we shall see, failed to convince those for whom it was intended and provoked only misunderstanding and disapproval. Superficially the whole question seemed at best tangential to the great issue which was coming to a head in 1642. Certainly, by bringing forward such a subject at such a time, Milton betrayed his lack of any sense for what might be politically possible of achievement. Yet in the long view nothing showed more strikingly whither the Puritan movement was tending under the influence of the ideas which the preachers were so industriously fomenting. At this very moment both the preachers and Henry Parker were arguing that the commands of King Charles were to be obeyed not because they were his but according as they corresponded to the law of nature and were approved by reason and conscience. Milton took cognizance of that argument in the 'Address to the Parliament with the Assembly' which he prefixed to the second edition of his first divorce tract. 'He who marries,' he there asserts, 'intends as little to conspire his own ruine, as he that swears Allegeance: and as a whole people is to an ill Government, so is one man to an ill marriage.' He has as much right to redeem himself from a private covenant as they from a public one, and on the same grounds, namely, 'reason, charity, nature and good example.' Milton like Parker turns to the myth and doctrine of the fall of man as the starting-point for his conception of the law of nature in the light of which all laws of God and man are to be understood and obeyed. In marriage that meant specifically that the law of nature took precedence over canon law. It meant too that all scriptural commands must conform to nature and reason. It meant that Christ's saying to the Pharisees, 'as it is usually expounded, can be no law at all.' Reason and nature forbade. If the denying of divorce for any cause but adultery had sprung from natural law, 'the Jews, or some other wise and civill nation would have pres't it,' whereas in fact Moses yields to 'a law ancienter, and deeper ingrav'n in blameles nature,' and Christ, rightly understood, does not overrule but confirms Moses.[47]

Milton reiterates his insistence on the supremacy of natural law, having only the good of man as its object. 'Nature her self the universal Mother intends nothing but her own perfection.' When the scriptures tell us, 'And the Lord said, It is not good that man should be alone,' God is presenting himself to us 'like a man deliberating' in order to show us that he intended to found marriage 'according to naturall reason, not impulsive command,' 'that the duty should arise from the reason of it, not the reason be swallow'd up in a reasonless duty.' It is in the light of this principle that in the first divorce tract but more fully in *Tetrachordon* Milton elaborates his interpretation of the Biblical account of the creation of man and woman and of the institution of marriage by the creator. It is another draft for a poem on the fall of man.[48]

The first thing that God named not good was Adam's loneliness before the creation of Eve. The first need he planted in the nature of man was for a woman, a wife, a helpmeet, and in order to satisfy that need he made Eve out of Adam's living substance. This was the one perfect and indissoluble marriage in the entire history of the human race. Adam in his innocence could make no mistake in the selection of a wife to comfort his loneliness; Eve could not fail her husband. The effect of their fall was not to abrogate the need of Adam's sons for fit wives, far from it, but merely to weaken and corrupt their natural powers to satisfy their need. They became liable to error in the choice of their helpmeets, and Eve's daughters to failure in their function of consolation. For all nature then became subject to change and difference. There is a 'twofold Seminary or stock in nature, from whence are deriv'd the issues of love and hatred,' and yet God and nature are engaged in bringing 'the due likenesses and harmonies of his workes together.' It is error or 'some evil Angel' which in mismated persons brings together 'the sleeping discords and enmities of nature . . . that they may wake to agony and strife.' That is to say, nature, which requires men and women to marry, does not make every woman fit for every man, and when as a result of the fall, unfit persons seek to join in wedlock, inviolable nature keeps them asunder. This must be true, and nothing that Christ says may be construed to the contrary, for it is of the essence of Milton's faith that Christ died not to save man from liability to error or from the necessity of effort and struggle but to set him free through experience of error to exercise faith and enlarge knowledge, the remedies of error and of all its consequences. The defenders of canon law in denying us our natural freedom to profit by the mistakes we make in the search for a fit helpmeet, 'would have us re-enter Paradise against the sword that guards it.' Better to follow 'what moral *Sinai* prescribes equal to our strength, then fondly to think within our strength all that lost Paradise relates.' [49] In other words, the way to regain the paradise that Adam and Eve enjoyed in one another before the fall is to marry and if need be to divorce and marry again. Thus the same law of covenant and renewal of covenant, which Parker and the defenders of parliament against the king were asserting as the basis of the state, Milton was putting forward as the true basis of marriage or the state in little.

IV

An Assembly of Divines
1643-1644

THE custom of monthly fast days began on February 23, 1642, with Calamy and Marshall preaching to the house of commons at St. Margaret's. A succession of preachers followed their example in exhorting parliament and people to obey the Lord even at the cost of disobeying the Lord's anointed. Lawyers and pamphleteers filled the press with reasons why the king's subjects might have to resist the king's commands. Milton was learning that for a man to be bound to an ill marriage was no different from being bound by a bad government. Civil war began in August and continued inconclusively through the summer and autumn. Edgehill on October 23 decided nothing except perhaps that the Powell family kept their daughter from going back to her husband in London. Charles set up his headquarters at Oxford where he had preachers, pamphleteers, and a press at his own disposal. But sermons and pamphlets served no better than force of arms to bring opposing parties to agreement, and attempts to negotiate peace during the winter months merely bred further distrust.

Fighting broke out again in April, but the triumph over the enemies of the Lord which the preachers had so confidently predicted was not yet forthcoming. On the contrary parliament's forces were met by a series of reverses in the field, and at the end of May a plot, authorized by the king, was discovered in the city only just in time to prevent the overthrow of parliament itself by violence. The immediate danger from Waller's plot, as it was called, having been overcome, parliament's first action was to order a day of thanksgiving to be held on June 15 with Stephen Marshall and Obadiah Sedgwick to preach to the commons at St. Margaret's and Edmund Calamy and Charles Herle

to the lords at the abbey.[1] All four preachers directed their hearers'
attention to images and 'types' of their present situation to be found
in the scriptures. Sedgwick showed them the fate of the contrivers of
the recent plot in Haman's fall. Herle drew upon the ninety-fifth
psalm for terms in which to rejoice at parliament's escape. He saw
Waller, the chief conspirator, prefigured in Achan and urged the
members of the house to emulate Joshua. Calamy, addressing the
lords, also turned to Joshua, but called up other 'types' as well—for
example Ahab and Samson—of chieftains faithful or unfaithful to their
special calling. His purpose was to drive home the lesson of Luke
12: 48—'unto whomsoever much is given, of him shall be much required'—and of the parable of the talents. The most notable of the
four sermons on this occasion was, as we should expect, Stephen
Marshall's discourse on Revelation 15: 2, 3, 4, *The Song of Moses
the Servant of God, and the Song of the Lambe.* Though his text was,
he said, part of the '*darkest* and *most mysticall* Book in all the Scriptures . . . yet time (one of the best Interpreters of Prophecies) hath
produced the *events* answering the *types* so full and clear, that we
have the whole Army of Protestant Interpreters agreeing in the generall scope and meaning of it.' He used the imagery of the Apocalypse
in order once more to bring the struggle of parliament against the
king and the prelates into line with the legend of the true church
beset by Antichrist and of Christ's expected advent and triumph. He
would have his hearers see themselves again in the most valid and
compelling of perspectives. The great stream of history, directed by
God from eternity to eternity, having reached its present point, would
inevitably go on, and they were called to be the agents and actors of
its next advance.

Everybody knew, of course, that the next thing John saw in his
vision, after the elect singing the song of Moses at the glassy sea, was
the seven angels pouring the vials of the wrath of God on the beast and
the whore, and Marshall concluded by telling his audience that parliament itself must be as one of the angels. What in particular he meant
by this doubtless needed no explaining. Parliament had so far successfully resisted the king's power to impede its own freedom of action in
the state and the Puritan brotherhood's freedom of utterance in pulpit
and press. The preachers had used their freedom in order to exploit

the scriptures for their provocative effect upon the public mind. But what had come of all this was as yet not a workable organization of power for making secure the freedom so far attained or for keeping the energies thus aroused within manageable limits but, as anyone might have guessed from Milton's tracts, simply freedom extending itself in various different and unexpected directions to incalculable lengths. Thus things had come to the point where parliament must commit itself to a course of action more concrete and constructive if the danger of imminent defeat was to be withstood. It must make certain of having an effective military force at its command, it must win the Scots to its side, it must establish its authority over the church and the press, and it must do all of these things if it was to be sure of accomplishing any of them.

The problem of the church came first. Parliament had cut off the authority of the bishops, ejected prelatical clergy, made way for preachers acceptable to the people, and established monthly fast days. But it had not yet taken final action upon the recommendation of the Grand Remonstrance and the ministers' petition of December, 1641, for the convening of an assembly of divines to consider what should henceforth be the doctrine and discipline of the church. A bill calling for such a body had been introduced in the commons in May, 1642; it had been considered and reconsidered many times, but a year later it was still pending. To reconstitute the church would, of course, be to revolutionize the whole life of the nation, and the king naturally refused his consent. But to act without his consent would be to abrogate the last vestige of his authority over the ecclesiastical as over the civil state, and this parliament had so far been unwilling to do. In June, 1643, however, both houses, disregarding the king's refusal, at last agreed upon an ordinance which called the Westminster Assembly into being.[2] Parliament at the same time invaded the prerogative of the crown in the closely related matter of the press. The king's power to enforce his constitutional authority over printing had, of course, lapsed with the fall of Laud and Star Chamber. The authority remained his, however, and his adversaries possessed no legal power to stop the flow of royalist pamphlets out of Oxford or satisfy repeated complaints of the Stationers' Company at the violation of its privileges. Parliament consequently now also passed an ordinance assuming the authority formerly held by the crown and entrusting to licensers appointed by itself the function of passing upon all printed matter before publication.[3] The decisions concerning the printing ordinance and the ordinance calling the Westminster Assembly were made just at the time of the thanksgiving observance of June 15 and the preaching of Marshall, Sedgwick, Calamy, and Herle.

The assembly convened on July 1 with a sermon by the prolocutor designated by parliament, the learned, elderly, and mild-tempered William Twisse, who had just written a preface for the English translation, about to be published, of his friend Joseph Mede's famous book on the Apocalypse.[4] A special fast day was at once declared for July 7 with preaching at St. Margaret's by Matthew Newcomen, one of the Smectymnuans, and Oliver Bowles. Yet since none of parliament's arrangements could be counted secure without the Scots, the assembly in effect marked time while a commission proceeded to Edinburgh to negotiate an agreement. Sir Henry Vane went as parliament's chief spokesman, with Stephen Marshall and Philip Nye to represent the assembly divines. The outcome was the Solemn League and Covenant, purporting to be a close military and ecclesiastical alliance between the two kingdoms against the king. It was approved by the Scottish parliament on August 17 and by the English with certain reservations early in September. Commissioners were at once dispatched from Edinburgh to the assembly at Westminster, and on September 25 the members of both parliament and assembly and the Scottish representatives subscribed the Covenant at a solemn meeting at St. Margaret's church with addresses by Philip Nye and Alexander Henderson. Up to this point, by order of parliament, the assembly had been confining its discussions to the thirty-nine articles. Now, with the Scottish commissioners present, it was directed to take up the question of church government. By the first of January, 1644, its members found themselves seriously at odds with one another, and the dispute, spreading presently to public, parliament, and army, eventually disrupted not only the assembly but the entire reform movement and the church itself.

The explanation of these developments is to be looked for first of all in the state of mind of the members of the assembly itself. The Scottish commissioners came to Westminster speaking what seemed the same language but, as we have seen, with meaning drawn from a very different national experience. Their conception of the church did not, at first thought at any rate, appear essentially different from that which had recently been set forth by Smectymnuus, Milton, and other assailants of prelacy. But unlike the English, Scottish reformers had worked out their ideas in the course of a long struggle in an unstable society with a regime at once more arbitrary and less secure. They had contended for nearly a hundred years not simply for freedom to preach but for control of the church itself and through the church for freedom to impose discipline and unity upon a whole nation. English Puritans, though there was no telling how many or with what reservations, might agree in principle that the church was to be acknowledged as an independent kingdom of the spirit in which sovereignty had been vested by Christ in his people and to which civil rulers like other men were subject. Scottish Presbyterians, however, had actually worked out a system of government and discipline embodying this principle, and recent Scottish history was filled with the ups and downs of their endeavor to put the system into effect. The Presbyterians had not yet succeeded. James had put the kirk once more into episcopal shackles, and Charles had attempted to rivet them on. Yet in spite of everything, Presbyterianism more and more permeated Scottish national life and shaped Scottish character. It sprang up again, stronger than ever, in the National Covenant in 1638, and it was brought to Westminster in 1643 by men determined to secure its establishment at last beyond the power of kings to prevent or deny.

Henderson, Baillie, Rutherford, and Gillespie, with the two lay elders who accompanied them, understood more precisely what they wanted, were much more clear-cut in their ideas, more unyielding, and in a sense, but perhaps only a Scottish sense, more constructive and practical, than the English they had now to deal with. The presbyterian system as they explained it required that every parish should have its pastor, its teacher, and its ruling elders, the last named being laymen. These composed the kirk session and were responsible for the souls, minds, manners, and morals of their people. The parish with its kirk session was comprised within the presbytery, composed of representatives, clerical and lay, of all the parish churches of a given district.

This body, which in effect replaced the episcopal diocese, was the key to the whole structure and the secret of its strength. The election of church officers gravitated under its control. It controlled the all-important function of ordination. It was always at hand to maintain the disciplinary powers of kirk session. It sent its representatives to the regional synod and to the general assembly, the representative body of the whole people, comprehended within the kirk.

The liberty valued under this system was not the freedom of individuals or particular groups to differ from one another within a stable society but the freedom of the church itself to instruct, admonish, and discipline all sinners alike, whoever they might be. Doubtless the society which resulted in Scotland would for good reason never have been endurable to most Englishmen. That, however, is beside the point. What it did for Scottish society was to give coherence and focus to the common life. It supplied a body of ideas, a vocabulary, a social instrument for the organized direction and expression of considered opinion. It brought the minister upon the stage with his people behind him, narrow and provincial to the point, sometimes, of being grotesque, but tenacious of principle and of his people's interests, nobody's fool, pawky, in a word, Scotch. This is the character we see, to the life, in the letters which Robert Baillie, pastor of Kilwinning in the presbytery of Irvine in Ayrshire, professor and principal of the University of Glasgow, wrote to his wife, parishioners, and friends from the Edinburgh General Assembly, from the camp of the Scottish army, from London in 1641, and from the Westminster Assembly. Much that he saw in England he could neither understand nor appreciate, and when Scottish judgment went wrong, it went very wrong. Yet whatever Baillie saw he faced squarely and stated honestly. He makes us perceive the force and solidarity of the society which stood behind him, which stood behind Alexander Henderson when he defied the king's orders at the Glasgow Assembly in 1638 and when later at Westminster he pled and argued and bargained with the dissident English on behalf of his people. He and Baillie and their fellow-commissioners had not come to England because they needed help in reforming their church or uniting their nation. They came as ambassadors to make certain once for all of the kirk's security. The stage they had been acting on all their lives may have been bleak and narrow, but on that stage they had learned to exercise authority, make decisions, and reach conclusions.

Not so the members of the Puritan brotherhood. The experience of the reform party in the English church since the accession of Elizabeth had been very different. Some, in the early stages of the movement and again after the Laudian repression began, had ventured direct attack upon government by bishops appointed by the crown, and some had made an abortive premature attempt to institute something like presbyterianism. But most Puritans, that is to say most men of earnest Protestant piety, accepted the royal supremacy and many submitted without objection to the principle of hierarchy in church government. They left the things of government alone and advanced their interests in the church by preaching and the promotion of preaching within the established scheme of things. Hence Puritanism had not developed in the way Presbyterianism had done in Scotland as a concerted endeavor by the ministerial order to take control of the church away from the crown but as a movement for setting forth a conception of spiritual life in the pulpit. Puritans became numerous and influential, and constituted authority undertook their repression, but they owed their success and whatever followed upon it to their personal address as leaders and spokesmen of self-conscious groups of questing souls brought together by what seemed spontaneous conviction and held together by nothing more than voluntary association.

And yet, naturally enough, when the time finally came for them to be asked what should be done about church government, a numerous segment of them, but by no means all, assumed that they should take up the power which had been struck out of the hands of the prelates and exercise it according to the principles that appeared to serve so well in Scotland. Their understanding of those principles, however, as compared to the clear practicality of the Scots, was theoretical and nebulous. Their first concern, as we have seen, had been not the replacement of bishops by presbyters but the liberation of the pulpit, the erection of a godly preaching ministry throughout the land and the driving of dumb dogs out of the church. They had come to insist on the extirpation of prelacy, even in resistance to the crown, but the reason was still the need to make sure of freedom to preach. Until they could be certain of that, they could not, with the best will in the world, really address themselves to the problem of instituting any sort of church government on a comprehensive national scale.

Which is to say they were never able to do so at all, because the movement they had promoted had already brought into being a mode of religious organization, elastic, protean in its adaptability to changing folk experience, and in the event quite ineradicable. That condition, later ridiculed by Dryden and admired by Voltaire, which permitted every Englishman, as one to whom liberty was natural, to go his own road to heaven at his own risk, had its beginning in those more or less unrecognized, unacknowledged, and sometimes disallowed groups of likeminded godly souls who, from about 1570 on, fell into the habit of joining together, for the most part within the church, in order that they might engage whom they would to expound the Word of God to them. Relatively few such groups under Elizabeth and even under James actually broke away from the church, and those that did were in their own time comparatively unimportant to the development of the whole movement. Even after the rise of Laud many Puritan preachers, men such as William Gouge or John Goodwin or the five Smectymnuans, had their people so solidly behind them that they had no need to remove themselves. Those who, like Thomas Goodwin and John Cotton, formed or joined congregations on the continent or in New England, in most cases still regarded themselves as of the church, purified and independent but not separate. Only as time went on and misdirected repression was followed by revolution did the divisive and anarchical tendencies in the Puritan movement run to extremes. Even so, before 1643, the leaders of completely independent 'gathered' churches or out-and-out sects were still for the most part not tinkers and tub-thumpers but university graduates and ordained ministers of the Church of England. Puritanism, far from being a strange aberration, was a deeply grounded continuous developing movement arising within the church itself, as English in its essence as Presbyterianism was Scotch. All the differences and hot disputes it engendered mattered less in the broad development of English life than the free access to the Word in print which no government was able to deny; that and a succession of men somehow gifted and trained to expound the Word according to their own lights. Granted such conditions, Englishmen fell into the habit of joining together as they chose or as circumstances might require for their souls' satisfaction with or without benefit of clergy in church, chapel, or conventicle, at home or in exile, in England, in foreign lands, in the American wilderness. Wherever they went, and they presently went everywhere, and however they differed, this they would all know how to do.

There was still another long-established reservation in respect to the church which also came into play to prevent the molding of English life into the stiff pattern of Scottish Presbyterianism. Since prelacy, whatever might be said for it, was a weapon in the hands of the king, his political opponents took advantage of the popular agitation against the bishops and reduced their power step by step to nothing. But the leaders of parliament were not disposed to yield to any other interest the control of the ecclesiastical state which they had just wrested from the crown or grant to the Puritan clergy an independence withheld from bishops. They took no more kindly than English kings had done to the notion of church and state as two kingdoms of equal though complementary jurisdiction. They did not intend the Westminster Assembly to take the place either of Convocation or of the General Assembly of the Church of Scotland. Its membership, fixed by parliament, consisted of 119 divines, chosen severally by the members of the house of commons, and thirty lay members, ten lords and twenty commoners, drawn from parliament itself. Parliament laid down the rules of procedure and the main subjects to be discussed. In a word, the assembly was vested with no independent jurisdiction; its express function was only to make recommendations which parliament might or might not approve on such matters as parliament might indicate. For the question of the church was crucial to the whole revolutionary movement, and discussion and settlement of the question could not be relegated to a company of godly divines set off by themselves.

Baillie observed with some justice from the Scottish point of view that the assembly was no assembly at all but merely 'a meeting called by the Parliament to advyse them in what things they are asked.' [5] And he bitterly complained that the perfect consummation of the assembly's work was thwarted by the lawyers of the house of commons. But the trouble went deeper than the unwillingness of lawyers to give way to a Scotch Presbyterian *jus divinum*. Baillie's reports of his countrymen's dealing with the English from his coming to Westminster in 1643 to his final departure in 1647 is the story of the increasing bafflement of Scottish expectations by English disagreements and compromises and of Scottish confidence by the indirection and inconsistency of the English mind and character. It is also the story, sharply depicted from a single point of view, of the break-up of the Puritan movement by spiritual forces generated within itself. But the story began promisingly enough for the Scots. The English for once were having to come to Edinburgh, asking favors. 'The Parliament syde,' Baillie wrote, 'is running down the brae . . . now when all is desperate, they cry aloud for our help.' He should, however, have taken warning from the character of the men parliament sent north to negotiate the desired alliance. He did indeed marvel at English 'slowness in all their affaires,' and he had suspicions of Nye as 'head of the independants.' But he admired Vane as 'one of the gravest and ablest of that nation' without discovering that he was also one of the most difficult to pin down, and the good Scot was dazzled as most men were by Marshall's eloquence.

The English were for a 'civill League' and 'keeping of a doore open in England to Independancie,' while the Scots were for a 'religious Covenant,' drafted by the practiced hand of Alexander Henderson.[6] Vane's management of the affair, whether the Scots were deceived or not, was characteristic and significant. The English agreed to the covenant but with a reservation. They agreed to endeavor the preservation of the Church of Scotland and the reformation of religion in England—'according to the Word of God, and the example of the best Reformed Churches.' What the Word of God signified in the premises was left for the future to determine. Nye, in his address before parliament and assembly on September 25, declared that what they had all agreed to was to preserve and reform religion, but if it should be found that England had done better in 'handling the word of righteousnesse' or that Scotland had done better in order and discipline or that some other church had 'learned Christ' better, they would all 'humbly bow, and kisse their lips that can speak right words

unto us in this matter.' Henderson, in the face of such slippery statements, dourly reiterated that 'Necessitie, which hath in it a kinde of
Soveraignty, and is a Law above all Lawes, and therefore is said to
have no Law, doth mightily presse the Church and Kingdom of
Scotland at this time.' [7]

But the English attitude was most sharply revealed in the rules
which parliament laid down for the assembly's procedure. Every
member was required to pledge himself 'not to maintain any thing but
what he believes to be the Truth and to embrace Truth in Sincerity,
when discovered unto him. . . . What any Man undertakes to prove
as necessary, he shall make good out of the Scriptures.' To these
prescriptions, of course, no one, Scots or English, could think of taking
exception, but they were followed by additional injunctions, in which
lay much of the meaning of the Puritan Revolution:

No Man to be denied to enter his Dissent from the Assembly, and his
Reasons for it, in any Point, after it hath first been debated in the Assembly;
and thence if the dissenting Party desire it, to be sent to the Houses of
Parliament by the Assembly (not by any particular Man, or Men, in a
private Way) when either House shall require it.

All Things agreed on, and prepared for the Parliament, to be openly
read and allowed in the Assembly; and then offered as the Judgment of the
Assembly, if the major Part assent; provided that the Opinion of any
Persons dissenting, and the Reasons urged for it, be annexed thereunto
(if the Dissenters require it) together with the Solutions (if any were)
given in the Assembly to these Reasons.[8]

The assumption behind these rules was obvious. It was supposed
that all the members of the assembly needed to do to arrive at agreement on all matters concerning the church was to examine the Word of
God and debate their findings freely. And this was in fact what they
did.[9] But the probable consequences became apparent in what followed
when on August 28 the assembly was asked by parliament for its
judgment as to the lawfulness of the Covenant. The formula 'according
to the Word of God' held the members in debate all day Monday.
Tuesday they concluded that they were ready to submit their approval
to the house. But Wednesday, being a fast day, they spent in prayer
and preaching, and on Thursday, just as they were about to wait upon
parliament with the results of their deliberations, Cornelius Burges

stood up to enter his dissent and demand time to submit his reasons. Lightfoot tells us, it was judged 'intolerable impudence, that the great affairs of two dying kingdoms, should be thought fit by him to stay and wait upon his captiousness.' [10] Nevertheless, this was not to be the last occasion on which the affairs of kingdoms and churches would be required to wait while preachers searched the scriptures, consulted their consciences, and exercised their gifts.

The Scots saw quickly enough that this was no way to get done the business they had come about. 'The like of that Assemblie I did never see,' Baillie wrote soon after his arrival, 'the like was never in England, nor any where is shortlie lyke to be.' He marveled at the 'learning, quickness, and eloquence . . . the great courtesie and discretion in speaking, of these men.' 'They harangue long and very learnedlie. They studie the questions well before hand, and prepares their speeches.' Their manner of conducting their meetings he finds admirable and worthy of imitation. But 'their longsomenesse is wofull at this time.' The prolocutor, for one thing, William Twisse, though admitted to be 'very learned . . . very good, beloved of all, and highlie esteemed,' was not a man to shut off discussion and force decisions. After long debates about pastors, doctors, elders, and deacons, the assembly spent two or three sessions discussing the duties of widows in the church, 'not,' Baillie complains, 'that we needed to stay so long on that subject, but partlie because everie thing that comes to the Assemblie must be debaited, and none of their debates are short.' After months of this, Scottish patience grew thin—'The unhappie, and unamendable prolixitie of this people, . . . either in Church or State: we are vexed and overwearied with their wayes.' 'The humour of this people is very various, and inclinable to singularities, to differ from all the world, and one from another, and shortlie from themselves. No people had so much need of a Presbyterie.' [11]

The question of presbytery was indeed, from the Scottish point of view, the crux of the whole dispute. Apologists for episcopacy had claimed that bishops, though owing their appointment to the crown, derived their authority from God. The Scots did not deny the principle of *jus divinum* but claimed the right for presbyters chosen by the people. This could mean in practice control of the church by a close-knit ministerial caste rather than popular rule, but theocracy in that form enabled the Scottish people to withstand feudal anarchy and royal oppression. The kirk stood, in a sense the English never knew, for unity and order within the nation, and its representatives at Westminster would not have been good Scotchmen if they had not tried to make certain that the security of Scotland should be sealed in the establishment of what Baillie frankly described as a 'Scots Presbytrie' in the English church.[12]

Their English colleagues in the assembly would hardly have been human if they had not been tempted to conclude, as many of them now did, that they and their order were to succeed to the same position and function to which the ministry had so long laid claim in Scotland. In England, however, the people had learned to look not to the church and its ministers but to the crown and parliament as the symbols and instruments of national unity and order. They had prospered under a government which had been ready to ignore differences it had no immediate interest in proceeding against, a government prepared to sacrifice a certain degree of consistency and uniformity of belief and behavior among its subjects for the sake of a general social and political stability. The present crisis resulted in some measure from the abandonment of that laxity. But the breakdown of the attempt to impose a more rigorous control made the religious problem not easier but more difficult than ever to deal with, especially for the preachers now called to consider it in the Westminster Assembly. Since Tudor times religion had been the great ground of difference, and they and their order had been the great promoters of that difference. Now, however, they were themselves confronted with the question of how unity and order were to be restored in the face of revolutionary conditions they had themselves done so much to foment.

ii. PRESBYTERIAN VS. INDEPENDENT

The members of the Westminster Assembly, in swearing to uphold the Solemn League and Covenant, pledged themselves to endeavor to bring the churches of the three kingdoms together in 'doctrine, worship, discipline and government.' The expressed intention was 'that we, and our posterity after us, may, as brethren, live in faith and love, and the Lord may delight to dwell in the midst of us.' [13] In the circumstances of the moment, this was a strategic affirmation of the ancient ideal of spiritual union, embodied and made operative among men in a visible church, comprehending the whole community. To establish the authority of the church was the one way to forfend both tyranny and anarchy. It was the certain way to attain peace on earth and salvation hereafter. And for a majority of the ministerial members of the Westminster Assembly, the presbyterian way of organizing the government and discipline of the church, as exemplified in Scotland, was the way prescribed by the Lord, revealed in scripture.

The problem, however, was to put that mode of government and discipline into effect, not in a backward, turbulent society only recently emerged out of the anarchy of a collapsing feudalism, but in an England which had felt the force of both Reformation and Renaissance. The problem was, in a word, to make presbyterianism work in a society which could bring to the cause of reform itself such characters as Milton and Cromwell. The Presbyterians, though they commanded a majority of votes in the assembly, fell far short of commanding undivided support among the people at large, in parliament, or even in the preaching order. The original make-up of the assembly reflected the opinions, neither unanimous nor clear-cut, of the members of the house of commons. Most of the divines who accepted parliament's call were Puritan preachers, well regarded and well established in their respective localities. They were naturally inclined to fall in with a plan designed to put the people under the domination of the church and the church under the domination of the ministry. But they were not to begin with a compact determined party, all of one mind. Some were more willing than others to compromise. Some were ready to insist that ultimate control of the church necessarily rested with parliament. A small but able and influential group, recently returned from exile in Holland, opposed from the beginning the centralizing tendencies of their associates. The lay members of the assembly, representing parliament, most notably Vane and Selden, were a constantly disturbing element. But the factors opposing presbyterianism within the assembly were as nothing to those at work outside. Some of the divines named by parliament, including men of episcopalian views, refused to serve or appeared very seldom. The New Englanders, John Cotton, Thomas Hooker, and John Davenport, who had been urged in

September, 1642, by a group including Cromwell and St. John to come back and help settle the church, for one reason or another stayed away.[14] But Roger Williams turned up, not to sit in the assembly but to give an important lead to an increasing host of dissenters of all shades of opinion. The Presbyterians were doomed to failure, and like many another defeated party, have been harshly judged. But as we seek to understand the reasons for their failure, we must keep in mind what they thought they were trying to accomplish. Confronted by the confusion and disruption of a revolutionary age, they were endeavoring to restore order to society in the one manner, as they thought, divinely appointed and most surely sanctioned by human tradition and divine authority. What they could not understand or admit was that all the forces of the age now upon them were making toward a society which was not to be brought under any single control by a religious discipline of any sort administered by a clerical caste within a fixed ecclesiastical framework.

But the first difficulty the Presbyterians encountered was that they could not now change their own habits of thought or undo what they and their kind had themselves brought about in the national life. This fact was brought home to them almost immediately by a small group of Independents in the assembly, consisting at first of Thomas Goodwin, Philip Nye, Sidrach Simpson, Jeremiah Burroughes, and William Bridge but joined later and from time to time in some degree by others. The five original Independents were noted preachers, possessed of the learning suitable to their position, and Goodwin, their leader and spokesman, was one of the most eminent and representative members of the Puritan brotherhood. He had been a student at Cambridge while the memory of William Perkins was still alive at the university. He was a disciple of John Preston and Richard Sibbes. With Sibbes, Thomas Ball, and John Davenport, he had edited Preston's numerous sermons for posthumous publication, and he had succeeded that famous preacher as lecturer at Trinity Church, Cambridge. He was a friend of John Cotton, and about the time that the latter had taken refuge in New England, Goodwin had betaken himself to an English congregation in Holland. He was now back in a London pulpit and had just reissued a collection of his sermons, called *A Childe of Light Walking in Darkness* (1636, 1638, 1643), a moving and eloquent treatment of the well-worn theme of regeneration, the familiar picture of the single soul on its lone dark pilgrimage, lighted within by grace. On April 27, 1642, he had preached on a fast day to the house of commons a sermon, called *Zerubbabels Encouragement to Finish the Temple*. 'Gods first and chiefe care,' the preacher said, 'was, to build up his Church *mysticall*, to make men Saints . . . and to that end he made a plentifull provision in matters of faith.' 'Matters of Order & Government,' on the other hand, came later in God's calculation; men 'often fall into the right, by seeing their errors by degrees.' 'Be sure you establish nothing but what you have full, cleare, and generall light for.' Otherwise you will 'but lay a foundation of a new rent and division in the age to come.' For there is a spirit, he says, 'even the Holy Ghost, who will not rest working in mens spirits, till the whole building be rightly framed.' [15]

'It were a thousand pities of that man,' Baillie said, 'I hope God will not permitt him to goe on to lead a faction for ren[d]ing of the kirk.' [16] But what Goodwin and the Independents proposed was simply that the church go on in the manner and direction which the Puritan brotherhood had been following all along. The majority of the divines in the assembly, under the urging of the Scots, were proposing that the disciplinary powers of the church and the all-important authority to ordain ministers and license preachers be vested in the presbytery or 'classis' made up of representatives from the various parishes of a given district. But they were forgetting the pit whence most of them had been digged. They were forgetting that they had risen to their present position through the opportunities formerly allowed them to enlist the support of converts and followers regardless of parish boundaries and independently of official central authority. Every Puritan group which at any time joined together to engage a lecturer tended to become a 'gathered church,' centered in its preaching minister and self-limited in membership to his convinced personal followers. Laud's effort to repress this tendency had merely served to intensify it, and his downfall had set it free to run its course unchecked. Hence the Independents in the assembly and a constantly increasing host of preachers and congregations outside looked with distrust on the proposal to curtail the liberty they had formerly and now again enjoyed in order that a limiting power such as parliament had only just revoked might be reestablished over them in the form of presbyterian 'classes.'

Yet although it was apparent that in any test of strength in the assembly the Independents would be voted down, it was also apparent that the recommendations of the Presbyterian majority were not likely to be adopted by parliament without question or amendment, and the less likely the longer decision could be delayed. Hence in order to prolong debate and, so it seemed to the Scots, to confuse and darken counsel with words, Goodwin and his adherents took full advantage of the rules which parliament had laid down and, hardly less important, of their opponents' scruples in favor of full and free discussion. Again and again Baillie had to note that, just as agreement was about to be reached on one point or another, Goodwin 'incontinent assayed to turn all upside downe' or 'carried it so, that all was dung in the howes.' But the most baffling thing of all was that the English themselves, try as they would, seemed unable to put a stop to such tactics. By April, 1644, Baillie was saying, 'We are almost desperate to see anything concluded for a long time: Their way is woefully tedious. Nothing, in any Assemblie that ever was in the world except Trent, like to them in prolixitie.' [17]

And yet the first decisive step, if not to terminate, certainly to alter the conditions of the dispute, was taken by the Independents themselves. For over two months, as Baillie says, they had been 'holding of[f] with long weapons, and debaiting all things too prolixlie which come within twentie myles of their quarters.' [18] They had even, it would appear, made overtures to the king,[19] and on the other hand, they had signed a paper, drafted by Marshall and subscribed by several leading Presbyterians, begging everybody to desist for the present from further gathering of churches until it should be seen what the assembly would decide.[20] But the five dissenting brethren, as they were called, did not themselves observe the counsel of patience. Early in January, without cognizance of the assembly, they made a direct appeal to parliament and, to make matters worse, immediately put their appeal before the public in print in *An Apologeticall Narration.*

Baillie stigmatized this manifesto as a sly and cunning plea for toleration.[21] It was in fact an adroit and timely expression of basic

English objections to theocracy patterned upon the Scottish model. The authors carefully dissociated themselves from extreme doctrinal views, but they pled in measured terms that, under any government which might now be set up in the church, allowance be made for persons like themselves and for groups such as they represented. They asked in truth for no more than the continuance under presbyterianism of the kind of latitude for preaching which they had enjoyed, with or without approval, before the Laudian repression and which they were in fact at the moment enjoying again in greater degree. More important, however, than anything said in *An Apologeticall Narration* was the fact that it was said at just this juncture in print. Goodwin and his associates thus carried their case from the assembly to parliament and into the forum of public discussion and by so doing set the example for all opponents of theocracy to do the same. Godly divines in the Jerusalem Chamber at Westminster might go on debating as long as they liked and finally produce a directory of worship and confession of faith for the Scots to take home with them. But among Englishmen, from this point on, the Presbyterians in the assembly were but one party to a dispute which had been shifted in spite of them to a broader arena and the outcome of which could as yet be neither foreseen nor controlled.

The Scots countered *An Apologeticall Narration* by a statement of their own, probably from the pen of Alexander Henderson, entitled *Reformation of Church-Government in Scotland, Cleered from some mistakes and Prejudices.* Again they showed how well they perceived the difficulty before them and how helpless they were to deal with it. Temperately, patiently, but none the less positively, they once more explained how reformation had been accomplished in Scotland and how their system really worked in practice. A more dignified or reasonable statement from the Scottish point of view would be hard to conceive. The writers saw clearly enough that their differences with the Independents sprang from the difference between English and Scottish experience. Reformers in England, they noted, had been 'either altogether, or for the greater part taken up with the Doctrine' whereas in Scotland, 'after the doctrine was established, which was speedily done,' reformers were chiefly occupied with discipline and government and with putting down opposition. The result, they claimed, was a system midway between anarchy and tyranny, and though they were willing 'to heare and learne from the word of God, what needeth further to bee reformed in the Church of Scotland: Yet God forbid, that we should never come to any certainty of perswasion, or that we should ever be learning, and never come to the knowledg of the truth.' [22]

Judging from their experience, therefore, the Scottish commissioners found the objections raised by the Independents chimerical if not disingenuous. The Independents professed to be afraid lest the authority of presbyteries be used unwarrantably against individual congregations and churches, and they contended that discipline would be sufficiently maintained if churches were left free to admonish and, if necessary, break communion with offending churches. But to the Scots, the danger their opponents feared seemed never likely to occur, and the fears it gave rise to resulted from failure to understand the representative character of presbyterian government. For their part they foresaw the much greater danger that would arise from failure to set any authority above the individual congregation. If every individual church were left free from control outside itself, then every church might differ with impunity from every other, and if no church need submit to any superior authority, why need any member of any church submit to the authority of the church itself? Only through the imposition of order and the maintenance of discipline on a national scale had the reformed church in Scotland made headway against disorder and repression. Any break in that system would mean not a gain in liberty for the church but an advantage to its enemies. There was little more that the Scots could add to the statement of their case except the usual detailed arguments from scripture and history and the usual disputatious rebuttal of the arguments of their opponents. Before the year was out Samuel Rutherford buttressed Scottish proposals with some seven hundred and sixty-eight pages of erudition in his *Due Right of Presbyteries*. Adam Steuart, Alexander Forbes, Baillie, Rutherford and Gillespie filled other pages with attacks upon the Independents and reports of the evil consequences of the English way of doing things.

For the English the implications of *An Apologeticall Narration* were more important than its explicit demands. Its authors, though a minority in the assembly, represented a large if confused body of opinion outside. In speaking, however moderately, against a too rigid application of presbyterian principles, they spoke for all who desired a certain latitude in the church, and they gave the signal for many to speak with less moderation for a wider freedom than they themselves conceived. Their associates in the assembly were thus compelled, while attempting to restore order in the church, to face the problem of reconciling the need for order with the desire for liberty, and the debate over liberty and order in the church, having been forced out into the public press, became at once part of a great outburst of discussion concerning the whole structure of human relations in every aspect of state and society. The men who made up the main body of the assembly, having had everything their own way from November, 1640, up to this point, were thus confronted by widespread disaffection in their own ranks and among those they had counted upon as their adherents. They found themselves suddenly put on the defensive by bolder spirits, readier wits, nimbler pens on their own side of the controversy they had themselves promoted with the king and the bishops. Before they could bring their deliberations to a close and let the Scots go home, most of the ideas which were to become the seeds and shibboleths of revolution for a long time to come had appeared on the London bookstalls in the pamphlets of the Presbyterians' critics and opponents. These publications have naturally engaged the interest of historians who have had small sympathy for theocracy and little taste for sermons. But the Presbyterians, that is to say, those members of the great Puritan preaching order who now found themselves more concerned for the interests of their order and the unity of the church than for the liberty of the individual, are not for that reason to be dismissed or ignored in any just account of Puritan revolutionary discussion. In opposing Milton, Roger Williams, and other champions of liberty in 1644, they may have sinned against the light, but it was a light they themselves had a hand in kindling.

They and their cause did not lack defenders in the press, but for getting first at parliament and then at the public their prime implement was still the pulpit. From now on until preachers from the victorious New Model had to be given a hearing, the men invited to address the members of the house of commons on regular fast days and on all special days of humiliation or thanksgiving were drawn from the assembly, and with few exceptions all sermons preached on such occasions continued to be published with the authorization of the house. Never did the men of the pulpit have such opportunity to direct opinion in such a crisis or to have their doctrines and claims tested so promptly and decisively.[23]

Up to the end of 1643 their sermons expressed, first of all, the hopes and expectations with which they addressed themselves to the work of reforming the church according to the Word of God. The unacknowledged mendicant evangelical organization which had brought them to where they were had been their recourse under frustration but not their ultimate plan and objective. Now the long struggle was near its close and the day at hand when the church would be restored and Jerusalem regained. One more bout with Antichrist, one more putting-forth by every saint of every talent in the service of the Lord, and the last age of the church would begin. The preachers' dominant mood when they first came together at Westminster was still apocalyptic, expressing itself once more in terms of the familiar English Protestant legend of church history and the familiar images of St. John and the prophets. Their own dialectic, however, betrayed the preachers into a position which swiftly advancing circumstances soon made untenable. The Lord, they held, would surely keep covenant with those who kept covenant with him. The end of the spiritual saga was sure to be a happy one. If the saints were afflicted, it was only that they might learn their own weakness, grow strong, keep straight on and strive harder. The will of the Lord was to restore his church. If the armies of parliament met defeat, and they had certainly not yet attained victory, the reason was that parliament had not yet seen properly to the great business of reform. Reform required first that the saints should apply themselves to the study of God's Word, and unless they were carried away by carnal desires and vain conceits, the Word would unfailingly lead them to perfect agreement and the parliamentary army to certain success.

So the assembly divines searched the scriptures and debated their findings. But what followed was not agreement but disagreement, not success but reverses in the field, plots in the city, a rival parliament, pulpit, and press at Oxford. And the initial exultancy of the preachers on being called together in the assembly had soon to be qualified. A note of anxiety is to be heard in Marshall's sermon at Pym's funeral on December 15, 1643—'Set selfe, and selfe-respects aside; Drive no designes of your owne; Count it reward enough, to spend, and be spent in this cause.' [24] The same note was heard again in his sermon at Christ Church on January 18 when the two houses, the lord mayor, aldermen, and common council, the assembly and the Scottish commissioners gathered to give thanks for escape from another royalist plot and marched afterward through the streets to Merchant Taylors' hall for a banquet in celebration of the event. Marshall turned I Chronicles 12: 38—'all these . . . came with a perfect heart to Hebron, to make David king over all Israel'—into an exhortation to unity under a godly ruler,[25] but Baillie's comment was, 'we wish the union in realitie had been as great as it was in shew.' [26] For everyone knew that the loud professions of harmony on that occasion were belied every day in the assembly by Goodwin and his fellow-dissenters and by their following of independents, separatists, anabaptists, and what not outside.

By the close of 1643 whoever managed such matters apparently thought that the time had come to give the Scots opportunity to try what a bolder tone could do at St. Margaret's to induce parliament to take sterner measures with dissenters. Baillie complained a little later that it was the English fashion 'to speake before the Parliament with so profound a reverence as truelie took all edge from their exhortations, and made all applications to them toothless and adulatorious.' [27] The Scots were expected to remedy this fault. Henderson was called to preach on the fast day in December, Rutherford in January, Baillie in February, and Gillespie in March. Henderson told his hearers in plain terms that it was their business as godly men and magistrates to make laws for the settlement of religion and 'to constrain their Subjects to the duties of Religion, and to coerce and stop them that they do nothing to the contrary.' [28] Parliament must not confine itself like Gallio to civil matters only or like Gamaliel resort to evasion and compromise. Rutherford on January 31 in his cloudy way said much the same sort of thing.[29] Baillie preached a sermon on February 28, *Satan the Leader in chief to all who resist the Reparation of Sion*, straight from the deepest springs of Scottish experience. 'Were our God a Novice,' he declared, 'in the great art of governing the world, and of the Church in the bosome thereof,' they might have reason to be amazed at the dangers that surrounded them. But they should reflect upon the state of Israel in the time of the prophet Zechariah. 'The people of God after a long captivity in *Babel*, after many yeers oppression both in Religion and civill liberties, at last by the hand of God were delivered.' Returning in joy to Jerusalem, they were still beset by enemies and afflictions. Nevertheless, when 'a hopelesse fainting had stupefied and taken away the wonted care of the publike, from the hearts both of their Princes, Priests, and people,' the Lord raised up Haggai and Zechariah to put new vigor into them so that they should not rest until the temple and the city were rebuilt. The enemy, of course, was as always Satan, whom Zechariah saw standing at the right hand of the high priest, whom the angel of the Lord rebuked, and whom Baillie saw at work in Arminians, Socinians, papists, and prelatists, but above all in those whom he calls antinomians, those, that is, who, under color of magnifying free grace and setting Christ on his throne, scoff at repentance and foster the flesh. These were the devils who were especially impeding the work of the assembly.[30]

'No Protestant Church to this day,' he told parliament in his dedicatory epistle, ever spent half the time reforming the whole body of religion 'as this Land hath already spent on some few points of Discipline alone.' If England or Scotland at the beginning of reformation had delayed until every minutest point had been scholastically debated, the work would have been defeated before the discussion was half over. And if now the assembly continued as it had begun, 'if every opponent must be heard on every point, to object, to reply, to double, to triple his exceptions,' then, he said, assembly and parliament will be a week of years before they can so much as lay a foundation of their building. Meanwhile Satan is busy. The result of 'this wearisome procrastination' is that 'millions of men and women, live as they list, in *Blasphemy* and *Drunkennesse, Chambering* and *Wantonesse, Strife* and *Envy, Ignorance* and *Impietie.*'

The other preacher called by parliament to the pulpit on February 28, 1644, was Milton's friend and former tutor Thomas Young. Probably it was not by accident that, a Scot by birth and education though an Englishman by adoption, he was invited to serve on this occasion, the only time the choice fell on him. His sermon on Psalms 31:24, called *Hopes Incouragement,* though rhetorically in a lower key than Baillie's, was similar in purpose. God's people, parliament was told, always wait patiently upon him. Those who wait patiently, no matter how sorely tried, 'rouse up themselves with strength and courage to wait further upon him,' confident that their courage will be thus increased. This lesson the preacher enforced by the doctrine of the talent, so well known to his famous pupil, as a command to believe and act, and of the covenant as certain assurance of the outcome. The application to the situation at hand in February, 1644, was that parliament must not lose patience or courage in *'the purging of* . . . [the Lord's] . . . *floore,* as it hath reference both to the *Church* and *Common-wealth.'* [31]

But Young had also something special on his mind. Earlier in his sermon he had reproved 'such as in their troubles waite not upon God for deliverance, but make use of unlawfull meanes to worke their freedome from the same,' words which at the moment clearly suited the predicament of his friend and former pupil as well as the behavior of the Independents. As he drew to a conclusion he addressed his hearers as 'publicke persons sharing in that *legislative* power, which hath influence upon the whole kingdome,' and he went on to urge them to make no laws against religion and piety, of which he cited certain historical examples, among them the following:

Eminent governours have stained the glory of their government by enacting Lawes which stand in opposition to Gods Law: *Valentinian* the great beginning to alienate his affections from his royall consort (the cause I spare to relate) casting his affection upon *Justina,* thereupon makes it free by Law for any, that would, to have two wives, and after the promulgation of that Law presently he married her: how inconsistent his Law was with the Law of God, I need not speake.[32]

One might wonder, since parliament had many things to think about besides the legalizing of plural marriage in any form, why Young chose to warn his hearers at just this time against offending in just this way. But the explanation seems obvious. The second edition of Milton's *Doctrine and Discipline of Divorce* had recently appeared with an address 'To The Parlament of England, with the Assembly.' The preacher no doubt knew the circumstances which had prompted this work and had probably discussed the subject with its author. From his point of view, his friend's proposal to legalize divorce on the grounds suggested seemed nothing less than a proposal to legalize 'digamy,' and he warned parliament specially against it. Milton could not have failed to see the point, whether anyone else did or not. Young clearly drew the story of Valentinian's decree from *Historia Ecclesiastica* of Socrates Scholasticus. But Milton too had read Socrates Scholasticus and had referred to the same story in his *Commonplace Book.* His note, under the heading 'Matrimonium vide de Divortio,' reads, 'Digamiam lege sanxit Valentinanus. Socrat. L. 4. c. 30. graec.' [33]

With the fast day sermons of Baillie and Young at St. Margaret's on February 28, 1644, the fire of that all-important pulpit was turned against the authors of *An Apologeticall Narration* and all who joined them in opposing presbyterianism. The Independents, for their part, perceived that the longer they could hold the assembly in debate the more they could count on the support of powerful forces outside. In parliament the setting up just at this time of the Committee of Both Kingdoms gave added strength to the faction, headed by Vane and St. John, which was most ready to sacrifice religious unity to the need for winning the war against the king. In the army, to which the religious dispute now also spread, Cromwell was coming forward both as a representative of the same point of view and as an effective commander. In these circumstances the strategy of the Presbyterians was to discredit the Independents by pointing to the errors and corruption now rife as the consequence of delay in reconstituting the church and as an obvious provocation of divine wrath upon parliament and its armies. For evidence of these evils and dangers, the spokesmen for the majority pointed to the flood of unlicensed, heretical, scandalous pamphlets now issuing from the press, for which in fact the Independents of the assembly had as little direct responsibility as their opponents themselves. The Presbyterians' earliest specific allusions were to Richard Overton's *Mans Mortallitie,* Roger Williams' *Bloudy Tenent,* and Milton's *Doctrine and Discipline of Divorce,* but it will be best to postpone discussion of these writings and of the opposition to presbyterianism in general outside the assembly until we have taken more complete account of the efforts of the Presbyterians themselves in that crucial year to exorcise the disruption they saw impending in the tactics of Thomas Goodwin and his associates.

The attack begun by Baillie and Young in February was resumed by their countryman George Gillespie at the next fast day preaching at St. Margaret's on March 27, and for the English it was finally taken up explicitly and in earnest by Richard Vines in a sermon called *The Impostures of Seducing Teachers Discovered*, preached before the lord mayor and aldermen at a special day of thanksgiving on April 23; by Thomas Hill in a fast day sermon before the same audience the following day, entitled *The Good Old Way, Gods Way*; by Hill again in a sermon called *The Season for Englands Selfe-Reflection* before the two houses at a special fast day for Essex in Cornwall on August 13; and by Herbert Palmer on the same occasion in a sermon called *The Glasse of Gods Providence towards His Faithfull Ones*. Baillie wrote that Hill and Palmer preached that day 'two of the most Scottish and free sermons that ever I heard any where,' that they 'laid well about them, and charge publicke and parliamentarie sins strictlie on the back of the guilty.' [34] As to who the guilty were, the preachers left indeed no doubt. Vines, in April, had charged that now every man made a shibboleth of his own private opinion. The ministry was assailed, mortality of the soul upheld, the subjection of believers to the moral law questioned, liberty of all sorts promised, including 'liberty of sensuall lusts, and fleshly loosenesse.' [35]

The next day Hill continued in the same vein and when he came to print added a special warning against dangerous books. He drove the point home in the epistle to his fast day sermon in August with a 'See Bloody Tenent' in the margin. Palmer spoke more openly in the pulpit itself. Some books, he said, clearly alluding to *The Bloudy Tenent*, '(*well worthy to be publikely burnt*) plead for *Popery*, *Judaisme*, *Turcisme*, *Paganisme*, and all manner of *false Religions*, under *pretense of Liberty of Conscience*.' Opinions not schismatical or contrary to good doctrine—'It is true that the name of *Conscience* hath an awfull sound unto a *Conscientious Eare*'—may patiently be borne with. Yet there are limits beyond which forbearance must not go. The plea of conscience against the taking of an oath before a magistrate, against bearing arms, or against civil government or property, must not be allowed. He includes another exception, which may be quoted in full:

If any plead Conscience for the Lawfulnesse of *Polygamy;* (or for divorce for other causes then Christ and His Apostles mention; Of which a *wicked booke* is abroad and *uncensured,* though *deserving to be burnt,* whose *Author* hath been so *impudent* as to *set his Name* to it, and *dedicate it to yourselves,*) or for Liberty to *marry incestuously,* will you grant a *Toleration* for all *this?* [36]

Palmer's sermon, delivered on August 13, was for some reason not registered for publication until November 7 and probably did not appear in print until shortly after that date. In the meantime, however, Prynne joined the attack on the Independents with *Twelve Considerable Serious Questions touching Church Government,* a copy of which was in Thomason's hands on September 16. In his eleventh question the author demanded whether independency was not a very seminary of schisms in church and state, a flood gate to let in 'all manner of Heresies, Errors, Sects, Religions, destructive opinions, Libertinisme and lawlessnesse.' He asked more explicitly whether the final conclusion, 'as Master *Williams* in his late dangerous *Licentious Booke* determines,' would not really be '*that every man, whether he be Jew, Turk, Pagan, Papist, Arminian, Anabaptist, &c ought to be left to his owne free liberty of conscience*' and so allowed to embrace and publicly profess any sort of '*false, seditious, detestable*' error he may choose. What the effect will be, he says, is made apparent by 'the late dangerous increase of many *Anabaptisticall, Antinomian, Hereticall, Atheisticall opinions, as of the soules mortality, divorce at pleasure, &c* lately broached, preached, printed in this famous City, which I hope our grand Councell will speedily and carefully suppresse.' [37] One other printed attack on *The Doctrine and Discipline of Divorce* appeared in 1644, the anonymous *Answer,* dated by Thomason November 19.

We must not infer that Milton's critics were chiefly occupied at this point in seeking the invidious immortality which has befallen them. There may have been pulpit attacks upon him of which we have no record, but from the evidence available in print it would seem doubtful whether, as Gardiner, depending too heavily upon Masson, says,

Milton's persistence in publishing his opinions upon marriage 'brought upon him a storm of obloquy daily increasing in volume and force.' [38] Milton himself testifies that the first printed notice his book received, 'after many rumors of confutations and convictions . . . and now and then a by-blow from the Pulpit' was Prynne's 'jolly slander, call'd *Divorce at pleasure,*' coming 'at the taile of *Anabaptistical, Antinomian, Heretical, Atheistical* epithets.' [39] His own complaint was that no one offered a considered reply to his argument until the second edition of *The Doctrine and Discipline* had been out a year. Palmer's brief allusion in his sermon of August 13, probably not published until some time in November, was not made until the first edition of Milton's tract had been before the public for at least a year and the second edition for over six months. This pulpit 'by-blow' was, so far as we know, the first public reference of any sort except Young's covert rebuke in his sermon on February 28. Prynne's slur came a few weeks after the delivery of Palmer's sermon but before its publication. The pamphlet called *An Answer to a Book, Intituled, The Doctrine and Discipline of Divorce* was not licensed for publication until November 14, 1644, and the attacks of Featley, Pagitt, Baillie, and Edwards did not appear before the following year and then only along with attacks on many other allegedly scandalous doctrines.[40] In none of the attacks on Milton's argument for divorce, finally, were his ideas discussed in such a way as to suggest that his critics had considered seriously what he had to say or had ever heard about his own marital difficulties.

The leaders and defenders of the Westminster Assembly in 1644 were mainly and properly concerned not with Milton's proposals in respect to marriage or with his private affairs but with the great problem with which he had himself at first been chiefly occupied, the reform of the church and its restoration to its place of spiritual leadership. If, to be sure, they had attended closely to what he said on that subject in his tracts against the bishops, they might have taken alarm at the practical implications of his reasoning on the relations of church and state. On that point, however, the book they came to regard as most dangerous and most necessary to repress was Roger Williams' *Bloudy Tenent*. The reason is clear. With every day that passed the need to put the ecclesiastical state in order seemed more imperative. The delay caused by the Independents' unwillingness to submit to the will of the majority in the assembly appeared to give scope for religious expression and organization among the people to take their course without tarrying for either magistrate or minister. Hence the Presbyterian majority felt compelled to call upon parliament to hold the forces of disruption in check until a plan could somehow be drafted, agreed upon, and set in operation. But parliament was not easily to be persuaded to grant to the ministers a degree of independent authority it had denied the bishops, and as the difficulty of imposing by force any sort of uniform control over religious life became more apparent so also did the practical advantages of passing over religious differences which did not immediately and measurably affect the security of the state and the conduct of the war. This had been the practice usually followed, though not acknowledged, under Elizabeth. It had made way for the rise of Puritanism in the church, and it was now being turned to account by Cromwell among the troops under his command. Nevertheless, to the earnest and devoted men who made up the majority in the assembly such a solution of the problem of the church seemed no solution at all but a plain neglect of duty and opportunity, and Williams' offense was to offer his friends in parliament a too plausible set of reasons for evading their responsibility for the spiritual condition of the people.

iii. THE RISE OF HERESY AND SCHISM

Fate set *The Bloudy Tenent* in a context of events ominous of the eventual failure of Presbyterian hopes. The military campaign of 1644 began in January shortly after the publication of the Independents' *Apologeticall Narration.* The Scots had then crossed the border and begun operations against Charles in the north. In spite of a humiliating reverse at Newark in March, they had kept the Earl of Newcastle engaged and with Fairfax's assistance had driven him behind the walls of York. There they had been joined by the army of the Eastern Association, led by Manchester with Cromwell as his commander of horse, and on July 2 the combined parliamentary and Scottish forces met and defeated the king's supporters at Marston Moor. The battle was decided when Cromwell, having routed Rupert on the parliamentary left, kept his troops under control, wheeled and struck the enemy again, this time from the rear. 'God made them stubble to our swords.' [41]

At such a moment *The Bloudy Tenent* appeared on the London bookstalls. All through the early months of 1644 Baillie had been praying for a Scottish victory to lend force to Presbyterian arguments, noting at the same time that Independency and worse was spreading in the English forces and that Cromwell, 'a known Independent,' was permitted by Manchester 'to guide all the army at his pleasure.' [42] Early in June Baillie was writing to his friends that 'one Mr. Williams has drawn a great number after him . . . denying any true church in the world, and will have every man to serve God by himselfe alone, without any church at all.' [43] Then on July 2 came the victory at Marston Moor, and Scottish hearts exulted, only to be dashed by the news that credit for the victory was claimed for Cromwell. Henderson and Vines, in their thanksgiving sermons on the eighteenth, had to content themselves with preaching against envy among brethren, though the former declared that 'it is a wonder that so intelligent a people, should be carried away with every winde, and scattered into so many Sects and Divisions.' [44] On July 15 a copy of *The Bloudy Tenent* was in Thomason's hands, bearing in its opening pages the blunt statement that civil magistrates should have nothing to do with the '*Christian state* and *Worship*,' that God commands freedom to be granted in all nations for 'the most *Paganish, Jewish, Turkish,* or *Antichristian consciences* and *worships*,' and that all efforts to enforce religious uniformity merely confound both the civil and the religious state. A few days later Baillie wrote that 'very many,' misled by his 'good acquaintance' Roger Williams, were now for 'a total libertie of all religions, and writes very plausible treatises for that end.' [45]

Events in the military campaign after Marston Moor did nothing to allay alarm and distraction among the divines of the assembly. As the army of the Eastern Association resumed its defense of the eastern counties, dissension arose between its two commanders and among their subordinates. Cromwell, having learned how to transpose faith into action and having tasted success on the battlefield, was all for pushing on to complete victory over the king. Manchester, full of not unjustified apprehension of what such a victory might bring forth, hung back. Cromwell, who was probably insubordinate, and Manchester, who was certainly jealous and overfearful, came up to London in September to lay their quarrel before parliament and the Committee of Both Kingdoms. They arrived at a critical moment, a moment which held in it, however, nothing but enhancement for Cromwell's prestige and influence. While the campaign in the north, thanks to him, was being brought to its triumphant conclusion, the efforts of parliamentary commanders in the midlands had come to nothing, and in August, Essex, the general most favored by the Presbyterians, got himself and his army into a dangerous position in Cornwall. On August 9 the assembly consequently sent a delegation to both houses, headed by Cornelius Burges and Stephen Marshall. The former presented a plea for a special fast day to intercede with the Lord for Essex and his army, now on the brink of disaster. Marshall presented a petition demanding that action be taken to prevent 'the spreading Opinions of Anabaptism and Antinomianism with that Turbulency, that it tends to a Division amongst them that join in the Owning of this great Cause.' With the petition was submitted a list of offenders, beginning with Hanserd Knollys. The name of Roger Williams, now safe beyond reach in America, was not included, but the house, having referred the petition to a committee, ordered that 'one *Williams* his Books . . . concerning the Tolerating of all Sorts of Religion' be publicly burned.[46] Thomas Hill and Herbert Palmer, as we have seen, seconded this condemnation from the pulpit on the special fast day which followed on August 13, and Palmer added the recommendation that Milton's book on divorce be accorded the same treatment.

Yet in spite of prayers and preaching, in spite too of petitions and orders for the repression of scandalous books, Essex left his army to surrender on September 2. The news reached London a week later, and the assembly at once entered upon a great searching of hearts to determine what sins of its own, of parliament, of the army, of the people had provoked the Lord to pour out his wrath, not as expected upon parliament's enemies but upon parliament's own army. It was 'the most free and strange par[ley]' Baillie had ever heard but, like so much talk he had listened to in that place, it was brought to nothing in the end by Thomas Goodwin and his faction.[47] Parliament meanwhile ordered a special fast day for September 12 and invited Thomas

Coleman and Matthew Newcomen to preach. The appointment of the former on this occasion, a consistent champion of the subordination of the church to parliamentary authority, could hardly have been agreeable to the majority of his colleagues.

The thoughts that troubled their souls were more fitly expressed by Newcomen. The preachers had been asking why the people were not yet redeemed from Babylon, why the reparation of Zion remained still incomplete, why Christ's kingdom had not yet sprung up in England as promised, why the seventh trumpet did not blow. The answer had been that the Lord was still chastising his people for not going faster about the work of reformation, and yet all the conditions causing delay were made steadily worse by the delay itself. 'When *Israel* was in *Egypt*,' Newcomen exclaimed, 'there was nothing they desired more then the Land of *Canaan;* when they were come out of *Egypt*, and were upon the borders of that Land, then they despised it, and wished themselves in *Egypt* againe. Ô that it were not so with us.' For discipline and government in the church now seemed to some a fiction, to others mere tyranny and persecution. Nothing would satisfy them but the toleration of all religions and of all opinions. Yet it was obvious that unity in religion was the very bond of all concord among men, diversity the very seminary of distraction and division. 'And in a little time, either a Schisme in the State begets a Schisme in the Church, or a Schisme in the Church begets a Schisme in the State.' 'Men will at last take up swords and speares in stead of Pens: and defend by Armes what they cannot doe by Arguments.' The answer to the question, what sin, by whom committed, had brought the anger of the Lord upon the parliamentary army in Cornwall, seemed therefore clear. Parliament and assembly had covenanted to extirpate heresy and schism; yet heresy and schism abounded more than ever, and nothing would placate the wrath of the Lord but their immediate suppression and the restoration of order, unity, and discipline in religion with parliament's support.

Newcomen was now ready to be as precise in his denunciations as any Scot could wish. 'There are two opinions,' he told his audience that day, 'which if encouraged, (& they are encouraged, if connived at) will open a door to *Turcisme, Judaisme, Atheisme, Polytheisme,* any monster of opinion.' The first of these, he said, is 'that every man is to be left to the Liberty of his own Religion,' a notion 'contended for by the *bloudy tenets, John Baptist, Liberty of Conscience*, and the like Pamphlets.' The other is that 'there is no *Jus Divinum* upon the Calling of the Ministry,' as lately set forth in a pamphlet 'bearing the Name of the *Compassionate Samaritane*.' [48] The first pamphlet here mentioned was, of course, Roger Williams' *The Bloudy Tenent of Persecution, for cause of Conscience, discussed, in A Conference betweene Truth and Peace*, which had appeared anonymously in July.[49] The next two were *Liberty of Conscience: or the Sole means to obtaine Peace and Truth*,[50] and *John the Baptist, Forerunner of Christ Jesus: or, A necessity for Liberty of Conscience*, both issued anonymously by Henry Robinson, the one in March, the other, it would seem, about the time of Essex's defeat (Thomason's copy is dated September 23). The last pamphlet on the list, also anonymous, was William Walwyn's *Compassionate Samaritane, Unbinding the Conscience*, of which the first edition had appeared some time in June or July.[51]

Two other members of the Smectymnuan group presently joined the hue and cry at St. Margaret's against the threat of disruption they saw in the abounding heresy and schism about them. On October 22 Calamy told the members of the house that they would themselves be reckoned anabaptists and antinomians if they failed to proceed against such notions as that all religions were to be tolerated by the state and that the soul was mortal.[52] On November 5 Spurstowe complained in the same place of blasphemies 'too tall for the Pen to deale with,' requiring to be 'cut downe by the power of your Sword.' [53] Thus by November, when Milton sent a copy of *Areopagitica* to his friend Thomason, each of his Smectymnuan associates had raised his voice before parliament in one way or another against the publication of erroneous opinions. None of them, however, except Thomas Young, made any allusion to their former coadjutor's divorce tracts, and none of them at any time took cognizance of his argument for unlicensed printing.

But more and more, as the disputes of 1644 continued unabated and unsettled, Cromwell, in his dual role as military leader and member of parliament, was becoming the decisive figure in the whole situation. His political alignment was with Vane and St. John, and this faction, abetted by the Erastian lawyers of whom Baillie so bitterly complained, was able to keep parliament from proceeding effectively against the opponents of presbyterianism and the authors and publishers of unlicensed pamphlets. Yet pending the final settlement of the problem of church government, something had to be done to maintain the preaching of the Word, and the longer present conditions continued the more difficult and pressing became the problem of finding suitable preachers to fill the pulpits left vacant by ejected or renegade clergy and to meet the ever-increasing demand for pulpit edification. On April 20, 1644, over the opposition of the Independents, the assembly submitted a proposed directory for ordination which, however, the house of commons made no haste to approve. It was still under discussion in parliament and between parliament and assembly when the house stopped to fast and pray and listen to Newcomen and Coleman preach on the occasion of Essex's defeat in the west. But this was also the moment when Manchester and Cromwell came up to Westminster in the course of their developing quarrel over the conduct of the war and the selection and management of the troops under their command. Cromwell was back in his seat the day after the fast day services at St. Margaret's when the house resumed its discussion of the proposed directory for ordination. The debate revealed once more the unwillingness of members to give way completely to ministerial pretensions. It was brought to an end by the passage of a motion, offered by St. John but prompted by Cromwell, referring the proposed directory back to the assembly with counsel of moderation and compromise. Appropriate committees of assembly and parliament and the Scottish commissioners were instructed to

take into Consideration the Differences in Opinion of the Members of the Assembly in point of Church Government; and to endeavour a Union if it be possible; and, in case that cannot be done, to endeavour the finding out some ways how far tender Consciences, who cannot in all Things submit to the common Rule which shall be established, may be borne with, according to the Word, and as may stand with the publick Peace, that so the Proceedings of the Assembly may not be so much retarded.

The chagrin of the Presbyterians, smarting under the disaster that had befallen their favorite Essex, could hardly have been lessened when the house went on to vote thanks to Cromwell for his fidelity to the parliamentary cause, in particular for his services at Marston Moor, where, it was said, 'God made him a special Instrument in obtaining that great Victory.' [54]

iv. THE LIBERTY OF UNLICENSED PRINTING

Cromwell and Manchester patched up their differences and went off with the other generals to the second battle of Newbury. The Accommodation Order had no immediate effect except to encourage the Independents in the assembly and dissidents of all sorts outside. The Presbyterians for their part, besides sermons and petitions, besides the burning of *The Bloudy Tenent,* attempted still another maneuver for discrediting their opponents. This was to invoke the printing ordinance of June, 1643, against Milton for his *Doctrine and Discipline of Divorce* and against the author, supposed at the time to be Clement Wrighter, of *Mans Mortallitie.* The crown, from the beginning, had claimed jurisdiction over printing as over coining and had exercised its prerogative by issuing permission to printers and booksellers either directly or through the Stationers' Company. From the beginning, too, it had sought to provide by a system of licensing for what we may call copyright, for the protection of the public from whatever seemed offensive according to the standards of the day, and for the security of government itself in state and church.

The breach between the Long Parliament and the crown did not abrogate these regulations but simply rendered their enforcement next to impossible. The parliamentary ordinance of June, 1643, was primarily an attempt to reinstitute control according to the pattern which had been set by Elizabeth's injunctions of 1559 and reaffirmed by a Star Chamber decree of 1637. The only essential differences were in the immediate purpose, which was to repress royalist publications emanating from Oxford, and the mode of administration. The function of censorship, formerly exercised under the crown by the Bishop of London and the Archbishop of Canterbury, was now assigned to licensers appointed by parliament, twelve ministers being designated to the all-important task of passing before publication upon books of divinity. The enforcement of the ordinance was still entrusted to the

Stationers' Company, but Star Chamber was replaced by parliament itself as the court of final jurisdiction. That the press should be absolutely unaccountable, no responsible person supposed, but the problem now as always was to determine to what extent in practice it should be held to account, in whose interest, and to what end.[55] The extreme import of the action proposed against Milton and the author of *Mans Mortallitie* would have been to put the press along with the church under the absolute control of the Presbyterian clergy, but there was little likelihood that any parliament would ever make any such surrender of what had always been regarded as part of the prerogative of the sovereign. The memory of Laud's action in 1637 against Prynne, Bastwick, and Burton was still fresh in men's minds, and Laud was now in the Tower by order of parliament.

Pamphleteers heeded the printing ordinance as suited their interest or convenience. Milton took the trouble to secure a license for his translation of Martin Bucer but not for either the first or second edition of *The Doctrine and Discipline of Divorce*. As though to show his disregard of the ordinance, he put his name to the unlicensed second edition and issued it with a prefatory address to parliament itself. Palmer's recommendation from the pulpit on August 13 that such publications deserved to be burned evoked no immediate response. The Stationers' Company, on the other hand, was persuaded to complain again to parliament of the lax enforcement of the printing ordinance. Under such pressure, on August 26, in the anxious days on the eve of Essex's surrender, the house of commons added several new members to its committee for printing and ordered the committee 'diligently to inquire out the Authors, Printers, and Publishers, of the Pamphlet against the Immortality of the Soul, and concerning Divorce.' [56] The reason for singling out these two pamphlets was their obviously scandalous subjects, and the purpose was of course to discredit the opposition to presbyterianism. Whether Overton was known to be the R. O. who acknowledged authorship of *Mans Mortallitie* is doubtful, but there could have been no mystery as to the authorship of the divorce tract, and probably none as to its printers, Thomas Paine and Matthew Simmons, whose initials and address appeared on the title page of the first edition. Nothing appears to have been done to carry out the order in respect to either publication. Parliament soon had much else to think about, and the next word on the printing ordinance came from Milton himself in the form of an address to parliament, published without permission sometime in November, with the title *Areopagitica; A Speech of Mr. John Milton For the Liberty of Unlicenc'd Printing*.

Nothing more, possibly, might have been heard of the demand for Milton's prosecution under the printing ordinance but for a barbed remark near the close of this address which described the stationers as 'old *patentees* and *monopolizers* in the trade of bookselling' and accused them of fraud.[57] Hence the company renewed its attack upon Milton, this time in a complaint to the house of lords. The circumstances leading to this complaint, if we may briefly look ahead in our story, show how nearly impossible it had become to enforce any control over the press. On December 9 the lords took sudden offense at the appearance of a surreptitious publication which they described as 'a scandalous printed Libel against the Peerage of this Realm,' and at once ordered the master and wardens of the Stationers' Company to report whether they knew the author and printer.[58] The stationers asked for time to make inquiries, and a few days later brought in a hosier's apprentice who told of finding, one morning, two and twenty copies of the offending paper thrust between the stall-boards of his master's shop, of conveying two of them to the lord mayor, of reading one of them, and unluckily of letting a number of others fall into the hands of unruly neighbors. The lords sent this information to the lord mayor with a request to know what he had done about the matter and a demand that some action be taken forthwith. The demand was repeated on December 26 and two days later, having had no response from either the mayor or the company, they sent a peremptory summons which at last brought the wardens to their door. The latter reported that they had tried to find out the author and printer of the offending paper but without success, 'the Letter being so common a Letter.' But they then went on for their part to complain of 'the frequent Printing of scandalous Books by divers, as *Hezechia Woodward* and *Jo. Milton*.' [59]

The lords at once directed the gentleman usher to arrest the accused persons and appointed two judges to examine them. Woodward was apprehended and questioned without delay and as promptly released on his own bond and his promise to reappear when summoned.

There is no record of his being called again. As for Milton, there is no record of his ever having been approached, apprehended, questioned, or further molested by either house or the stationers for anything he had ever printed with or without permission. He himself testified to the fact in the address to parliament prefaced to *Tetrachordon* in March, 1645. It is generally known, he there says, how and by whom parliament had been instigated to attack *The Doctrine and Discipline of Divorce*, but he declares that, in spite of 'furious incitements,' nothing 'hath issued by your appointment, that might give the least interruption or disrepute either to the Author, or to the Book.' 60

The meaning of this episode in the situation at the close of 1644 is clear enough. Neither the lords nor the stationers were really bent on prosecuting Milton or Woodward. The lords, their jealousy provoked by attacks on Essex and Manchester, pounced upon an anonymous libel as one way of making their resentment known. The stationers may or may not have been unable to find out who was responsible for that publication, but neither they nor the city authorities were inclined to submit to the lords or to be drawn into a political dispute the outcome of which was by no means certain. When finally pressed, the stationers drew a red herring across the trail by putting upon parliament itself some of the blame for the notorious failure to restrain the press. Why they did not proceed against Milton under the ordinance, as they might have done, is hard to explain except upon the supposition that they had no real hope of success, knowing that they could not proceed far without encountering insuperable opposition.

The stationers complained of Woodward because, only a few days before on December 23, he too had defied their authority, and they carried the complaint farther in his case because, probably, he was a more vulnerable target. He was a somewhat absurd eccentric who attempted to compose the differences of the moment by confused counsels of peace and charity. When he had finished three of the projected six parts of his *Inquiries Into the causes of our miseries*, he took them to the licenser, who approved the second and third but not the first. Yet no rebuff could stop the man's rage for utterance. He published the forbidden first part of his tract, none the less, and when in consequence the stationers secured a warrant from the lords forbidding him to print the second part, though previously approved, he defended himself in still another unlicensed tract. 'I am a free man,' he declared, 'and may take my liberty, not standing charged as servants do, not to *answer again.*' On the whole issue of free speech, however, Woodward was as confused as he was irrepressible. He was all for obeying the law and putting down blasphemy and false teaching. When in error, he welcomed correction by the censor's hand. His intention had been to clear the Independents of the charge 'that they hold forth the *licentiousnesse of wicked consciences; Tolerations of all sorts of most detestable Schismes, Heresies, and Religions.*' So he issued his defense of the Independents against the imputation of favoring liberty of conscience, 'warranted,' he said, in default of any other license, 'by the God of Heaven.' '*Truth,* and *Reason,* the old Licensers of old, have licenced my words all along.' [61]

The attempt of the Presbyterians to embarrass and discredit their opponents by getting the stationers to invoke the printing ordinance against Milton and Woodward came to nothing. For in taking upon itself the authority claimed by the crown over the press, parliament fell heir to all the difficulties, doubly compounded, that had formerly beset its enforcement. There had never been a time when writers, printers, and booksellers had not found it to their advantage to supply, legally or otherwise, an appetite for print which grew by what it fed on. No government had ever been able for long to maintain strict control. There had been prosecutions from time to time on behalf of the stationers or the privileged printers, and when powerful interests felt themselves endangered, offenders were severely handled. But over the years such cases were not numerous, and their effect was always at best uncertain. Not less remarkable than the ruthlessness with which the Marprelate press was put down was the fact that it took Elizabeth's government so long to catch up with the men responsible for it. Not less impressive than the punishment meted out by Laud to a handful of hostile pamphleteers was the ineffectiveness of the measures taken and their rebounding upon his own head. The truth was that control over the press, never complete, was already disintegrating when parliament put the finishing stroke to the work by wiping out Star Chamber and sending Laud to the Tower. Unlicensed publications could be smuggled in from Holland or Scotland. Copies could be altered or added to after the licenser thought he had done with them.

Imprimaturs could be falsified. Printing presses could be set up in odd corners and moved from place to place beyond reach of the stationers' agents. Broadsides and tracts could be hawked about by unauthorized persons. Authors, printers, and booksellers could avoid putting their names to their work. Most important, especially after parliament assumed jurisdiction, licensers had no consistent notion as to what ought or ought not to be allowed. More authoritative than any decree of the crown or order of parliament were the prevailing ideas and convictions, largely bred by the pulpit and the literature that flowed from the pulpit, concerning reason, conscience, and expression. The presumption that anyone who could quote scripture for his purpose must be permitted to speak and so to print whatever the spirit prompted him to utter was difficult to resist.

For what hope could there be without the Word, which was to say the Word in print? The whole point and meaning of the movement which had been so assiduously fostered by the brotherhood of preachers had been to convince men that the decisive experience of each man's spiritual life should center in his reading of a book, one certain book above all others but inevitably others too. Never wholly prevented from preaching, the Puritans had not been prevented from printing what they preached. Almost half the books printed in England before 1640 dealt with religion in some form or other, and the nearer 1640 approached the greater the number of books of all kinds published and in circulation and the greater the proportion with a religious purpose or coloring. Men learned to read the Bible for a key to their inner lives and a rule for family, church, and state, and though they did not always find what they looked for, though they certainly did not all find the same thing, they learned to read with imaginations aroused, and they did not stop with the Bible. Nothing did more to foster the production of books than the enormous literature of edification, comment, and controversy which the Bible evoked. Here was the all-sufficient book, supplying the prime apparatus of thought and expression concerning not only the inner drama of the breast but also the great drama of the world's affairs. Yet printers and booksellers flourished by publishing everything that people would buy. God was revealed in his works as well as in his Word, in nature, history, and the life of man. Hence all books might be of use, even to the Bible's devotees, and the same books which furnished the minds of poets and dramatists might be drawn upon to confirm, illustrate, enrich, and corrupt the teachings of the pulpit and of the Bible itself.

Under such conditions the problem, always difficult, of enforcing adverse control over the activities of the press had become by 1643 practically insurmountable. The disagreement and confusion of mind which became promptly evident in the assembly manifested themselves just as promptly among the ministers appointed by parliament to pass upon books dealing with the all-important subject of divinity. One licenser might take the attitude that, if he was not to make himself responsible for other men's sins, he must protect the people from contamination with error. But another might assume that he must allow every man's light to shine, even with some admixture of darkness, provided it was drawn from the scriptures and put forth peaceably. The former point of view was represented by James Cranford's statement that he approved Thomas Edwards' *Gangraena* in order that readers might discern the mischief of ecclesiastical anarchy and the monstrousness of toleration. The latter was illustrated by Charles Herle in licensing the Independents' *Apologeticall Narration*. Herle was the author of several pamphlets in defense of parliament against the king. He had preached more than once at St. Margaret's. In May, 1643, he had published a temperate but cogent attack on the Independents, called *The Independency on Scriptures of the Independency of Churches,* and he opposed them in the assembly. Even in giving them leave to print, he declared himself inclined to 'the Presbyteriall way of Church Government.' Nevertheless, he gave them leave and commended what they wrote as 'seasonably needfull' for the vindication of the Protestant party in general from 'the aspersions of Incommunicablenesse within itselfe' and of the writers 'both against misreportings from without, & some possible mistakings from within.' Their words, he said, were 'full of peaceablenesse, modesty, and candour.' [62] No wonder, in the face of such scrupulous care lest any opposition offered in the spirit of godliness should fail to get a hearing, that the Scots despaired of ever getting the church reformed.

The state of mind represented by Herle was carried to further extremes by John Bachiler, a licenser after the Independents' and sectaries' own hearts. Edwards' account of him as 'Licenser general of

Books, not only of Independent Doctrines, but of Books for a general Toleration of all Sects,' was hardly an exaggeration. 'If the Devill himselfe should make a book,' Edwards declared, 'and give it the Title, A plea for liberty of conscience . . . and bring it to Mr. *Bachiler,* hee would license it, and not onely with a bare *Imprimatur,* but set before it the commendations of *A usefull Treatise,* of *A sweet and excellent booke,* making for love and peace among brethren.' [63] Acting upon such principles, Bachiler authorized the publications of John Goodwin, beginning with *Theomachia,* and of John Saltmarsh, beginning with *Dawnings of Light,* and he made a practice, as indeed did other licensers, of adding his commendations to the books he approved, whether he agreed with them on every point or not. He defended himself against Edwards' strictures in a statement accompanying his imprimatur to Goodwin's *Twelve Considerable Cautions,* a statement which throws an interesting light on the whole licensing system. He insists that he has authorized nothing contrary to the gospel, the authority of parliament, or the public peace. But 'in this discussing and Truth-searching age,' he holds it his duty as a man and a Christian '(in all sober and calm disputes from Scripture and reason, where the contention seems to be for Truth, and not for Victory) to suffer faireplay on all sides, and to yeeld that liberty to every free borne subject which . . . the Law of God, of Nature, and this Kingdome gives.'

But there were limits beyond which even Bachiler would not go in suffering fair play to all sides. One might infer from the statement just quoted that he had been reading Milton or Roger Williams were it not that we have his own assurance to the contrary. Defending himself further against the charge that he had approved dangerous books, contrary to his own opinions, he declares,

the Books which meet the harshest censure, such as the *Bloudy Tenent,* the Treatise about *Divorce,* and others that have Affinity with these, I have been so farre from licensing, that I have not so much as seene or heard of them, till after they have been commonly sold abroad; and how many such like I have refused to license, some scores can witness.[64]

Thus by the end of 1644 the divines of the assembly had failed to silence opposition in the press as completely as they had failed to secure agreement among the members of their own order. The Independent minority in the assembly still held out against centralized control over individual preachers and congregations. Writers with ideas repugnant to Presbyterian interests and orthodox beliefs were able to get permission to print from one licenser or another or, if not, to publish anyhow with little risk. Milton could assail the printing ordinance itself with impunity, indeed without attracting much attention. The truth was that there was no effective action parliament could take to enforce its own regulations, and its members were unwilling to do the entire bidding of the Westminster divines in this or any other matter. The preachers had done their pulpit-work well, but with practical results that few of them had looked for and many of them deplored. They had sown the Word without foreseeing the harvest they had now to reap. They had preached the doctrines of calling and covenant, evinced by faith, manifested in action, to be crowned by success here or hereafter, and they had thus planted in many minds dreams of new heaven and new earth. But it is one thing to launch men on a quest for the New Jerusalem, quite another to stop them when they have gone far enough. The preachers selected by parliament came together at Westminster, expecting to reconstitute the church in the light of the Word. In the light of the Word, however, the New Jerusalem took more shapes than one, and the members of the assembly promptly fell out among themselves. The light could not, moreover, be limited in its shining to the chamber where the assembly met. Thanks to pulpit and press, the Bible was in everyone's hands and anyone could quote it for his purpose. Hence all attempts in 1644 to impose a presbyterian frame upon revolutionary Puritanism served simply to evoke the many-headed hydra of English dissent.

V

The Honest Liberty of Free Speech

1644

THE Accommodation Order of September 13, 1644, directing the Westminster Assembly to make provision for tender consciences, foreshadowed the eventual frustration of all efforts to reconstitute the church. Milton's attack on the printing ordinance signalized the breakdown of all efforts to reestablish control over the press. Both were disregarded, and yet the nearer the assembly came to fixing a new church-order the wider grew the breach within its own ranks, the more active and outspoken the opposition outside. The truth was that the English people on their way out into the modern world were not to be held within the limits of any single discipline or fixed pattern of belief. But this condition was due not so much to the intransigent particularism of Independents and dissenters or to the unyielding intolerance of Presbyterians as to the state of mind of the people at large. It was the result of many compelling changes in all the conditions of life, not least important the change in the modes and temper of religious life, brought about by the spread of a vernacular culture depending upon free expression in and out of the pulpit, the accumulation of printed books in the people's hands, and free access to the printing press.

The divines of the assembly were confronted by the incalculable future they had labored to bring upon themselves, and the fact became evident in the number, intensity, and diversity of the attacks upon their proposals which followed the publication of *An Apologeticall Narration* in January, 1644. The intricacies and asperities of the disputes which accompanied that manifesto we may safely pass over, but not the portents of the age to come which it also provoked. These are especially to be seen in the writings and activities of certain figures who stand out among the various critics and opponents of presbyterianism in 1644. Each of these men springs from the common English Protestant background. Each illustrates the unlooked-for working of the common ferment of ideas for which the Puritan movement was largely responsible. Each illustrates too in some degree the intermingling with Puritanism of other influences. Each represents a point of view which was to play an important part in the further unfolding of Puritan revolutionary activity and discussion. John Goodwin, going far beyond Thomas of the same name, becomes the most articulate exponent of the principle of the 'gathered church,' the herald and theorist of that dissidence of dissent which was to be a normal condition of English religious life from that time on. Roger Williams, having applied the same principle with startling results to the unprecedented conditions of the American frontier, brings the lessons of his experience to bear upon the crisis in England. Henry Robinson takes up the argument from the point of view of an English merchant who has lived and done business abroad and is convinced that England's destiny lies in expansion overseas. William Walwyn and Richard Overton push on from a conception of the spiritual communion of saints to conceive of a natural communion of citizens in a democratic society. Milton, whom we have seen attempting to transfigure the institution of marriage in the light both of Puritan faith and of humanistic reason, now endeavors also to transfigure the state in the same way. The contribution of each of these men to the debate over the church in this critical year is as authentic an expression of Puritan ideas as that of any of the Westminster divines. What these men thought and said in 1644 took on unforeseen importance as the frustration of parliamentary military effort under Presbyterian generals gave way in the following year to success under Fairfax and Cromwell.

i. THE GATHERED CHURCH: HENRY BURTON, JOHN GOODWIN, WILLIAM PRYNNE

Thomas Goodwin and his faction gave voice in the assembly to forces that had always been present and active in the Puritan movement, but they did not themselves represent those forces in the form most dangerous to the authority of the ministerial caste. Presbyterian theocracy had more to fear from members of the preaching order, such as Henry Burton and John Goodwin, who had not been named to take part in the assembly. The head and front of Thomas Goodwin's offending was indeed that he gave countenance and encouragement to such men as these. Burton, on his triumphant return to London in 1640, went about regaining his old pulpit at St. Matthew's Friday Street, where he was finally restored in 1642 as lecturer.[1] When parliament in May, 1641, attempted to bind its members by a 'protestation' to defend religion as 'expressed in the Doctrine of the Church of *England*,'[2] he published *The Protestation Protested*, an assertion of that conception which from now on was to bedevil all plans for establishing order in and through the church. God, he began, had put irreconcilable enmity between the seed of the woman and the seed of the serpent, between the elect and the reprobate. The elect were the church, and 'a particular Church, or congregation rightly collected and constituted, consists of none, but such as are visible living members of Christ.' But the Church of England was not such a congregation, and the saints could not in conscience bind themselves to defend it. To be sure, Burton admitted, 'where ever the Gospel commeth in its power and purity, it will kindle coales, and stirre up debate,' but this was only a necessary incident to 'zeale and plaine dealing in reproving of sinne.'[3] His subsequent quarrel with Edmund Calamy illustrates the kind of predicament into which the preachers were frequently led by such principles. In 1636 Calamy had been silenced by his bishop as lecturer at Bury St. Edmunds. In 1639 he had been chosen by the vestry as rector of St. Mary Aldermanbury. But in 1645 a committee of 'underwriters' engaged Burton to deliver a regular 'Catechisticall Lecture' in the same church, and the lecturer used the opportunity to preach independency and draw together a flock of his own. He soon found himself locked out of the church at Calamy's instance, and took to print in order to point out the close parallel between the treatment now accorded to him and that which Calamy himself had formerly suffered at the hands of a bishop.[4]

The case of John Goodwin was even more revealing. He had been vicar of St. Stephen's, Coleman Street, since 1633, but by January, 1645, he had gathered another group of followers about him in the same place on the basis of personal conviction. He then fell into dispute with his regular parishioners, among them Isaac Pennington, as to who should or should not be admitted to the sacrament, and the upshot was that in May he was ejected from his living by the parliamentary Committee for Plundered Ministers. He continued, however, as pastor of his 'gathered church,' meeting in the same neighborhood and maintaining friendly relations with the members of the parish and their present minister. In 1647 they petitioned parliament that they might have him back as lecturer. In 1649 he was restored as vicar, and not only that, but his independent congregation was then invited to come with him, sharing in his ministry and in the use of the church.[5]

Goodwin was able to make the most of both systems, but except for that rare good fortune, rather indeed by reason of it, he gave striking evidence of the anomalous state of affairs which the Puritan preachers brought upon themselves. Whether as parson of a parish or head of a conventicle, Goodwin knew how to conduct himself only as a preacher of the Word, a fisher of men, a shepherd of souls from hither and yon. The church was always for him a 'gathered' church, that is a voluntary group brought together by the voice of the preacher. There were many others like him, and more and more as events moved on, but he was the most consistent, uncompromising Independent of them all, the most articulate and before long the most conspicuous. For Prynne, Edwards, Vicars, and all such he became the prime butt of abuse, the arch-sectary and schismatic, the great red dragon of Coleman Street, the gargantua of error.

He was indeed a great master of both the rhetoric and the dialectic of his profession, the most adroit and persuasive champion of the purest congregationalism. His point of view in the debate initiated by the Independents of the assembly was first expressed in print in *M. S. to A. S. with a Plea for Libertie of Conscience in a Church way* (1644, dated by Thomason May 3, second edition July 11). This was a reply to *Some Observations and Annotations upon An Apologeticall Narration* by Adam Steuart. Goodwin's own assault on presbyterianism was made from the pulpit on the special fast day, September 12, after Essex's surrender in Cornwall. On this day, as we have seen, the house of commons heard Matthew Newcomen at St. Margaret's deliver still another attack on heretics and sectaries.[6] Goodwin on the same day defended all such in two sermons, the substance of which, 'with some necessary Enlargements,' he presently published with the title θεομαχια; or *The Grand Imprudence of men running the hazard of Fighting Against God, In suppressing any Way, Doctrine, or Practice,*

*concerning which they know not certainly whether it be from God or
no* (1644, dated by Thomason, October 7). Judging from the fre-
quency and violence with which this work was assailed, from the number and nature of Goodwin's succeeding writings, from the number
of his adherents and the role they played in later developments, *Theomachia* was one of the most important publications of the entire period.

The argument was, of course, grounded upon scripture, but the
preacher was a man steeped also in humanistic learning, one who
wielded the scriptures in the spirit of Acontius and in the tradition of
Colet and Erasmus. He had previously argued that Christ's gift to
man in the atonement was not perfect righteousness or perfect knowledge but the power to progress toward both through faith and the
exercise of reason.[7] He did not deny that truth was revealed in the
scriptures; he denied the authority of any man to say certainly what
that truth was. But humanism did not, in his case, lead to unmitigated
rationalism or unchecked skepticism. Having, like John Hales, said
good-bye to Calvin, he turned as others at Cambridge were to do to
Neo-Platonism. If he had not relinquished his fellowship at Queens
in 1627, possibly he and not Whichcote, who had just enrolled at
Emmanuel,[8] would have been remembered as the earliest of the Cambridge Platonists. His position, set forth with all the prolixity of his
kind and age, is clear. 'There is no sight so lovely, and taking to the
eyes of all ingenious and sincere hearts, as naked truth.' So much we
know through faith. But truth exists to be discovered by reason, planted
in us by the creator for that purpose. It is 'a jewell which lyes out of
sight, as it were, in the bowels of many reasons, men must search for
it, that wil find it out.' [9] It cannot be discovered at a single leap, once
and for all, or by one or a few for the rest of mankind, but must be
sought by every believer for himself, through ceaseless inquiry, continuing 'as long as meats or drinks, silver or gold, houses or lands,
friends, or other Relations, Magistrates, or Ministers, Bibles, or other
good books, yea as long as habits of Grace and Holinesse, yea as long
as Jesus Christ himself as Mediator, shall be anything at all unto the
Saints.' God, who is Alpha and Omega, could, if he had wished, have
made himself all the intervening letters of the alphabet as well. But
it is his method and the method of nature to proceed from the less
perfect to the more perfect. Goodwin is, as always, pat with his quota-

tions from holy writ. 'The first man is of the earth, earthy: the second man is the Lord from Heaven. . . . For we know in part, and prophecy in part. But when that which is perfect is come, then that which is in part, shall be done away.' [10] But exactly when imperfection and change will be no more and God all in all, when nothing will any longer intervene or mediate between reason and truth, no man can tell.

It was of the essence of Puritanism that faith should be expressed instantly in action, ideas in laws and institutions. In *Theomachia* Goodwin brought both the authority of scripture and his idealistic conception of truth to the support of his plan for reducing church government to a point where every person would be free to seek truth under whatever preacher and in whatever company seemed to be proceeding in its direction most surely. He began his sermon with Achan (Joshua 7), whose sin, preachers frequently reminded their hearers, had brought defeat upon Israel. This was, of course, but to raise the burning question of the moment, what sin, committed by whom, had brought the wrath of God upon the parliamentary army at Lostwithiel? Newcomen, in his sermon before parliament on the same text on the same day, answered for the majority of his colleagues in the assembly. Goodwin answered for the independent sects and congregations by a brilliant, in the eyes of his opponents an infuriating, application of the words of Gamaliel in the fifth chapter of Acts. Everybody, of course, knew the story. After Pentecost, the apostles preached and worked miracles in Jerusalem, and the people believed and were healed. But the priests and rulers were angry and threw the apostles in prison. They, however, escaped and preached again because, Peter said, they must obey God and not men. Whereupon Gamaliel a Pharisee spoke, 'Refraine your selves from these men, and let them alone: for if this counsell or worke be of men, it will come to nought; but if it be of God, yee cannot destroy it, lest yee be found even fighters against God.' [11] What Goodwin made of this famous passage hardly needs to be explained, or how he called up other texts, equally potent and familiar, to support his interpretation. It all came to this, that the Lord was not in the wind or the earthquake or the fire but in the still, soft voice. That is to say the Lord was in 'every Way, Doctrine, and Ordinance of his' by which 'he communicates and imparts himself graciously unto the world.' Therefore, it was madness in men to attempt 'to suppress such wayes or courses as they are not able to demonstrate, but that they are Wayes of God indeed.' If they are not his, he will scatter and destroy them in his own time, but if there is anything of him in them, then to oppose them is to fight against God himself.[12]

The Lord may have been in the still, soft voice, but for Goodwin the voice was generally to be heard, preaching, expounding, debating, in the 'gathered' group of like-minded souls, whether within the church or in a conventicle outside. He filled many pages with learned, subtle, intricate dialectic in support of an essentially latitudinarian doctrine. Nevertheless, the religious congregation remained for him the appointed means for approaching that completeness and certainty of knowledge which were the end-all of spiritual endeavor. The issue raised by Goodwin and by the increasing cloud of his disciples and emulators concerned, however, something much more than the liberty of congregations to partake in their own way of the Word of God. It concerned the place and function of the church in the community, its relation to spiritual and intellectual life in general, above all to public opinion made articulate and pervasive by new instruments and conditions. The issue involved the whole question of the relation of liberty to law, of the individual to the community.

Yet the discussion is not to be understood as a simple or clear-cut conflict between oncoming democratic freedom and outmoded tyranny. Every party to the dispute may be said to have had liberty in some sense as its professed aim and to have made some contribution to the complex of ideas and practices which came finally to be lumped under that name. The difficulty was to agree on the nature and extent of the liberty to be sought and the means of incorporating it in a common order. That the hydra-headed press and the clashing machinery of party politics would soon come to be accepted as the indispensable apparatus for the exercise of liberty in society occurred as yet to few. To the Presbyterians, above all to the Scots, the prime organ of liberty was the church, and the object was to free the church to do its work in the nation. Hence they sought to persuade the civil power that both its duty and its interest lay in supporting the church as they conceived it, and their conception prepared them to resist and overthrow the civil power if it refused. But this was to acknowledge that in the civil power lay the ultimate source of danger to the church, and hence the real offense of the Independents was to weaken the church in the face of parliament.

The implications of that offense and the gravity of the danger it entailed were illustrated, somewhat paradoxically, by the attitude taken at this juncture toward both parties by William Prynne. After his release from prison, he resumed his former war upon prelacy and took personal charge of the prosecution of his old enemy Laud. Then, following Parker's lead, he poured forth hundreds of pages of uncritical erudition against royal supremacy in his *Soveraigne Power of Parliaments and Kingdomes* (1643). Now he unleashed his pedantic fury against Independency. He was a fanatic, emancipated by his past sufferings from any suspicion of fallibility, licensed in his own esteem to speak at inordinate length without contradiction, but he was a fanatic on behalf of parliament. His position was simply that, since unity of the church was essential for the people's salvation and since presbyterianism was laid down in scripture as the means to that end, the enactment and enforcement of presbyterianism was the business of parliament, which was the embodiment of the people in the state. This was to offer less comfort to Presbyterian ministers than they wished, but it was to offer still less to the Independents. For Prynne saw clearly that if the latter were allowed to have their way, all possibility of control of religion by parliament or any other authority would be gone. If every minister were to be allowed 'to congregate what Church hee pleaseth,' why, he asked, should not 'particular persons' have the same liberty to form whatever governments they pleased. Papists, Arminians, Anabaptists and Arians, heretics, sectaries, and enthusiasts, would 'erect new Independent Churches of their own . . . uncontroulable, unsuppressible by any Ecclesiasticall or Civill authority.' 'We shall have,' he concluded, 'almost as many severall heresies, sects, Churches, as there are families, persons.' Moreover, the same men will next demand the same liberty to elect 'what civill forme of government they please . . . and to cast off all . . . civill Governours, Governments, Lawes at pleasure.' [13] He had recently taken note of one who demanded nothing less than 'divorce at pleasure.' [14] What he meant by all this was, of course, that the establishment of religious uniformity, if it was to be attained at all, would have to be the work of the civil power. What the activities of Independents such as Burton and John

Goodwin made clear was that the church had reached such a pass that, left to itself, it produced nothing but difference and disunion. That agreement might not be possible of attainment even by action of the civil power, that in the interest of civil peace the state might have to ignore religious differences or even religion itself, these were alternative conclusions Prynne could not admit.

ii. CHURCH AND STATE IN NEW ENGLAND:
JOHN COTTON AND ROGER WILLIAMS

They were, however, ideas which had been injected into the discussion by Roger Williams as an incident to his own controversy with John Cotton and the authorities, ministerial and civil, of Massachusetts Bay. The story of that controversy has passed into the legend of American liberty, but the debate between Williams and Cotton also became part of the general debate instituted by Thomas Goodwin and his associates in the London press in 1644. In New England the consequences of Independency which Prynne apprehended with such alarm had developed with a clarity and intensity due to the unforeseen simplifications of a Utopian experiment under frontier conditions. John Cotton, sometime fellow of Emmanuel and a friend of Thomas Goodwin, had betaken himself in 1633, when conscience forbade him to yield to his bishop, from Lincolnshire to Massachusetts. An important group of converts accompanied him or followed soon after. There was, however, a difference between leading a flock of gathered saints across the ocean and leading it to a Dutch city, still more to another meeting place in the same London street. New England, far from being the forbidding land pious legend has made of it, was a natural environment to which its first settlers quickly and prosperously adapted themselves, and they proceeded in an incredibly brief time to launch a civilization. When Cotton arrived, he found a society in which the saints were masters. Accepting a call to preach to the Boston congregation, he became at once something like the primate of the pulpit brotherhood and keeper of the conscience of the civil magistrate. In England he and his fellows had been the leaders of minorities, each in some degree at odds with both civil and ecclesiastical authority. Here, they were rulers of the church and at one with the state. Hence they fell into the age-old temptation of clerics to use their peculiar kind of power for the support of the *status quo* and the advantage of their own order. The brotherhood of preachers hardened into a tight theocracy and the congregations of the godly congealed into an ecclesiastical system differing more in details of organization than in spirit or effect from the rigidest presbyterianism.

But this transformation by no means stifled the dynamics of Puritanism. The vitality of the movement was in the preaching of the Word, and John Cotton the high priest was confounded by John Cotton the evangelist. Too often and too convincingly had the latter set forth the great doctrine of regeneration—the doctrine, that is, that although every child is justly doomed to die for the sin of the old Adam, any sinner whatsoever, man or woman, may nevertheless at any time be called by the grace of God to be redeemed, to receive the new Adam, to be reborn in Christ. There were, of course, trials to be endured, means to be used, covenants and halfway covenants to be employed, qualifications and compromises to be argued about and refined upon, but when all was said that could be said in the pulpit, the regeneration of the individual sinner was the essential human meaning of every preacher's words. The essence of hope was in searching the breast by the light of truth revealed there and in the scriptures. The essence of salvation was in believing that one could be saved. The essence of the church was the communion of the elect.

Along with these doctrines, there came to New England the characteristic heterodoxies which everywhere dogged them. The preachers might make clear that the multitude of sinners were lost souls and the elect but few. The pulpit depended, indeed, on persuading a multitude that this was everybody's condition and that everybody should, therefore, watch and pray for those inner signs which brought assurance of grace. But the grace which the preachers taught people to look for in themselves, people naturally found, or if not, they sought ways to relieve their spirits of the terrible burden laid upon them. They readily concluded that, if all men were bad, all were at any rate equal, and one man's claim or chance to divine favor was as good as another's. From the belief that all but a few were condemned by God's wrath and that those few were excepted only by his favor they passed easily to the notion that the generality of men enjoyed God's favor from birth and that only those were damned who willfully rejected his love and the love of their fellow men. But the confusion of doctrine did not stop there. In teaching the people to read the Bible, the preachers did not intend them to read with no, still less with erroneous, instruction—to use it as a mirror wherein to see their own wild notions reflected back to them. In telling people always and at all costs to heed the voice of conscience, the preachers did not mean that men should hearken to nothing else, least of all that they should mistake their own impulses and desires for the indwelling of the Holy Spirit. In leading the godly, by the light of the scriptures and in the name of conscience, out of the jurisdiction of the bishops, the preachers for the most part did not wish the people to think that they were separating from the church and not merely from its corruptions. In setting up independent congregations, they were by no means inclined to concede the same liberty to dissenting groups that might spring up among themselves. In restricting communion to approved saints, they did not propose to allow the unenlightened to escape beyond reach of discipline and edification. In persuading the civil authorities to admit only church members to vote and hold office, they did not of course absolve the rest of the people from civil obedience.

Yet the preachers found these limitations upon the spiritual energies they had themselves evoked impossible to maintain even in the ranks of the most eminent of the godly. Mrs. Hutchinson, who scandalized them by gathering a conventicle to listen to the revelations privately vouchsafed to her by the Holy Spirit, was the spiritual child of John Cotton himself. Roger Williams, who outraged them by pushing congregationalism to the extreme of separatism, was himself one of the brotherhood and had on his arrival in Boston been offered and had declined the post of teacher to the church which Cotton later accepted. These were two notorious disturbers of the peace of Zion, but since, for very practical reasons, the unregenerate had to be admitted along with the regenerate, the godly had always the ungodly to contend with, and the colony was torn by heresy and schism from the moment of its founding. The frontier, moreover, recognized no difference between orthodox and heterodox, but offered unimagined scope and room to both. When Hugh Peters was asked what they did with heretics in New England, he replied in effect that the problem was there very simple—they put them over the river.[15] When John Cotton under-took to refute the charge that he had procured Roger Williams' banishment, he contended that banishment was hardly punishment in a country 'where the Jurisdiction (whence a man is banished) is but small, and the Countrey round about it, large, and fruitfull.' It was not, he said, 'so much a confinement, as an enlargement, where a man doth not so much loose civill comforts, as change them.' [16] Williams, when driven to the woods in January, 1636, probably did not wholly appreciate the truth of this remark, but there was a significant measure of truth in it. When orthodoxy in Massachusetts pressed harder upon men than they were willing to bear, there were other places to go to—Rhode Island, Connecticut, New Hampshire, and points west. There, with variations, they could start the same process over again, generate new churches, new orthodoxies, new schisms, new exoduses to newer and newer promised lands. Thus in America the dreaded disruption of the ecclesiastical state facilitated the rapid planting of one new community after another. A continent offered itself for the diaspora of the church to deploy upon.

Under such conditions the unacknowledged or disallowed implications of all those doctrines of predestination and election, of fall and redemption, of conscience and the communion of saints, which the Puritan brotherhood had exploited to such effect in the pulpit, developed unchecked to conclusions that in another generation were to seem axiomatic. But with these conclusions in 1644—the logical enough result of the impact of American experience upon a sanguine, imaginative, adventurous mind, indoctrinated with Puritan ideas—Roger Williams startled and shocked the brethren in London. Upon his arrival at Narragansett Bay, his problem had been to make certain of his personal safety. He must, first of all, have a suitable understanding with the Indians, and for that he was singularly well prepared. From one point of view they were at best Canaanites or at worst imps of the evil one with no rights which the chosen people were bound to respect. At least they were not entitled under natural law to more land than they could occupy and make use of.[17] Williams, however, took the point of view that, 'God having of one blood made all mankind,' there is 'no difference between *Europe* and *Americans* in blood, birth, bodies, &c.' and therefore all are naturally the children of wrath. But by the same reasoning the Indians had as good a title to God's favor as other men in their condition.

> Boast not proud *English*, of thy birth & blood,
>   Thy brother *Indian* is by birth as Good.
> Of one blood God made Him, and Thee & All,
>   As wise, as faire, as strong, as personall.

> By nature wrath's his portion, thine no more
>   Till Grace *his* soule and *thine* in Christ restore
> Make sure thy second birth, else thou shalt see,
>   Heaven ope to *Indians* wild, but shut to thee.[18]

Unimpeachable doctrine, perhaps, but when it led Williams to argue that the King of England had no right to grant the Massachusetts Bay Company a patent to the Indians' lands, he was going too far to please those whose charter and whose land titles were thereby called in question. The same principles, however, prompted Williams to make friends with the Indians, to study their ways and learn their language, in the hope of winning them to the true faith. On his voyage back to England in 1643, he occupied himself with composing *A Key into the Language of America*,[19] which he put into print soon after his arrival, one of the most unusual documents in the literature of the doctrine of grace and one of the earliest in the literature of the noble savage.

Williams was, however, not alone in seeking refuge in the Narragansett country. The region was a bateable land, lying between Massachusetts Bay and Plymouth on one side and the Connecticut settlements on the other, to which many unruly spirits came fleeing from orthodoxy and from law and order as understood in Massachusetts. The gathering together, under such conditions, of such 'a Colluvies of wild Opinionists' [20] resulted in a society whose dissensions gave some color to the accusation that only anarchy could result from the disruption of church discipline. But the greatest danger that the quarreling groups in Rhode Island had to fear came not from one another, and certainly not from papist or Jew or Turk, but from the congregationalists of Massachusetts. The remedy was obvious. The safety of every group lay in union against the common enemy, but the only possible union that all could hope for had to be purely civil. Where there were so many different opinions, no opinion could be recognized or utilized as the basis of union except at the expense of all the others and the certain risk of disrupting the civil union itself. Thus sheer necessity, if nothing else, forced religious liberty upon the Rhode Islanders as a policy of state, and what may be called their first act of state was to dispatch Williams to England for the purpose of procuring a charter from parliament which should confirm their union and validate their claim to immunity from further interference from Massachusetts. He arrived shortly before the swearing of the Covenant at the end of September, and he presently addressed both parties in the Westminster Assembly in *Queries of Highest Consideration.*[21] The real point of this little pamphlet was stated in the dedicatory epistle to parliament. Williams' experience convinced him that any attempt by the civil power to reform the church was bound to result in endless confusion. 'Right Honourable, your *Wisdomes* Know the *Fatall Miscarriages* of *Englands Parliaments* in this point; what *setting* up, *pulling* downe, what *Formings, Reformings,* and againe *Deformings,* to *admiration.*'

But he would have been untrue to his cloth if he had not been able to put up an argument in terms of religious doctrine as well as of political expediency in defense of the policy which served Rhode Island so well. His affair, moreover, was not directly with Presbyterians and Independents but with Massachusetts, whose emissary he found in London petitioning for an extension of that colony's patent to include the Narragansett country. His main argument, therefore, was directed in print against his old friend and adversary, John Cotton. Cotton was obviously the kind of man who feels compelled to square his interests with his conscience but who must also square his conscience with his principles by the aid of his dialectic. He wrote to Williams after the latter's trial and banishment, setting forth the usual objections, with scriptural proofs, to the separatist principles Williams had championed, namely that no power on earth can determine what a man believes except the man himself and that no man can join in church fellowship except with others whom he knows to be true believers like himself.[22] Thus began an interchange of replies and counterreplies which led to the publication in July, 1644, of Williams' *The Bloudy Tenent, of Persecution, for cause of Conscience, discussed, in A Conference betweene Truth and Peace.* Cotton replied in 1647 with *The Bloudy Tenent, Washed, And made white in the bloud of the Lambe.*

In 1651, when Williams had to come to England a second time to defend Rhode Island against Massachusetts, he reopened the debate in *The Bloudy Tenent Yet More Bloody* (1652).

The passage of time, in justifying so completely one party to this dispute, has made it seem as though both might have said all they had to say without filling so many hundreds of pages with the dialectics peculiar to their time. Given his own premises, Cotton found himself in the predicament of the unwary liberal called upon to say just where the limit should be put on the practical application of liberal principles. He could not, of course, deny conscience—that is, the right to profess and to practice what one believes—without repudiating his own past or his own faith. So he had to qualify the liberty to be allowed. It was not lawful, he said, to persecute any who differed for conscience' sake, providing conscience was rightly informed. It was not lawful to persecute any who differed for conscience' sake even upon important points, until admonition had been given once or twice. It was not lawful to persecute for minor errors, if they were put forward in a spirit of meekness and love. But if an erring person persisted in the face of correction, he must be counted as acting contrary to conscience, and if he persisted in a tumultuous manner, that is, by attempting to mislead others contrary to command, he must be counted a danger to civil peace and treated accordingly by the civil magistrate. The arbiter of truth and error was, of course, still the church, which was to say in effect the ministers.

To Roger Williams, this was to deny the logic of the whole movement for reform. 'In vaine,' he says in his address to the reader in *The Bloudy Tenent*, 'have *English Parliaments* permitted *English Bibles* in the poorest *English* houses, and the simplest man or woman to search the Scriptures, if yet against their soules perswasion from the Scripture, they should be forced (as if they lived in *Spaine* or *Rome* it selfe without the sight of a *Bible*) to beleeve as the Church beleeves.' In a sense the writer of these words was the least peaceable of men. At any rate, he was not one to abide quietly any challenge to his own conception of truth, let alone any admonition to keep silent about it. Truth existed and was revealed in scripture, and nothing was so important as to find it and declare it, except to act upon it, regardless of consequences. But this responsibility was one which every person must bear for himself and which none could assume for another. The true church was not here and now, in this church or that, in England or New England, a thing to be possessed and obeyed; it remained like truth itself an end not yet attained but always to be waited and sought for. But if no particular church, so-called, was qualified to determine what the simplest man or woman must believe, 'against their soules perswasion from the Scripture,' then how could civil magistrates tell what church or what religion they must enforce for their people's good? Rulers, like other men, 'must judge and punish as they are perswaded in their owne *beleefe* and *conscience,* (be their *conscience Paganish, Turkish,* or *Antichristian*).' [23] If every ruler were to punish all of his subjects whose consciences were persuaded otherwise than his own, the effect would be to suppress Christianity and '*civility,*' and bring all things to confusion.

Thus Williams perceived as clearly as Prynne that Independent principles, carried to their logical conclusion, left the ministers no means of controlling the effect of the Bible, or indeed of the pulpit itself, on the popular mind, no means of restoring unity to the church, except the forcible intervention of the state. But his New England experience, illuminated by a more imaginative grasp of history and a sharper prescience, told him that not only was it impossible for the state to do this but that the attempt must produce, though in the name of Christ and the church, nothing but endless strife and confusion. 'Who knowes not in how few yeares the Common weale of *England* hath set up and pull'd down? The Fathers made the Children Hereticks, and the Children the Fathers.' [24] What the enemies of truth do against its lovers, they 'vermillion' over as justice against heretics. 'Yea, if they kindle coales, and blow the flames of *devouring Warres,* that leave neither *Spirituall* nor *Civill State,* but burns up *Branch* and *Root,* yet how doe all pretend an *holy War?* He that *kills,* and hee that's *killed,* they both cry out, It is for *God,* and for their *conscience.*' [25]

Williams drove his point home by prefacing *The Bloudy Tenent* with a succinct summary of his contentions, so clear, so unequivocal, so outspoken, that his opponents hardly needed to read the book in order to condemn it. The crucial and most startling point was that every civil state was declared to be essentially and exclusively civil and that 'it is the will and command of *God,* that . . . a *permission* of the most *Paganish, Jewish, Turkish* or *Antichristian consciences* and *worships,* bee granted to *all* men,' in the expectation of their conversion by spirit-ual means. Enforced uniformity and the denial of such freedom were said to confound both civil and religious peace.

Thus the principles plainly implied in Milton's tracts and John Goodwin's sermons and gingerly advanced by Thomas Goodwin in the Westminster Assembly and by John Cotton in New England were explicitly carried to their logical practical conclusion.[26] At the moment when *The Bloudy Tenent* was being published, Williams was safely on his way back to Rhode Island with a charter in his pocket from parliament, permitting him to continue his attempt to found a state which denied on principle all responsibility for the faith and salvation of its citizens. He was to have his will in one corner of New England while his opponents were to have theirs in another, but the matter did not stop there. Every English community in the new world carried the seeds of dissent in its bosom, and the frontier had no special favors to offer to any. Williams' part in the debates of 1644 was to express common Puritan principles with the special force and meaning which accrued to them under the strange conditions they encountered across the Atlantic.

iii. TOLERATION AND TRADE'S INCREASE: HENRY ROBINSON

But the horizon of English experience was widening in more than one direction, and Puritanism could be made to fit mercantile as well as colonial enterprise. Prynne and the advocates of presbyterian reform were almost as much scandalized by Henry Robinson as by Roger Williams and for much the same reason. The author of *Liberty of Conscience*[27] was a prosperous merchant, descended from a line of merchants, engaged in foreign trade. He had lived abroad, in Con-stantinople, Italy, and the Low Countries, and in 1641 published two pamphlets which revealed his main interest and objective, *Englands Safetie in Trades Encrease* (August) and *Libertas, or Reliefe to the English Captives in Algier* (October). He continued in the same vein in 1650 in *Briefe Considerations Concerning the Advancement of Trade and Navigation*. These writings show that the dream of mer-cantile empire rather than of the New Jerusalem had first claim upon Robinson's imagination. For him, England's future lay in invention, manufacture, export trade, and foreign exchange, in fisheries, shipping, and the navy, in travel, communication, and the suppression of piracy. He entered the dispute over the church because the promotion of these interests could not go forward until Presbyterians and Independents had settled or put aside their differences. In 1644 he published *Liberty of Conscience: or the Sole means to obtaine Peace and Truth* (March 24) and *John the Baptist, Forerunner of Christ Jesus: or, A necessity for Liberty of Conscience* (September 23). He also issued rejoinders to Prynne and Steuart and took exception to John Dury's well-meant attempt to make peace between the two parties in the assembly, as among Protestants everywhere, by obscuring the issues that divided them.[28]

Robinson's temper and experience led him to assume, so far as possible, a neutral, that is, a latitudinarian stand in religion, and for the same reason to side with the Independents against the Presbyterians in the disputes of 1644. But, as in Williams' case, he fixed upon those features of independency which pointed most clearly in the direction of his own interests. Though identified with no sect, he quickly reached a position indistinguishable from that of extreme separatism. He accepted the doctrines of scriptural infallibility, authoritative conscience, and individual responsibility for the cultivation of God's gifts. Every man, he held, possessed some gift—one talent or ten did not matter—for discovering truth in scripture. God left the scriptures in the unclear condition in which we have them in order that we should exercise our ability to understand their meaning. Knowledge abounds according as we apply ourselves to the search for it. In spiritual as in civil affairs, every man understands his own business best and every man's business thrives best when he looks after it himself.[29] To be sure, men generally believe what they are bred to believe, but what they are bred to believe, whether Lutherans, papists, Jews or Turks, they believe to be true and cannot be compelled to believe otherwise. Compulsion induces hypocrisy, as when papists at church in England stop their ears or Englishmen at mass in Italy send their eyes gadding after beauty. 'Men doe not imbrace errours otherwise than as they account them truths,'[30] and they will defend one as pertinaciously as the other. Moreover, though conscience be the excuse, the motive of war and persecution is usually covetousness. 'Few have been yet so mad to put people to death meerly for Religion sake.' [31] So, the true cause of the struggle between king and parliament is the contention of the clergy not for the salvation of the people but for possession of the tithes and livings of the church. 'He that putteth not into their mouthes, they even prepare War against him.' But why must people pay for 'the chaffer of these Clergie-merchants?' Would not their encroachments, in any other trade, be damned for a monopoly—'the greatest infringing of the Subjects propriety?' [32] Robinson grants that ministers must be maintained, but the laborer should be worthy of his hire, and men should be free to buy truth where it suits them best. Thus the lesson of the current unhappy situation seemed clear. 'The powers of the Civill State and Church may not be confounded.' The magistrate must not interpose in matters that affect only the church's peace, nor the church in things that touch only the civil peace. If either 'shall take upon them to usurpe the weapons, or intermeddle in matters which concerne the other; it will not only disturbe the peace of both, but bring them infallibly by degrees to take up armes upon pretence of defending their respective bounds and jurisdiction.' [33] The end of such strife can only be the destruction of both church and state.

But Robinson's experience and his practical conclusions paralleled those of Williams in still another respect. Prynne, the majority of assembly divines, and the Scots made much of the magistrates' duty to repress heresy in order to appease God's wrath, protect the faithful from contamination, and avoid responsibility for the sins of other men. Robinson demolished this notion with unconcealed delight by *reductio ad absurdum*. Obviously, he pointed out, according to such reasoning, whenever the ministers and the magistrate failed to agree, the magistrate must suppress either himself or the ministers. If his duty was to protect his subjects from the contamination of false doctrine, where should his efforts stop? When he had put down all papists, anabaptists, Brownists, and the like at home, there would still remain many more such abroad. Must he make war on all the world in order to convert or compel unbelievers and misbelievers everywhere to the true faith? If not, he must at all costs keep them out of England, for if he admitted them, he would have to grant them, at his own and his people's peril, a freedom to err which he denied to his own people for their own protection. He would, on the same grounds, have to keep his own people at home. But if this were done, if all communication with heretics and infidels were forbidden, how could the faithful in England heed the divine command to go forth and preach the gospel to all the world? And how could they engage in foreign trade or build an empire?

iv. REASON AND LOVE: WILLIAM WALWYN

But the effects of the gospel as the Puritan brotherhood had been preaching it for three generations were many and incalculable. Of all the opinions condemned by Newcomen in his fast day sermon for Essex's surrender, none was more alarming than the contention put forward in *The Compassionate Samaritane* that there is no *jus divinum* in the ministry.[34] This was to challenge not the authority of the gospel but the exclusive right of the ministerial caste to preach it. The challenge was put forth by one who represented with rather startling clarity the effect which the translated scriptures and the flood of other English printed books were having upon alert and independent minds under the conditions of the time. William Walwyn, the anonymous author of *The Compassionate Samaritane,* was born in 1600, the younger son of a Warwickshire squire. Forty years later he was a silk merchant, member of the Merchant Adventurers, with a family, a house in Moor-fields, a garden, and a library, where, he said, he liked to entertain a discoursing friend. He was to become, a little later, one of the principal spokesmen and organizers of the movement for a democratic state, but his political opinions and activities sprang from his earlier religious experience and the thoughts and convictions to which it led. These came to light in the series of pamphlets in which, beginning in 1642, he brought his point of view to bear with engaging and disarming candor upon the issues arising from the preachers' efforts to secure their hold upon the church and the hold of the church upon the people. His earlier pamphlets appeared anonymously, and he obviously preferred to work quietly and trust to the methods of rational good-natured persuasion, but the effect of his tactics in the end was to make him the object of suspicion not only to the Presbyterians but to Independents and sectarians as well. In his endeavors to defend himself against his critics, he put into print eventually a singularly explicit and detailed account of the development of his own ideas and course of action.

Walwyn's thinking took its primary impulse and direction from the Puritan pulpit itself, but the development of his thinking showed how unstable a compound of ideas Puritan doctrine was proving in the circumstances to be. Puritan doctrine, whatever else it imposed or implied, required acceptance of the authority of the Word, and Walwyn's story like that of Williams showed how easily the interest and intention of the pulpit in preaching the Word could be undone by the effect of the Word upon its own believers. The preachers told the people that under the law of Moses all men were condemned for the sin of Adam but that under the gospel some were saved through the merits of Christ. The one doctrine made all men equal; the other set a limited number free. Both doctrines, however, were supposed to be plainly set forth for every man to read and confirm for himself in the scriptures. In the scriptures was made plain every step in that operation of grace in the breast which no man could initiate for himself, but for the signs of which every man was exhorted to watch and pray and by which he might surely know that he was one of the chosen ones. In the scriptures too, preachers insisted, the saints could find assurance that grace, having once been granted to them, would surely be fulfilled.

Yet its very success in winning the people to acceptance of such doctrines put the ministerial caste into an ambiguous and critical position. Its members were, they said, merely the ministers of the Word, but according to the logic of their own position, as the Word did its work, there remained less and less for them to do. How soon, in the case of any given sinner, let alone mankind in general, the work of the Word might be presumed to be complete and the ministry of the pulpit no longer needed, was a question difficult to decide, easy to be mistaken about, and certain to breed dissension. But the fact was that, as men grew more assured of grace under the gospel, they grew less fearful of condemnation under the law; as they grew more alive to the righteousness imputed to them through Christ, they grew less concerned for the guilt imputed to them through Adam; and so, becoming more confident of salvation and more practiced in the dialectic of faith, they grew less dependent upon the preaching order, more critical of preachers. And from that point, they fell readily into the notion that, instead of all men being damned for the sin of Adam and only those few saved whom God chose to save for no cause in them, all men were put in the way of salvation through Christ's atonement and only those were lost who themselves rejected grace and contrived their own ruin. If men were equal in their liability under the law, why not in their title to grace? If any were to be liberated by faith in Christ, why not everyone? Why should any man be supposed to stand condemned for any fault or by any decision save his own?

Such questioning was, moreover, additionally prompted in the circumstances by influences from outside the pulpit for which the pulpit had nevertheless prepared the way. The preachers had done more than any other group to promote the production of books. They held, to be sure, that though they themselves in the exercise of their special calling needed to know languages and the arts, the people, even those of meanest capacity, needed nothing more for saving knowledge than to read the scriptures. So the people read the scriptures, and the book trade, fostered by popular demand for the Bible and for books of explication and edification arising from the Bible, went on also to put all sorts of literature into English print. The result was the increasing intrusion into public life of men untrained in the schools, literate only or mainly in the vernacular, but far from unread, uninformed, uncritical, or inarticulate. Since, moreover, they had heard many sermons from many pulpits, they were not unprepared to take the measure of any preacher. Laud in 1638 had had such a one to deal with in John Lilburne. Now in 1644, with Lilburne away in the army, working for Cromwell against Manchester, the assembly divines were confronted by another man of similar background though of different temper in William Walwyn.

Walwyn had at one stage suffered from that perturbation of mind which the preachers commonly sought to induce as the necessary condition for the experience of spiritual rebirth which was expected to come, if it came at all, with the assurance of grace, bringing hope of liberation from sin and guilt. He was, he tells us, 'very serious and sincere in my application of things to my own conscience,' with the result that he found 'much disconsolation therein, great uncertainty, and at last extream affliction of mind, the Law and Gospel fighting for victory in me.' [35] Was he an elect soul set free by Christ or must he expect like most of the children of Adam to languish indefinitely under the condemnation of the law? If his spiritual experience had followed its expected course, his anxiety on this point should have continued, daily renewed and never fully allayed short of a deathbed triumph over the evil one, to be memorialized finally in a funeral sermon with an appended edifying account of his life-long spiritual struggle. Walwyn was not, however, by natural inclination a twice-born soul or a Puritan saint but a man of common sense and good will with an inquiring mind and an independent but equable temper. So, while continuing to observe with interest the many varieties of religious opinion and behavior displayed about him, he stopped agonizing over his own soul and looked about him to see what he might do to ameliorate the general conditions of life in his time. 'I abandon all nicities and uselesse things,' he said in 1646; 'my manner is in all disputes [,] reasonings and discourses, to enquire what is the use: and if I find it not very materiall, I abandon it.' [36] And in 1649 he claimed that he had long since found 'more ease and freedom, then others, who were entangled with those yokes of bondage, unto which Sermons and Doctrines mixt of Law and Gospel, do subject distressed consciences.' The formula by which he rationalized his escape from such distress was, he tells us, 'that part of doctrine (called then, Antinomian) of free justification by Christ alone.' [37] That is to say, he learned, as others were to do, that by a simple logical inversion, transposing positives to negatives and negatives to positives, one might easily turn the grim doctrine of predestination about so as to still the fears, nourish the hopes, and give free play to the energies which the doctrine itself, as preached from a hundred pulpits, had evoked.

The first begetters of Walwyn's emancipation from Puritan orthodoxy may be said to have been the preachers themselves who by their very success invited his critical scrutiny. Their endeavor, overriding all restraints and all other purposes, was to win converts, and hence every preacher tended to gather about him, regardless of parish boundaries, his own particular flock of adherents. But the unavoidable complement to this tendency was that unconvinced and anxious or merely restless and curious souls roamed from church to church in order to listen hopefully to this preacher and that, making perhaps unwelcome criticisms and invidious comparisons. By April, 1644, Richard Vines was complaining in a sermon to the lord mayor and aldermen of a kind of person he calls a nomad or walker, 'who will not endure to sit at the feet of a constant godly ministry' but who 'wanders away the Sabbath by peeping in at Church-dores, and taking essay of a sentence or two, and then if there be no *scratch* for his *itch, lambit & fugit,* he is gone.' [38] No observant and reflecting person who listened to many sermons by different preachers could, of course, fail soon to discover that the pulpits in general were by no means in complete agreement and that not all they gave forth could reasonably be taken for gospel. The dissension which presently arose in the Westminster Assembly reflected a confusion already present and rapidly increasing among its members. The preachers were further betrayed by the defensive self-righteousness they assumed under criticism. They had learned too well how to fit infallible texts to the dogmas they preached and dogmas to the support of their own interests. They were too confident of being able to show that any opinion which differed from their own differed also from the Word of God. They were too prone to attribute to moral obliquity and calculated malice any questioning of their authority or doubt of the entire purity of their motives. Hence they incurred the peculiar odium which besets successful churchmen who, under color of defending nothing but the true faith, seem to contend for nothing so much as their own privileges and perquisites.

Walwyn, clearly, was one of the 'nomads' or 'walkers' of whom Vines complained. The Presbyterian Thomas Edwards in 1646 called him a 'Seeker,' 'a strong head,' given to asking questions designed to unsettle men's faith in their ministers.[39] The sectarian preachers in 1649 described how on the Lord's day he would lead his followers from one church to another, staying in each only long enough to hear something said from the pulpit 'which he may through his art . . . render ridiculous and weak.' [40] Walwyn's art was—'with a soft foot, and with much slight of hand'—to puzzle his victims with such subtle guileful queries as 'How can you prove the Scriptures to be the Word of God?' or to call in question the reasoning and the motives of ministers. He would take young men to his home in order to work on them in the pleasant conversational intimacy of his garden or library. The story was told that on one such occasion he drew Lucian from the shelf with the remark, 'Here is more wit in this . . . then in all the Bible.' [41] A friend of Walwyn's, writing in his defense, denied not that such an episode occurred but only that any such comparison was made, pointing out besides that it was not for wit that the Bible was to be preferred.[42] Walwyn himself, while avoiding publicity, made no concealment of his opinions and practices. He took an active part, when the Long Parliament convened, in reforming the church of the parish in which he lived. He maintained communion with the church through all the changes of the time and, although he joined no sect or separate congregation, he had, as he freely admitted, made it his business 'to know and understand all the severall doctrines and ways of worship that are extant, and for that end have taken liberty to hear and to observe all.' [43]

He had, that is, even before the Long Parliament, made it his affair to learn not only what duly licensed and presumably orthodox ministers had to say in established pulpits but also to seek out the disallowed sectarian groups which had managed somehow to survive through all phases of repression. He endeavored to learn their beliefs and practices but also the reasons why they were condemned and persecuted. Which sects in particular he frequented or which of their leaders especially affected him is impossible to say. Various congregations of separatists still held together at home in England as well as in exile in Holland or America. A considerable group of Baptists, followers of John Smyth, led by Thomas Helwyss and John Murton, had returned from the continent to the neighborhood of London about 1612. The Family of Love, according to report, still persisted, and teachings similar to theirs were to be heard from such men as John Everard and John Eaton. Most of these groups and their leaders, though as apt as their orthodox rivals to differ from one another, shared certain common characteristics. Each drew in some degree upon long-accustomed modes of Christian mysticism. They were much influenced by the *Theologia Germanica* and by continental mystics like Sebastian Franck and Nicholas of Cusa. They tended to place greater reliance upon direct inspiration than upon learning or even the scriptures. They were more likely to assert that Christ brought redemption to the generality of mankind than simply to a small body of the elect. But they were also inclined to limit church communion to confessed and admitted believers, and to institute such communion at once without waiting for the magistrate. Yet no account of the opinions and activities of the sects would be accurate or sufficient which failed to take note that the errors —antinomian, anabaptist, or what not—for which they were most commonly condemned were precisely those notions which seemed to spring most directly from orthodox doctrine, when zealously and elaborately set forth. John Preston, for example, Master of Emmanuel, would have denied the doctrine of free justification, and yet no one preached the immanence of Christ in the breasts of believers more convincingly than he except perhaps his friend John Cotton, whose disciple Anne Hutchinson, from sitting too long at his feet, became overpersuaded of the Christ within and concluded unhappily for her that she was therefore free to reveal him directly to any who cared to come to her. She was a mystic of sorts, an enthusiast, and no doubt a troublesome woman, but her state of mind was a portent of the disruption which was springing up everywhere in the wake of Puritan preaching. Walwyn, no mystic or enthusiast but what may best be described as a vernacular humanist, gave even more important premonition of what was to come. Having listened to many sermons, orthodox and heterodox, he too had finally arrived at 'that *unum necessarium,* that pearle in the field, free justification by Christ alone!' and had consequently found himself, he said, 'master of what I heard, or read, in divinity' and 'working by love . . . master of my affections, and of what ever I read in humane authors.' [44]

But if, as he said, the doctrine of free justification taught him how to think for himself about what he heard and read, it was also true that what he read greatly strengthened his confidence in the doctrine and in himself. When put upon his defense by ministerial critics, he appealed first, as we should expect, to scripture, but, as his critics perceived with more heat than penetration, he read the scriptures like a man who had read something besides. The account of his reading, which his critics drove him into giving, is a particularly illuminating page in the history of the Puritan Revolution. Roger Williams brought to bear on the issues of 1644 the lessons he had learned from applying Puritan faith to the problems of a new society on the American frontier. Henry Robinson had done the same with the implications of advancing foreign trade. Walwyn, who never put foot out of England and knew no language but English, showed what might be the effect of ideas now opening up to common men in the books, foreign and ancient as well as English, profane as well as godly, which had by this time been put into English print. He admitted that he could not construe three lines of Latin or do more than quote a few common proverbs in that tongue. Nevertheless he had, he says, been reading humane and divine authors in his native language for some twenty years. The authors he names give indication of the general course of his thinking. 'Some of Mr. Perkins works, Mr. Downhams divinity' and 'those peeces annexed to Mr. Hookers *Ecclesiasticall pollicy*,' [45] these, he says, he had 'as it were, without book.' Which of William Perkins' writings—of which Fuller observes 'it is a miracle almost to conceive how thick they lye' [46]—Walwyn particularly read, it would be difficult to say. Perkins was the great popularizer of Puritan divinity. His *Armilla Aurea* of 1590, translated with the title *A Golden Chaine: or, The Description of Theologie, Containing the order of the causes of Salvation and Damnation, according to Gods word* was an exposition of Christian doctrine for the general public, covering the whole sequence of creation, innocence, fall, redemption, and judgment. Reprinted many times, it provided the substance for innumerable sermons and the model for many similar works, of which *The Summe of Sacred Divinitie . . . Published by John Downhame* (1630?), to which Walwyn refers, was an example. [47]

What readers such as Walwyn got from such books can easily be understood, though it was not what the authors intended. Perkins demonstrated that the salvation of the elect and the damnation of the reprobate had no cause but God's own will and pleasure and that the destiny of each was fixed and clear. But the dire fate in store for the multitude of the damned was held forth in order that everyone should realize the happy destiny of those whom God had chosen to save, always with the understanding that he might choose anyone whomsoever. That men should fear to be damned was necessary in order that they should desire to be saved, and that they should desire to be saved, though their desire was only a possible sign and not a determining cause of grace, was of course necessary if they were properly to understand each link in the golden chain that led the saints back to God. Walwyn was one of those who learned this lesson perhaps too well. In him as in others the lively apprehension of the process by which grace might come to anyone led to the conclusion that it could in reason be denied by a loving God to no one. The inclusion, among the books Walwyn remembered along with Perkins and Downame, of 'those peeces annexed' to Hooker's *Ecclesiastical Polity* is significant. For bound up with that work was 'A Learned Discourse of Justification' [48] in which one could read that faith is not to be separated from charity and hope and that 'they are not all faithlesse, that are weake in assenting to the truth, or stiffe in maintayning things any way opposite to the truth of Christian doctrine.'

Thus the doctrine of free justification, by extending the incidence of grace to correspond more nearly with the limits of charity, enabled Walwyn to recover his equipoise. He found ease for spiritual perturbation in another quarter as well. We learn that among the writings which he 'had, as it were, without book' was 'Doctor Halls meditations, and vowes, and his heaven upon earth' and that he was in the habit of 'using Seneca, Plutarch's *Lives,* and Charon *of humane wisdom,* as things of recreation, wherein I was both pleased and profited.' We are also presently told of an author to whom he was even more addicted. 'I blush not to say,' he declares, 'I have been long accustomed to read Montaigns *Essaies.*' Quoting Montaigne through several pages, he concludes, 'I recite these passages, because I am in love with them.' [49] Seneca and Montaigne, it is clear, meant much, as much as Perkins and Downame, in Walwyn's development. Montaigne he read in Florio's translation, Seneca—the epistles—in that of Thomas Lodge. As for Hall's *Meditations and Vowes* of 1605 and *Heaven upon Earth* of 1606 and Pierre Charron's *De la Sagesse,* translated with the title *Of Wisdome* by Samson Lennard, they merely served up similar ideas with more acceptable unction. [50]

What neo-stoicism offered to one who had heard his fill of sermons by men who, it seemed to him, worried so much about the fall of man and its consequences that they lost sight of the good of which men are still capable can be briefly stated. The apparent simplicity of Seneca's teachings and the candor of his approach were important elements in an appeal which was all the greater since he too, like the preachers, was chiefly occupied in prescribing appropriate attitudes to be taken in particular cases arising under a predetermined general scheme of things. That scheme is nature; nothing contrary to nature can be called good; that which in the nature of things distinguishes man as man is reason. 'For man is a reasonable creature; his good therefore is consummate[d], if he hath fulfilled that to which he was borne.' And what does reason require of him? 'An easie matter; to live according to his nature,' of which the governing principle is still reason, which, Seneca says, 'is no other thing than a part of the divine Spirit, infused and plunged in our humane bodies.' 'What is reason?' he asks again. 'It is an imitation of Nature,' and 'What is mans chiefest good? It is to doe all things according to Natures will.' He who does thus will be unshaken in mind and exempt from fear.

There are excellent and perdurable goods prepared for every one of us . . . there is the tranquillity of the soule, and a perfect liberty disclothed of all errors . . . Not to feare men or Gods, neither to will that which is dishonest, nor desire over-much, and to have the greatest power over himselfe. It is an inestimable good for a man to become his owne.[51]

Thus Seneca and such exponents as Hall and Charron of Stoic doctrine mixed with Christian piety showed Walwyn how to contain his soul in peace while the preachers fomented anxiety and disagreement. But the writer who explicated nature and exemplified reason most engagingly was Montaigne. A Roman Catholic, to be sure, yet Walwyn in exasperation finally tells his ministerial critics that they should go to this 'honest Papist' to learn 'civility, humanity, simplicity of heart; yea, charity and Christianity.'[52] Montaigne's undogmatic temper, his gay skepticism, his intellectual curiosity, his speculative enjoyment of men and ideas, his tolerance, delighted Walwyn and moved him to emulation. In the same spirit he went about among the sects and churches or brought men home for quiet talk in his garden and library, passing or seeming to pass no judgments but asking questions that called every fixed judgment of the time in doubt and sooner or later aroused the suspicions of the godly. His sympathies were engaged by the people around him and his intelligence by the problem, his own as well as theirs, of living in the kind of world they had to live in. Nothing but love, he concluded, was the fulfillment of the law, and a loving creator infused the power of reason into every human breast.

Thus the doctrine of free justification supplied Walwyn with an acceptable basis for arguing that there was nothing to prevent men from solving all their difficulties if they would. Neo-stoicism assured him that the good of man required simply that men live according to nature and follow reason. Montaigne offered the engaging picture of noble savages in their unspoiled primal innocence actually living after that fashion. Not less important, he gave many examples of humane, rational, virtuous behavior from classical historians and other ancient writers. Walwyn was also presently reading Plutarch, Thucydides, Lucian, and probably other ancient and foreign authors in their current English translations. But Montaigne, having introduced Walwyn to the noble savage and the antique Greek and Roman, also showed him a way of approaching controverted issues and, with Seneca, a style of discourse which, in refreshing contrast to current modes of preaching and debate, seemed so disarmingly colloquial, so simple and ingenuous, and yet so effective that it presently brought upon Walwyn the accusation of Jesuitism.[53] Under such influences he mingled the idea of liberty under the gospel with romantic naturalism, tempered both with civic idealism, balanced them with a feeling of responsibility to the community, and went about like Socrates or Montaigne insinuating doubt as to the *jus divinum* of the Puritan ministry, the entire devotion of its members to the public cause, their purity of motive, and their practical good judgment.

Walwyn first presented his case in two anonymous tracts, one in November, 1642, called *Some Considerations Tending to the undeceiving those, whose judgements are misinformed,* the other in September 1643 called *The Power of Love.* In the former he pleads the cause of the abused sectaries, as Lord Brooke had done, not as being one of them but as a Christian and a good citizen, striving to promote the public good by persuading men to put aside their differences and depend upon good will and common understanding to overcome their difficulties. *The Power of Love* purports to be a Familist sermon put into print with an address to the reader by someone who has had the courage and the patience to learn 'what kinde of people these are, and what opinions they hold?' It opens, significantly, with the text (Tit. 2:11, 12): 'The grace (or love) of God that bringeth salvation unto all men hath appeared, teaching us to deny ungodlinesse and worldly lusts, and to live soberly, righteously, & godly in this present world.' It goes on to interweave Paul's words with Solomon's statement 'that God made man righteous, but he sought out many inventions' and with Montaigne's picture of the happy peaceful existence of cannibals in the state of nature. 'By all which,' the writer says, 'it plainly appeares that God ever intendeth unto man a pleasant and comfortable

life,' that 'he made him naturally a rationall creature, judging rightly
of all things, and desiring only what was necessary.' What was necessary God made ready at hand and easy to use, but now in these latter
days, men esteem nothing but their own inventions, whether in diet,
dress, buildings, or furniture. And it is in spiritual things as in natural.
There is nothing 'necessary either for the enlightening of our under-
standings, or the peace of our mindes' but what God 'hath plainely
declared and manifestly set forth in his Word.' Yet again 'we have our
inventions.' We will not content ourselves with the love God bestows
upon all his children. We will not trust the powers of understanding
he has given us. We will not trust one another. We will not have
salvation to be as easy to understand as God made it. We require learned
men, bred in universities, to multiply our fears, difficulties, obscurities,
and perplexities, to mislead us and make trouble—'nay make you even
ready to cut one anothers throates; or by this division prepare you for
your common adversaries to cut both yours and theirs too.' [54]

The attacks of the Presbyterians in 1644, following *An Apologeticall Narration*, on opponents of all sorts, provoked Walwyn to return
more cogently than before to the defense of the separatists and of the
principles of love and reason. His pamphlet, *The Compassionate Samaritane*, opens with an epistle addressed to the house of commons
complaining that the printing ordinance, which he says was intended
only to restrain the publications of the king and his agents, is being
used to stop the mouths of good men, 'who must either not write at
all, or no more than is suitable to the judgments and interests of the
Licensers.' He writes 'without boldnesse and without feare,' assured
that it is every man's duty 'to furnish You with what we conceive will
advance the Common good, or bring ease or comfort to any sort of
men that deserve well of their Countrey.' The authors of *An Apologeticall Narration* had asked for toleration only for themselves; he,
again asserting that he himself is no separatist, bluntly demands toleration for everybody. ' 'Tis common freedome every man ought to aime
at, which is every mans peculiar right so far as 'tis not prejudiciall to
the Common . . . and no man [is to] be punished or discountenanced
by Authority for his Opinion, unlesse it be dangerous to the State.' [55]

Walwyn argues his case more succinctly, more tellingly, to a conclusion more apposite to the immediate situation, than either Robinson

or Williams. The state should grant freedom of conscience, because, first of all, whatever a man's reason concludes to be true or false, agreeable or not to God's Word, he cannot choose but believe. The objection that the people are incapable of rational judgment, he dismisses as coming from 'some politike Bishop, or Dr. Ignorant University man, or knave Poet.' All knowledge is uncertain, and 'Fathers, Generall Councells, Nationall Assemblies, Synods, and Parliaments in their times have been most grossly mistaken.' But the cause of division in the community is not the toleration of errors and differences but the attempt to compel everyone to think alike. 'If you will use Club Law, . . . you arme men with prejudice against you.' The bishops repressed 'Puritane and Sectary' in order to trample upon the people and serve their own worldly interests. The Presbyterians wish to do the same for the same reason, setting up distinctions between civil and ecclesiastic and between lay and clergy, persuading people that ministers are called by God, that they alone are learned and can know and judge. Walwyn had no illusions left concerning preachers. No one expressed more vividly the resentment which the brotherhood of the pulpit, having so long exalted the Word, brought upon itself when it decided that the flood of words had gone far enough and must be stopped. Now, Walwyn declares, they so manage that only they may speak, condemning without contradiction whom and what they please. In their pulpits

they brand men with the name of Hereticks, and fasten what errours they thinke are most hatefull to the people, upon those men they purpose to make odious: There they confute all opinions, and boldly they may doe it, for as much as no liberty of reply or vindication in publike is allowed to any. . . . And that men may not vindicate themselves by writing, their next interest is to be Masters of the Presse.[56]

This brings him to his concluding point. Whatsoever is not of faith is sin, but faith rests upon reason, and as every man must believe for himself so he must think for himself. Men may differ from one another, sect from sect, ministers from ministers, synods from synods, but such differences are not in themselves evil, and schism does not concern the commonwealth unless one party stirs up hatred and oppression against another. Thus, from his experience with the multiplying differences that arose in London in the course of the Puritan movement, Walwyn came to the same practical conclusion that Williams reached from his experience on the American frontier and Robinson from his observation of men and faiths at home and abroad. The ecclesiastical state had ceased to be a workable instrument or significant symbol of social union. It had become the arena of social conflict. Hence the interest and the responsibility of the civil state lay in enforcing not agreement but peace among the warring particles into which the church had dissolved. But where should men look for means to regain the sense of solidarity they had lost? The author of *The Compassionate Samaritane* draws to a close by affirming as positively as Prynne the principle of parliamentary sovereignty, but more clearly with less heat in far fewer words. The next step in the argument was that, by the grace of God which brings the possibility of salvation unto all men and by the law of nature to which all are subject, all men should be equal also under the laws of England and have an equal voice in making them. Walwyn was to take this step a year later when the occasion offered to play Samaritan to John Lilburne, back from the war and again in trouble for too freely speaking his mind.

v. FREEDOM AND EQUALITY: RICHARD OVERTON

Among the unlicensed pamphlets condemned by the preachers in 1644 as evidence of the consequences of delay in reconstituting the church was *Mans Mortallitie*. It appeared in January shortly after *An Apologeticall Narration* and not long before the second edition of Milton's first divorce tract. It was mentioned with the divorce tract in the stationers' complaint to parliament of August 24 against unlicensed publications.[57] Milton later incorporated the particular heresy set forth in the work into his own system of divinity, but there is no evidence and little likelihood that he had any acquaintance with the author. The R.O. who appears on the title page of *Mans Mortallitie* was without doubt Richard Overton, a Baptist, at any rate in his beginnings, associated with John Cann and precisely the kind of person who might have attracted the notice of William Walwyn. He and his book gave striking additional evidence of the unprecedented conditions and the strange new forces which now confronted the godly divines of the assembly. Overton, with a knack for rough abusive satire in the Marprelate manner, had taken part in the hue and cry against prelacy in

1641–1642. He now transposed the heresy of free justification into the metaphysics of popular revolution, identifying Christian liberty with natural, the elect of God with the common people, the privileges of the saints with the rights of man. But, though in his conclusions he does not differ greatly from Walwyn, he is more abstract and dogmatic in his thinking, more assertive and far less equable in temper. He was also probably humbler in his social origins and certainly less prosperous. He became, with Walwyn and Lilburne, one of the three outstanding Leveller pamphleteers, but was probably never admitted as one of the leaders of the party.

In 1644 Overton spoke for the increasing number of those who felt Puritan orthodoxy to be an affront to their self-respect and common sense. It leveled all men in sin but then set up an elite in an order of grace for which its proponents demanded special recognition and authority in the social order. Men were, admittedly, born with equal claims to God's favor which none could of his own motion advance a jot, but this equality was relegated to the corrupt order of nature. Natural liberty, shared equally by all, ended in death; Christian liberty, which led to life and happiness, was reserved for those whom God alone had determined to save. This meant, or so it seemed to men in Overton's position, that the many were damned while an appointed, not to say self-appointed, few were saved for no just reason that anyone could comprehend. Such an arrangement seemed obviously unreasonable and inequitable if one happened to belong not to the few who sat pontificating at Westminster but to the many who milled about the streets, taverns, conventicles, and bookstalls of the city, under threat of being perhaps pilloried and jailed for claiming the same freedom of speech which the assembly cherished for itself and its apologists. If all men sinned in Adam, surely all should be saved in Christ. Justification should be for everyone. There should be but one liberty, one equality, for all.

Mans Mortallitie is an attempt to work out a conception of the nature and destiny of man in accordance with such ideas and at the same time, of course, with the scriptural account of man's creation, fall, and redemption. Though Overton may have been influenced indirectly by Socinian thought, the principal immediate source of his ideas, of much of his information, and of the references to ancient philosophers with

which he sprinkled his pages was obviously George Wither's translation, published in 1636, of *The Nature of Man* by the fourth-century
Greek father Nemesius. Wither's preface to this work was almost as
important for Overton as the work itself. It asserts that man's nature,
though depraved by the fall, was not denied the capacity to be renewed.
We should all have perished, thanks to Adam, but for the fact that
'the second Adam . . . benefited us without our own *righteousnesse,*
as much as the first . . . harmed us, without our *personall sinne.*'
Hence, if we now forfeit a second time the power thus restored to us,
we lose it through our own doing, not through the defect of nature.
'By the first *sinne,*' Wither says, 'we lost, indeed, our *light,* but not our
eyes,' and light being renewed to man in Christ, only those are condemned who reject it. If now we have eyes that see not, ears that hear
not, hearts void of understanding, it is 'even for want of knowing what
power wee have given us, and how wee are to exercise that *power.*'

So much Overton got from Wither's preface. What he got from
Nemesius himself is equally obvious. *The Nature of Man* undertook to
reconcile the idea of an overruling providence with that of man's free
will and the immortality of the soul. It gave, however, a clear account
of classical physiology and psychology and of the opinions of the leading ancient philosophers concerning the relation of soul and body. To
the information he thus derived from Nemesius, Overton added what
he could learn on the same subject from the English translation, published in 1634, of Paré's great work on anatomy and surgery,[58] and
he used what he learned in this way to support a notion of conditional
immortality which in turn supported the doctrine of free justification
and the equating of Christian with natural liberty. The whole performance afforded another example of the way in which the multiplication and accumulation of printed books of all sorts in the vernacular was raising up an increasingly literate articulate breed of thinkers
and writers to plague and scandalize the representatives of traditional
learning and orthodox thought.

Overton is never anything but bold and clear in stating the conclusions to which his assertive dogmatic mind led him. The thesis of his
book is that man's being is single and entire. Soul and body are one,
subject together to the same natural laws of procreation, growth, and
death. To these laws Christ subjected himself in becoming man, and

through them he is one with every man and every man with him. Consequently, as he shared mortality with us, we share immortality with him, unless of course we choose to reject it—'So that none can be condemned into Hell, but such as are actually guilty of refusing of *Christ.*' [59] Thus Overton committed himself to the notion that the soul dies or sleeps in the grave with the body and is received again into life at the resurrection according as it has accepted or denied Christ. Such an idea, though by no means new when put into print in January, 1644, was assailed by the preachers as evidence of the need for restoring order in the church. The implications of the idea presented in *Mans Mortallitie* were indeed ominous. By rejecting any distinction between the state of grace and the state of nature, Overton was denying the basis for any claim to authority by the assembly or its members and asserting the innate title and capacity of men in general to think, speak, and act on any issue in church or state. He was saying in effect that all men were born free and equal in the eyes of God and were therefore entitled to equal rights on earth. The full force of such ideas would be felt the following year with the organization of the New Model army at the instance of Cromwell and with the rise of the Leveller party under the leadership of Lilburne and Walwyn, supported by Overton's fiery pen.

vi. THE LIBERTY OF UNLICENSED PRINTING: JOHN MILTON

Presbyterians had linked Milton's *Doctrine and Discipline of Divorce* with Overton's *Mans Mortallitie* and Williams' *Bloudy Tenent* as evidence of the deplorable effect of delay in reconstituting church government caused by the tactics of their Independent opponents. Milton's personal associations, however, had not been with such men as Williams and Overton but with Thomas Young and other leaders of the dominant faction in the assembly itself. He had contended along with them for reform of the church on presbyterian principles or at any rate on principles that seemed to be at one with theirs. To be sure, if they had attended closely to what he wrote against the bishops, they should have seen that his views as to the proper treatment of religious differences by the state approached those of *The Bloudy Tenent* and his attitude toward the *jus divinum* of the ministry that of *The Compassionate Samaritane*. But they might also have seen that, if he fell into what they took to be dangerous errors on such matters, it was only because he insisted on carrying to extreme conclusions principles he shared with them and indeed derived in some part from them. Certainly he could claim that his proposals concerning marriage were consistent with the teachings of the Puritan pulpit, that his arguments were based upon scripture, and that he could cite eminent authorities, such as the reformers Fagius and Bucer, in his support. He expected, therefore, that the ministers would consider his arguments on their merits and either accept them or join issue with him on common ground. Their failure to do anything of the sort caused him the most acute and indignant astonishment.

But though the reception of *The Doctrine and Discipline of Divorce* was not what he expected, neither was it exactly what it has sometimes been represented to have been. Thomas Young, surely, must have tried to argue his former pupil out of his errors before undertaking to warn parliament against 'digamy.' The vulgar, as Milton said, 'the brood of Belial, the draffe of men,' no doubt did 'laugh broad . . . to see so great a strength of Scripture mustering up in favour, as they suppose, of their debausheries.' And some preachers did soon, probably, begin 'to inveigh and exclaim on what,' he was informed, 'they had not read.' [60] No one, however, let alone any learned divine, paid any explicit attention to Milton's tract in public or in print until it had been out about a year, and then the preachers merely girded at it in the pulpit and finally, as we have seen, egged the stationers to take action against it. The continuing burden of Milton's complaint was, not unjustifiably, that all the 'sound argument and reason' he had offered had been 'put off, either by an undervaluing silence, or the maisterly censure of a rayling word or two in the Pulpit.' [61] Why the men of the pulpit held off so long we can only speculate. Conceivably, they held back out of consideration for a friend in error. Conceivably, too, they attached less importance to John Milton's ideas than John Milton did or than we do, and they took them up only when and as it suited their own polemic occasions. Unquestionably, they had at the time much else to think about.

But Milton would have been less astonished at their attitude if he had had a more practical understanding of human motives. For *The Doctrine and Discipline of Divorce*, appearing just as the Westminster

Assembly was about to convene, assailed the age-old jurisdiction of the church over one of the most vital of institutions at the very moment when control of the church seemed about to pass finally into the hands of the ministerial order. The second edition, prepared while the ministers were falling out among themselves in the assembly, appeared early in 1644, just after the publication of the Independents' *Apologeticall Narration*. The prefatory address, 'To the Parlament of England, with the Assembly,' and the similar addresses, headed simply, 'To the Parlament,' which introduced *The Judgement of Martin Bucer* and *Tetrachordon* were in effect appeals to parliament from the judgment and authority of the assembly. That is to say, Milton appealed, as he thought, from entrenched, self-regarding, clerical prejudice to disinterested, enlightened, secular intelligence. He had learned that '*New Presbyter* is but *Old Priest* writ Large.' He had had his first taste, hard upon the frustration of his marriage, of disillusion and defeat, his first practical lesson in the hazardous, equivocal, contingent nature of freedom.

Areopagitica, a copy of which 'ex dono authoris,' was in the hands of George Thomason by November 24, was the first positive expression of his reaction to that experience. His immediate provocation was, of course, the stationers' complaint of August 24 against the divorce tract, and the work was described on the title page as 'A Speech of Mr. John Milton For the Liberty of Unlicenc'd Printing.' In form it was a plea to parliament, published contrary to regulations, for revocation of the printing ordinance. This did not mean, however, that Milton felt himself to be in any real danger of prosecution. He knew that any attempt at strict enforcement of the printing ordinance was now, in his phrase, like trying to pound up the crows by shutting the park gates. To make much of the threat of the stationers against him and the gallantry of his rejoinder, to think of him as a sort of Independent David laying the Presbyterian Goliath low with one pamphlet from his mighty pen, is to misrepresent the facts and mistake the real place of *Areopagitica* in the debate provoked by the disagreements of Presbyterians and Independents and in the development of Milton's own ideas.

His choice of form in which to express his ideas at this juncture was itself significant of a change in his attitude. The methods of disputation which convention had imposed upon him in his former tracts had been distasteful and doubtfully effective. When he said that in prose he had the use only of his left hand, he meant especially that kind of prose. He was at his best, and knew it, when he dropped the disputant and assumed the more congenial role of orator and prophet, as he had done in the carefully contrived eulogy of parliament near the close of his *Apology*. His old disdain for the methods of dispute taught in the universities was intensified by his recent experience as a pamphleteer and found expression again in the reply he had just made to Hartlib's request for his views on education. It was not the 'ragged Notions and Babblements' of the schools, he believed, but the 'organic arts' of logic, rhetoric, and poetry which 'inable men to discourse and write perspicuously, elegantly, and according to the fitted stile of lofty, mean, or lowly.' Commanding such arts, 'whether they be to speak in Parliament or Counsel, honour and attention would be waiting on their lips.' [62] Honor and attention had not waited on Milton's pamphlet-pen, and in *Areopagitica* he wrote not another polemic of the conventional type but an oration constructed according to the rules of classical rhetoric. He might not address parliament in person from the floor or from the pulpit of St. Margaret's but, modeling himself upon Isocrates, he could try what a written speech could do to persuade the parliament of England to fulfill the role to which England was called by her historic destiny. To the assembly's plan for a presbyterian theocracy, he could in this way oppose most effectively, perhaps, his own idea of the Puritan Zion, transfused with his Utopian conception of the antique humanistic republic.

In the politics of the moment this was to take sides with the Independents and sectaries against the Presbyterians, with Cromwell against Manchester. The contemporary reader would have seen explicit acknowledgment of that fact in Milton's praise of Lord Brooke toward the close of his oration. Brooke's attitude toward the church had been that of one reared like Milton in the tradition of humanism. Though not himself a sectary, he had come forward as the high-minded upper-class champion of toleration on idealistic grounds and in the interest of unity in the state. His conception of the proper relation of church and state resembled Milton's and may have owed something to the latter's tracts against the bishops. Milton could mention him 'for

honours sake' without breach of decorum because he had recently died
in battle, but the praise accorded him should have caused Thomas
Edwards, if he read *Areopagitica*, to cry antinomian. Milton said that
Brooke's words were so full of meekness and charity, so mild and
peaceful, as to be like those of Christ himself. 'He . . . exhorts us to
hear with patience and humility those, however they be miscall'd, that
desire to live purely, in such a use of Gods Ordinances, as the best
guidance of their conscience gives them, and to tolerat them, though
in some disconformity to our selves.' [63]

Milton's main concern in *Areopagitica* was not, however, to defend
the sects against intolerance any more than it was to defend himself
against the futile threat of prosecution under the printing ordinance.
He wrote not at all as an apologist, but as a man of learning and vision,
seizing upon the furor over the breakdown of the printing ordinance
in order to present the problem of the press, of the church, of the sects,
indeed of England, in the perspective of history and in the light of
Christian faith as he understood it. He was trying to direct the attention of parliament, now momentarily under the spell of Cromwell's
leadership, to the larger meaning of the situation which unrestricted
access to books had brought about among the English people. The timid
and the envious might, to be sure, 'prognosticat a year of sects and
schisms,' fearful lest men be diverted from their catechisms and Christian walking by the whiff of any ill-considered pamphlet. The assembly
might jangle over dependencies or independencies. Sects and parties
might contend against repression. He for his part spoke for none of
these but for the nation he thought his countrymen at least had it in
them to become. Parliament must be made to see that the most important fact it had to deal with was the rise of that 'disputing, reasoning,
reading, . . . discoursing' public which the pulpit, the printing press,
and all their works had called into being. Here was the inescapable
condition under which government must henceforth operate. Liberty,
which parliament had assured to the people, had 'enfranchis'd, enlarg'd and lifted up [their] apprehensions.' They could 'grow ignorant again, brutish, formall, and slavish' only if their rulers did the
same. There could be no turning back at any other price, no suppression of 'all this flowry crop of knowledge and new light.' 'Beleeve it,

Lords and Commons,' he exclaimed, 'they who counsell ye to such a suppressing, doe as good as bid ye suppresse your selves.' [64]

'Where there is much desire to learn,' he declared, 'there of necessity will be much arguing, much writing, many opinions; for opinion . . . is but knowledge in the making.' Did his critics expect that 'after all this light of the Gospel . . . all this continuall preaching,' after 'all the Sermons, all the Lectures preacht, printed, vented in such numbers,' after all the books published, 'to the contempt of an *Imprimatur*,' by the preachers themselves—did they expect the people to remain 'an unprincipl'd, unedify'd, and laick rabble?' Must the cruse of truth run no more oil? He and Smectymnuus had formerly argued that the free passage of the gospel in the age after the apostles had been stopped by the Roman church. Now he argued that the free circulation of books in the ancient world had been brought to an end by the censorship of the Inquisition. And as he and his party had contended that by the grace of God the Reformation had been instituted first in England and would there be consummated, so by an adroit leap of logic, which many contemporaries would have balked at, he made the free circulation of books in England seem part of God's design for the redemption of the world. This is the point of the famous passage, so often taken as the supreme expression of the moral egoism of Milton and his countrymen:

Now once again by all concurrence of signs, and by the generall instinct of holy and devout men, as they daily and solemnly expresse their thoughts, God is decreeing to begin some new and great period in his Church, ev'n to the reforming of Reformation it self: what does he then but reveal Himself to his servants, and as his manner is, first to his English-men.

This, of course, whether it became them to say so or not, had been precisely what the preachers also had told parliament time and again in the pulpit. But Milton once more drew the unpalatable corollary to Puritan principle, namely that to censor whatever God's Englishmen chose to commit to print was, to borrow John Goodwin's phrase, the grand imprudence of running the hazard of fighting against God. [65]

There was, of course, as Milton knew, excellent historical ground for believing that to attempt to restrain the press was to try to undo and unsay very nearly everything that had been done and said in England for a hundred years or more. Thanks to the politic, unacknowledged, uncertain, but always measurable tolerance observed by Elizabeth, grumbled at but submitted to by James, vainly revoked to his cost by Charles and exploited by his enemies, the English people had enjoyed a large if undefined liberty of thought and expression even before they were called upon to contend for it or theorize much about it. And thanks to a press, which had never been consistently or completely restrained, they found themselves in 1640 fully prepared for the war of ideas which revolution provoked. Milton, grasping the meaning of all this, his imagination set afire by the promise which freedom to print held out to men like himself, spared no effort that his rhetoric could supply to make the members of parliament realize the apocalyptic fulfillment in which they were called to take part. What he tells them is, of course, not sober analysis of a political crisis but a poet's expression of the excitement of a people, carried away by revolution, intoxicated by words and ideas and the hopes they inspired. He would have his supposed listeners see their countrymen as 'a Nation not slow and dull, but of a quick, ingenious, and piercing spirit, acute to invent, suttle and sinewy to discours, not beneath the reach of any point the highest that human capacity can soar to'; 'a knowing people, a Nation of Prophets, of Sages, and of Worthies'; a people taken up even in the midst of war, 'with the study of highest and most important matters to be reform'd.' He would have them see London as 'the mansion house of liberty,' full of anvils and hammers beating out the instruments of war, but not less full of pens and heads, 'sitting by their studious lamps, musing, searching, revolving new notions and idea's wherewith to present, as with their homage and their fealty the approaching Reformation.' [66]

But granted that the liberty of the people to read and know and speak was now less than ever to be denied, how was that liberty to be managed in the state? This was, indeed, the fundamental constitutional question of the whole Puritan Revolution, and Milton's specific answer to it must not be misunderstood or misjudged. He had begun by thinking of the church as truly the implement of liberty, and in a sense he never totally relinquished the idea that freedom could be incorporated only in a religious community. But he had now concluded that in such a community no special function of government or privilege of speaking must be accorded to any ministerial caste or ecclesiastical organization. Yet he did not on the other hand anticipate the development of all that apparatus of schools, newspapers, political parties, and popular elections which has come to seem the indispensable machinery of popular government. It would have been strange indeed if he had done so. He was not, like Lilburne, himself one of the people, with the ideas and the idiom of the street, the shop, the tavern, and presently the army camp at his tongue's end. He had been reared in sheltered circumstances to take his place among the most eminent, orthodox, and respectable of the brotherhood of preachers. He had undertaken the role of a private scholar and man of letters, still bent, nevertheless, on putting his gifts and learning at the service of the church and his country. He knew himself to be master of the arts of discourse, of the history of states and the church, of the scriptures and the classics. He was planning to write a series of English heroic poems and, by this time too in all probability, a history of his country from the beginning, and a summation of Protestant doctrine. All this is to say that he brought to bear on the issues of 1644, not the political ideas of 1775 or even 1688 but the blended culture and idealism of Reformation and Renaissance at their height. Political democracy was not so much contrary to his principles as outside his knowledge and experience. The kind of parliament he conceived as standing at the center of power in the state was not that called for three years later in the Levellers' Agreement of the People but an Areopagus, a great council of worthies, hearkening at all times to instruction and admonition from those who had learned from the best authors and the Word of God how to distinguish 'what is infallibly good and happy in the state of mans life, what in it selfe evil and miserable.' [67] Who could be better qualified to speak to rulers or for the people?

The Long Parliament was not destined to become the senate of a humanistic Utopia, transfigured by the Puritan Zion. Neither, to be sure, did England become anything like a parliamentary democracy for at least two hundred years. But that, so far as Milton is concerned, is beside the point. In *Areopagitica* he put before parliament certain principles upon which the government of free people in England must henceforth rest. Puritan that he was, he could not fail to assert the sole sufficiency of the scriptures in all things, but it must be remembered that poets and philosophers had taught him what human meaning to make of Moses and Paul, which is to say of the sacred epic of man's fall and redemption. He had learned that truth exists, one and entire, but revealed to man in his fallen state only in partial glimpses and reflections, mingled always in some degree with its opposite, that reason, by ceaseless searching, testing, choosing, can gain knowledge of truth, and that creation is the theater, experience the term, error the function, and liberty the necessary condition for the exercise of reason and the attainment of knowledge. Knowledge, gained, can be communicated by discourse, and communicated, can be understood; truth can be distinguished, bit by bit, from its opposite, proclaimed, and heeded, to the continuous and progressive benefit of man and the state, 'ev'n to the reforming of Reformation it self.' 'And perhaps this is that doom which *Adam* fell into of knowing good and evil, that is to say of knowing good by evill.' [68]

The condition which provoked all that activity of heads and pens and printing presses, of sects and schisms, by which the Long Parliament was confronted, was nothing less than the condition into which all men fell with Adam and in which they must expect to remain until the second coming of Christ, the condition, in a word, from which no government on earth was exempt. 'Assuredly we bring not innocence into the world, we bring impurity much rather: that which purifies us is triall, and triall is by what is contrary.' Hence the absurdity, upon which Milton lavishes his gift for ridicule, of treating authors as though the writings of grown men were no better than schoolboy themes not to be sent forth 'without the cursory eyes of a temporizing and extemporizing licencer.' [69] Governments must expect to govern as men must expect to live; they must expect that things will be bad, but bad as they are, that they will grow worse or better. Governments must expect to learn like the rest of us, and therefore they must submit to the instruction of circumstance and of any book from which anything can be learned concerning the mystery of good and evil. This is the principle that should govern all parliament's decisions, and Milton therefore, faithfully observing the rules of his rhetoric, opens and closes by stating both principle and the practical inference to be drawn from it. 'For this is not,' he says in his exordium, 'the liberty which wee can hope, that no grievance ever should arise in the Commonwealth, that let no man in this World expect.' And in his peroration—'This I know, that errors in a good government and in a bad are equally almost incident.' Either may be misinformed, mistaken, or misled. But there can be no hope or excuse for rulers who, forgetting they are men, refuse the opportunity to learn. 'But,' he says on his first page, 'when complaints are freely heard, deeply consider'd, and speedily reform'd, then is the utmost bound of civill liberty attain'd, that wise men looke for.' And again on his last, 'to redresse willingly and speedily what hath bin err'd, and in highest autority to esteem a plain advertisement more then others have done a sumptuous bribe, is a vertue (honour'd Lords and Commons) answerable to Your highest actions, and whereof none can participat but greatest and wisest men.' [70]

Milton did not repeat the experiment of trying to match sermons and pamphlets with a classical oration. *Areopagitica* appears to have gone completely unnoticed. Prynne, the next year, in his *Fresh Discovery of some Prodigious New Wandring-Blasing-Stars, & Firebrands*, replied in characteristic fashion to attacks on the printing ordinance by Henry Robinson, John Lilburne, and Richard Overton but made no mention of Milton. Enforcement of the ordinance continued lax as before but clearly not because of the force of Milton's reasoning or the splendor of his rhetoric. This apparent ineffectiveness was not surprising. The advocates of free speech and liberty of conscience who won immediate attention in 1644 were those who spoke in the language of the time on behalf of recognizable sectarian and partisan interests. Milton spoke for no faction but for English Protestant humanist intelligence. But speaking thus, in a language of his own, he dealt more purely and in broader terms with the fundamental question at issue between the Westminster divines and all who opposed their endeavor to call a halt to the revolutionary process they had themselves set in motion. Putting aside merely polemic considerations, he addressed himself to the great central problem, how the principle of liberty was to be incorporated within the state, the liberty of the Word as the Puritans had preached it, but also of the word in print. That is to say, the great body of ideas about man, his nature, history, and place in the scheme of things which had been brought into English life through the agency of printed books.

The godly divines who assembled at Westminster in July, 1643, were caught in a predicament not uncommon in revolutions. They had instilled a peculiarly dynamic faith in a great but indeterminate body of disciples and followers. Liberated at last from the particular ecclesiastical controls which had formerly impeded their preaching, they naturally hoped to safeguard their ministry by instituting new controls of which they and their order would continue masters. In other and simpler circumstances, as in Scotland or New England, their expectations might have met some measure of fulfillment, but not now in England. Puritanism had not been permitted to develop in isolation, shielded from the impact of other influences bearing down upon English life from different quarters. And the dynamics of Puritan doctrine itself, under such conditions, proved too great for its own proponents to arrest or to direct to any simple calculable end. The preachers were only at the beginning of their troubles when they found themselves freed at last from the restraints of a discredited episcopacy. They were free but, such was the nature of the faith they had embraced, they were unable to agree what to do with their freedom when confronted by the erupting energies aroused by the interplay of Puritan faith with ideas and modes of experience beyond their comprehension. Thomas Goodwin and the other opponents of presbyterianism in the assembly could presently be voted down. Not so John Goodwin, Williams, Robinson, Walwyn, Overton, and Milton. Each in his own way spoke for people who, in spite of anything the assembly could do, were being more and more exposed to all the winds of doctrine blowing from pulpits, conventicles, and bookstalls through the streets, shops, churches, and taverns of the city. While the godly divines of the assembly went on disputing over church government and preaching against heresy and schism, the people at large were becoming more and more irretrievably committed to diversity in faith while growing more and more practiced in the expression and organization of opinion as a basis for common action within the body politic. The outcome of this development, foreshadowed in the tracts of 1644, now became evident in the army.

VI

The Word of God in the New Model Army

1645-1646

By the end of 1644 the Puritan divines were at loggerheads with one another in the assembly and with an increasing host of critics and opponents outside, including many renegades from their own ranks. Meanwhile their cause appeared to fare no better in the field. After the great defeat of Essex in the west at the beginning of September, parliament drew its remaining forces together, including those led by Manchester and Cromwell, for another attempt upon the king in the midlands. By the end of October, however, the campaign had come to an end at Newbury in bafflement and dissension. Charles withdrew to Oxford with his forces intact, and Cromwell came up to Westminster to press his quarrel with Manchester, his commanding officer. Parliament and assembly now found themselves in a difficult position. They could have peace at the risk of letting the crown regain some measure of control over the church. They could go on with the war at the cost of seeing religious differences among their own partisans deepen and spread. They could in fact settle nothing in either church or state so long as Charles kept the field and the danger of defeat hung over English and Scots, parliament and assembly, Presbyterians, Independents, and sectaries alike.

The predicament was, as it were, made for Cromwell. Even in the matter of religion and the church, his attitude and that of the army under his leadership were presently to become more decisive than the desires of either assembly or parliament. Everything that had happened to him up to this point in the war had served to build up his faith in himself. The events of 1644 made him known as the most effective military leader on the parliamentary side. He now came forward as the most effective political leader as well. The campaign over, he returned to his place in the house of commons and initiated the series of maneuvers which culminated in the spring of 1645 in the reorganization of the army with Fairfax as commander but according to Cromwell's ideas and with him still as its driving force. The result, prompt and complete, was to be the victory which the preachers had looked for as the sign of God's favor upon their efforts to reform the church, but victory under conditions which made the problem of reform insoluble and the fulfillment of their plans impossible. For Cromwell's success in war and politics sprang from his gift for drawing upon those spiritual energies in himself and others which the Puritan pulpit had evoked but which the representatives of the ministerial caste now in control in the assembly were endeavoring to keep within bounds, if not to repress. He led the way toward the creation of the army which brought victory to the side of parliament and assembly, not by curbing and containing the Puritan spirit but by giving it free play, by granting full scope to its characteristic modes of expression and organization. Thus, in an extraordinary but indubitable sense, he became also a great spiritual leader, and under his leadership the army was destined in the end to overrule both assembly and parliament in the great contention over church and state.

Hence the next chapter in the history of the Puritan Revolution centers in the army, and it begins like every other chapter with the preaching of the Word. The army, of course, had had plenty of preaching before Cromwell came to dominate it. Many noted ministers, as we have seen, went out with the regiments under Essex in 1642.[1] After Edgehill, however, most of them found other matters to attend to, first of all their city pulpits and by midsummer the great business of the assembly. Baxter charges his colleagues with having quit the army out of desire for an easier and quieter life,[2] but the cause of their defection lay deeper than that. Revolutions have a way of outstripping the calculations of their promoters. The preachers who had done so much to bring about the unprecedented situation in which they found themselves in 1642 were slow to grasp the full implications of what they had done, and the reason is indicated by Baxter's own attitude. He tells us that, at the beginning of the war, the officers of Cromwell's newly raised troop of horse at Cambridge, 'that famous Troop which he began his Army with . . . purposed to make their Troop a gathered Church, and they all subscribed an Invitation to me to be their Pastor.' He rejected the invitation with a reproof, in which he made plain 'wherein my Judgment was against the Lawfulness and Convenience of their way.' [3] So he heard no more of them and apparently thought no more until after Naseby.

Baillie, realistic as ever, saw very soon that victory, if it were to advance religion and settle peace according to Scottish ideas, would have to be won by Scottish arms. Yet as the months went by and his countrymen won no battles, he had to record, along with the obstructive maneuvers of Independents in the assembly and of Erastian lawyers in parliament, the multiplying activities of sectaries in London and the growth of heresy and schism among the parliamentary troops. By May, 1644, he had heard that 'more than the most part of my Lord Manchester's armie are seduced to Independencie, and very many of them have added either Anabaptisme or Antinomianisme, or both.' After Marston Moor in July he had suffered the chagrin of having Major Harrison come from the battlefield, trumpeting the praises of the army Independents, 'making all believe, that Cromwell alone, with his unspeakable valorous regiments, had done all that service.' As to Cromwell, Baillie admitted with his unfailing candor that the man was 'a very wise and active head, universallie well beloved, as religious and stout' and that 'most of the sojours who loved new wayes putt themselves under his command.' [4]

What he failed to understand was that the ways favored by Cromwell and his men were not really so new as they appeared. They were the natural fulfillment of the Protestant movement in England, and they were supremely apposite to the situation now opening before the English people. Baxter, after the Restoration, thought that all the mischief that had befallen in his time had begun with the seduction of honest, ignorant men in the army by a few fiery self-conceited fellows, 'hatcht up among the old Separatists,' and that all might have been prevented if ministers of sufficient learning, sound doctrine, and moderate temper had remained with the troops from the beginning. But his notion that 'then all the Fire was in one Spark' and might easily have been stamped out was a delusion, no matter how many learned, godly, judicious divines may have devoted themselves to the work.[5] Actually, not all the ministers did leave the army after 1642; not all who remained or joined later were extreme separatists and heretics; not all who deviated in some degree from orthodoxy were ignorant and conceited firebrands.

But aside from that, those who did desert would probably have been no more successful in quenching the fire kindled by the Word as preached among the soldiery than they were elsewhere. Not every recruit, at the time he enlisted or was pressed into the New Model, was a Puritan saint, but the men Cromwell favored for positions of trust and leadership generally had the root of the matter in them, and the others knew what saints might expect to feel, how they were supposed to behave and what rewards they might look for here and hereafter. All were familiar with the common procedures of the godly for banding together in order to help themselves to edification by the Word. Opportunity and success drove these lessons home. Not presbyterianism as conceived by the Westminster divines on the Scottish model, with its rigid parochialism and its tight apparatus of classes and synods, but independency or congregationalism in all its protean manifestations —the spontaneous irrepressible aggregation of like-minded saints in shifting voluntary groups within or without the traditional ecclesiastical frame, or what was left of it, seeking comfort and enlightenment for themselves from the gospel—this was actually, or was rapidly becoming, the accustomed English way, a way of organizing religious life adaptable to strange conditions, such as civil war or the American frontier. Not its least merit was that it gave scope for variations upon the doctrine of grace, better suited, or so it seemed, to the spiritual needs of men under such conditions than strict Calvinistic orthodoxy. Hence it was that Cromwell's men understood how to form themselves into what they chose to call gathered churches, and though Baxter refused their invitation, they were at no loss to find preachers to serve them, ministers and graduates as well as men from their own numbers, officers and common soldiers, graced with gifts for expounding the Word and not uninspired, of course, by unnumbered sermons previously heard from clergy lips.

The New Model had hardly got under way when parliament gave

expression to the misgivings aroused in many by such goings-on. It had withdrawn its members from the army, all, as things turned out, except Cromwell. It had its Independent faction, and it was unwilling to give the Presbyterians of the assembly all the authority over the church which perhaps they desired. But neither was it prepared to let the church dissolve into shifting flocks of believers responsible to no one but themselves. It had had before it for some time a proposed ordinance for stricter control of unauthorized preaching, and this was now, April 26, pressed through to adoption. No one was to preach unless he had been ordained or had been approved as a person intending to enter the ministry and wishing to make trial of his ability. The order was duly issued in print, and Fairfax was enjoined to see that it was strictly obeyed in the army. It could hardly have reached him, however, when it appeared again in print, with the usual phrase, 'according to order,' but this time with the addition of an anonymous qualifying but significant 'vindication.' The public was now assured that parliament had no intention of repressing godly instruction in the army at a time when the need for and the shortage of preachers were both so great. True, the preaching of formal sermons with opening, dividing, and applying of texts, was work only for ordained ministers. But others were not forbidden to read and expound God's Word for the edification of those under their charge, 'as suppose a Master to his Family, a Captain to his Company, a Collonel to his Regiment, a Generall to his Army, a King to his People, if he hath the grace to do it.' Nor were men forbidden to gather for prayer and mutual instruction or to use and improve their talents as occasion might arise, each in his proper sphere.

You therefore Gentlemen of the Souldiery in the field . . . you may both *pray and speak* too in the head of your Companies, Regiments and Armies, you may deliver the piety of your souls, the wel-grounded confidence of your hearts, the valour of your minds, *in such Orations, in such Liberties of speech,* as may best enspirit the men that follow you, with such a religious and undaunted animation as may render them unconquerable before the proudest enemy.[6]

The New Model took the field in the spring of 1645. On June 14 it overwhelmed the king at Naseby. A year later it had brought every remaining royal force and stronghold to surrender or destruction.

Shortly after the victory at Naseby, Baxter, who had spent the interval as lecturer to the garrison at Coventry, went to the army on business of his own and saw with consternation what he took to be the consequences of his own and his fellow ministers' neglect. He found, he says, hot sectaries, Cromwell's favorites, in the chief places of command, and when he met Cromwell in person, he was coldly received and expostulated with for his former refusal to serve the now famous victorious regiment. His conscience so troubled him at all this that he accepted an appointment as chaplain to Whalley's regiment and stuck to his post throughout the remaining stages of the war up to the fall of Worcester. According to his own account he preached and disputed as long as his strength endured, and then, exhausted, ill, and alone, believing that death was upon him, he bent his thoughts, he says, 'on my Everlasting Rest.' [7] His intention was to spend his last hours drawing up his own funeral sermon, but when he had completed what amounts to sixty-eight printed pages on Hebrews 4: 9, he found himself still alive and still full of his recent experience and the thoughts it provoked. So he kept on writing and produced the remaining 788 pages of *The Saints Everlasting Rest*. But even this was not enough. He continued, up to the Restoration, preaching and writing against the errors and confusion which, he believed, had grown with Cromwell's rise to power, and in the first part of his autobiography (said to have been 'Written for the most part in 1664,' [8]) he gave a circumstantial account of the state of mind prevailing in the New Model at the moment when it was about to assume the dominant role in the revolutionary movement.

In a letter written in June, 1646, which found its way into Edwards' *Gangraena*, Baxter says he found the army preachers telling the soldiers that Christ judges only by the heart and that magistrates have nothing to do with the conversion of sinners or the reformation of the church. The law of 'Love and Liberty' was to be observed 'that there may be an equality.' Ministers needed no authorization save the anointment of the spirit and the acceptation of the saints. Universities were useless, tithes should be abolished, and blasphemy, being a sin against God, should be left for God only to punish. [9] In his autobiography, Baxter says that honest men of little knowledge and weak judgment 'made it too much of their Religion to talk for this Opinion and for that,' arguing for democracy, now in the state, now in the church, talk-

ing about 'Free-grace and Free-will, and all the Points of Antinomianism and Arminianism.' But 'their most frequent and vehement Disputes were for Liberty of Conscience, as they called it; that is, that the
Civil Magistrate had nothing to do to determine of any thing in Matters of Religion, by constraint or restraint, but every Man might not
only *hold*, but *preach* and *do* in Matters of Religion what he pleased.' [10]

The most distressing thing about such notions, and the most difficult to deal with, was that not one of them but seemed a distortion of
or fallacious deduction from some truth which the pulpit had been
laboring to set forth for the enlightenment of precisely such men as
composed the army and were now making such havoc of what they
had been told. Baxter's *Saints Everlasting Rest* illuminates the error
he abhorred as well as the truth he embraced and shows how near akin
the two were to one another. The five opening chapters, which contain
the substance of that work, conclude with the assurance that now, 'by
the line and plummet of Scripture,' we have been shown 'the Christian
safely landed in Paradise.' The vital element in Baxter's belief was
the conviction that Christ had entered into his soul and given him the
power both to know and to do what God desired of him. Blest by grace
with the ability to act in the light of faith, he felt assured, though as he
thought on his deathbed, of his place in paradise. There he would have
no more need to fast or weep or watch or pray; 'nor will there be use
for Instructions and Exhortations: Preaching is done; The Ministry
of man ceaseth; . . . The Unregenerate past hope; the Saints past
fear, for ever.' His imagination takes wing in describing the condition
of saints redeemed and the process by which they may come to know
that supreme good which swallows up all lesser goods. How noble a
faculty, he exclaims, is the soul's power of understanding.

It can compass the Earth: It can measure the Sun, Moon, Stars, and Heaven:
It can fore-know each Eclipse to a minute, many years before: Yea, but
this is the top of all its excellency, It can know God who is infinite, who
made all these; a little here, and more, much more hereafter. Oh the
wisdom and goodness of our Blessed Lord! He hath created the Understanding with a Natural Byas, and inclination to Truth, as its object, and to
Prime Truth, as its Prime Object.[11]

For to Baxter, as to Lord Brooke, to Milton, and as we shall see to
Saltmarsh, indeed to all Puritan enthusiasts who had come under the
spell of Paul and Plato, truth was something that could be apprehended,

paradise was a state that could be regained—by little and little, it might be, but none the less certainly in the end.

But the too lively apprehension of predestined bliss in the hereafter could lead overeager souls to misunderstanding and trouble in the here and now. Baxter concedes that, even before coming to his everlasting rest, the saint by long gazing may on occasion rise to the third heaven and glimpse the unutterable. But this only by anticipation; attainment must await the second coming, the final resurrection, the last judgment, the crowning and enthronement in glory. The trouble was, however, that there were too many men in the army who, overpersuaded that they had Christ within, were deluded into thinking that they had but to reach forth their hands and retake paradise, or whatever else they might conceive to be rightfully theirs, at once, just as they had taken Bristol or Basing House or Worcester. That is to say, from Baxter's viewpoint, they were, poor simple souls, plunged into mortal error—from which he felt compelled to rescue them if he could—on the crucial point of justification. His anxiety is illustrated at the close of the sermon he prepared for his own now fortunately receding funeral. Describing the exaltation of the saints, he undertakes to state the meaning of the parable of the talents, and this brings him suddenly back to the vexed question he had just been disputing in the army. Drawing a line across the page, he remarks 'a great difficulty riseth in our way.' The difficulty was to determine 'in what sence is our Improvement of our Talent, our well doing, our overcoming . . . alledged as a Reason of our Coronation and Glory?' What is the relation of faith to works and of both to our salvation and reward? How soon may we expect the master to return and say, 'Well done good and faithful Servant, thou hast been faithful over a few things, I will make thee Ruler over many things?' [12]

The fact was that the Puritan preachers had done their work too well. They had made too certain that common men should understand that the vocation of the saints led inevitably to their justification and ultimate triumph and that their calling was sealed to them in the gifts entrusted to them by the Lord. At any rate, fired by such doctrine, the men of the New Model had shown that, whether gentlemen or not, they had a gift for winning battles and, whether ministers and graduates or not, a talent for expounding the Word. Hence, or so it seemed to Baxter, they jumped to the fallacious and dangerous conclusion that the effect of grace was immediate, absolute, and total, that the coming of Christ was instant or at least proximate, and that the liberation and crowning of the saints was to be looked for not in the indefinite future or upon terms but at once and unconditionally.

The full effect of all this did not become apparent until 1647 when parliament supplied the men of the New Model with a material grievance and pamphleteers and agitators had showed them how to transpose their faith into political as well as military action. Meanwhile Baxter recovered from his illness, if not from his fears, and finding the difficulty concerning justification too great to be handled in *The Saints Everlasting Rest,* undertook to settle it, first in a duodecimo of five hundred pages, called *Aphorismes of Justification* (1649), and finally in a larger work of four hundred and sixty-two pages, called *Rich: Baxter's Confession of his Faith* (1655). But every effort of his all too fluent dialectic to draw men away from the antinomian pit of free justification while stopping short of the popish slough of justification by works invited misunderstanding on both heterodox left and orthodox right. He was in the unhappy position of one who in a time of crisis seeks to promote reform and yet avoid extremes and conserve essentials. He accounted for his unhappy predicament by saying that 'every ignorant, empty braine . . . hath the liberty of the Presse.' For Baxter could not exult as Milton did in the vision of a whole people reading, discoursing, disputing their way toward knowledge of the truth.

Some think the truth will not thrive among us, till every man have leave to speak both in Presse and Pulpit that please: God forbid that we should ever see that day! If ten mens voyces be louder then one, then would the noyse of Errour drown the voyce of Truth: . . . For the godly, compared with the ungodly, are not neer so few as the men of cleer understanding, in comparison of the ignorant: And they are most forward to speake, that know least.[13]

ii. THE ARMY PREACHERS

Who accepted the invitation which Baxter rejected to dispense the Word to Cromwell's troopers we do not exactly know. Nor can we point to any particular sermon in print before 1645 which we can say that either Cromwell or his men actually heard. There is, however, no lack of evidence as to the preachers who were carrying all before them in the New Model at the moment of its triumph over the king or as to the nature of their utterances. Baxter, Edwards, and other contemporary witnesses supply us with a considerable list of men whose sermons and tracts were eagerly heard or read by the soldiers and the populace directly after Naseby. Two in particular Baxter found holding sway at headquarters, namely John Saltmarsh and William Dell, and of these the former seemed the prime source of that antinomianism which, he thought, led to the anarchy which presently ensued. Baxter was indeed moved to write because he saw Saltmarsh's 'Flowings of Grace' (*Free-Grace: or, The Flowings of Christs Blood freely to Sinners*) 'so exceedingly taking both in the Country and the Army,' 'especially when I saw how greedily multitudes of poor souls did take the bait, and how exceedingly the Writings and Preachings of *Saltmarsh* and many of his fellows did take with them.' [14]

Saltmarsh, a graduate of Magdalene College, Cambridge, and the author of a volume of poems in English and Latin (1636), was on the eve of the Long Parliament the conforming incumbent of a Yorkshire parish, but after a spiritual awakening, described in *Holy Discoveries and Flames* (1640), he embraced the Puritan cause. Thomas Fuller, with whom he quarreled, conceded that he was 'of a fine and active fancy, no contemptible Poet, and a good *Preacher*,' though 'a violent oppressor of *Bishops* and *Ceremonies*.' [15] Under the parliament, Saltmarsh was appointed to a rectory in Kent, but by 1646 joined the army. The nature of his preaching is to be seen in a dozen or more tracts, issued, some of them more than once, between January, 1645, and May, 1647, the year of his death. They have such titles as *Dawnings of Light, Free-Grace, Smoke in the Temple,* and *Sparkles of Glory.* As Baxter, and more particularly, as Rutherford with tireless pedantry, did not fail to set forth, there could be no mistaking the antecedents of Saltmarsh's ideas. They represented the current version of the type of heterodoxy which, to go no further back, had beset Calvinistic orthodoxy from Geneva to Naseby. They were in line with the *Theologia Germanica* and the sixteenth-century continental mystics, with Henry Nicholas and the Familists, and with such English preachers as John Everard and Giles Randall, who had been active in London for many years, and John Eaton who had but just published his *Honey-Combe of Free Justification* (1642).[16]

These men had also awakened the interest and sympathy of the courtly idealist, Lord Brooke, and of the middle-class humanist and humanitarian, William Walwyn. The truth was that Antinomians, Anabaptists, Familists, Arminians, or whatever they might be called, and however they might be assailed as upstart, unruly, ignorant eccentrics by members of the ministerial caste, represented as ancient and vital a form of Christian piety and doctrine as the most orthodox adherent of the Westminster Assembly. Had not the people been told time and again that, unless grace came to them by the will of God through Jesus Christ, they could not hope to be saved from judgment upon the sin to which they were born? Had not the preachers described the experience by which a man might tell that grace had indeed come to him? Saltmarsh was simply one of the long succession of those who find liberation and strength by pressing on to the conclusion that the grace men are told to look for is actually theirs for the taking. Why need they wait for learned but disputatious divines to settle all points of difference among themselves? It was enough to know and love Christ in their own hearts, in their fellow men, and in God's creation. Salvation comes by 'Experiment of *Jesus Christ*,' to each man for himself within himself, each man's experience being of equal validity with that of every other, and the sufficient key to the mysteries of God's printed Word. 'The *spirits* of such as possesse *Christ*,' are the 'Counterpane' of the scriptures, wherein '*truth* answers to *truth*, as in *water face answers to face*.' 'And the more *Christ* is known, and that *love of God to the Sons of men* which was *manifest* in the *flesh*, the more that *glorious liberty* from the *Law, Sin*, and *Satan*, is manifested in that soul.' [17]

Though there is no truth but Christ and no Christ but the Christ within, yet he manifests himself to no man once and for all but to each only by degrees. Truth, single and entire, 'shines forth in many *streams* of *glory*, and opens like *day*.' The kinship of Saltmarsh's conception to that of Brooke, of Milton, indeed up to a point of Baxter himself, is obvious.

All outward *administrations*, whether as to *Religion*, or to *natural, civil*, and *moral* things, are onely the *visible appearances* of God. . . . And God does not *fix* himself upon any one *form* or outward *dispensation*, but at his own *will* and *pleasure* comes forth in such and such an *administration,* and goes out of *it,* and leaves it, and takes up *another.* . . . The *pure, spiritual, comprehensive* Christian, is one who grows up with God from *administration* to *administration,* and so walks with God in all his *removes* and *spiritual encreasings* and *flowings;* and such are *weak* and in the *flesh* who tarry *behinde,* worshipping in that *form* or *administration* out of which God is departed.[18]

It follows that truth does not prevail by argument or force but only through successive revelations of itself in the spirits of men. The error of ministers and churches is not in thinking they possess truth but in thinking that they alone possess it and that they possess it once and for all in its entirety. The magistrate may not forbid the light to shine as it will in any man. His part is simply to maintain peace so that every man may seek truth for himself and make it known in his own way. Hence every man should be at liberty to preach, and for those who have no pulpits the press should be free. Hence, too, no man should be despised either for gifts and learning or for lack of them; 'the spirit is in Paul as well as Peter, in both as well as one.' [19]

Though Saltmarsh professed to lay aside both the method and the spirit of controversy and condemned the matching of text with text, argument with argument, his challenge to the ministerial caste was unmistakable. The practical purport of his preaching was to reduce the ecclesiastical state to the purest democracy, not to say anarchy. William Dell preached to the same effect more concretely. His sermons show how easily the saints of the New Model could pass from the knowledge that Christ was immanent in their breasts to the certainty that God was present in their ranks. Dell, Master of Arts of Emmanuel College, had joined the army in 1645 as chaplain under Fairfax. Not long before Naseby he published *Power from on High, Or, The Power of the Holy Ghost Dispersed Through the whole body of Christ, and communicated to each Member according to its place and use in that body. Delivered in two Sermons, on Acts 1.8. and now published, for the instruction and use of those that are Spirituall* (1645). A year later on June 7, before an assemblage of officers, soldiers, and people at headquarters, he preached a sermon called *The Building and Glory of the truely Christian and Spiritual Church* (1646). A few days later he officiated at the marriage of Cromwell's daughter to Henry Ireton. On November 25 he preached by invitation before the house of commons at St. Margaret's.

The sermons published by Dell in the spring of 1645 with the title *Power from on High* and dedicated to the Countess of Bolingbroke, wife to a cousin of Cromwell and of Oliver St. John, give us a sample of the spiritual meat fed to the New Model on its way to victory. The preacher does not refer directly to the Westminster Assembly, but in his dedicatory epistle he takes pains to distinguish between the form of godliness, which he says is very common in his day, and the power of it, which is very rare. In the text of his sermon, he says,

And as Souldiers that are under a wise and carefull Commander, when they are neere an ingagement, are not suffered to run rashly upon the enemy, nor permitted to goe forth to battle till they are armed and mounted: so Christ would not suffer his Disciples to goe forth in his warfare . . . till first he had armed them with the Holy Ghost.

Christ still gives power to his servants as he did to his apostles in the beginning, more to some than to others but to each enough for the task in hand, and a little 'will inable a man to doe great things, far greater then the world suspects or imagines.' The conclusion seemed inescapable and incontrovertible. 'We may judge of our calling to any businesse'—we may know, that is, that we are really doing the Lord's work —'by the power we have received from Christ for it,' which amounted to saying, by the success of our efforts.[20]

The preacher is speaking at this point of ministers of the church, but his words applied as well to the embattled saints of the New Model. A year later, he prefaced the printed version of his sermon preached at headquarters just before the fall of Oxford with praise of the army plainly directed at its Presbyterian critics. The once despised army of sectaries, united as one man in humility, faith, and prayer and in unfailing devotion to the good of the state had belied all suspicions and accusations.

I have seen more of the *presence* of God in that *Army,* then amongst *any people* that ever I *conversed* with in my life . . . we have seen his *goings,* and observed his very *footsteps:* for he hath *dwelt* among us, and *marched* in the head of us, and *counsel'd* us, and *led* us, and hath *gone along* with us *step* by *step,* from *Naseby.*

Dell did not fail to apply this belief in the power of the indwelling
Christ and the free justification of the elect to the problem of the church
over which parliament and assembly, to the despair by this time of
many besides the Scots, were still boggling. The true church, he declared, consisted only of those who have the spirit within them, and
the spirit, though it manifests itself in a diversity of gifts and dispensations, is the same spirit in all and brings all together in love and
peace, with no intermingling of the profane, the unbelieving, and the
carnal. This, he says, is no new doctrine. The new doctrine is that the
church

> *should be made up of all the people that live in a Kingdom; and that all*
> *that are born in such a Nation, should necessarily be stones for the building*
> *of the new Jerusalem. . . .* For God doth not now make any *people,* or
> *kindred,* or *nation* his *Church;* but *gathers* his Church *out* of every *people,*
> and *kindred,* and *nation:* and none can be *stones* of *this* building, but those
> that are first *elect,* and after made *precious,* through a *new* birth, and the
> *gift* of the Spirit.[21]

This meant, of course, that there could be no true church which was
not a 'gathered' church composed of none but visible saints. It was to
proclaim the disintegration of the ecclesiastical state and to extend indefinitely the individualism which had triumphed in the army. In
his fast day sermon before parliament at the end of November, 1646,
Dell declared that, since only Christ in his own time and way can deal
with sin, the reformation of the church must await Christ's continuing, progressive triumph over the evil which harbors in the breasts of
sinners. Against Antichrist the magistrate is as helpless as any other
man, and any effort of his to govern or reform the church is doomed to
failure and defeat. A false *'Clergy-power,'* by crying *'Destroy one,*
Destroy both,' had formerly endeavored to get itself upheld by temporal authority. The prelates too were wont to say *'No Bishop, no*
King.' So now 'their *successors* in the Kingdome of *Antichrist* still cry,
No Minister, no Magistrate.' And Dell, having thus identified Presbyterian divines with Antichrist, admonished parliament not to suffer the
victorious saints of the army to be oppressed by their adversaries, 'who
would use *your power* against *us,* not for *you,* but for *themselves.'* [22]
His words were ill relished by many in his audience. The afternoon
preacher on the same day, Christopher Love, a Presbyterian extremist,

later executed for treason, at once attacked him in the pulpit and followed up the quarrel in the press.[23] The house, contrary to custom, voted no thanks or invitation to print to either preacher, and fell back for its next fast day on Marshall and Newcomen. Dell nevertheless published his sermon, uninvited and unlicensed. Under the Commonwealth he was made Master of Gonville and Caius.

Thus in November, 1646, parliament heard from the pulpit of St. Margaret's the same doctrine it had heard so roundly condemned two years before when set forth in *The Bloudy Tenent* and *The Compassionate Samaritane*. The final effect of following Cromwell's leadership in reorganizing the army was to remove the last restrictions upon preaching in both the army and the community. Practically every one was now free to use whatever gifts he had for attracting listeners eager to hear that Christ was at hand, that no matter what the learned or the well-placed might say to the contrary, they were his chosen ones, his true church. Sects under such conditions multiplied and flourished as never before. Though many of their preachers were renegades from the Puritan clergy, the true sect was not primarily derived from or necessarily associated with a parish church or settled congregation. Nor had the sects in general yet become the firmly organized dissenting communions of a later period. They were many of them as yet shifting and amorphous groups of people, uprooted and confused by change, revolution, and civil war, congregating loosely about individual preachers and flocking from one to another. The preacher was all-important, and given a leader with the necessary qualifications, the group presently consolidated itself and might even cohere with other groups of like mind, similarly circumstanced and led.

The first essential was that the preacher evoke in his disciples the sense of having shared an experience which set them apart from the generality of men. An important device of organization was some form of covenant, binding upon all, to which all must agree. The numerous sectarian groups known as Baptists required baptism, which was to say rebaptism, as an initiatory rite which they administered by immersion and denied to any but approved saints and hence to children. These practices had of course the effect of emphasizing the separatist character common to all sects and were resented as disloyal and subversive. What the sect offered its proselytes was always the sense of distinction and security to be found in becoming one with a peculiar people, called to enter the ark of salvation in a doomed and perishing world. An important element in this was the assurance that they, the saints, lowly and despised, were soon to see their present situation reversed when Christ should come to rule the world, purified and renewed. There was also another attitude, not actually very different in practical effect, to which belief in the indwelling of Christ and in the essentially spiritual nature of the church frequently led. The saint might remain unconvinced by the claims of any single group to be the true church spiritual, even though he might admit the presence of Christ's spirit in some measure in each. In that case he must wait, content to possess Christ within himself while seeking for visible manifestation of him according to his own will in his own time. Practically speaking, this was to resolve the institution completely and finally into the individual, every man becoming a church to himself.[24]

The differences and peculiarities which developed among the various sects do not concern us at this point, as they did not concern their critics, who were occupied rather with the common danger to be seen in all of them taken together. The principal sectarian leaders, assailed by such writers as Edwards and Baxter, were frequently university graduates and clergymen who had betrayed their cloth and their class. All voiced, in whatever terms, the conviction, so dynamic in its effect, that God had chosen not the great, the wealthy, and the learned to be heirs of his kingdom but common men, rich in faith. Christ had blessed the poor and promised that the kingdom should be theirs, and Daniel and John had prophesied that the kingdom was at hand.

Hanserd Knollys, graduate of Cambridge, ordained in 1629, had put these notions into print in 1641, at about the time of his return from New England, in *A Glimpse of Sions Glory.*[25] The mischief that, according to Edwards, he did in the Earl of Manchester's army is to be seen in his *Christ Exalted: A Lost Sinner Sought, and saved by Christ: Gods people are an Holy people* (February 18, 1646). Another Cambridge man, ordained in 1630, who turned Baptist, left his living, and joined the army was Henry Denne, author of *The Man of Sin Discovered: Whom the Lord shall destroy with the brightnesse of his Coming*, issued in 1645 along with an attack on Stephen Marshall and Daniel Featley, called *Antichrist Unmasked*. Edwards tells us that

Denne's usual themes were that believers in Christ were surely saved, that Christ died for all men, for Turks and pagans as well as Christians, for Judas as well as Peter, and that no one should be required to pay tithes.[26] Still another army preacher with a Cambridge education, Master of Arts of Emmanuel College in 1625, but apparently not ordained, was Francis Cornwell, who published *The Vindication of the Royall Commission of King Jesus* in 1644 with a preface to parliament in which he declared that it was 'not the voyce of the Assembly [of divines], but Christ only in the Assemblyes, we have covenanted to listen to.' Edwards says that copies of this tract were handed to members of parliament at the door of the house.[27] A notorious example of the kind of man lacking academic education who found opportunity in the army to wage war in the pulpit as well as in arms was Paul Hobson, a tailor and a Baptist, who rose to be major in the regiment commanded by Robert Lilburne.[28] The nature of his preaching can be seen in *Practical Divinity: Or a Helpe Through the blessing of God to lead men more to look within themselves, and to unite experienced Christians in the bond and fellowship of the Spirit* (1646) and in *A Garden Inclosed, and Wisdom Justified only of her Children . . . discovering the Glory, Beauty and Perfection of the Love of God to Saints that are so comprehended, and in such a glorious inclosure* (1647).[29]

Hugh Peters, the most famous of all the army preachers, was the perfect indispensable counterpart to Saltmarsh, Dell, and the swarm of Baptists. He sprang from the same origins, subject to the same influences, as other members of the brotherhood of preachers. After he had taken his degree as Master of Arts at Trinity College, Cambridge, in 1622, he was struck, he tells us, with a sense of his sinful estate upon hearing a sermon at St. Paul's. He was then presently 'quieted' by Thomas Hooker, further enlightened by Sibbes, Gouge, and Davenport, and set up in a lectureship at £30 a year by a convert, who is described as 'a Chandler, and died a good man, and Member of Parliament.'[30] About 1629 Peters fled to Holland, and emigrating thence to New England in 1635, he became pastor to the congregation at Salem in succession to Roger Williams. He was soon intimate with the Winthrops, father and son, to whom he was related by marriage. He witnessed the examination and trial of Mrs. Hutchinson. An active preacher, approved by his congregation, he also busied himself in public affairs and was sent back to England in 1641 as a colony agent. In 1642 he went as chaplain with Lord Forbes's expedition to Ireland. In 1643 he supplied a prefatory epistle for a defense of New England congregationalism by Richard Mather, *Church-Government and Church-Covenant Discussed*. In the same year parliament sent him to Holland to raise money on its behalf and upon his return voted him £100 in cash and a like sum in books, the books to be supplied out of Archbishop Laud's library.[31]

In the campaign of 1644 Peters served as chaplain in the army and as an emissary from the commanders to parliament. He joined the New Model in 1645 and was probably present at Naseby. He and Edward Bowles went as chaplains under Fairfax on the expedition that immediately followed for the recovery of the west. Both preachers held forth to the troops the day before the storming of Bridgwater (July 20–22) and Peters is said to have been up and exhorting the men in the early morning, just before the assault.[32] He was sent up to London with the news of that victory and was rewarded by parliament with £100.[33] He performed the same service after the taking in rapid succession of Winchester and of Basing House. After Winchester, Cromwell wrote to Speaker Lenthall that Peters would present considerations from the army 'not so fit to be committed to writing.'[34] The Commons Journal now referred to him as Cromwell's secretary. Along with the news of victory the house that day heard him tell also of the army's need for men and money and of the people of Winchester's need for godly preachers. Peters' reward on this occasion was £50. His report after Basing carried another plea for consideration of the soldiers' interest. In January, he was out with the army again, making himself especially useful in persuading the Cornishmen to lay down their arms. In January he reported to parliament the capture of Dartmouth and on March 21 the end of all resistance in the west. Parliament on this occasion invited him to preach along with Joseph Caryl at a special thanksgiving service at Christ Church on April 2 before both houses, the assembly of divines, the lord mayor, aldermen, and common council. After the sermon, published with the title *Gods Doings, and Mans Duty*, it voted him the usual thanks and request to print and presently passed an ordinance providing him with an estate of £200 a year out of the lands of the Earl of Worcester.

Baillie early recognized and deplored the 'malapert rashness' [35] which, along with his interest in affairs and his gifts of utterance and of showmanship, made Peters invaluable to the army commanders, especially Cromwell, for representing their interests to parliament and to the public at large. Thus he became the chief exponent and defender of their policies and acts in both church and state and one of the main butts of the hostility they aroused in whatever quarter. 'This man is an Ubiquitary,' Edwards wrote in February, 1646, 'here and there, in this countrey, and that countrey, in the Army, and at *London.*' 'Solicitor Generall for the Sectaries,' he calls him, '*Vicar Generall and Metropolitane of the Independents both in New and Old England,*' 'the new Arch-Bishop of *Canterbury.*' [36] When Peters visited Lilburne in the Tower in 1649 in a vain effort to placate that champion of liberty and master of the art of political publicity, he was told, 'Mr *Peter,* . . . you know that I know you to be one of the setting-dogs, or stalking horses of the great men of the Army.' He was, Lilburne said, one of their principal guides and spokesmen; he lay in their bosoms, knew their secrets, and was used by them 'to trumpet abroad their Principles and Tenents.' [37] The final result of all these stirrings and appearances on behalf of the new masters of power was that, of all the preachers who had spoken and written against the king, even including John Goodwin, Peters was the only one who was made to pay the supreme penalty at the Restoration.

'I confess I did what I did strenuously,' he wrote at the end. 'By my Zeal (it seems) I have exposed my self to all manner of reproach.' [38] Naturally the reproach for the zeal he so strenuously embodied produced a rich crop of legend, not without some color of truth, but much of it apocryphal, and little of it free of satirical intent. He was pictured as Cromwell's tool and adviser, as preacher, clown, busybody, conspirator, and traitor. Yet notwithstanding his notoriety none of his army sermons was ever authentically published, and he issued no edifying tracts based upon sermons. The principal contemporary account of the manner and content of his preaching in these years is that found in Edwards' *Gangraena.* His publications up to this time had consisted chiefly of news reports of the army's successes with commendation of its commanders. The only sermon which Peters himself sent to the printer was apparently the thanksgiving sermon of April 2, 1646, already referred to, and that performance was itself related to the report, published shortly before as *Master Peters Messuage from Sir Thomas Fairfax*, of the victory it commemorated. It also foreshadowed the two tracts which Peters issued later on behalf of the army and its commanders, namely, *Mr. Peters Last Report of the English Wars* (1646) and *A word for the Armie. And two words to the Kingdome* (1647).

Peters did not address himself in *Gods Doings, and Mans Duty* directly to the task of expounding free justification, but we are not to conclude that that doctrine meant little to him. "We know no more,' he said later, 'than we Practise, yet we shall never practise without Knowledge.' [39] Knowledge as he conceived it and as he and the army preachers had set it forth to the New Model had been confirmed by practical results, the force of which there was no mistaking. The business was not now to find religious motives for effective military action. The problem was to compose the differences, religious and other, which the army's success had exacerbated and complicated. The problem for which the army leaders, especially Cromwell, felt a peculiar responsibility was to make peace, and Peters' task for the moment was to present their view of that problem to parliament and the public. He did not, therefore, expatiate on Christ's coming to his faithful ones, emancipating them from the old law, renewing their spirits, clearing their minds and senses, uniting them in obedience to himself within themselves and in the love of him present in one another. That could be left to Saltmarsh and the Baptists. Peters bluntly reminded his hearers of what the army had accomplished, drawing the obvious deduction that the principles that had worked so well in the war might work to everyone's advantage if applied to the problem of the church.

He begins by enlarging in the way his audience would naturally expect on Psalms 31:23, 'Love the Lord all ye his Saints: for the Lord preserveth the faithful, and plenteously rewardeth the proud doer.' He makes the triumphant application that all the endeavors of the enemy have come to nothing: 'the Parliament is not destroyed, the City stands, the Gospel is preached. . . . Oh, my Lords, you are not at *Oxford,* led up and down as *Sampson,* to be looked at by children.' Next he recites the 'speciall Providences' which have befallen since the Bishops' Wars by means of the army and its commanders.

You have the Army you wished for, and the Successes you desired. Oh the blessed change we see, that can travell now from *Edenburgh,* to the lands end in *Cornwal*, who not long since were blockt up at our doors! To see the highwayes occupied again; to heare the Carter whistling to his toiling team; to see the weekly Carrier attend his constant mart; to see the hils rejoycing, the vallies laughing! [40]

But finally he comes to his main point. In the army men had found a way to exercise their gifts, sink their differences, unite their efforts in the face of imperative need. Were the issues that divided the church so important as to set parliament against the men who had procured the liberty and safety of the kingdom? 'You are still buzz'd in the ear with a desperate encrease of Errour,' but there would be fewer differences, errors, sects, if they did not think them so many. The only enemy is Antichrist, the only error pride, the only remedy love. He concludes by urging four significant practical steps for the promotion of peace: encourage preaching, relieve the poor, reform the laws, regulate the press. But preaching, not discipline or polemics, still comes first. 'If I know anything, what you have gotten by the sword, must be maintained by the word, I say the word, by which English Christians are made.' [41]

The same points appear in *Mr. Peters Last Report of the English Wars*, written after the fall of Worcester and Oxford—not in fact a report at all but a succinct statement of the army's answer to the practical problem of the church. 'Let the present Church-government,' meaning the presbyterian system laid down by parliament on the recommendation of the assembly, 'goe on,' but let it 'walke softly and tenderly.' Let no one speak against either presbyterianism or independency without knowing what he is talking about. 'Let us remember *England*, as it was never conquered but by faction, so it can never be ruled but by love; the same Last will not fit an *English* and a *Scotish* foote.' He concludes, therefore, with the demand the Puritan brotherhood had made when the Long Parliament first assembled. '*England* is devout,' he says, 'and Religion of one kind or another carries most prevalency, and . . . therefore that which hath been our wound must be our cure (preaching and Preachers I meane).' [42] Compromise and moderation were his answer to the problem of the church, that and a sufficiency of itinerant ministers to preach the gospel in every county. In effect, this would have meant something like a resumption of the old unacknowledged expedient tolerance of the days before Charles and Laud.

Busybody though he was, no mystic or dialectician, certainly no mystagogue or heresiarch, possibly a bit of a buffoon in the pulpit,

Peters nevertheless, as the editors of his autobiography said of him, 'had a Root of Grace' in him or, changing the figure, 'the Fountain was clear from which ran so savoury a stream.' That root of grace, the bottom of sheer godliness in the man, without which he could not have gained and held Cromwell's confidence, appears unmistakably in the little posthumous work called *A Dying Fathers Last Legacy to an Onely Child: Or, Mr. Hugh Peters Advice to his Daughter* (1660). As Baxter had done, but more simply, more directly, not with Baxter's superabundant rhetoric but in the less elaborate style of John Dod, Peters also with death at hand undertook to describe the regeneration of the saints through union with Christ, their foreordained triumph over death, and their admission to glory. Nothing could have been more in the true vein of traditional piety in the Puritan manner. The child is told above all things to be 'perfect in *Romans* 8,' which was the starting point for so many sermons and treatises. From one point of view, no conception of man's destiny could offer less hope to the generality of men, but to resilient saints like Hugh Peters, even while waiting to be hanged, drawn, and quartered, nothing could be more inspiriting. In that eighth chapter, the child is to mind especially the first verse—'there is therefore now no condemnation to them which are in Christ Jesus'—and the twenty-eighth—'we know that all things work together for good to them that love God.' 'The Preaching of these Truths,' he says, 'have been my greatest Advantage, and of most benefit to Others.' For Peters, though in New England he had taken sides against Mrs. Hutchinson, in Cromwell's army made the easy *démarche* from orthodoxy to the notion Baxter found so alarming that Christ comes to his chosen ones without limiting conditions and that his chosen ones are not the few but the many, the poor, and the simple. Christ sends to fetch the fatherless child from the ditch and, leading him step by step from humiliation to glory, seats him at the heavenly table.

The child for whom the book is written is also instructed, with many homely lightsome similitudes and pithy proverbial sayings, in the traditional discipline and code of behavior that went with the doctrine of effectual calling. She is to gather 'a Little *English* Library' of approved authors; the authors recommended are the chief worthies of Puritan edification—Dod, Sibbes, Preston, Gouge, Thomas Hooker,

Thomas Goodwin, Baxter himself, and others. She is to 'keep a Book
. . . in which, every Night before you sleep, you set down on the one
side, the Lords gracious Providence and Dealings with you; and your
dealings with him on the other side.' She is to bear in mind that affliction keeps us waking, 'as the Thorn to the singing Bird,' that conscience calls us up to labor, 'as the Day the Lark, and the Lark the
Husbandman.' Being a woman, she is to keep at home and not to
be like a squirrel, 'leaping from Tree to Tree, and Bough to Bough.'
She is to realize that marriage 'hath many Concernments in it, where
Goodness and Suitableness are the primary ingredients,' and that the
conjugal yoke 'must still be lin'd with more Love to make the draught
easie.' As 'the little Needle will draw a long tail of Thread after it,'
so 'little sins may be followed with great sorrows,' but 'a very very
little Grace (if true) is saving: a little Growth (if right) is comfort-
ing,' and 'a little little grain' of faith, 'like Mustard-seed will do Wonders.' But perhaps nothing, really, illustrates better the temper which
enabled such sanguine, forth-putting, executive spirits to turn the doctrines and the piety of Paul, not without overtones of Ecclesiastes and
the stoics, to their own uses than Peters' disquisition on the vanity of
earthly things while awaiting the executioner.

Many dying men speak much about the Vanity of the World: But truly,
as I would not die in a pet, so I would not quarrel with, or leave the World,
because I could be no greater in it, but because I could not do, nor be better
in it, and that God is pleased I should leave it for a better: I wish I had never
been vain in a vain World, but I appeal to, and plead with, Christ for my
peace. *So use the World, as if you used it not:* for the World hath a principle
of decay in all the glory of it: Dote not on it, my poor Child.[43]

iii. CROMWELL AND FREE JUSTIFICATION

But the greatest witness to the doctrine of free grace was Cromwell himself, as authentic a Puritan saint as ever confounded the Puritan brotherhood with the consequences of their own teachings. Following the
formula set forth in a hundred pulpits, he was able by 1638 to declare,
'my soul is with the congregation of the first-born, my body rests in
hope, and if here I may honour my God either by doing or by suffering, I shall be most glad.' He could say this while confessing that he

formerly loved darkness and hated light. 'I hated godliness, yet God had mercy on me.' [44] Many men after such an experience took to preaching. But Cromwell was an East Anglian squire, one of an extensive clan of kinsmen, friends, and neighbors, and such men became, rather, the patrons of preachers and the secular leaders of the Puritan movement. He continued a twice-born soul, holding himself accountable for the gifts that fell to him, but his spirit found expression and relief in vehement public activity, in his neighborhood, in parliament, and finally in war and the organization of victory. He had heard Marshall, Calamy, and others preach that the Lord had laid his command upon parliament and had covenanted to acknowledge obedience with victory. Cromwell had taken to heart the argument that the law written by God in the breast must be heeded even at the cost of resisting the king. These principles were enough, and having no taste for speculation or debate, he went off in the summer of 1642 to raise a troop of horse, which, as we have seen, formed itself also into a 'gathered' church.

By the time Presbyterians and Independents had locked horns in the assembly, Cromwell was well on his way to determining, by the same pragmatical test to which the preachers themselves were appealing, what elements in their teachings were valid and useful in the situation immediately at hand. Protracted civil war, with armies of the size and character presently required, was something the Puritan brotherhood had not anticipated and was not prepared to cope with. But the habit men had learned of forming independent spontaneous groups for the purpose of helping themselves to the preaching of the Word was as though designed to meet the situation resulting from the dragging out of the armed conflict. Cromwell's own position on the question of the church seems to have approximated most closely that of the seekers who found themselves unable to accept in full the claims of any group to be the true church visible. But this position, to one who enjoyed the conviction of grace, was entirely compatible with the principle of the 'gathered' church, by accepting which Cromwell was able to enlist the kind of men he needed to forge an effective instrument of war. That he knew very well, as Baxter inferred,[45] what he was about, his own words testify. 'You must get men of a spirit,' he told John Hampden after Edgehill, 'or else I am sure you will be beaten still . . . I raised such men as had the fear of God before them, and made some conscience of what they did.' [46] How completely he was himself committed to the faith he looked for in the men who fought under him appears in his letters after victory and in the memorable letter to his daughter at the end of October, 1646.[47] No clearer expression of the type of spiritual experience which gave the Puritan movement its essential meaning and vitality is to be found in Puritan confessional literature from Richard Rogers to Baxter, Bunyan, and beyond.

In Cromwell, however, as in other converts to the doctrine of grace, the dynamics of Puritan faith outran the restraints of Puritan discipline. The man who, in September, 1644, when things looked black, wrote, 'the Lord is our strength, and in Him is all our hope. Pray for us'; or who, in April, 1645, while the outcome still hung in the balance, wrote, 'God is not enough owned. We look too much to men and visible helps'; or who declared after Naseby, 'Sir, this is none other but the hand of God; and to him alone belongs the glory,' [48] had the root of true godliness in him, as the most orthodox would have had to admit. But he showed what strange alarming fruit that stock could produce. His first concern, always, was to get the business of the Lord, as faith gave him to understand it, done rather than defined or thought out to its remote implications and consequences. Yet his need to act and to defend what he had done or proposed to do compelled him as he went on to take more and more extreme positions, which he arrived at pragmatically but none the less consistently with the logic and historic drive of the whole Puritan movement. Thus he became the exponent in action of those startling conclusions to Puritan doctrine foreshadowed in Milton's and Lord Brooke's tracts against the bishops and explicitly set forth in the pamphlets of Williams, Robinson, Walwyn, Overton and others. He adduced the proof and emphasis of military success to the support of the most revolutionary contentions of these writers—the equality of men under God, the immanence of the Holy Spirit in the individual and its sufficiency without other mediation than scripture and the light within, the liberty of conscience, the moral imperative involved in gifts and opportunities, the instant unfailing supervention of providence in human affairs. These principles, with their obvious corollaries as to church and state, pointed especially to the attenuation of the ministerial function in religious life and of the state's responsibility for the integrity of the church. One would not dare to say that Cromwell had thought all these principles out to their remotest consequences before undertaking to raise a troop of horse (if indeed he ever did), or that he kept strictly to them when he took responsibility for restoring order in church and state into his own hands, but the logic of events drove him to acknowledge and act upon them until victory was accomplished.

His acknowledgments are recorded in some of the most famous statements of his letters and speeches. 'I had rather have a plain russet-coated captain,' he wrote to the Suffolk committee in August 1643, 'that knows what he fights for, and loves what he knows, than that which you call a gentleman and is nothing else. I honour a gentleman that is so indeed.' [49] 'Ay, but the man is an Anabaptist,' he wrote to Crawford in March, 1644, 'Admit he be, shall that render him incapable to serve the public? . . . Take heed of being sharp, or too easily sharpened by others, against those to whom you can object little but that they square not with you in every opinion concerning matters of religion.' [50] 'He that ventures his life for the liberty of his country,' he wrote to the house of commons in June, 1645, after Naseby, 'I wish he trust God for the liberty of his conscience, and you for the liberty he fights for,' and again 'when I saw the enemy draw up and march in gallant order toward us, and we a company of poor ignorant men . . . I could not (riding alone about my business) but smile out to God in praises, in assurance of victory, because God would, by things that are not, bring to naught things that are.' [51] And in the well-known dispatch to parliament after the taking of Bristol in September, he put into a single paragraph every essential point of the argument for religious liberty under the protection of the state. Parliament's soldiers rejoice 'that they are instruments to God's glory and their country's good,' but the war has been won by all who have wrestled with God for this blessing. 'Presbyterians, Independents, all had here the same spirit of faith and prayer . . . they agree here, know no names of difference: pity it is it should be otherwise anywhere. All that believe, have the real unity, which is most glorious, because inward and spiritual, in the Body, and to the Head.' Every Christian, he goes on to say, for the sake of peace, will do as much for outward uniformity in religion as conscience will admit, yet 'from brethren, in things of the mind we look for no compulsion, but that of light and reason. In other things, God hath put the sword into Parliament's hands, for the terror of evil-doers, and the praise of them that do well.' [52]

In December, 1644, when the house of commons suddenly approved the self-denying ordinance as first proposed, Baillie wrote 'as yet it seems a dream, and the bottom of it is not understood.' [53] After Naseby at least part of the meaning was clear. It was Cromwell's will, Baillie then wrote, 'to desyre the House not to discourage these who had ventured their life for them, and to come out expressly with their much-desyred libertie of conscience.' [54] Cromwell, as Baxter observed, had brought all the sectaries in the army together on the common principle that the state had nothing to do with determining the faith of its subjects, 'by constraint or restraint,' and he had won over those whom Baxter calls the 'sober party' by professing to seek only 'the Universal Interest of the Godly, without any distinction or partiality at all.' [55]

Thus before the Presbyterians could settle their differences with the Independents in the assembly, with dissidents of all sorts outside, or with the Erastians in parliament, the army struck up a *modus vivendi* in religious matters which enabled it to put an end to the war which had borne down upon all parties alike. But that was all. The victory of the New Model, far from solving the problem how to reconstitute English society, complicated every old issue and created new ones. The sword had not in fact been put into parliament's hands, whether for the praise of those who did well or for the terror of those who did evil. It remained where Cromwell was certain God had put it, in the army's own hands, and an army dominated by men who believed in free justification through the indwelling Christ was not likely to surrender its sword lightly to a parliament intolerant of such notions. Unprecedented and anomalous as such a development might seem, the army was in the way of becoming an organ for the discussion and expression of fundamental principles of state and for consequent action, and neither parliament nor assembly had power to disregard or resist its decisions.

VII

The Dissidence of Dissent

1645-1647

FROM its victory at Naseby on June 14, 1645, the New Model army went on to suppress all remaining resistance to the new order of things whatever that might be or by whomsoever determined. At the end of April, Charles gave up the struggle and took refuge with the Scottish forces at Newcastle. Yet the approach of victory and the conclusion of war merely meant that the unresolved issues of the Puritan Revolution grew more pressing and dissension among the victors more acute and ominous. The army under Cromwell's leadership had found a way to obviate differences and achieve unity of purpose in effective action. The assembly on the contrary grew more divided than ever, and its disagreements became more and more sharply reflected in parliament and the public. Parliament's order of September 13, 1644, directing the assembly to provide accommodation for tender consciences, was disregarded. For convinced and zealous Presbyterians to compromise with Independency while the outcome of the war was still in doubt was to invite defeat, and to draw back after victory was to give up within sight of the promised land. For the Independents to submit while the army was advancing from one success to another was humanly impossible. Hence, with both parties taking more and more extreme positions, all attempts at accommodation and compromise on questions relating to religion and the church came to nothing. In December Parliament rejected the pleas of the Independents; [1] in January, 1645, it approved the Directory of Worship proposed by the assembly; and in the months that followed it authorized the successive parts of the presbyterian system of government and discipline.

To give practical effect to these decisions was another matter. In April the assembly ordered Thomas Goodwin and his faction to submit definite alternative proposals. Realizing, however, that anything that they put forward would be summarily voted down, the 'dissenting brethren' virtually withdrew from the assembly. In September, when parliament published Cromwell's letter on the fall of Bristol, omitting the plea for toleration, they at once put the full text into print.[2] In October, instead of the report demanded by the assembly, they submitted a remonstrance, shortly published, in which they refused to commit themselves to any comprehensive scheme of church government and argued for still wider congregational autonomy than before.[3] In March, 1646, the Presbyterian faction induced parliament to decree the establishment of presbyterian government throughout the realm. In June, just as the army was bringing its work in the field to a conclusion, the house of commons ordered that presbyteries be put into actual operation in London; and in September, with their plans still unrealized, the Presbyterians introduced in parliament a fearsome ordinance for the ruthless suppression of heresy and blasphemy, which was not, however, finally adopted until May, 1648, when any possibility of enforcement was out of the question.

The failure of the Presbyterians was not due simply to their inability to anticipate the Toleration Act of 1689. So far as success in battle was believed to indicate divine approval, parliament could be said to have made good its claim to hold rulers responsible under law. But representative government as it was to develop after 1689 did not come into being and acceptance with the army's triumph over the king in 1645. That success merely brought an already anomalous situation to still greater constitutional confusion. With the power of the crown in abeyance, who should say where the authority of parliament stopped? Who should call the men now sitting as a parliament to account even as they had called the king? Who was to determine the rights and obligations of individuals and institutions, whether of utterance or action, within the state? The traditional procedures for parliamentary election were in suspension. The modern apparatus of party organization was not in being. The press as an instrument for the direction and expression of popular judgment on public issues was still in large measure unfamiliar, if not suspect, though in fact irrepressible and increasingly active. In the general confusion, only one thing seemed certain. The church surely had authority to instruct and admonish all men freely and without exception in their duties as men and Christians.

To the Puritan preachers and their followers, the final success of the revolutionary cause in the war meant that the liberty which was God's peculiar gift to his people was brought at last within the bounds of possible realization. The only remaining problem was the practical one of making liberty, above all the liberty of the church, which was to say of the pulpit and the preaching order, secure and operable within the body politic. The proponents of the Directory of Worship and the system of government and discipline which accompanied it did not, however, assume that the liberated church would be required to tolerate error or compromise with the forces of disruption. They believed, on the contrary, that liberty could be maintained in the community only through the church, reformed but also restored to its position as the single comprehensive organ of spiritual life on earth. The authority of the church, derived from God and vested in his people, was to be exercised in the people's behalf by their chosen presbyters. Ministers, specially called and ordained, were to preach the Word, and since the Word was free, they must be free to instruct and admonish whomsoever they judged to be in need of their ministrations, not excepting the rulers of the state. Moreover, doctrine without practice, admonition without discipline, authority to instruct without power to exact obedience was, as Milton said before he realized the import of such ideas, 'but shooting at Rovers.' [4] And rulers who failed to heed the Word might expect to forfeit the obedience of their subjects.

Up to a point there was, of course, little in all this which Puritans in general, sectaries and Independents as well as Presbyterians, would have wholly rejected at least in principle. All agreed that the true church was a communion of souls having authority to call whom they would in some fashion to minister to them, and all conceived the church's function to be to dispense the Word, having authority to require obedience. So long as prelatical government held, the most doctrinaire Presbyterians had acted in some degree independently of constituted authority. When prelacy came to an end, every Puritan group, whether its members still kept within the traditional parish boundaries or gathered from hither and yon about a preacher of their choice, expected to govern its affairs through its own leaders by whatever name they might be called. Thus in a sense every group, whatever abstract or ideal notion of the church its members might subscribe to, found itself, practically speaking, to be both presbyterian and independent, and precisely where any given group or individual might stand in theory or practice as between the two extremes had up to now been difficult to tell. Now, however, the triumph of the army confirmed the break-up of ecclesiastical order so that every resulting particle or fragment of the church as a whole, whether parish congregation or gathered flock, was left actually independent of every other and a law to itself.

Nothing like this had happened in Scotland. Nothing like it had been in the minds of English reformers at the inception of the Puritan movement or even of most Puritans at the convening of parliament in 1640. At that time most of them had assumed, as Milton had done, but without much knowledge or reflection, that the logical and necessary alternative to prelatism would be some form of nationwide church government based upon presbyterian principles. Many had insisted that the adoption of such a system was a necessary condition for victory over the king. And now that victory had been won, the solid phalanx of divines who controlled the assembly still insisted that the need for such a system was more imperative than ever. Civil rulers, they held, were appointed by God so to govern his temporal kingdom that the ministers of his spiritual realm might care for the souls of all his subjects without exception. The necessary condition for the exercise of their function by the church's ministers was spiritual independence of the secular power whose material support was nevertheless expected and required. Pressed to the extreme, this was taken to mean that the church at large, acting through its presbyteries, should be free to deny communion to any who would not submit to its authority, and the magistrate must sustain the church in its judgments.

But to implement spiritual liberty in the community after any such fashion would have been to allow the ministerial caste the privilege of reaching into every conscience, every household, every shop and counting room. Neither gathered congregation nor parish church, neither pulpit nor press, neither parliament nor army, could have counted itself free from surveillance and censure. The effect of the proposals of the Presbyterian faction, as their full implications became apparent, was to inflame dissension and confusion even beyond anything known so far. So far not every Puritan who looked for some sort of presbyterian settlement had been utterly uncompromising in his attitude toward Independency. Not every Independent had up to now been unwilling to stop short of unlimited congregational liberty. But from this time on Independents were pushed farther into nonconformity and dissent. Sectaries were fired to greater activity. Men of moderate temper and humane outlook grew critical, skeptical, and contemptuous of the pretensions of clerics and preachers of all persuasions. Parliament itself, though dominated more and more by the faction hostile to the army, still held back from giving Presbyterian extremists all they asked for. It approved the Directory but as to excommunication, control of which made all the difference between what Baillie described as a true Scottish and a lame Erastian presbytery, it reserved final judgment to itself. The fact was, of course, that nothing either parliament or assembly decided about anything could now be put into effect contrary to the will of the army.

Thus the stage of discussion which attended the army's triumph over the king was the prelude not to peace in the church and the nation but to further strife among the victors. Danger of defeat had so far kept the inner tensions of the Puritan movement from disrupting the movement itself. Now the incompatible aspirations which Puritan preachers had labored so hard to evoke were given free play beyond the preachers' power to control. The Presbyterians, Scots as well as English, continued to uphold their cause before parliament from the pulpit, and their sermons and treatises circulated in print. Pamphleteers such as Thomas Edwards at the same time assailed all opponents of Presbyterian plans with hitherto unheard of virulence. The opposition, however, was nothing if not varied. In the assembly Thomas Coleman, himself a learned divine, betrayed his cloth by maintaining the church's dependence on the state, and Selden turned the shafts of his wit and the weight of his learning against clerical pretension. Outside, Prynne girded at everybody, Presbyterians as well as Independents, who resisted the claims of parliament to absolute supremacy in all things. Milton, having delivered a final blast against the ministerial critics of his divorce tract, gave up pamphleteering for the present but set himself to fortifying his conception of liberty, virtue, and truth from the scriptures and the history of his country. Thomas Goodwin and the assembly Independents lay low and awaited events but made good use of their turn, when it came, in the pulpit at St. Margaret's. John Goodwin, though still vicar of St. Stephen's, instituted his 'Coleman-street Conclave,' as Vicars dubbed it, to serve as a kind of center and seminary, counterassembly or insurgent synod, for dissenters in general. Baptists of all sorts flourished and multiplied outside the army as well as within. John Lilburne, who was in some fashion one of them, came back from the war full of the conviction of grace and of zeal for his former role of martyr, folk hero, and champion of the rights of Englishmen. William Walwyn set about organizing Lilburne's sympathizers into something like a concerted movement for legal, economic, and social reform, and Richard Overton loosed his reckless rationalizing pen against all oppressors in church or state, assembly or parliament.

i. THE PRESBYTERIANS, SCOTS AND ENGLISH: EDWARDS' *Gangraena*

In attempting to recount the disintegration of the Puritan movement from January, 1645, to the breach between parliament and the army in the spring of 1647, we had best begin for the sake of clarity with the Scots. They had come to Westminster with the single purpose of gaining English adherence to such a disposition of authority in church and state as would assure the security of their people embodied in the kirk from oppression by the crown and the bishops either at home or from over the border, and this purpose they never lost sight of. In the assembly and its committees, in the pulpit when occasion offered, and in the press with exhaustless erudition and solemn perseverance, they set forth that conception of the two kingdoms, spiritual and temporal, each with its distinct though complementary right and function, which had been the basic principle of the Scottish Reformation. Their most learned and voluminous expositors were Rutherford and Gillespie, their most effective polemicist was Baillie, but their clearest head and most forceful speaker was Henderson. In a remarkable sermon before the house of lords on the eve of Naseby (May 28, 1645) he explained what to the Scottish mind Christ meant when he told Pilate that his kingdom was not of this world. Christ's kingdom, Henderson declared, may be not *of* this world, but it is certainly *in* it. The magistrate must not preach

or administer the sacraments or exercise discipline, but he must see
that all these things are accomplished. The minister must not sit in
judgment, but he must teach and exhort that justice be done. The
two should be like the will and the understanding, the temporal sword
commanding the spiritual, the spiritual exhorting the temporal, to do
its work, but neither should usurp the function entrusted by God to the
other. Disruption and tyranny must follow if either power failed in its
duty or transgressed its proper sphere.

But what was to be thought of a people who, having escaped from
prelatical oppression, ran into 'such a *Chaos* of Anarchy, Libertinisme,
and popular confusion, as now covereth the face of this Kingdom?' [5]
The frustration of Scottish aspirations, the bewilderment of the Scottish mind at the ways of the English and, as things turned out, of the Al-
mighty, continued to find liveliest expression in Baillie. When parliament in January, 1645, had voted approval of the new Directory of
Worship, he went back to Edinburgh and told the general assembly
what great things the Lord had done for Scotland. That an English
assembly and an English parliament should abolish the service book
and adopt a Scots presbytery, 'such stories,' he said, 'latelie told, would
have been counted fancies, dreams, meer impossibilities.' They were
dreams indeed. On his return to London in April, he wrote, 'all the
ports of hell are opened upon us.' [6] In the house of commons the faction led by Selden, glorying in his Jewish learning, was holding up the
establishment of presbyteries and synods. In the army, new-modeled,
Independents and sectaries were in command. There was nothing now
for the Scots to rely upon save their own army, which must be strengthened and, of course, win battles, and to this end there must be a minister in every regiment and a half dozen of 'the most gracious, wyse,
and couragious' over the whole army, 'for . . . wherever that army
is, Scotland, and the Protestant party of this isle, must be saved or
lost.' But weeks passed, victories came not to the Scots army but to
the English while Montrose and the plague descended upon Scotland.
That the Lord should thus cast the enemy down in England and set
him up in Scotland, 'it is one of the deeps of divine wisdome, which
we adore'—but obviously found hard to bear.[7] After the fall of Glasgow to Montrose (1645) Baillie had to wait weeks before hearing

what had happened to his family and friends.[8] Meanwhile on July 30 in a sermon before the house of lords, called *Errours and Induration,* he grappled with the question why God should inspire the English to overthrow prelacy and then allow them to fly off into anarchy. The indefatigable man was at the same time compiling *A Dissuasive from the Errours of the Time* (1645), to be followed by *An Historicall Vindication of the Government of the Church of Scotland* (1646), and *Anabaptism, the True Fountaine of Independency, Brownisme, Antinomy, Familisme, and the most of the other Errours, which for the time doe trouble the Church of England* (1647). In March, 1646, just before Hugh Peters' triumphant sermon at Christ Church, he wrote home, despondently, that the English now seemed inclined 'to have no shadow of a King; to have libertie for all religions; to have bot a lame Erastian Presbyterie; to be so injurious to us, as to chase us home with the sword.'[9]

By 1646, however, the brotherhood of preachers—those who held fast to what they believed was the true purpose of the Puritan move-ment, namely to establish Christian liberty by restoring unity and order in the church—found themselves in an impasse and a dilemma which made their plight at least as difficult as that of the Scots. The frustration of all their efforts to restrain heresy and dissent threw some of them into a condition of panic which found expression in Edwards' *Gangraena.* That frenzied polemic, however, gives a distorted im-pression of the state of mind of the brotherhood as a whole. Their very real discomfiture of spirit is better seen in the sermons they continued to address by invitation from time to time to parliament and other pub-lic bodies. In the pulpit we see these earnest well-meaning men at their best, entrapped in an unforeseen situation largely of their own creating, victims of their own success in their own calling. They still clung to the belief that God was determined, as Marshall told the lords in March, 1645, to bring out a new edition of his church and that the reformation of England was, as Palmer told the commons in Septem-ber, 1646, the expectation of the world.[10] But these men were not statesmen or philosophers but preachers, and when called to transpose the exhortations and visions of the pulpit into laws and institutions, they were still preachers and put preaching first. The preaching of the

Word, Marshall had long since told parliament, was the chariot on which salvation comes riding into the hearts of men.[11] Now once more he declared:

This Church of God is then built, when the doctrine of *Jesus Christ* is made known, the new and living way to life by him is opened; when Ministers and Ordinances are given, the elect called in, Churches gathered, and established, the worship and government of Christ set up, for the perfecting of the Saints, for the work of the Ministery, for the edifying of the body of Christ, till all the Saints come in the unity of the Faith, and of the knowledge of the Son of God unto a perfect man, unto the measure of the stature of the fulnesse of Christ: when the Curtains of the Church are thus enlarged, and the Tents of it made firm; when God doth thus prosper and blesse the Church of Christ, then doth hee build up Zion.[12]

But the rich convolutions of pulpit rhetoric always came back to the same point. In October, 1646, Marshall preached to the lords on the text, 'Out of the mouth of Babes and Sucklings hast thou ordained strength.' He would, no doubt, if pressed, have held that the strength ordained by the Lord had to be funneled through the pulpit of a church governed by presbyters. But mounted in his own pulpit, he declared the babes and sucklings to be all those weak things in the world who are made invincible by the sword of the spirit coming forth of their mouths.[13]

Marshall had a gift for soaring beyond difficulties in a dazzle of words, but the fact was that the sword of the spirit awakened by the pulpit was issuing from many mouths in many places and uttering many notions in the name of truth which could not all be true. Thomas Goodwin pointed out what no one would have denied that the Lord had raised up such a multitude of saints in England, faithful, called, and chosen, as the world had never seen.[14] The trouble was that the greater the multitude of saints the more surely the Puritan Zion seemed to fall apart in endless confusion. 'Happie were it for the Church,' said Thomas Case, 'if the oppositions and Set-backs of her Deliverance were managed onely by her *Enemies*.' [15] 'It is a sad thing to me,' said Henry Wilkinson, 'to think that they which look on one another as Saints, should behave themselves each to other as the Jewes had wont to doe toward Heathens.' [16] Infidels and apostates, said Richard Vines, are visible to the eye, but the heretic who 'holds some *planks of truth when the ship is broken,* is more hardly to bee knowne.' [17] 'If we had sworne,' said John Lightfoot, 'to have promoted and advanced Errour, Heresie, and Schisme, could these have growne and come forward more, then now they have done, though we swore against them?' [18]

What sober gracious heart would not bleed, Matthew Newcomen demanded, 'to see how many under pretence of pursuing *truth* and *liberty,* have clean *forgot* that there is any such thing . . . as unity: Everything that *to them is new,* is in their apprehension *truth,* and everything which they thinke *truth,* they presume they have a *liberty to hold,* and to *hold it forth* without any regard to *unity.*' 'I know,' the same man declared in a later sermon, 'it hath been said by some, that because a *heart* to *know* and *embrace* the *truth* is the *gift of God,* and the *Magistrate* cannot by *forcible means work* such a heart in men, therefore the Magistrate must use no *compulsion* or *coercion* in matters of Religion.' But does this mean that the magistrate may not '*compell* men to *attend* upon those *meanes* where *God* doth *usually give that grace*' or is forbidden to '*make Laws* to *restrain* and *punish errours and blasphemies* that are against truth?' [19] To Newcomen as to many other men, the practical efficacy of grace and of the spiritual liberty it conveyed seemed to depend upon nothing so much as order and unity in society, and unity and order seemed unattainable outside the historic framework of the church. One did not need to be a hysterical fanatic like Edwards or Prynne to think of toleration not as the necessary condition to peace within the state but as the latest and deadliest stratagem of Antichrist to promote strife and confusion among Christ's own people.

The preachers who spoke before parliament or other public bodies on behalf of presbyterianism in these years were on the whole temperate and restrained in their attacks upon heretics and sectaries. This was not true of some of their supporters who vociferated their alarm in the pamphlet press. The most notorious of these writers and in his way the most effective was Thomas Edwards. He had been forced from his post as university preacher at Cambridge in 1628 for assailing the order then prevailing in the church, but he had compounded for his violence against bishops by his later violence against all who sought the New Jerusalem at a faster rate than he or in a different direction. 'For we instead of a Reformation, are grown from one extreme to another, fallen from *Scylla* to *Charibdis* . . . one disease and Devil hath left us, and another as bad has come in the room; yea, this last extremity . . . is far more high, violent and dangerous in many respects.' [20] In this mood, he had published *Reasons against the Independent Government of Particular Congregations* (1641) and *Antapologia* (1644), an attack on *An Apologeticall Narration*. Edwards' confutation of the assembly Independents, we learn from Baillie, was so highly regarded that 'all the ministers of London, at least more than a hundred of them,' agreed to set up a weekly lecture for the author at Christ Church, 'where he may handle these questions, and nothing else, before all that will come to hear.' [21]

Christ Church in Newgate Street, formerly belonging to the Greyfriars, was a large structure where the two houses of parliament, the lord mayor, aldermen, and common council were in the habit of meeting on important occasions. Edwards appears to have published none of the sermons or lectures he delivered in that place, but early in February, 1646, with encouragement from Baillie and other ministers, he carried his war against the Independents and all their auxiliaries into print in *Gangraena: or A Catalogue and Discovery of many of the Errours, Heresies, Blasphemies and pernicious Practices of the Sectaries of this time, vented and acted in England in these four last years*.[22] Among the persons attacked in this work were John Goodwin, Saltmarsh, and Walwyn, three men who may be said to represent the progressive stages by which the movement for reform of the church was now swiftly transforming itself into a movement for political revolution. Each was quick to reply, Goodwin in *Cretensis* (March 19), Saltmarsh in *Groanes for Liberty* (March 10), and Walwyn in *A Whisper in the Eare of Mr. Thomas Edwards* (March 13) and *A Word More to Mr. Thomas Edwards* (March 19). Edwards countered with the two hundred and twelve pages of *The Second Part of Gangraena: or, A Fresh and further Discovery of the Errors, Heresies, Blasphemies, and dangerous Proceedings of the Sectaries of this Time. As Also . . . A Reply to the most materiall exceptions made by Mr. Saltmarsh, Mr. Walwyn, and Cretensis* (May 28). Goodwin made an elaborate rejoinder in *Anapologesiates Antapologias* (August 27), Saltmarsh replied to Edwards and several of his numerous other critics, in *Reasons for Unitie, Peace, and Love* (June 17); and Walwyn ridiculed his opponent in *An Antidote Against Master Edwards His old and New Poyson* (June 10), *A Prediction of Mr. Edwards his Conversion* (August 11), and *A Parable, Or Consultation of Physitians upon Master Edwards* (October 29). Undaunted by all this, Edwards went on to publish *The third Part of Gangraena. Or, A new and higher Discovery of the Errors, Heresies, Blasphemies, and insolent Proceedings of the Sectaries of these times* (December 28), a work of some three hundred pages, and in the following year he issued the two hundred and eighteen pages of *The Casting Down of the last and strongest hold of Satan, or, A Treatise against Toleration And pretended Liberty of Conscience* (June 28).

Milton wrote,

> Men whose Life, Learning, Faith and pure intent
> Would have been held in high esteem with *Paul*
> Must now be nam'd and printed Heretics
> By shallow *Edwards* and Scotch what d'ye call.

But the numerous counterattacks upon *Gangraena* testify to the immediate effectiveness of shallow Edwards' work. What especially attracted attention was that, instead of attempting to controvert error with argument, he attacked heretics and sectaries, all he could hear of, by name, reporting what they said and did, with no scruples in the gathering and handling of evidence. 'Such discoveries,' he declared, 'are a more sensible practicall way of confutation . . . then so many syllogismes and arguments.' [23] He supplied 'a Catalogue of errours now in being, alive in these present times,' a hundred and seventy-six of them, with four added in a postscript to the first edition of Part I, fifteen more in an appendix to the second edition, twenty-three more in Part II, and fifty-three in Part III. The one hundred and fifty-fourth error listed in Part I is Milton's proposal concerning divorce, with an injunction in the margin to see his *Doctrine and Discipline*. One looks in vain for any reference in *Gangraena* to Milton's marital misadventure, or indeed to any other personal circumstance, but we do learn that two gentlemen of the inns of court heard a certain she-preacher recommend his book, the woman having an unsanctified husband from whom she had run away with the husband of another woman. She and one of 'Master *Goodwins* and Master *Saltmarshs* Saints' were also said to preach that all devils should be saved. [24] We hear more of Mrs. Attaway farther on in *Gangraena* but nothing which has anything but the most adventitious connection with Milton. The references to Mrs. Attaway and to Milton are but extremely minor details in Edwards' account, which he claims represents only a small part of the heresies, blasphemies, and schismatical practices with which the land was being deluged.

Edwards was, of course, a contender against the light his age was learning to honor. But there was this to be said for him, that he did not look on the disintegration of ecclesiastical order as a necessary step in the liberation of mankind. He believed rather that society was breaking up before his eyes, and he wrote in a rage against the authors of the disruption he was witnessing. Though he pours out his evidence with the most uncritical profusion, his total picture of the situation at which the Puritan movement had arrived by 1646 bears the marks of actuality. 'You have made a Reformation,' he tells parliament in the opening pages of his book, 'but with the Reformation have we not a Deformation, and worse things come in upon us then ever we had before?' [25] Not one of parliament's ordinances for the restraint of sectaries but is slighted and scorned. Lay preaching was never more in request; presbyterian church government never more preached and printed against; unlicensed printing never more prevalent.

He did not, like the Scots, analyze or trace to their sources the errors he was engaged in cataloguing. His purpose was to show how the Independents and the rag-tag of sectaries employed these notions to carry on the organized betrayal from within of the reform movement itself. In the first two years of parliament, he says, Independents were few in number and were freely admitted into the city churches and the assembly. But not content to wait for the working out of a new frame of church government, they started at once to gather new churches, even soon to rebaptize the people, and to resist every concerted and ordered measure of reform. Having preached and printed contrary to parliamentary ordinance, having drawn people away from their obedience to pastors and governors, they next thrust themselves into places of honor, profit, and command in the state and the army. With astonishment and dismay, Edwards describes the tactics of the semiconspiratorial revolutionary faction, steadily cohering on its way to power. These men are 'Polupragmaticall, indefatigably active, stirring, restlesse night and day.' They have their agents everywhere. They have an eye to everything, a hand in everything, that may be to their advantage. 'Out-acting and out-working all the Presbyterians, they deal with this man to take him off, and worke with another man to qualifie him.' They have won over most of the news-writers, and they have their emissaries working for the election of members of parliament favorable to their cause. 'They observe all mens tempers, humours, and accordingly deal with them all, some with offices and places, some by holding out principles suiting their lusts.' [26] Though they make up, he is sure, only a fraction of the army, yet they claim credit for all the army's achievements and begin to talk of what the army under the right leadership might do about church government.[27] Whereas presbyterianism 'goes against the grain, and crosses men's lust,' the sectaries allow anybody to preach, to question preachers, and to vent opinions, brooking no interference by any authority. They are against tithes or any form of public maintenance of the ministry, and they are for popular government of churches. They would have every congregation independent of all others. They believe in 'the personal visible raign of Christ[,] that outward glorious Kingdom[,] which shall be on earth.' And to all these wild notions they add carnal seductions such as the encouragement of long hair and new fashions of apparel, a 'free and frolick kinde of living.' No wonder that many godly persons fall away, 'it being the ready way now to get great gifts, offices, or some place to turn Sectarie.' The sectaries, Satan assisting, 'are in the warm Sun, having the South-wind blowing upon them, and golden showers . . . falling into their laps,' while godly, orthodox, Presbyterian ministers are reproached and deserted.[28] It is, perhaps, not surprising that, shortly after his fourth and final blast in this vein, published in June, 1647, Edwards betook himself to the continent—tradition says from fear of the resentment he had aroused.[29]

ii. THE ERASTIANS: COLEMAN, SELDEN, PRYNNE

Not all the opposition to giving the ministerial caste a free hand to impose their authority upon the church came, however, from the kinds of persons assailed by Thomas Edwards and his likes. The unwillingness of parliament to admit the Presbyterian claim to a *jus divinum* found at least one champion in the ranks of the assembly itself in Thomas Coleman, rector by parliamentary appointment of St. Peter's Cornhill and reputed for his Hebrew learning. In July, 1645, just when the assembly had been having to take time to refute and condemn the particularly heinous errors of Paul Best and John Archer, Coleman further outraged his colleagues by speaking some obvious home truths in a fast day sermon to the house of commons. 'There was never Sermon preached on these publike Fasts,' he tells us, 'that was received with such contrary affections, and censures, as this.' [30] The house withheld the usual vote of thanks but ordered him to print his discourse 'as near as he can, as he preached it.' [31] Gillespie preached against him before the house of lords on August 27 in a sermon which he published with a more specific rebuttal. This in turn provoked an interchange of several polemics.[32] Coleman's argument, pressed with a certain cogency and an air of common sense, was of the sort to be heard frequently from now on and from various quarters. 'Establish,' he said to parliament, 'as few things *Jure Divino* as can well be.' Ministers have enough to do with teaching and preaching without having to conduct a government or administer judgment. 'I could never yet see, how two coordinate governments exempt from superiority and inferiority can be in one state.' What the church needs is not power to exclude sinners from communion but more ministers to preach the gospel, better maintenance for them, more schools to train them. Lacking such, the ministry is becoming 'the refuge of men that faile.'[33] As for excommunication, 'What will your censure doe?' asks Coleman's friend Hussey; 'it will shame a few whores and knaves . . . a boy in the streets can doe as much.' [34]

The most formidable and exasperating critic of the Westminster divines was John Selden, the head, according to Baillie, of the Erastian faction in parliament, but a member also of the assembly itself, privileged like other members to debate and vote on all questions that came before it. The use he made of this privilege is recalled in the story that, sometimes, when the ministers took to citing scripture, he would tell them, 'Perhaps in your little Pocket Bibles with gilt Leaves (which they would often pull out and read) the Translation may be thus, but the Greek or the Hebrew, signifies thus and thus.' [35] Needless to say, not all of Selden's ministerial colleagues were as unlearned as this story implies, but all shared the same embarrassment of having to carry on their discussions in the presence of one who, though not of their cloth, was recognized to be one of the most learned scholars of the age on all matters it most concerned them to know. Historian, lawyer, and member of parliament, he was, besides, more experienced than they in the ways of men in deliberative assemblies. He had been long acquainted with the clerical mind, and he observed the unguarded pretensions of the Westminster divines with an amused detachment which no doubt often put them at his mercy in debate. He was not above taking pleasure, as Aubrey says, in being a thorn in their sides, in using his knowledge to baffle and his wit to vex them.[36] Hence Baillie's repeated complaints of his arrogance, his glorying in his Jewish learning. One might think to demonstrate the *jus divinum* of presbyteries from the example of the Jewish Sanhedrim, but Selden was ready with proof 'that the Jewish State and Church was all one, and that so in England it must be, that the Parliament is the Church.' [37]

Everything, indeed, that Selden heard in the assembly he must have felt that he had heard before. He had been over the same ground with the clergy in the days of the bishops, and to him new presbyter was much the same as old prelatist. His *History of Tythes,* published in 1618, furnishes the key to his attitude toward the church in 1645. At thirty-four he had made himself famous as the author of works on English, oriental, and classical antiquities. He was the great English Protestant humanist scholar, fit rival to Grotius. He did not repudiate the appeal to the scriptures, but he pressed that appeal to discomforting logical conclusions. Rejecting tradition and putting no credence in personal revelation, he mastered languages and compared texts in order if possible to determine what actually the scriptures were and said. He undertook to gather, weigh, and sift historical evidence in order to determine as nearly as one could what were the facts, in order to understand scripture in the light of history, and to judge men and institutions in the light of both. Usually his scholar's zeal led him to educe his evidence beyond the limits of the modern reader's patience. But on the subject of tithes it happened that he was attacked by churchmen who either missed his point through ignorance or misrepresented it through self-interest. Hence he was provoked in the preface to his book to state his meaning, for once, simply and briefly, though with

Olympian condescension as for fools and ignoramuses, and he continued in the same vein in a reply to his chief antagonist, in a letter to Buckingham, and in a brief apologia, 'Of my Purpose and End in writing the History of Tythes'; but none of these things was he allowed to publish.[38] He was no more concerned, he said, with the question whether tithes are due to the church under the law of God than Aristotle or Theophrastus had been. That was a matter not for historians but for divines to determine, and he was a historian. His book pretended to be nothing 'but it self, that is, a meer Narration and the *Historie of Tythes.*' He sought nothing but knowledge of truth without venturing his credit 'to make or create Premisses for a chosen Conclusion, that I rather would than could prove.'[39]

Nevertheless, the conclusion upon which Selden bore down with four hundred pages of evidence was that from Hebrew times to the present, wherever tithes had in fact been levied, it was always by the authority and under the laws of the state. To assert the contrary was to call in question the laws and customs of the realm. To argue 'from affirmative Canons only to Practice,' that is from a decree that a thing ought to be so to the conclusion that it is so, is equal 'to the proving of the practice of a Custom from some consonant Law of *Plato's* Commonwealth, of *Lucians* men in the Moon, or of *Aristophanes* his City of Cuckoes in the Clouds.'[40] There could really, of course, be no mistaking the point of all this. The accumulation of so much evidence that the church had always, everywhere, depended upon the state for the enforcement of its claims to material support implied, overwhelmingly, that the church had no other reliance and that what the state granted the state might, if it wished, take away. But what made *The History of Tythes* doubly hard for the clergy to stomach was the tone of it. According to Tillesley, one of the two archdeacons who undertook to refute the work, there was no part of the preface but what was 'fraught with supercilious contempt and full of the Rhetoricke of a censorious overweener.'[41]

Selden had to learn that irony, the weapon of men who know too much, is not an altogether safe weapon to handle. He was called before members of Star Chamber and the privy council and forced to sign a submission in which he expressed regret for having published his book, without, however, having to admit that he was mistaken in any part of it. The book itself was suppressed and the author forbidden to print anything in reply to his critics. Though he was not like Eliot one who thought to serve truth by dying for it, yet the rebuffs he received left their mark upon him. He was, he said, an English common lawyer, but might not a lawyer be wedded to 'true *Philologie* the only fit Wife that could be found for the most learned of the Gods?' 'Who of the Learned knows not,' he asked, what light lawyers had given 'out of their studies of *Philologie,* both to their own and other Professions . . . in rectifying of Story, in explication of good Authors, in vindicating from the injury of time both what belongs as wel to sacred as prophane studies?' [42] In the parliaments of 1626 and 1628 he brought his own legal learning, thus illuminated, to the support of Eliot, Hampden, and Coke in the struggle against the pretensions and encroachments of Charles. He introduced the Petition of Right, and he pointed out to the house that 'there is no law to prevent the printing of any book in England, only a decree in the Star Chamber.' For a man to be imprisoned and his goods taken from him on such ground and on such authority seemed to him a great invasion of the liberty of the subject.[43]

Selden himself, for his part in the actions of parliament in 1629, spent the next two years in prison. Upon his release he went back to his studies and his comforts, and in 1635 took up the argument against Grotius for the sovereignty of the English crown at sea. The event would show, however, that there was no inducing him to admit any claim to authority, whether of the crown, the bishops, or the clergy, derived from a supposed absolute right rather than from law, embodied in parliament and resting upon mutual convenience and agreement, confirmed in practice and ascertainable as recorded fact. Heylyn reports that he was a frequent guest at Lambeth and that Laud did all he could to win him over to the king. But it was probably true, as Heylyn says, that Selden 'had not yet forgotten the affronts which were put upon him about his History of Tythes (for in the notion of affronts he beheld them alwaies).' [44] The two archdeacons, like the Oxford divines who attacked Gibbon, had been permitted by arbitrary power to assail not the faith but the fidelity of the historian, and the historian was not the man to forget that fact when the bishops took to arguing for episcopacy by divine right.[45]

Undependable and unpredictable as only a scholar in politics can be,

Selden found Presbyterian pretensions to divine right no easier to swallow than he had those of Episcopalians before them. The substance of what he said when he came to sit in the Westminster Assembly is preserved in *Table-Talk: being the Discourses of John Selden Esq; or his Sence of Various Matters of Weight and High Consequence Relating especially to Religion and State.* This was compiled by Selden's secretary, Richard Milward, who says, 'I had the opportunity to hear his Discourse twenty Years together, and least all those Excellent things that usually fell from him might be lost, some of them from time to time I faithfully committed to Writing.' Selden died in 1654, Milward in 1680, and the book, not surprisingly, remained unpublished until 1689.

'In reading,' the compiler said, 'be pleas'd to distinguish Times, and in your Fancy carry along with you, the WHEN and the WHY, many of these things were spoken; this will give them the more Life, and the smarter Relish.' It was surely an ironic fate that brought the author of *The History of Tythes,* friend of Ben Jonson and sponsor of the Petition of Right, to the Jerusalem Chamber in 1643. According to Clarendon he might, the year before, have thrown in his lot, as Lord Keeper, with the king, but, it was said, he would not make a journey to York or lie out of his own bed for any preferment.[46] He lived at his ease, among his books and learned projects, in the household of the Earl and Countess of Kent, exempt from the needs as well as the ambitions that beset most men. What it is that makes such men nevertheless put themselves upon the stage of affairs where they are compelled to contemplate the transparent follies of others is hard to say, but once committed to the part of observer at that spectacle, it probably mattered very little to Selden on whose side he sat. Listening to the Westminster divines, he was confirmed in the same rational, critical, skeptical attitude which had been previously fixed in his mind by his brush with their rivals and former oppressors.

Hence one easily understands why *Table-Talk* came to be an admired book in the eighteenth century. 'Men say,' Selden observes, 'they are of the same Religion for quietness sake,' but he doubts if any three men can be found anywhere who agree on all points. 'Religion is like the fashion'; every man has one as he has a doublet, but one man wears his slashed, another laced, another plain. 'Wee differ about the trim-

ming.' Religious disputes will never end because there is no rule
by which to end them. One man says one thing and another another,
like Inigo Lanthorne disputing with his puppet in *Bartholomew Fair*.
The Word of God is the rule, says the Puritan, but he means himself.
It is called the Word of God, 'yet it was writ by a man a mercenary
man, whose coppie either might be false or he might make it false.'
'The Text serves onely to guesse by. Wee must satisfye our selves fully
out of the Authors that lived about those times.' As for councils of the
church, 'the truth is, the odde man is still the holy Ghost.' And as for
the clergy, they are like the woman who cried to her husband, 'What
will you beleive your owne eyes, before your owne sweet wife?' 'Chaine
up the Clergie on both Sydes.' Equally mad are those who say that
bishops must be continued *jure divino* and those who would have them
abolished for being antichristian. 'All is as the State likes.' But, 'never
any King drop'd out of the Clouds.' 'A King is a thing men have made
for their owne sakes for quietness sake.' The way to peace is through
law, and 'every Law is a Contract betwixt the Prince & the people.' [47]
Thus in Selden learning and common sense converged to defend individual liberty under the established law of the state against pretensions
to authority for which no provision could be found in law or record in
history. Law and history were for Selden merely two sides of the same
shield. But to the great question with which Presbyterians were in
their own way trying to deal, how to organize and implement spiritual
liberty in the society confronting them, the great lawyer and scholar
did not address himself.

For final decision on that question the assembly divines had of necessity to look to parliament, and parliament's ability to enforce decisions
was gravely altered by the events of 1645. The handful of men still
sitting at Westminster were all that remained of civil authority in
the state; yet they were hardly any longer a parliament in the historic
meaning of the term. Their continuance could be justified up to this
point by the armed resistance which the king offered to the constitutional claims put forward against him in 1641–1642, but as soon as
that resistance was brought to an end, there ensued a situation of extraordinary constitutional confusion. Parliament, what was left of it,
had by that time become a self-perpetuating revolutionary regime
which there was no legal way to remove or replace without its own

consent. This was not forthcoming. Important interests had sprung up during the civil war which now had large stakes in the retention of power. There was the phalanx of Presbyterian divines, expecting to take over the church and the universities. There were the city merchants who, having helped to finance the war for parliament, looked for a return on their investment. There were the committees with their functionaries and hangers-on which had the disposal of church lands and confiscated royalist estates, and there was finally, in the members who had stuck to their posts through everything or been recruited to take the places of others who had lost heart and deserted, the habit of power and the fear of losing it. Thus the parliament in which Cromwell presently resumed his seat and with whose agents Milton had to deal in connection with his own business affairs was in make-up and temper nothing like the body which had first come together in 1640, let alone that serene senate of worthies Milton thought of himself as addressing in *Areopagitica*. To be sure, parliament, such as it was, still held back from putting spiritual life completely under the control of presbyteries, but by the same token there was now left no recognized or legitimate authority in church or state to keep parliament itself from overriding any man's liberty. Under the customary forms of government and in the name of law, it could be as absolute as Charles had ever aspired to be. Under such a regime, it was obvious that the vaunted presbyterian discipline could be made an instrument of intolerance and oppression as violent and complete as prelatism under the crown.

This fact in all its implications was at once made plain beyond mistaking by Prynne, who, from hounding Laud to his doom, had turned to hunting for enemies of parliamentary supremacy in other quarters. Almost at the moment when his former persecutor was laying his head upon the block (January 10, 1645), Prynne was issuing another of his portentous tirades, a hundred and fifty-six pages, called *Truth Triumphing over Falshood, Antiquity over Novelty. Or, The First Part of A just and seasonable Vindication of the undoubted Ecclesiasticall Jurisdiction, Right, Legislative, Coercive Power of Christian Emperors, Kings, Magistrates, Parliaments, in all matters of Religion, Church-Government, Discipline, Ceremonies, Manners: Summoning of, Presiding, Moderating in Councells, Synods; and ratifying their Canons,*

*Determinations, Decrees: As likewise of Lay-mens right both to sit
and vote in Councells; (here proved to be anciently, and in truth none
other but Parliaments, especially in England) both by Scripture Texts,
Presidents of all sorts, and the constant uninterrupted Practices, Examples, of the most eminent Emperors, Princes, Councells, Parliaments,
Churches, and Christian States, (especially of our owne) in all ages
since their embracing the Gospell.*

The title tells us all we need to know of the contents of this work.
Prynne was here pleading with parliament not to let the church get out
of its own hands and into those of John Goodwin, Henry Burton, and
their like. But he was just as insistent that parliament should maintain its supremacy also in the face of Presbyterian claims. In August
he challenged the assembly divines with *Foure serious Questions of
Grand Importance concerning Excommunication and Suspention from
the Sacrament.* No matter who his opponent, Prynne always argued
like the litigious lawyer he was in a torrent of unsorted, unconsidered
precedents and citations. If one did not fit, another might. He was at
once a grotesque caricature and the antithesis of Selden. He never
forgot the affront that had once been put upon him, and since he had
lost his ears in the cause of right, he could not possibly ever be wrong.
Disagreement was outrage; all ministers must be made to keep the
place assigned to them under the law; presbyteries must bow to parliament; the church must serve as the state's obedient arm in policing
the moral and spiritual life of its subjects; dissenters of all persuasions
must give way or be exterminated. The fullest expression of this fanati-
cal Erastianism came from his pen in March, 1647, in *The Sword of
Christian Magistracy Supported: Or A Full Vindication of Christian Kings and Magistrates Authority Under the Gospell, To punish
Idolatry, Apostacy, Heresie, Blasphemy and obstinate Schism, with
Pecuniary, Corporall, and in some Cases with Banishment, and Capitall
Punishments.*

iii. THE SECULAR HUMANIST: MILTON

The conception of church and state so lucidly and cogently set forth
by Henderson in his sermon to the house of lords on May 28, 1645,
that notion of two complementary but distinct jurisdictions, each ab-

solute in its own sphere, was not for England. Even if all the independents, separatists, and seekers, all the heretics of whatever sort, listed in Edwards' *Gangraena*, could have been suppressed, parliament was still not likely to have acknowledged without reservation a *jus divinum* in presbyteries. But the fact was that opposition to presbyterian theocracy, far from being suppressed, was flourishing more freely than ever, and Puritan doctrines were being carried to more extreme conclusions. How far and in what different directions, we may see both in the course which Milton now set for himself and also in the steadily developing activities of John Goodwin, John Lilburne, and their respective disciples and associates.

Milton took no part in the pamphlet war now raging against Presbyterian intolerance, but his abstention was not due to indifference. The immediate problem was not so much how to bring about toleration in the modern sense as how to preserve or regain spiritual unity among a divided people. The Presbyterians could conceive only one way of accomplishing that purpose, the restoration of ecclesiastical uniformity according to the scheme agreed upon by their representatives in the assembly. Independents and sectaries rejected not the principle of comprehension but the attempt to impose centralized control over spiritual life under a closely knit system of government and discipline. In the end of course every party to the dispute was compelled by circumstances to abandon all hope of making its conception of the church prevail, whether by force or persuasion, and to accept the protection which the state alone could afford to each against its rivals. But in 1645 the time for that had not yet come, and every group was free to contend for mastery or, since mastery was not to be had, for survival. Yet even so, few minds were prepared to think of such a condition as the rational and permanent solution of the problem. General adherence to the principle of liberty of belief for every law-abiding person under the jurisdiction of the state had to await the development of a civil government sufficiently sure of itself to guarantee such liberty. In the meantime the compelling need of all those who rejected presbyterianism was security for whatever group, congregation, sect, or party to which they happened to belong.

Milton now found himself aligned with no group in the dispute over the church. Church-outed, so to speak, a second time, and this time by his own former associates, he turned to no particular denomination or preacher. He felt no need for any mediation between himself and the truth of the Word which his own reason could not supply. Personal experience and the study of history had taught him to suspect the motives and distrust the habits of mind of all clerics of whatever order in all ages. New presbyter was always turning out to be but old priest. The contention between the divines of the assembly and their various opponents, the great debate over 'dependencies and independencies how they will compound, and in what Calends,' [48] seemed to him chiefly a struggle for position and power in whatever ecclesiastical system might presently come to be established. The plight or the program of no party to that dispute was any concern of his, and he wrote nothing on behalf of any of them or of their cause.

In Milton the Puritan revolutionary emerged as the secular humanist concerned less with reforming the church than with liberating men's minds from error and superstition. After *Areopagitica* he looked for the godly commonwealth or humanistic Zion to be accomplished by the great senate of worthies who had issued the Accommodation Order to the divines of the assembly and then presently went on to institute the New Model army. And while the army went about the business of winning its holy war against the king, Milton turned not to polemics against the Presbyterians but to pursuits which should enable him to serve the commonwealth in his own chosen role. That is, he must satisfy his own mind and so prepare himself to satisfy others of the validity of his ideas by a systematic study of the scriptures and of the history of England. The final fruit of these studies was the *De Doctrina Christiana* and *The History of Britain*. This was none the less the case though the relevance of both works to the situation in which their author found himself in the period after 1645 has been somewhat obscured by the fact that neither was finished when he was called from his studies in 1649 to be secretary to the Council of State.

De Doctrina Christiana, begun not later than 1646 and worked over in succeeding years, was not completed before 1657 and not published until 1825. There is no telling when any particular part, as we have it now, was composed, but there can be little doubt that the governing idea and purpose of the work took form following Milton's controversy with the assembly divines over the liberty of marriage and of printing.

His argument on those matters had led him to assert that freedom was the inescapable condition—the doom that Adam fell into—for the attainment of good in this life in any form. His doctrinal treatise simply went on from the point he had reached in *Tetrachordon*. In its extant form, especially in the chapters on creation, fall, and redemption, it elaborates conclusions foreshadowed in 1645. Milton addressed himself to the task of clarifying out of Biblical materials an idea of God, man, and nature, consistent at every point with belief in man's ability to understand himself and his universe sufficiently to permit him to govern himself and determine his own destiny. These convictions Milton felt he must state and prove out of God's Word, namely, that the universe is governed by divine law, that man by his disobedience brought punishment and servitude upon himself under the law, and that Christ set him free again to distinguish true from false, good from evil, and so to obey the law if he would and redeem himself from his subjection to death. Every man had Adam and Christ within him, and every man's fate depended upon the outcome of the struggle of those two with each other and with the evil one. Thus scripture could be made to justify rejection of interference by church or churchmen with freedom to marry, learn, think, and speak. But thus, also, Milton could justify his belief that no order of men, no institution or law of state or church, should come between any man and his free obedience to the higher law revealed to him in scripture, in creation, and in his own mind and conscience.

Yet the will of God was revealed in history as well as in scripture, and Milton's other chosen occupation in these years was the writing of a history of England, still with the purpose of sustaining his own convictions and enlightening the minds of his countrymen. 'I undertook,' he said, 'a history of the nation from its remotest origin; intending to bring it down, if I could, in one unbroken thread to our own times.' [49] By the close of 1646 he had probably completed the first two books, bringing the story down to the end of the Roman period. By the end of the second civil war in the summer of 1648, he had completed the third book, dealing with the struggles of Britons and Saxons. He himself tells us that, when in March, 1649, the Council of State asked him to take the post of Latin Secretary, he had finished the fourth book, which concluded with the rise of the West Saxon kingdom.

By that time, too, he had again turned his historical learning to the uses of polemic in *The Tenure of Kings and Magistrates*. After that, official duties and pamphleteering caused further work on *The History of Britain* to be suspended until his partial retirement from office in 1655.

Milton's approach to the writing of history was that of a Renaissance scholar who was also first and last an English Protestant. In his tracts against prelacy, in *Areopagitica* and the divorce tracts, he had held to the common conception of England's role in the history of the world. As a patriotic Protestant Englishman he began with the conviction that England had always, even in Saxon and British times, been the special instrument of divine providence, replete with men of faith and virtue. Her past should, therefore, be a most fit subject for a historian. It was glorious, Sallust said, to serve the state with deeds, but it was also not to be despised to serve with words. Milton had echoed this idea more than once in his previous writings. But if, as Sallust said, Athens had had her small deeds made known as great by her eloquent writers, England's great achievements had been made to seem small by the unskillful handling of monks and mechanics. Milton set himself to remedy this fault, to make the illustrious deeds of her virtuous leaders, and along with them of course the baleful acts of her wicked or weak ones, at last suitably known. For, he said, even the greatest hero is aware that when he has conquered all things else, he cannot conquer time or detraction and, 'wisely conscious of this his want as well as of his worth . . . honours and hath recourse to the aid of Eloquence . . . by whose immortal Record his noble deeds, which else were transitory, becoming fixt and durable against the force of Yeares and Generations, he fails not to continue through all Posterity, over *Envy*, *Death*, and *Time*, also victorious.' Only by virtue can liberty be maintained, and the historian, by keeping alive the memory of noble deeds, does as much as the hero to promote the one and preserve the other. Heroes and historians, performing different but not unequal services, have to be something like equal in their powers and should be equal in renown. 'For worthy deeds are not often destitute of worthy relaters: as by a certain Fate great Acts and great Eloquence have most commonly gon hand in hand, equalling and honouring each other in the same Ages.' [50]

'To relate well and orderly things worth the noting, so as may best instruct and benefit them that read' was, then, the professed purpose of *The History of Britain*.[51] Within the limits of that purpose and of the resources at his disposal, Milton's method was thorough and sound. He made use of the standard authorities of his time and of such primary sources as were then available, and he permitted none of them to go unscrutinized by critical judgment. As one who thought that the scriptures must submit to be read in the light of reason, he could demand no less of Geoffrey and Bede. But if worthy deeds called for relaters no less worthy, a worthy relater might fairly look for deeds worthy to be immortalized. Neither British deeds, however, nor the original recorders of them seemed to Milton to deserve remembering. In the period before Caesar he found chiefly fables. When he came to the Roman period and Roman writers, he felt that his story was arriving where things might be seen in their true colors and shapes, but the yield of British worthies in Roman times was not much greater than before. A few Romans—but not Caesar, a tyrant justly slain—answered to his conception of the virtuous ruler, and a few Britons showed 'magnanimitie, soberness, and martial skill,' but these were the exception. In the affair of Boadicea the British showed themselves to be right barbarians, 'no rule, no foresight, no forecast, experience or estimation, either of themselves or of thir Enemies,' nothing but 'the wild hurrey of a distracted Woeman, with as mad a Crew at her heeles.' Barbarous too, absurd, and unnatural was the British custom of polyandry, though Claudius was hardly less contemptible, letting Agrippina sit at a Roman triumph, 'public in her Female pride among Ensignes and Armed Cohorts.' The Romans, Milton said, 'beate us into some civilitie,' but as Roman virtue decayed, Roman liberty and civilization declined. 'And with the Empire fell also what before in this Western World was cheifly *Roman;* Learning, Valour, Eloquence, History, Civility, and eev'n Language it self.'[52]

Britons and Saxons did little that was worth remembering and produced no historians capable of recording whatever might have deserved not to be forgotten. 'Dubious Relaters,' he calls them, 'and still to the best advantage of what they term holy Church, meaning indeed themselves: in most other matters of Religion, blind, astonish'd, and strook with superstition as with a Planet; in one word, Monks.' They report few examples of virtue and liberty flourishing together, little of anything but the error and ignorance of venal churchmen leading the people into tyranny and servitude. At the collapse of the empire, the Britons at first bestirred themselves, but soon 'remitted thir heat, and shrunk more wretchedly under the burden of thir own libertie, than before under a foren yoke.' Backward against foreign foes, they were eager and prompt for civil broils. Kings were anointed not of God's anointing and soon after put to death by their anointers to be replaced by others still more fierce and proud. Full of contempt for such writers as Nennius, William of Malmsbury, and Geoffrey of Monmouth, Milton questions the very existence of Arthur and all his wars and conquests. After the supposed victory at Badon, at any rate, the Britons were no better than before. Drawing upon Gildas, whom he finds with reservations the most credible of their historians, Milton depicts their clergy as

Unlerned, Unapprehensive, yet impudent; suttle Prowlers, Pastors in Name, but indeed Wolves; intent upon all occasions, not to feed the Flock, but to pamper and well line themselves: not call'd, but seising on the Ministry as a Trade, not as a Spiritual Charge: teaching the people, not by sound Doctrin, but by evil Example: . . . deadly haters of truth, broachers of lies: . . . slightly touching the many vices of the Age, but preaching without end thir own greivances, as don to Christ; seeking after preferments and degrees in the Church more then after Heav'n; and so gain'd, make it thir whole study how to keep them by any Tyranny. Yet lest they should be thought things of no use in thir eminent places, they have thir niceties and trivial points to keep in aw the superstitious multitude; but in true saving knowledge leave them still as gross and stupid as themselves; bunglers at the Scripture, nay forbidding and silencing them that know; but in worldly matters, practis'd and cunning Shifters; in that only art and symony, great Clercs and Maisters, bearing thir heads high, but thir thoughts abject and low.

He has no better to tell of the Saxons and their monkish chroniclers. The best he can do with Bede is to pick out 'from among his many Legends of Visions and Miracles' not a history but a mere calendar of kings, of whose wars we hear much but of whose wisdom and justice nothing. One after another, Milton says, they left 'thir Kingly Charge, to run thir heads fondly into a Monks Cowle.' [53]

What was happening to Milton as he went on with his *History of Britain* in the years from 1645 to 1649 is plain. He had intended to follow Sallust's example and relate nothing but facts 'with plain, and lightsom brevity,'[54] free from hope and fear and partisanship, expecting that the story he was to tell would furnish examples of virtuous rulers, promoting and preserving liberty, and of wise teachers, instilling virtue by spreading knowledge. As he proceeded, however, his expectations were disappointed and his intentions became impossible to fulfill. Reformer and humanist that he was, he could not restrain his disgust with the doings of Britons and Saxons or his contempt for their chroniclers. But that was not his only disappointment at the moment. When the preachers had rejected his ideas concerning marriage without consideration and, he believed, from venal motives, he had turned to parliament. But parliament was working out to be equally corrupt. The body of men who, after approving the Accommodation Order and launching the New Model, went on to approve the Directory of Worship and set themselves more and more against the army, was no such senate of worthies as Milton had addressed in *Areopagitica*. It was rather the body whose committees mulcted and humiliated him when, his interrupted marriage having now been resumed, he had to appear as suitor for the recovery of his royalist father-in-law's sequestered property. The historian, consequently, could not help seeing in the affairs of Britons and Saxons a parallel to the things happening about him in his own time and found it impossible to keep this fresh disillusion out of his book. *The History of Britain* as it goes on becomes an indictment of parliament and assembly on the eve of the second civil war, one more expression of Milton's scorn for the faithless clergy of any age or order—old priest or new presbyter makes no difference—and of civil rulers who submit to be corrupted by them. 'Civility,' as he calls it, always declines, and ignorance, superstition, contention, and corruption flourish, whenever the church and its ministers betray their true spiritual calling in order to reach after temporal power. Thus from emulating Sallust, Milton takes to anticipating Gibbon and Voltaire.

He was especially prompted to such bitter reflections when he came to tell how the ancient Britons, liberated at last from Roman rule, found no use for freedom except to fall into strife among themselves and finally into subjection once more to foreign enemies. Reaching that point in his narrative in 1646 or 1647, Milton found the parallel to the behavior of parliament and assembly at the moment of his writing too striking to be passed by in silence. For was not the whole movement for liberation and reform in his own time in danger of breaking up for the same reasons in frustration and confusion? The army's victory had put an end to tyranny and oppression. But to what avail? Parliament with its committees was more concerned now with the perquisites of victory than with reforming the state or securing the rights of its own supporters and deliverers. The divines of the assembly were less concerned with preaching the gospel than with getting benefices, lectureships, and masterships of colleges for themselves and with persuading the secular power to impose their authority upon the people by force. The people for their part, 'who had bin kept warme a while by the affected zele of thir pulpits,' were becoming more cold and obdurate than before, turning to lewdness and atheism. We might well consider, Milton said, why the Britons, having been given their liberty 'should let it pass through them as a cordial medcin through a dying man.' The answer was that 'libertie hath a sharp and double edge fitt onelie to be handl'd by just and vertuous men.' [55] At the close of 1648 it was clear to Milton where just and virtuous men were now to be found, and he dropped *The History of Britain* in order to resume pamphleteering and defend the actions of the army leaders against the strictures of the Presbyterian ministers.

iv. THE INDEPENDENTS: THOMAS GOODWIN, JOHN GOODWIN

The proponents of the Westminster confession of faith and directory of church government sought to give effect to the idea that agreement upon a common creed embodied in a united comprehensive church was essential to an ordered and stable national existence. In this they had the support of substantial citizens who hoped soon to restore civil and ecclesiastical order, of the city authorities, and of a majority in parliament. But there were also in parliament and the city not a few who took the side of Independents and sectaries, and there was always a certain number of men of cooler judgment and conciliatory temper ready to make allowances for differing minds and tender consciences.

The fact was, of course, as Milton and Selden in their several ways made evident, that a deep-running tide of opinion was setting in against the very idea of an all-inclusive authoritative church, whatever institutional shape it might assume. And Lilburne and his associates, as we shall see, were at hand to represent the same oncoming force in a more concretely disturbing form. Yet another fact not to be lost sight of was that the influences making for the rejection of the traditional conception of a universal visible church continued at work within the ministerial order itself. The opponents whom the Presbyterians found most difficult to deal with in 1645 and for some time thereafter were still Thomas Goodwin and the 'dissenting brethren' within the ranks of assembly divines, backed by John Goodwin and the increasing host of 'gathered churches' and shifting groups swayed by preachers of more or less irregular ordination in the army, the city, and the country round about.

Both houses continued as a rule to select members of the Presbyterian faction of the clergy to address them on fast days and other occasions, Marshall being always by far the greatest favorite. But as the reports of victory kept coming in from the army and parties became more sharply defined in parliament, the spokesmen for other factions and points of view also occasionally got their turn to speak. What the army preachers, Peters and Dell, found to say in the pulpit of Christ Church or St. Margaret's, we saw in the last chapter. Members of the dissenting minority in the assembly, on the rare occasions when they too were called upon, gave further significant evidence of the growing reaction against the uncompromising attitude of the close-knit group of divines now riding high in the assembly. The tactic of Presbyterian extremists was to visit upon the Independents full responsibility for the worst extravagances of the most extreme sectaries and eccentrics of the moment. The response of the Independents was not to defend but to disavow the extremists on their side of the quarrel and to counter the violence of their assailants with a plea for peace in the national interest to be arrived at by the exercise of charity among the faithful toward one another even at the expense of complete doctrinal agreement or uniformity of practice. In pursuing this line the Independents were, of course, moving with the trend of thought and feeling which was eventually to prevail. The Presbyterians had overplayed their hand. Like all Puritan preachers they had taught that salvation sprang from the experience of faith within the breast. They could not now set up as the measure of faith mere assent to doctrine or loyalty to system. Their intransigence called their own motives in question and brought discredit upon their own intellectual methods. Already they had reason to complain of those whom one of their number described as 'Sermon scorners . . . who to this day *hear Sermons,* in the very same *posture* they were wont to *see Stage-plays.*' [56]

Thomas Goodwin's usual theme in the pulpit was the mystical regeneration of the saints. In his fast day sermon on Revelation 17:14 before the house of commons in February, 1646, he went on from that subject to the predestined triumph of the Lamb and his saints, 'called, chosen, and faithfull,' over all who make war against him and them. The preservation of the saints was the great interest of states and kingdoms, and nowhere and at no time had there been such a multitude of saints as now in England. 'If we had stood at Gods elbow when he *bounded out the Nations* . . . we should not have known,' the preacher said, which to choose 'in respect of the enjoyment of the Gospel, and the communion of Saints, more then . . . this kingdome wherein we live.' And yet, 'consider,' he says, 'it is not simply having Saints, and multitudes of Saints, *called, faithfull,* and *chosen,* but it is the using them *kindly,* and *dealing well* with them, that is the interest of a Nation.' He is careful to state that he is pleading only for the preservation of saints, not 'for a liberty of all opinions,' and yet he adds, 'when I say *Saints,* I mean no one party of men.' This was not toleration in the modern sense, but it was something which probably came home to Goodwin's hearers with greater force. 'England is a mighty Animal,' he tells them—'an *Aphorisme* of the late Queens'— 'which can never die except it kill it selfe.' Saints do and will differ in judgment among themselves and will hardly ever agree. The apostles themselves could not prevent it. But let English saints be reconciled and united by the rule of charity, notwithstanding differences, and Christ will rule, Antichrist will be undone, and England will stand secure.[57]

Jeremiah Burroughes had elaborated the Independents' argument for peace to the length of three hundred pages the year before in *Irenicum, to the Lovers of Truth and Peace.*[58] In August, 1646, he preached a fast day sermon to the house of commons on the fourth beatitude. Let parliament hunger as it should after righteousness; the hunger it was called upon to satisfy was the need of all who had served its cause faithfully. 'Let not those who live peaceably, and labour to know the minde of Christ to the uttermost that they are able, be accounted the troublers of the Nation,' even if 'they can come no neerer to their Brethren then they doe.' [59] People cannot be forced to believe, he told the house of lords in November, before they are taught. To attempt force 'is to seek to beat the nayle in by the hammer of authority, without making way by the wimble of instruction.' If the wood is sound, the nail will bend or the wood split. 'Consider you have to deale with English consciences; there is no country so famous for firm strong okes as England; you will find English consciences to be so.' 'There is a great outcry,' he says in conclusion, 'against the toleration of all religions, & we are willing to joyn against such a toleration,' but his hearers are not to let their power be used to further the selfish designs of men: 'be faithful with God, encourage those that fear him, & God wil take care of your honors.' [60]

In the midst of all the sound and fury raised in these years by extremists on both sides of the dispute over church government, the argument advanced by the Independents for a religious peace based upon common sense, mutual forbearance, belief in the fewness and clearness of the things necessary to salvation, and willingness to compromise in the common interest began to be heard more and more with whatever variations from divers quarters. John Owen, a preacher now rising to fame and soon to be one of Cromwell's spiritual advisers, took a similar position in his fast day sermon before the commons in April, 1646, as did William Bridge, another of the 'dissenting brethren,' before the lords in October.[61] In June, 1645, the same argument had been cogently though temperately set forth in an anonymous pamphlet called *The ancient Bounds*. In March, 1647, Ralph Cudworth told the house of commons that 'Christ came not into the world to fil our heads with mere Speculations; to kindle a fire of wrangling and contentious dispute amongst us . . . whilst . . . our hearts remain all ice within toward God.' [62] At almost the same moment on the other side of the great schism in national life Jeremy Taylor in his famous *Discourse of the Liberty of Prophesying* was saying that 'since *we know in part, and prophesy in part, and that now we see through a glasse darkly,* wee should not *despise* or *contemn* persons not so knowing as ourselves.' [63] And all this time William Walwyn in his own unobtrusive way was insinuating notions of love and reason into the minds of men whom he was at the same time organizing into a party for the support of Lilburne and a political solution of the human problem resulting from revolution and civil war.

But the man whom the earnest advocates of an authoritative theocratic church establishment justly regarded as their most troublesome opponent outside the assembly was John Goodwin. He had not himself happened to be nominated to the assembly, as he well might have been. He had become instead the great lawgiver of dissent and metropolitan of gathered churches. Early in January, 1645, in *Innocency and Truth Triumphing together,* he took up the argument against Prynne's contention for presbyterian church government as the instrument of parliamentary absolutism. Prynne at once issued the counterblast which he called *Truth Triumphing over Falshood,*[64] and Goodwin fired back in *Calumny Arraign'd and Cast* (January 31, 1645). In May the parliamentary committee for plundered ministers sequestered him from his living,[65] but he still continued as preacher to an independent congregation in the same neighborhood, and in February, 1646, he published *Twelve considerable serious Cautions,* remarkable for its brevity as well as for its incisive statement that the Presbyterians could no longer hope to prevent the gathering of independent congregations and the only effect of their trying to suppress the many already in existence would be to plunge the whole reform movement into conflict within itself. In March, Goodwin took up the cudgels against Thomas Edwards in *Cretensis: or a Briefe Answer to an ulcerous Treatise,* demonstrating as good-humoredly as possible that the author of *Gangraena* was an ill-willed ass. In August, Goodwin exposed the badness of Edwards' grammar, logic, and doctrine in the two hundred and fifty pages with preface and index of *Anapologesiates Antapologias.* In September the introduction in the house of commons of the notorious ordinance threatening heretics with capital punishment provoked a series of rejoinders from Goodwin's friends and sympathizers. Goodwin lent his own weight to the attack in February, 1647, in a pamphlet called *Hagiomastix, or the Scourge of the Saints Displayed.* How, he asked, can the civil magistrate know the truth revealed in the Word so certainly that he may proceed against any who think differently without peril to his own soul?

But the discussion led Goodwin on to ask, what are the scriptures which men must believe on pain of death and what is meant by believing them? Is the English translation the Word of God? Or the original Greek and Hebrew, and if the latter, in what text? Or must men take as the intent of the Holy Spirit whatever their teachers tell them? Goodwin's answer was the same as Milton's. The scriptures were the Word of God, but that which must be believed as such was what reason alone was able to apprehend in the light of human knowledge and experience —which in Goodwin's case as in Milton's included wide acquaintance with the poets, philosophers, orators, and historians of classical antiquity. The result was that the author of *Hagiomastix* was promptly accused of denying the scriptures altogether and had to explain his meaning over again, briefly in 1646 in *A Candle to see the Sunne* and *A Post-script, or Appendix to . . . Hagio-Mastix* and at length in *The Divine Authority of the Scriptures Asserted,* which appeared in December, 1647. His final move against the threat of persecution was to see to the publication in February, 1648, of a translation of the first four books of Acontius' *Satanae stratagemata,* called in English *Satans Stratagems, or the Devils Cabinet-Council Discovered.* Meanwhile the Independents with the army behind them were now masters of the situation in parliament and the city, and the Presbyterians were making ready for armed revolt. *Satans Stratagems* was issued with three dedications, one to the two houses of parliament, one to Fairfax and Cromwell, one to the lord mayor of London. An address to the reader by Goodwin himself begins:

Amongst the many strains of that unreasonableness in men, which renders the days we live in, so calamitous and sad, there is scarce any more deplorable or comporting with our misery, then for men to have their mouths wide open in declaiming against what they are pleased to call Errors and Heresies, and their ears fast shut against all Christian means and directions, either for the discovery and eviction of them to be such, or for the suppression of them, being so evicted.

Goodwin was for the Presbyterians the more formidable opponent because he was himself one of the Brahmin caste, a match for any of the brotherhood in the arts both of debate and of edification. He knew how to take advantage of the freedom of disputation which was the convention of the school in which they had all been reared. He was master of the intellectual method of the Protestant divine, which consisted in applying a supposedly infallible dialectic to the supposedly infallible scriptures for the extraction of authoritative canons of judgment and rules of conduct. In the art of fitting scripture texts to dogmatic premises and so of gaining as well as giving assurance that not only his premises but all his consequent demonstrations, conclusions, and applications were logically irrefragable, he had no superior. With such assurance, one had but to take one's opponent's case apart, proposition by proposition, and expose his failure at the same process, his disagreement with scripture. In theory each disputant asked simply to be shown wherein he was at fault in order that he might revoke his error in a spirit of humility. In practice few were able, in proportion to their zeal and prowess in such disputes, to refrain from concluding that an opponent who remained unconvinced and who refused to admit his error was willfully turning away from truth, that his disagreement sprang from malice, rooted in sin, which conscience required should be rebuked. Hence all argument ran more and more to refutation, refutation ran to the exposing of error upon error, and the exposing of error gave way to personal attack upon the motives and character of one's opponent. Debate, which was supposed to lead without fail to harmony and agreement, plunged all parties more and more deeply into disagreement and contention; the more deeply embittered the longer the dispute continued.

Goodwin himself, humanist, Platonist, devotee of Acontius, understood well enough how all this came about. He understood how easily men grow angry in intricate and difficult disputes when their arguments are rebutted. And with scripture to appeal to, what argument could not be rebutted? He understood also how quickly zeal for truth corrupts into mere pride of opinion, lust for power, and fear of change. How sad it is, he exclaims, 'to see what commotions, tumults, and combustions' are raised up in the minds and spirits of men by the appearance of any truth which threatens to 'rack them from off the lees of their old customes, or compell them to a restitution of what they have unjustly taken, and peaceably injoyed for a long time . . . to see what

hurryings up and downe, what ingaging of parties, . . . what rem-
bling over Authors old and new, . . . what evading substantiall and
cleare interpretations of Scripture . . . what casting abroad of calum-
nies and reproaches . . . what shiftings, what blendings, what colour-
ings, what pretendings, what disgracings, . . . what appealings to fire,
sword, prisons, banishment, confiscations, and all to turn a beam of light
and glorie, into darknes & shame, to keep a new-born Truth from ruling over them.' [66] But though he understood all this, he himself could
not stop disputing or keep from growing choleric in deploring choler
and calumny in others.

Truth, for Goodwin as for Milton, surely existed, one and entire, and
was revealed in the scriptures. Not that the scriptures were clear and
consistent in all their parts or that any text or version or interpretation
of scripture in any language or translation was to be taken once and for
all as the literal authentic Word of God. Revelation was an unfinished
but progressive process of indefinite duration in which all men were
called to participate. Yet truth was not on that account less certainly
revealed. It was the more certainly made known because it was revealed
to reason, because, that is, it had to be searched for, pieced together,
applied and proved, every item of it, in discourse—discourse prolonged
until every point had been cleared and all differences composed. God
gave gifts of reason and understanding to men along with the scriptures,
'whereby to throw downe the mountains, and to fill up the valleys that
are in them, and to make the rough things plaine, to make a clear peace
between things that seeme to be at variance.' [67] This meant that every
idea suggested to Goodwin's mind by the scriptures had to be set forth
in rounded, cadenced, intricate periods and that every branch and twig
of argument had to be run out upon to the very tip and its strength
or weakness determined and demonstrated. It meant too, unhappily,
that after he had explained a point, Goodwin had often to explain the
explanation, so that Walwyn said of him that 'he spent much time . . .
to make plain things difficult to be understood, and then labour'd again
to make them plain and easie . . . but he had so perplex'd them, as
that he could not.' [68]

Nevertheless, whenever he stopped laying about him in point by
point dueling with the assailants who sprang up about him the more
numerously the oftener he refuted them, Goodwin gave striking ex-

pression to the ideas of liberty and equality implied in Puritan dissent. No one, he declared, who said 'unto men excellently gifted by God . . . and ardently desired of men, for the work of the Ministry, *Preach not in that Name*, except you will preach in our name also,' could be said to speak according to the Word of God which is free.[69]

The true and proper *foundation of Christian Religion* is not inke and paper, not any book, or books, not any writing, or writings whatsoever, whether *Translations*, or *Originalls*; but that substance of matter, those gracious counsells of God concerning the salvation of the world by Jesus Christ, which indeed are represented, and declared, both in Translations, and Originalls, but are essentially and really distinct from both, and no waies, for their natures and beings, depending on either of them.[70]

Saving knowledge depends upon nothing but the individual's faithful exercise of the ability given him by grace to learn the truth, and the scriptures are so conveyed to us as to reveal most to those who strive most to understand them. In giving us the gift of reason, God calls upon us to make use of it, and he covenants with us not to let it fail of its reward.

Here was Christian humanism, formulated in the doctrine of calling and covenant and brought to the defense of the conventicle. Goodwin's congregationalist conception of the church was clearly grounded on an idealistic conception of truth. His method for getting at the knowledge of truth was the free exercise of reason in discussion based upon scripture. His instrument of free discussion was the congregation of believers with their chosen guide, preaching, disputing, and it might be dissenting and separating in peace. Order and unity were to be attained not through the forcible imposition of authority and repression of differences but through the mutual forbearance of equals in unrestrained joint quest of truth. The magistrate had nothing to do in all this except, as a man like other men, to take such part as he might choose or be able to take in the congregation. The separation of powers between church and state and the identification of the church with the voluntary spontaneous aggregation of faithful seekers after knowledge could hardly have been carried farther or been more learnedly, elaborately, and at best eloquently argued. But this meant that in its practical working out the goal of all Goodwin's arguing and exhorting was still the little band of true believers apart from the whole body of men, such as they are—the sect, not the community.

VIII

The Rise of the Leveller Party

1645-1647

THE course of events from January, 1645, when parliament approved the Directory of Worship, to midsummer of 1647, when the army finally marched into London, made clear that the new system of church government and discipline could not be enforced. Parliament had become little more than a self-perpetuating revolutionary junto whose continuance depended upon the army. The army was certain not to support any settlement of the church without ample reservations in the interest of the independent sects and congregations. The immediate result was the failure of the Presbyterians even to get the new system started. The final outcome was the failure of the Puritan movement to bring about any permanent constructive change in the organization of the national church. So far as the structure of the church was concerned, the effect of the Puritan Revolution would be strictly negative. Certain giants and dragons in the way would be laid low, but all the travail of the Puritan spirit to attain the New Jerusalem would get no further in the end than what critics in later generations would despitefully name the dissidence of dissent.

But Puritan preachers had long since put the duty of awakening men's souls to the immanence of grace ahead of the need to reform church government. In the church, true, their wars brought nothing about. In the pulpit, however, and in the press, their teachings had a profound and far-reaching effect upon all Englishmen whatever their eventual alignment on the question of the church. The people learned to believe, regardless of disagreements, that all men were equal, equal in sin but also in their claim to redemption. They learned to look within themselves and to themselves for liberation, confident that the incalculable forces of existence, natural and supernatural, would not betray them in the end. They learned to assume that in the war of Christ and

Antichrist, which filled the whole of history and was now surely approaching its climax, Englishmen had a special role to play. They were assured that they could confirm the truth of these beliefs for themselves from the scriptures and that further confirmation, unnecessary though it might be, was to be found in the other books which the press was bringing them in such abundance. The Puritan effort to reform the church would be discredited as well as rejected, and the Presbyterians would receive their full share of the misunderstanding and abuse which befell Puritans in general after the Restoration. Nevertheless the teachings of the Puritan pulpit came to many men in the revolutionary period with an effect which lasted long after the defeat of the Puritan movement and lost none of its force when leaders of the movement themselves attempted to restrain the energies they had themselves called forth.

The sequence of discussion up to this point must be kept in mind. We have seen that in January, 1644, the small Independent faction in the assembly, knowing that they were certain to be outvoted in that body, appealed for support to parliament and public through the press. They were at once assailed by the Scots and other champions of presbyterianism, and they were seconded by John Goodwin and the gathered churches. But the contention between Presbyterians and Independents within the assembly and outside drew into the discussion such men as Williams, Robinson, Walwyn, Overton, and Milton, men of Puritan convictions whose experience and whose ideas had by 1644 taken them far beyond the purview of godly divines of almost any persuasion whatsoever. After 1644 the army preachers, Saltmarsh, Dell, Peters, and the rest, were spreading ideas even more alarming to the Presbyterians. The pamphlets of the former group, discussed above in Chapter V, and the exhortations of the latter, discussed in Chapter VI, foreshadowed in one way and another the next stage in the development of Puritan revolutionary thought. After 1644 the spiritual dynamic of Puritanism made itself felt more and more in the activities of men who, though not as a rule themselves preachers, were determined without delay to push the beliefs they had derived from the pulpit to extreme practical conclusions. Articulate and demonstrative, conscientious and uninhibited, with something admirable, even heroic, and yet too something preposterous about them, at times startlingly prescient and at other times fantastic and eccentric, but always in deadly earnest and often in hot water, each in his way represents the secular revolutionary springing out of the Puritan reformer.

i. THE FREE-BORN ENGLISHMAN: JOHN LILBURNE

The army preachers in 1645–1646 went on filling soldiers' heads with notions of free justification. The pamphleteers who had challenged the assembly divines in 1644 took various courses. Roger Williams went back to Rhode Island. Henry Robinson, after contending for a time with Prynne, took up several physiocratic Utopian projects in association with Samuel Hartlib. Milton, having committed himself to the idea of England as a humanistic commonwealth, withdrew to scholarly pursuits outside the arena of public debate. Walwyn and Overton, however, now came under the spell of John Lilburne, and these three joined forces to give a radically new turn to Puritan revolutionary discussion. Lilburne,[1] who had been lieutenant colonel in Manchester's regiment, came up to London at the close of the abortive campaign of 1644, expecting to support Cromwell in the dispute with Manchester which led to the organization of the New Model the following spring. No one was more sure than Lilburne of the spirit within him or more determined to obey its calling regardless of consequences. He might have been expected at this juncture to have become the leader and prophet of another gathered church or sect of true believers, but he chose a different course. With Walwyn to manage the organization and Overton to formulate ideas in clear dogmatic prose, he became instead the chief rallying figure of what may be best described as a popular revolutionary political party. The leaders of this group spoke the language of Puritan godliness, and they supported the demand of Independents and sectaries for toleration. Their objective, however, was not simply the toleration of religious differences or even the spiritual redemption of mankind but the promotion of justice for common men by common effort in the body politic. With such a program, they came to exercise a decisive influence on the course taken by the army in 1647 and so on the final disruption of all plans for the restoration of national order under parliament and assembly and within a presbyterian ecclesiastical frame.

The Levellers, as they came to be called, have attracted attention as early proponents of political ideas which became of the greatest importance in the next age. Lilburne, whether looked upon as a demagogue of a type democracy was to breed in abundance or as a hero in the cause of popular liberty, became a legendary figure. Our concern here, however, is not with Lilburne as a prototype or herald or originator of things familiar in the time to come but as a participant in Puritan revolutionary discussion after his return from the army at the close of 1644. We must not attach a kind and degree of significance to his ideas which they may not have had in their own time. He was not a consistent or systematic thinker but first and last a popular leader with a gift for putting himself and his sense of need and right before his public and for getting his public to see its own case dramatically represented in his. We shall understand his contemporary significance best if we begin not with his ideas but with the man himself as he acted out his ideas in the circumstances and the idiom of his own time.

Lilburne was a north country man, born of a family long settled in county Durham. When the royalists arraigned him at Oxford in 1642, he insisted that he was not a yeoman but a gentleman. Like many another young gentleman, however, he grew up as a London apprentice and found himself about 1637 having to strike out for himself and make his way in a difficult time. He was the kind of person likely sooner or later to seek comfort and company and perhaps scope for his abilities among sectaries, the kind Cromwell drew to himself after war began, and he became the epitome of all those implications in the teachings of the army preachers which so alarmed Baxter a few years later. After being whipped and pilloried in April, 1638, for his part in publishing Bastwick's attack upon the bishops, he was kept a prisoner in the Fleet until his release by the Long Parliament. But while a prisoner, he still managed to put his protests into writing and to record both his sufferings and the spiritual compensations he derived from them. Some of these writings at once made their way into print by the help of friends; others he himself published after his release. They are fiery polemics interspersed with stirring accounts of the author's personal experience, variants upon the familiar themes of Puritan spiritual autobiography.

By the time parliament assembled in November, 1640, Cromwell had heard of Lilburne, and early in the session presented a petition for his release. According to contemporary report, one might have supposed from Cromwell's speech on this occasion that the very government itself was endangered by Lilburne's predicament.[2] Freed by order of the house, Lilburne took part in the popular demonstrations of 1641, witnessed the arraignment and execution of Strafford, helped organize the apprentices in support of the petitions against prelacy, and had a hand in the 'no-bishops' riots in December. Meanwhile he had married and got started in the brewing trade, but when war began in 1642, he enlisted as a captain in the regiment of Lord Brooke, fought at Edgehill, was taken prisoner at Brentford, and in December was arraigned at Oxford for treason. He seized this occasion to stage a reckless defiance of his prosecutors, who would probably have hanged him in exasperation if parliament had not insured his release by threat of reprisals leading to an exchange of prisoners.

Back in London, Lilburne received £300 from the Earl of Essex and was offered a government post, which he refused. Instead, he went off to Lincolnshire and joined the army of the Eastern Association. He had in excess exactly the kind of spirit Cromwell was learning to make use of in waging war. He welcomed Lilburne's adherence and soon found ways to turn his zeal and his special talents to account. He was commissioned as major under Colonel King, an officer whose loyalty and competence Cromwell held suspect. Lilburne confirmed Cromwell's suspicions, and the outcome was that King was presently shelved and Lilburne promoted to be lieutenant colonel in Manchester's regiment of dragoons, while still Cromwell's partisan and agent. In the campaign that followed Marston Moor, he seized Tickhill Castle, contrary to Manchester's orders but with Cromwell's connivance, and Cromwell's favor doubtless saved him from being court-martialed. In the quarrel between the two commanders which came to a head after Newbury, Lilburne supported Cromwell and came up to London eager to testify in the latter's behalf before the house of commons. Now, however, began a rift in their relations. Cromwell, bent upon a clear-cut decision in the war, dropped his quarrel with Manchester for sake of winning parliamentary approval for the reorganization of the army, but Lilburne, refusing to compromise or desist, continued his attack upon both Manchester and King. When parliament voted to require officers of the New Model to subscribe the covenant, he resigned his commission on the ground that conscience would not let him serve on such terms. But the truth was that conscience had committed him to another and different kind of war, one which gave his peculiar genius greater scope and freer play.

He began at once in January, 1645, by challenging the position taken by Prynne in *Truth Triumphing*. Prynne's furious campaign against everybody who refused to submit to parliament's absolute authority over church and press offered Lilburne the same kind of provocation which had engaged him on Cromwell's side against Manchester and earlier on that of Prynne's associate Bastwick against the bishops. The quarrel appeared to Lilburne simply another episode in the age-long struggle of Christ and Antichrist. This theme he must often have heard harped upon in the pulpit, and he may have been stirred by it in Milton's tracts, but like Milton he had certainly imbibed it from Foxe's *Actes and Monuments*, the so-called 'Book of Martyrs.' From Foxe Englishmen learned to think of the history of mankind as being centered upon the resistance of the church against the assaults of the evil one and of the history of their own country as being centered upon the very special part that England, as the appointed instrument of Satan's overthrow, was required to play in that struggle. Englishmen of Lilburne's station and temperament had their attention fixed by Foxe particularly upon the role of common men in the story, humble, unlearned, discountenanced, but illuminated none the less by grace, simple soldiers of Jesus Christ, standing up against priests and tyrants, rejoicing and triumphing in the flames of persecution, with clouds of witnesses about them and all heaven looking on. This story, always the same with whatever variations, Lilburne had first reenacted and put into print in 1638 and reprinted after his liberation in 1640.[3] Now in 1645, he published another account of it, written in 1638 from the Fleet, that 'fiery Furnace . . . [in which] I stand *Sentinell* night and day, to defend Sion the City of the living God . . . desiring all my fellow brethren, that professe the same truth with me, as valiant and worthy Soldiers of Jesus Christ to lend me their best and corragious assistance.'[4] And going back to the same story yet again, still later in 1645, he published still another account, also written in the Fleet in 1638, of the grace which had, he said, been first manifested to him at the time of his public suffering, of the strength it had given him to fight the evil one and all his agents, and of the spiritual joy that followed.[5]

Here was Lilburne's spiritual autobiography, a martyr's tale told in the spirit of Foxe by the martyr himself, and as he went on enacting new episodes of martyrdom, he went on publishing the story over and over in old and new versions. He knew himself to be one reborn into the holy community of the elect, and that fact, concerning which there could be no argument, gave him a basis for arguing with anybody on any issue that concerned him—free conscience, free speech, free press, free trade, free vote. It gave him a title to be heard by bishops, preachers, parliament, the public, Prynne, Cromwell. Antichrist, he declared, was always endeavoring to overthrow Christ's kingdom by corrupting the priests of the church and through them all kings and magistrates in order that the civil sword should be used to repress Christian liberty and the authority of Christ over the souls of his elect. But Christ still ruled. Lilburne had tasted the exhilaration of testifying and suffering for Him at the cart's tail and in the stocks before an audience; he had just come from fighting and arguing for Him in the army. Now he brushes aside all of Prynne's cases and precedents. True, King Henry had jostled out the pope, but on the advice of the clergy he had then tried to thrust himself upon Christ's throne, and his successors have done the same. But they have never been able to overcome the true saints, who have still triumphantly opposed them, from the martyrs burned in the time of Queen Mary to 'my selfe and many others, that have suffured worse then death in King *Charles* his dayes.'

This is the great Controversie, that God contends with the whole Earth for, and for which God will make the greatest of Princes and States to *tast a Cup of trembling* . . . And if *England* drinke yet deeper of this Cup, amongst other causes, they may thanke Mr. *Prinne* for it who hath incited them to wage war with the King of Saints . . . For *Sir*, let me tell you, it is the incommunicable Prerogative of Jesus Christ alone to be King of his Saints, and Law-giver to his Church and people, and to reigne in the soules and consciences of his chosen ones.[6]

Thus the doctrine of the indwelling Christ, which was to be preached with such effect in the New Model army, was brought by

Lilburne into the arena of discussion in London just as the New Model army was embarking on its victorious campaign and parliament and assembly were doggedly putting through the new Directory of Worship. His immediate preoccupation was the same as the preachers' had been at the beginning of the struggle, namely to make certain of the freedom to speak. But he was not a preacher, and the doctrine of the liberty of the saints served him as ground for demanding the right of free discussion and a free press for common men like himself. Parliament at its beginning, he said, had opened the press to the use of all 'that so the freeborne *English* Subjects might enjoy their Liberty and Priviledge, which the Bishops had learned of the *Spanish Inquisition* to rob them of, by locking it up under the Key of an *Imprimatur.*' Now Prynne and the '*Blacke-Coates* in the Synod' were attempting to stop the press against men who had hazarded their lives for parliament and the subject's liberty. But Lilburne, 'having received a Talent from the Lord,' declares, 'I conceived my selfe bound in Conscience to imploy it, and lay it out for my Masters best advantage.' This was the same talent and the same temper which had formerly made him declare in the stocks that, knowing himself for a free-born Englishman and a soldier of Jesus Christ, he would speak his mind freely, come what come would. So he confronts Prynne with five propositions 'upón which I will dispute with you, hand to hand before any Auditory in and about the City of *London.*' The propositions, well buttressed by scripture references, sum up the case for Christian liberty as he conceived it. The law of the Old Testament was set aside by Christ. Christ has a kingdom in this world 'where visibly and spiritually he governeth, ruleth and dwelleth,' but its 'matter, forme, Lawes, Worship, Ordinances and Administrations' are every one of them spiritual and not carnal. 'No Parliament, Councell, Synod, Emperour, King, nor Majestrate' has any authority over it or its subjects. Persecution for conscience' sake is not of God but the devil.[7]

'*Sir*,' Lilburne concluded, 'it may be instead of satisfying my desire, you'll run and complaine to the Parliament and presse them upon their Covenant to take vengeance upon me.'[8] This is exactly what Prynne did. Lilburne, in challenging his opponent to debate the issues as he stated them and in putting the challenge directly into print without license, was in effect calling in question that absolute supremacy of the existing parliament of which Prynne was the most egregious advocate. The result was not a debate but a duel between two congenital martyrs fought before the parliamentary Committee for Examinations and in the press. Lilburne would be summoned before the committee, ordered to Newgate after a noisy scene, and presently released. At some point, however, he would publish without license an inflammatory account of the affair, and so be summoned again before the committee and again sent to Newgate.[9] Besides this quarrel there was his claim for the reparations authorized by parliament but still unpaid. There was his need to get started in trade of one sort or another. There were movements and meetings of citizens for the reform of this or that. There was the charge of treason he felt bound to press against Colonel King.

Yet the contention with Prynne gave Lilburne a definite issue and a particular case with himself as principal upon which to focus public attention. It enabled him to find his public, one might say to call forth his natural constituency. The masters of merchant companies, the lawyers, the well-placed ministers, the gentry, all those who in a word thought their interest likely to be best served by the continuance of the present parliament, these men were not as a rule for Lilburne or he for them. His appeal was to the apprentices and young men just out of their apprenticeship, the journeymen, artisans, and distressed tradesmen, men who like himself had their way to make and found it blocked or impeded in a world made more difficult and confusing by revolution and civil war. They flocked from church to church, from conventicle to conventicle. They milled about the shops, taverns, and bookstalls of the city and its suburbs. They read, discussed, and often took a hand at writing the pamphlets daily spawned by the press with or without license. And they followed Lilburne's exploits with interest and delight. Though they might not stand by him in every pinch of circumstance, they saw him as their man, while he gained from them the new sense of power that came from playing the martyr before a visible audience of fellow citizens as well as the audience of saints above, the part of martyr, folk hero, and demagogue. '*Behold how great a matter a little fire kindleth,*' Prynne exclaimed, quoting St. James, '*And the tongue is a fire . . . and is set on fire of hell:* which I may truely apply to *John Lilburns* tongue, and much more to his pen,' kindling combustions among the ignorant vulgar, 'who adore him as the onely *Oracle of Truth.*' [10]

Lilburne's challenge to Prynne was the opening episode in his renewed campaign against Colonel King and the Earl of Manchester. Cromwell might withdraw from that quarrel, but Lilburne now pressed the charge of treason which the citizens of Lincolnshire had brought against King the preceding August. King retaliated in April, 1646, by suing his accuser for 2,000 pounds and obtained his arrest on grounds of slander. Lilburne then addressed and of course published a plea to Justice Reeves of Common Pleas, denying the jurisdiction of that court in his case and appealing to the house of commons.[11] But this appeal, though directed against King, alluded also to the latter's patron, Manchester, and Lilburne was at once summoned (June 11) before the house of lords.

The affair which followed showed his mastery, in the new idioms and mediums of his age, of the ancient art of making trouble for unwary rulers. With reckless disregard of what might happen to himself, he defied the lords in a dramatic scene, or rather a series of scenes, and—most important—put the whole drama as it unfolded before the public in print. The public was at once informed how he was summoned from his bed at six in the morning, how he made his way to Westminster meditating upon his defense, and how, with God directing him in 'his wonted manner,' he contrived with 'my own brain, without any humane help in the world, a *Protestation* and appeal.' At the bar of the house, when asked what he knew about the offending pamphlet, he demanded to be told what offense he was charged with, and when ordered a second time to answer the question, he handed the clerk his written 'Protestation,' insisting upon his right as a commoner to be arraigned and tried by none but his own peers and fellow commoners. The exasperated lords committed him to Newgate 'for bringing into this House, at this Bar, a scandalous and contemptuous Paper.' [12]

But they had not heard the last of Lilburne. Writing from Newgate, he immediately published his account of the affair, calling it *The Free-Mans Freedome Vindicated* (dated by the author June 11, 1646) and including as frontispiece a portrait of himself with prison bars across the face and a legend which read 'The Liberty of The

Freeborne English-man, Conferred on him by the house of lords.' A few days later (June 16) he sent an appeal to the house of commons. On June 22 he was again summoned by the lords. When the summons reached Newgate, he locked himself in his room, composed an address to the chief keeper of London prisons and sent it out by his wife and a friend to be delivered and, of course, printed. Dragged by main force to the bar of the lords, he refused to kneel and was remanded to Newgate for contempt of the house.[13] There he remained until July 11 when he was once more dragged to Westminster, to answer now for all the publications and appearances in which he had been defying the lords' authority. According to his own account he marched boldly into the chamber with his hat on. According to the journal of the house he again refused to kneel and, when the clerk read the charge against him, stopped his ears with his fingers. He was not, however, prevented from making a speech in which he again denied the lords' jurisdiction, appealed to the house of commons, and declared that, if his hearers persevered in their endeavor to destroy the fundamental laws and liberties of England, 'I will venture my life and heart-blood against you to oppose you, with as much zeale and courage as ever I did any of the Kings party, that you set us together by the eares with.' The lords ordered *The Just Mans Justification* and *The Free-Mans Freedome* to be burned by the common hangman; and they committed the author to the Tower for seven years under fine of £2,000. They also reiterated an order they had previously issued, forbidding him the use of pen, ink, and paper and the visits of wife and friends.[14]

There was, however, no way of forcing Lilburne to keep silent for long in any prison. Practical difficulties made strict enforcement of such an order next to impossible in the face of such resistance as he knew only too well how to make. Scruples and hesitancies of one sort or another kept his oppressors from taking extreme measures against him. There was in the man a determination and an ability for putting his case before the public which his adversaries hardly knew how to deal with. The Protestant martyr was turning into the popular political leader and folk hero. This is the meaning of the complicated story of his controversy, first with the lords, then the city authorities, and finally the house of commons. As a prisoner Lilburne was supposed to provide for his own personal necessities, and his wife and friends expected to visit him for that purpose and as things turned out to get his appeals and protestations into print. Every attempt to put him incommunicado gave him another righteous grievance, another occasion for circumventing the ineffective and half-hearted restrictions imposed upon him. When his wife was not permitted to come to him at Newgate or enter the prison yard so that he could talk to her out of his window, she spoke with him from a neighbor's window across the way. When the jailer threatened to board up the window of his room, he threatened to tear down the boards and set fire to them, even though that might be to burn down the building. When the jailer threatened to shut him up in a place where there was no possibility of seeing anybody whatever, Lilburne told the man that that would surely get him his liberty, for he had friends who would then stir themselves to save his life. And when the lieutenant of the Tower told him that, again, he should be permitted no private interview with his wife, he was ready with a protest to which his enemies had no reply except compliance.[15]

The lieutenant was under orders to make certain that his prisoner should 'neither contrive, publish, or spread any seditious or libellous Pamphlets, against both, or either of the Houses of Parliament,'[16] but these instructions could hardly be carried out unless the prisoner's wife could be kept away from him or at least put under strict watch whenever she was admitted. Yet nobody could deny, certainly not the handful of pious men who now made up the house of lords, that God made woman to be a meet help to her husband. A wise and merciful creator, Lilburne declared, had so knit himself and his wife together— 'made us so willing to help to bear one anothers burdens'—that he would rather his brains were beat out than that she should be kept from him. The house of lords was attempting to divorce him from the wife God had given him, and such a breach of divine law was not to be submitted to without violent protest.[17] Elizabeth Lilburne appears indeed to have been a faithful wife according to the injunctions of the apostle and the ideals she may or may not have learned from Milton. She bore her husband's children, shared his thoughts, and ran his errands. She it was who conveyed his petition from Newgate to the house of commons in July,[18] and he had not been long in the Tower when the house received 'The Humble Petition of Elizabeth Lilburne, wife to Lieu. Col. John Lilburne, who hath been for above eleven weeks by-past, most unjustly divorced from him, by the House of Lords, and their tyrannicall officers, against the Law of God, and (as she conceives) the law of the Land.' She was presently to be found—'with eight Gentlewomen more of her friends'—waiting at parliament's doors for an answer to this appeal, and when none came, there followed a petition from Lilburne himself.[19] On September 16, 1646, the lords quietly capitulated to these importunities and to the law of God by ordering the lieutenant of the Tower to permit 'the Wife of Lieutenant Colonel *John Lilbourne* to come to him, and reside with him, when and as often as he shall desire.' [20]

Lilburne's appeal from the jurisdiction of the lords to that of the commons put the members of that house into a quandary. Though jealous of the privileges of commoners, they were not eager to quarrel with lords. On July 3, 1646, they referred his petition and that of his wife to a committee previously appointed to consider such matters. On July 9 they named a special committee with Henry Marten as chairman to determine the facts concerning his imprisonment. On October 27 and again on November 6, this committee called Lilburne in for a hearing but still postponed decision. He, however, was not the man to wait quietly for any committee to make up its mind. In *An Anatomy of the Lords Tyranny*, dated November 9 and published in total disregard of the printing ordinance, he reported in detail what had been done to him since his first committall to Newgate in June, how he had tussled with his jailers, how he had defied the lords at the bar of their own house, what he had said to the commons' committee. That is to say, having appealed from the lords to the commons without result, he appealed from both through the press to the public.

He was, to be sure, still a prisoner, and so he remained until parliament in 1648, for reasons of its own, revoked the sentence against him. But imprisonment in the Tower did not so much impede his activities as enable him to focus public attention upon them. It gave him something like leisure to read, reflect, and elaborate his case. It fixed him for the time in a place where other men with grievances and ideas could rally about him to some purpose. It gave him a stage on which he could make the most of his gift for dramatizing the common cause in his personal predicament. The lieutenant of the Tower, who loved his duty less than he did his fees and gratuities, could be bought off. Lilburne let no one forget that the lords had tried to divorce him from his wife, separate him from his friends, deny him the right of free utterance in his own defense, and require him to pay for his own maintenance while a prisoner of state. Nevertheless, he was soon enjoying freedom of movement within the precincts of the Tower, the use of books and writing materials, and abundance of visitors. Nor was it long before he was able to resume the campaign he had begun the year before on behalf of his particular constituency.[21]

The men who now looked to Lilburne were men faced by a predicament characteristic enough of a burgeoning mercantile economy but aggravated by revolution and civil war. Although the licensed monopolies of an earlier period had presumably been reduced, certain privileged companies still remained, and indeed the Merchant Adventurers had been given special advantages by the Long Parliament in return for financial aid. But beyond that, the fact was that, as trade and wealth increased, control of mercantile organizations tended to fall into relatively fewer hands. At the same time the number grew of men who saw their opportunities for getting ahead in the world, let alone acquiring wealth, steadily diminish as the result of what they naturally believed to be unjust and illegal restraints. Thus Lilburne, upon leaving the army in 1645, found himself debarred from entering the wool trade because he could not hope to compete with the Merchant Adventurers.[22] Here, surely, was another invasion of the native rights of Englishmen like the monopoly of the Stationers' Company over the publication of books and like that attempted by the Presbyterian divines over preaching. Thomas Johnson protested against such practices in *A Discourse Consisting of Motives for the Enlargement and Freedome of Trade* (April 23, 1645) and Lilburne took up the argument in *Englands Birth-Right* (October, 1645) and in *Innocency and Truth Justified* (January 6, 1646).

But this quarrel like others was soon with his help given concrete political application. Political authority and economic power in the city had, not surprisingly, gravitated into the same hands. The city government, that is, was dominated by the lord mayor and court of aldermen, representing the great mercantile interests, while the more popularly representative common council was permitted less to say, and men of the class represented by Lilburne were kept out of city elections. On April 15, 1645, the lord mayor, aldermen, and common council received a petition from 'divers Citizens' proposing that greater scope be given to the council and begging for various popular reforms. Nothing came of this petition, except that Lilburne published it in *Englands Birth-Right* in October, but the accompanying discontent did not subside and Lilburne in the Tower was ready in his own way to foment, justify, and express it.

The story as he tells it is as follows. On September 29, 1646, the day appointed for the election of lord mayor, a certain citizen of London, 'a Watch-maker in Cornhill, (a man that in these late wars, hath freely and gallantly adventured his life for the preservation of the present Parliament, and Englands Liberties),' presented himself at Guildhall with divers other citizens and demanded the right to vote. He was denied and excluded in a noisy scene but not before he had submitted a 'Protestation' against such treatment on behalf of the 'Free-men, Citizens, and Commonalty of . . . London.' Lilburne at once heard of this affair, if indeed he had not helped to bring it about, and went immediately, he says, 'to old Mr. *Colet,* the Record-keeper of the Tower, and asked him, if hee had the originall Records of the Charters of *London;* and understanding he had them; out of my penury, I bestowed three or foure pound for the Copies of those that were most usefull for me.' He also sent for 'an antient book' of which he had heard, printed 'above 100 yeares agoe, containing many of the Liberties and Franchises of London.' His next step was to get a friend to translate the French and Latin of both book and records for him. Within a month, also, he had dispatched to the printer a pamphlet of seventy-two pages, *Londons Liberty in Chains discovered,* subscribed 'From my prerogative, and illegall imprisonment in the Tower of *London,* this present Octob. 1646.' [23]

Nothing could better illustrate Lilburne's sense of journalistic time-liness, his gift for exploiting each occasion as it arose for advancing his cause and for suiting his argument and story to the mood of his public. Starting off with several verses from Jeremiah—'Shalt thou reign, because thou closest thy selfe in Cedar?'—he printed King John's charter, with a translation, authorizing the 'Barons' of London

to elect one of their number each year as mayor, and he followed this
with an account of the recent fracas at Guildhall, including the text of
the excluded citizens' 'Protestation.' Thus he committed himself to the
principle that the responsibility of the state for the welfare of the
people required the election of governors by the equal vote of its
citizens and that this right of suffrage had been the law of England,
approved by king and parliament, since the first founding of the
monarchy by the Saxons. Having made his position on that principle
clear beyond mistaking, he added a long account of the injustices that,
as a member of the commonalty, he was having to suffer at the hands
of the lords, the Merchant Adventurers, the Presbyterians, the lieutenant of the Tower, and John White, one of the warders, who had
accused him of writing certain scandalous pamphlets of which, it
happened, he was not the author. *Londons Liberty in Chains discovered* concluded with the petitions of Elizabeth Lilburne and her
husband to the house of commons. In *The Charters of London: or,
The second Part of Londons Liberty in Chaines Discovered*, published
in December, 1646, Lilburne backed up his argument for the popular
election of city officials by printing the texts, translated into English
and attested by the record-keeper of the Tower, of charters granted to
the city by Henry V and Edward II. At the same time he renewed his
attack on what he deemed the illegal monopolistic practices of the merchant companies.

One thing was evident in all this. Parliament, becoming more
deeply involved in controversy with the army, was unable to make up
its mind what to do with Lilburne. All through the early months of
1647 the committee appointed to consider his case still withheld
decision, while he maintained his clamor against the injustice of his
imprisonment. One evening in the Tower, as he was lighting a caller
to the gate, he was brusquely ordered to his room, and the result was
another pamphlet, *The Oppressed Mans Oppressions . . . In which
the oppressing cruelty of all the Gaolers of England is declared, and
particularly the Lieutenants of the Tower* (January 30, 1647). Included for good measure were a reply to Thomas Edwards' *Gangraena*
and a general attack on the Presbyterians. A few days later (February
8) the commons committee for the suppression of scandalous unlicensed pamphlets summoned Lilburne to answer for this publication,

but he refused to reply to any question until the chairman ordered the doors opened and gave him permission to make a speech. So, he says, 'I lifted up my soule to my old and faithfull Counceller, the Lord *Jehovah*,' and spoke in his now well-known vein not so much to the committee as to his accustomed public. A full account of the affair appeared in *The resolved mans Resolution,* signed and dated by the author, April 30, 1647. In the meantime, he had joined with Richard Overton, now in Newgate at the behest of the lords, in another address to the house of commons, called *The out-cryes of oppressed Commons* (February 28). The purport of this appeal was summed up in the statement, 'what by the wills of the Lords is done to us today, may be done to any Commoner of England tomorrow.'

Thus Lilburne in February, 1647, once more raised the issue concerning the responsibility of rulers and the rights of subjects with which the struggle had begun five years before. The preachers at that time had justified resistance to the king on the ground that Charles opposed the reformation of the church as required by the Lord, of whose will revealed in scripture they were the acknowledged spokesmen. The apologists for parliament had done the same on the ground that Charles had betrayed the people, for whom parliament professed to speak. But Lilburne was one of the people, and if parliament now denied him and them their just and legal rights, was he not bound in law and conscience to protest and resist as formerly parliament had done against the king and the bishops? And were not the people required to protect themselves by whatever means they could against the renewal of oppression from any quarter?

In February, 1647, when he raised these questions, Lilburne was in a very different position from that in which he had been when he challenged Prynne in January, 1645. He had, to be sure, spent much of the interval in prison, but he had been able to use prison as a post of vantage from which to press his appeal and make himself and his wrongs known, and the longer the house of commons delayed decision on his case the more difficult it became to quell him or his influence. He was no voice crying in the wilderness. The notions of right and the sense of needs unfulfilled to which he gave utterance were becoming the familiar obsession of a considerable or at any rate very vocal part of the public. His sympathizers and followers in the city had their links with the rank and file of the army. And parliament was soon to furnish the army with a grievance which would add the soldiery to Lilburne's constituency and give his ideas and his example sudden new great force and meaning. It was the army, indoctrinated by Lilburne and his party, which would put the final decisive veto both to the existing parliament's claim to absolute authority and to the assembly's plan to impose presbyterian government and discipline on the church.

Different though his position was, Lilburne was still the same man when he turned against parliament in 1647 as when in 1638 he had been whipped and pilloried for speaking out against the bishops. His ideas had not changed so much as they had unfolded and set under the stress of soldiering and controversy. He was still the man who had won Cromwell's sympathy and some measure of his confidence. He was still the Puritan saint. Or rather, he was what the Puritan saint and sectary became, once he had emerged from the conventicle, taking his Puritan calling, his conscience, and his assurance of grace with him. Grace abounded for Lilburne as for others, but spiritual warfare in his version of the story became directed against the evil in human institutions rather than in the heart of the sinner himself. The end sought was not personal conversion, but the general good. The struggle of Christ's redeemed ones became a struggle for the redemption of the state. The holy community, the New Jerusalem, came to be conceived rather as a going community of free citizens than a withdrawn though visible congregation of the elect. It was a conception not too different in principle from Milton's ideal of a humanistic Puritan commonwealth, but far less remote from the actual conditions of English society.

Yet Lilburne's endeavor to realize his spiritual aspirations on the secular plane led to a significant development in his intellectual activity after his return from the army. In his attacks upon the bishops, he had thought and written almost entirely in the apocalyptical terms he drew from Revelation and the prophets under the inspiration of John Foxe. When his war with Antichrist in the persons of Prynne, Manchester, King, and the lords landed him in the Tower, he used his enforced leisure to read something besides Isaiah, Daniel, and John. The preachers, seconded by Milton, had brought history to the support of scripture in their contention against prelacy. The lawyers had cited law against the king. Englishmen of Lilburne's class were prone to litigation, familiar with courts of law and the forms of legal pleading. At the same time they thought of law as derived from past experience rather than from abstract principles, and they thought of scripture less as a precise code of rules than as a record of experience from which rules were to be deduced. Hence royalists and parliamentarians alike, when they came to the brink of civil war, resorted to arguments of legality grounded upon custom, precedent, and the analogy of scripture. The literature of that discussion was of course already known to Lilburne when the lords sent him to jail, but in Newgate and the Tower he found time to read it more systematically than he had ever done before. The result was that he learned to extend his role as martyr in the cause of the indwelling Christ to include that of advocate at the bar, contending for popular rights embodied in English law, sanctioned by the Word of God, handed down from the immemorial past, and acknowledged and asserted by his opponents and oppressors themselves.

This is not, of course, to say that he ceased to present himself always in the perspective of English Protestantism. He still put himself forward as but the latest in the long line of English martyrs for conscience' sake which stretched back through the pages of Foxe to Wycliffe and the Lollards. But now he raised the question whether the faith for which the martyrs and he suffered was not all one with the law of reason and conscience which God had written in the breasts of common men—the law which by natural necessity, as he read in St. German's *Doctor and Student,* took precedence over and was not to be superseded by any contrary rule of state. Was this law not the same as the great natural law of self-preservation which, he read in Parker's *Observations,* prompted men after the fall to bind themselves by covenant to obey their chosen rulers, which bound their rulers to serve them and which also required them to protect themselves and maintain the state whenever rulers, as for example King Charles, betrayed their trust? On these principles parliament itself, which Parker held was in essence the people, had justified its resistance even by force against the king, as Lilburne read in the book he generally refers to as 'The Book of Declarations,' more precisely *An Exact Collection of all Remonstrances . . . and other Remarkable Passages betweene the Kings most Excellent Majesty, and his High Court of Parliament* (1643).

But this was not all. Parliament in 1642 had ordered the publication of the three parts of Coke's *Institutes of the Laws of England,* which the king had kept from the press. Here Lilburne read again that the essence of law was reason written by God in the breasts of the people. And here he also read that the common law of England, emanating from the people and declared by judges in particular cases as they arose, was the fundamental law of the state, superior to prerogative, statute, and all forms of arbitrary power. Every individual case and every enactment of rulers was to be judged by the law revealed in antecedent cases, running as far back as it might prove necessary or possible to go. Coke's search for precedents took him back in the second part of the *Institutes* to Magna Charta and from Magna Charta, by the aid of a unique thirteenth-century document he had the luck to turn up at Cambridge, to the reputed laws of the Saxons. This latter work, entitled *Mirroir des Justices* and commonly attributed to Andrew Horn, told how the Saxons, having by God's command reduced Britain to order, came together and drew up a set of laws, by which they agreed to govern and to be governed. The author of *Mirroir des Justices* knew nothing, really, about the Saxons, but he took this way to express the common human wish that the laws of the state and their administration should conform to principles of morality derived from the scriptures. Coke, however, seized upon the *Mirroir des Justices* as documentary evidence of the true origin of the laws of England.[24] Sprung from the hearts of the Saxons, handed down by Alfred and Edward, overridden by the Norman conqueror, recovered by the people in Magna Charta, they had been maintained ever since in the courts of common law and by parliament. The exaltation of the legendary Saxons led Coke also to exalt the English language and to demand that it should at last displace French and Latin as the language of English law.

The errors of fact and confusions of thought involved in such notions as these need not concern us. The important thing was that in these years Lilburne was devouring the books which had been brought forth at the beginning of the struggle in defense of parliament's revolutionary action against the king. He had made peculiarly his own the doctrine that a special responsibility rests upon rulers in respect of rights which, through the grace of God and in the order of nature and according to the laws of England, inhere in the people. To this principle he appealed in one way or another in the various reports and pleas, already recounted in these pages, which he contrived to issue in the course of his contention with the lords. The same idea was set forth at greater length and in more considered detail in certain pamphlets also issued in these years by Lilburne himself or by others writing under his direction or influence. In 1645 there appeared an anonymous tract called *Englands Birth-Right Justified Against all Arbitrary Usurpation, whether Regall or Parliamentary, or under what Vizor soever*. Thomason dated his copy October 10 and wrote on the flyleaf, 'Supposed to be Lilbournes or some friends of his.' The work opens with a quotation—'there is in Laws an equitable, and a literall sense' —from the manifesto issued in defense of parliament in 1642 with the heading 'A Question answered: How Laws are to be understood, and obedience yeelded?' [25] Without law to express the people's will and serve their needs, the writer of *Englands Birth-Right* declares, there can be no true freedom but only oppression. Law apart from the equity which is its reason and end is 'a shell without a kernell, a shadow without a substance, and a body without a soul.' This principle holds for parliament no less than for a king. So the writer, surely Lilburne, pours out his indignation that, after all that has been said and done, the distresses of the people are still unrelieved, their wrongs unrighted. The preaching of the Word is still engrossed by the ministers in their black coats, the trade in wool by the Merchant Adventurers, the printing of books by the Stationers' Company, the administration of justice by lawyers and judges, 'theeves *cum privilegio*.' The pages of this pamphlet are well sown with references to Coke, Magna Charta, and of course the scriptures.[26]

In his reply to Prynne early in January, 1646, *Innocency and Truth Justified*, Lilburne urged the same ideas in the same mood. He confronted the author of *The Soveraigne Power of Parliaments* with the argument drawn from Parker's *Observations* and St. German's *Doctor and Student*, that men cannot be compelled to obey any commands contrary to that fundamental law which requires all men to seek their own interest and safety. In November, Lilburne's pleading for his rights under the law of England and of nature was again recorded in lawyerly fashion in an anonymous tract, perhaps by Henry Marten, certainly by someone with a technical knowledge of the law, called *Vox Plebis, or, The Peoples Out-cry Against Oppression, Injustice, and Tyranny. Wherein the Liberty of the Subject is asserted, Magna Charta briefly but pithily expounded. Lieutenant Colonell Lilburnes Sentence published and refuted. Committees arraigned, Goalers condemned, and remedies provided.* To the argument from Coke, from the *Mirroir des Justices,* Magna Charta, and the Petition of Right, were here added illustrations from Roman history, Lucian, and the story of Reynard the fox, together with the shrewd warning that governments which invade their subjects' liberties in violation of law 'incite the people to find out and invent wayes unusuall, and of innovation, to free themselves from their oppressors.' [27]

Lilburne's case was argued yet again in January, 1647, in an anonymous pamphlet of over a hundred pages, called *Regall Tyrannie discovered: or, A Discourse, shewing that all lawfull (approbational) instituted power by God amongst men, is by common agreement, and mutual consent.* If the author of this extraordinary performance was not Lilburne himself, it was surely someone who had talked long hours with him in his Tower room. Once more we hear the story of his contention with the lords. Again we hear the application to his case of the argument parliament had used against the king five years before, set forth with the headlong inconsecutiveness of excited speech, going on and on. The argument is supported with an outpouring of quasi-historical proof from the Old Testament and English chronicle history. All men, it is said, are sons of Adam, by nature equal and free under God, the sole absolute universal ruler, who has written his law—the ten commandments—in the hearts of all men. The sin of Adam did not abrogate the natural freedom and equality of men but put upon them the need for protecting themselves from one another. This they did by delegating power in trust to magistrates. The writer runs through a number of scripture cases in proof of this notion and then adds a long account of English history. In Saxon England the people were said to have exercised their natural sovereignty under God through representative popular assemblies until they were conquered by William the bastard. He and his successors tyrannized over the people by arbitrary laws in a foreign tongue and by the prerogative of crown and lords. The people, however, rising in their own defense, wrung from their conquerors an agreement—Magna Charta—to rule by law in obedience to natural right. This right and this agreement have been violated first by the bishops and then by the lords in persecuting and imprisoning Lilburne. They must be restored and his appeal granted if the house of commons is truly to fulfill its trust as the people's chosen representative body.

Power is originally inherent in the People, and it is nothing else but that might and vigour, which such and such a Society of men contains in it self, and when by such and such a Law of common consent and agreement, it is derived into such and such hands, God confirms the Law. And so man is the free and voluntary author, the Law is the instrument, and God is the establisher of both.[28]

Thus Lilburne learned to derive his conception of agreement as the basis of law from the legend of Adam's fall, to read both legend and doctrine into English history, and so to make both history and scripture support the conclusion that parliament owed its being under God solely to the people. This was a conception which many men now found difficult to resist, at least in principle, but Lilburne went on to raise a practical question, which he made no less difficult to evade, namely, who in particular at the moment were the persons whose consent was necessary to the state and to whom parliament owed its being? The depleted band of members, with their hand-picked recruits, whom there was no recognized means of replacing at Westminster, were they the people or did their writ run indefinitely? Or did the people consist only of the parties interested in the continuance of these men in power? Or were the saints the people, elect souls liberated by grace and known visibly as such, they and no others? Or did the people comprise the multitude of common men who on the morrow of victory over the king found their wrongs, as they believed, still unrighted, their needs of livelihood, their expectation of new heaven, new earth, still unsatisfied? And what of the ungodly, the unbelieving and the misbelieving, were they not also sons of Adam, equal and free by nature?

Here were difficulties, paradoxes, and dilemmas to alarm rulers and puzzle philosophers, but Lilburne and his party do not appear to have been much troubled by the question where Christian liberty left off and natural liberty began. For immediate practical purposes the people to whom and for whom Lilburne held parliament responsible were all those whom he could induce to see themselves in him, all those, in short, whom he could reach through the exercise of his talent for getting himself, his wrongs, his sufferings, his demands and arguments, known and talked about by making scenes in public places and by getting his story somehow into print. But he presented his own case always as everybody's case, and he was ready on that ground to go to any extreme to make certain that it should be heard. He stood for the poor Johns of England. If the law *salus populi suprema lex* was to hold at all, it must hold for him. If justice were not done in his case, instantly and completely, how could anyone be certain that it would ever be done for anybody?

ii. THE RIGHTS OF MAN: RICHARD OVERTON

Lilburne was a figure about whom the various groups and factions opposed to presbyterian government and discipline in any form could rally and for a time unite. His exploits against the bishops and in the war, thanks largely to his own telling, were well known. His own religious experience, of which also he made no secret, won him the approval of independents and sectaries, particularly those who looked to John Goodwin for spiritual leadership. His challenge to Prynne in January, 1645, opened a series of attacks on Prynne and the Presbyterians by Goodwin himself and by Walwyn and Overton.[29] Lilburne took a prominent part in a meeting at the Windmill Tavern about the first of June which appointed him one of a committee to draft a petition begging parliament to order the members of the assembly home, ostensibly to rouse the people against the king, actually, according to Prynne, to break the assembly up.[30] When the lords shortly afterward sent Lilburne to Newgate, we hear of a petition to the house of commons in his behalf, signed by two or three thousand persons.[31] He apparently kept quiet in January, 1646, when the London ministers issued a manifesto against toleration, to which Overton and Walwyn, however, made quick and sharp reply,[32] but we hear of him again in May when the lord mayor, aldermen, and common council, after loud debate at Guildhall, sent a petition and remonstrance to parliament calling for the instant establishment of presbyterianism, the suppression of heresy, and the conclusion of peace by negotiation with the king.[33] Before this demand could actually be delivered (May 26), Lilburne, for the moment out of prison, was seen at Westminster distributing a manifesto against it, entitled *A Word in Season* (May 18). This was the work of Walwyn's pen, and John Goodwin's followers subscribed fifty shillings for the printing of 10,000 copies.[34] When Lilburne presently found himself in the Tower, he was indebted to Goodwin and his people, more, he says, than to other congregations, for 'large kindnesses manifested unto me in this my present imprisonment in supplying my necessities.' [35]

Thus various opponents of presbyterianism came together in support of Lilburne as he embarked upon his campaign for his rights as a free-born Englishman. One of his principal necessities, of course, was to get his numerous pleas and protestations into print. John Goodwin's people may have been helpful in this as in other things, but there was probably by this time no lack of printers and booksellers ready to do his business for him out of sympathy as well as for profit. Richard Overton, author of *Mans Mortallitie, The Araignement of Mr. Persecution,* and other pamphlets, had a hand in the clandestine press which appears to have printed most of Lilburne's productions.[36] William Larner was a bookseller who was clearly not above making a penny out of the sale of publications which, as Edwards assures us, 'being unlicensed and of such kinde of Arguments, sell dear.' [37] On March 20, 1646, there came into Thomason's possession a copy of an anonymous pamphlet of eight pages, called *The Last Warning to all the Inhabitants of London,* full of the violent rhetoric characteristic of Overton. Without liberty of conscience, the writer declared, we should have no army, and we should have neither an army nor liberty of conscience, if the Scots and the clergy are permitted to play their old game of cozening and dividing parliament and people. Two days later agents of the Stationers' Company caught Larner with several copies of this production in his shop, and the Committee for Examinations called him in for questioning. His story was that, in the usual manner of his trade, asking no questions, he had 'bought 25, of the said books, not knowing what they were for matter, or examining the

Person, what he was that brought them, or where was his aboad, not suspecting any danger in them.' Though the thing had not been licensed, he makes the point that neither had it as yet been prohibited. At any rate he refused to answer the committee's questions on the ground that he had been charged with no offense, and when a committee of the lords also presently summoned him, he followed Lilburne's cue and appealed from their jurisdiction to the house of commons. The lords sent him to Newgate, where, however, he prepared and sent to the printer *A true Relation* of these proceedings which, the title page tells us, 'comming to the hands of some of his, and the Commonwealths friends, are Published by them to the view of the World.' [38]

Larner's fate did not, however, stop the activity of Overton's pen or press. Shortly after the lords had sent Lilburne to the Tower in June, 1646, he issued *A Remonstrance of Many Thousand Citizens, and other Free-born People of England, To their owne House of Commons. Occasioned through the Illegall and Barbarous Imprisonment of that Famous and Worthy Sufferer for his Countries Freedoms, Lieutenant Col. John Lilburne* (July 7).[39] This was followed a few weeks later by *An Alarum To the House of Lords: Against their insolent Usurpation, of the Common Liberties, and Rights of this Nation. Manifested by them, in their present Tyrannicall Attempts against that Worthy Commoner, Lieutenant Col. John Lilburne* (July 31). The author and printer of such reckless attacks upon authority could not escape detection indefinitely. Betrayed apparently by a fellow printer, Overton was arrested at his lodgings in Southwark on August 11 and dragged before a committee of the lords. There, following Lilburne's example, he denied the jurisdiction of his examiners and refused to answer questions. The lords committed him to Newgate, whence he dispatched an account of the affair, dated August 17, to be printed apparently at the same press as before by his wife and brother. The title begins *A Defiance against all Arbitrary Usurpations Or Encroachments, either of the House of Lords, or any other, upon the Soveraignty of the Supreme House of Commons.*[40]

But the man's recklessness was still not exhausted. In October he issued another violent pamphlet, called *An Arrow Against All Tyrants And Tyrany, shot from the Prison of New-gate into the Prerogative*

Bowels of the Arbitrary House of Lords (dated by the author October
12). Next he appealed to the house of commons, and on November 3
he appeared before the committee, headed by Marten, on commoners'
liberties. The hearing over and the committee having come to no
decision, he refused, as a commoner, to move hand or foot and had to
be dragged through the streets back to Newgate. There his jailers
took from him the second part of Coke's *Institutes,* firmly clasped to
his belly, by main force. The authorities next went after his wife and
brother for continuing to operate his printing press. Brought to the
bar of the lords in January, 1647, they also defied the house and were
remanded to prison, the wife to Bridewell, whither she refused to take
a step and had to be dragged bodily, though quick with child. But still
her husband was not to be silenced. The story of her defiance and of his
own before the commons committee was soon put out in print with
the title, here much abbreviated, *The Commoners Complaint: Or, A
Dreadful Warning From Newgate, to the Commons of England.*[41]

Thus loudly emulating Lilburne, Overton got himself dragged off
to Newgate with Magna Charta in his embrace. To readers better
attuned to eighteenth- than to seventeenth-century modes of expression
in such matters, his writing and his ideas seem more intelligible and
original than Lilburne's. This was not the case with contemporaries.
One man was a fiery embittered reckless pamphleteer, but the other
was the English Protestant martyr, setting himself up to be attorney
for Everyman. The one makes modern readers think of Tom Paine;
the other made men of his own time think of Foxe and of Coke and
St. German. That is to say, Overton indicates more positively the
direction to be taken in future by the ideas he shared with Lilburne,
but his contemporary importance was not on that account greater, nor
did he actually go much further in his thinking. He followed Lilburne's
lead as Lilburne had followed that of the preachers and lawyers in
justifying revolution by the doctrine that civil obedience springs from
a covenant dictated by natural necessity. The difference was that
Lilburne pled for his rights under the social contract as an Englishman appealing to the laws of England and as a regenerate saint according to the doctrine of holy scripture, while Overton, though he made
some play with Magna Charta and quoted scripture now and then

like other men, laid claim to the same rights as the universal rights of man, revealed to man in nature.

In *Mans Mortallitie*, the tract which had earned disapproval in 1644 along with Williams' *Bloudy Tenent* and Milton's divorce tract, Overton had argued in effect that, thanks to the atonement, all men were equal and that their natural powers were sufficient for them to avail themselves of grace if they would. Justification was free, and free justification was taken to mean that nature revealed to reason all that men needed for their own good. Overton did not much concern himself to supply scriptural and historical proof of these principles, but having asserted them as obvious truths, he went on to draw practical conclusions from them with all the dogmatic assurance of the revolutionary doctrinaire. In *A Remonstrance of Many Thousand Citizens* he asserted that parliament men held their position in trust for the people—'Wee are your Principalls, and you our Agents' [42] —and that the present body should provide for a new parliament to be elected each year. In *An Alarum to the House of Lords* and *A Defiance against all Arbitrary Usurpations* he protested against the invasion of the people's rights by the lords, by the clergy, and by monopolists of one sort or another. In *An Arrow against All Tyrants*, he asserted without qualification that since all men

are delivered of God by the hand of nature into this world, every one with a naturall, innate freedome and propriety (as it were writ in the table of every mans heart, never to be obliterated) even so are we to live, every one equally and alike to enjoy his Birthright and priviledge; even all whereof God by nature hath made him free.

No officer of state or church holds his authority directly from God. God's will is expressed only in nature, only in the needs and powers he has implanted in every individual, and these no man can forego even by his own consent, 'Every man by nature being a King, Priest and Prophet in his owne naturall circuit and compasse, whereof no second may partake, but by deputation, commission, and free consent from him, whose naturall right and freedome it is.' As for the writer himself, for Lilburne, and for others in their predicament, Overton declares, 'It is but the just rights and prerogative of mankind (whereunto the people of England are heires apparent as well as other Nations) which we desire.' [43]

iii. THE LEVELLER PARTY: WILLIAM WALWYN

John Goodwin's people supplied Lilburne's necessities. Overton or some of his connections saw to the printing of his protests and manifestoes. But the organization of the movement which now rallied about Lilburne in the Tower was not the work of a sectarian of any sort or of a reckless emulator of Lilburne's own tactics. It was in the first instance the work of William Walwyn, who claimed to belong to no particular religious group but to be simply a devotee of love and reason, interested in his fellow men and in all the varieties of their beliefs and opinions. While still using a sufficient admixture of the language of godliness, he exploited Lilburne's notoriety in order to hold up to men not merely the assurance of grace but the expectation of serving common needs and securing common rights by common action in the circumstances immediately at hand. In January, 1645, when Lilburne was getting back from the war and Prynne was blasting Independency in *Truth Triumphing*, Walwyn was standing up for Baptists and the like in the second edition of his anonymous *Compassionate Samaritane*, and in the ensuing months he took part with Lilburne and with John Goodwin's people in the argument for liberty of conscience. The two men probably came together at the meeting at the Windmill Tavern about the first of June, which proposed, temporarily at least, to dissolve the assembly. They were certainly both present at a meeting of the parliamentary Committee for Examinations on July 19. Walwyn was there as one of a group of citizens who were pressing charges of corruption against Speaker Lenthall and his brother. Lilburne was there on business of his own. Prynne, who was also on hand, seized the occasion to get Lilburne locked up once more in Newgate, and Walwyn presently defended him in a tract called *Englands Lamentable Slaverie* (October 11), which recommended the prisoner's anonymous *Englands Birth-Right* (October 10) but demurred at his too strictly legalistic argument.[44]

From this point on, it would appear, Walwyn devoted his very special talents to Lilburne's cause, each man serving as a foil to the other.

Lilburne's gift was for taking the center of the stage and focusing attention upon himself as representative and spokesman for his audience. Walwyn's preference was to stay behind the scenes, direct the play, write the lines, and prompt the actors. He maintained his anonymity as long as possible on the ground that whatever a man said in print should be accepted or rejected for its inherent credibility alone. He was, however, unable to escape attention, and the attacks of his enemies, taken together with the replies in which he defended himself, enable us to put together a fairly precise picture of his character and activities. Bastwick first describes him as he waited with his companions outside the Committee for Examinations as 'the most remarkable and taken notice of' in the entire group. He was, it was said, 'mighty diligent about the Common-wealth that day, and the Priviledges of the Subject, and all the fraternity came flocking about him.' [45] Edwards in *Gangraena I* (February 26, 1646) put him down for 'a Seeker, and a dangerous man, a strong head,' given to asking questions which confused weaker heads.[46] *Gangraena II* (May 28) gave more details of the same sort and the promise of a whole book to be issued presently about Walwyn and his associates. In *Gangraena III* (December 28) Edwards shifted his attention from the religious heretics who had occupied him earlier to the army preachers and the men who were lining up in support of Lilburne. Walwyn in reply laid aside his anonymity in a frank but restrained account of his own career and opinions, which he called *A Whisper in the Eare of Mr. Thomas Edwards* (March 13, 1646), and this he followed up by a series of brilliant satirical attacks.[47] Of all the men who attempted to defend themselves against *Gangraena* Walwyn alone countered suspicion and slander with good-humored irony, analyzing and describing the human condition of his enemy with clear-eyed penetration. He alone was able to understand with a certain charity the unhappy state of one who was so afraid of what he took to be evil that he saw danger everywhere hemming him in and believed he could overcome it only by seeking the destruction of everyone he suspected of not sharing his delusions.

But Walwyn's chief concern was not to controvert his critics but to elicit and organize support for the cause he believed that Lilburne represented. Lilburne went on expounding Coke and Magna Charta to his visitors in the Tower while continuing to contend with the lords, to appeal to the commons, and to tell his story to the public in unlicensed print. In the meantime Walwyn went about the town reasoning with men of differing beliefs and opinions, leading them from sermon to sermon, asking them questions, taking them home for talk in his garden or library, putting books into their hands and doubts into their minds. He went to meetings, stirred up discussion, and at the right moment brought all talk to a head in shrewdly drafted petitions, certain to be rejected by parliament but equally certain to provoke still more discussion and discontent. For himself, as we have seen, he had solved the spiritual problem by embracing the belief that men share equally in the grace of God and are free to accept or reject it as they choose, each after his own fashion. His attitude toward the sects was equivocal. At the moment when they were most alarmed at the threat of persecution and most glad to receive support from any quarter, he attacked the proposed heresy ordinance and championed toleration. But he remained essentially a secular vernacular humanist, an admirer of Montaigne, attached to no close communion of saints of any persuasion whatever. Hence the leaders of the sects, perceiving how definitely he was not one with them, naturally concluded that he was against them, as at bottom he was. He tells us that as early as 1645 'some leading people of master John Goodwins'—he instances especially John Price—constituted themselves a committee to gather evidence against him, but seeing that he took up the defense of Goodwin, under attack for *Hagiomastix*, they withheld their hostility for that time.[48] In 1649, however, Price, Kiffin, and others published their account of his character and methods in a pamphlet called *Walwins Wiles*. Though Humphrey Brooke in *The Charity of Church-Men* (May 28) and Walwyn himself in *The Fountain of Slaunder* (May 30) and *Walwyns Just Defence*, a little later in the same year, endeavored to refute this attack, they substantially confirmed and indeed extended the picture of Walwyn's activities.

He had immediately come to Lilburne's defense when the latter was sent to Newgate by the lords on June 23, 1646. In four lucid incisive pages, called *A Pearle in a Dounghill* (June 30), he summed up the main points of Lilburne's argument and story. No clearer statement could have been made of the issue which parliament and assembly had now to face. The bishops, he said, had stopped the press, silenced the preachers, and punished men for obeying their consciences. Then parliament had set the people free, and Lilburne had suffered and fought in their and parliament's cause. Was he now to be punished, and were men to be silenced by parliament itself as formerly by the bishops? Were they to be put down by the house of lords while the commons stood by as a cipher? The answer was plain and ominous.

The People are become a *Knowing* and *Judicious* People, *Affliction* hath made them *wise*, now *Oppression* maketh wise men mad. . . . It is all one to them who oppresseth them, *oppression they cannot but hate*, and if *Parliaments* do in deed and in truth really deliver them, they will love Parliaments . . . *otherwise they will abominate them*, because, for a People to be made slaves, *by, or in time of Parliament*, is like as for a man to be betrayed or murthered by his own father; *which God of his mercy preserve both People and Parliament from, and that for ever.*[49]

The authors of *Walwins Wiles* observed that one of the great masterpieces of Walwyn's craft and subtilty was in the framing, ordering, and managing of petitions.[50] The practical outcome of his activities was the drafting and promoting of a series of petitions in the spring of 1647 which were circulated in and about London and submitted to parliament just as parliament was coming to loggerheads with the army. Their initial purpose was to secure Lilburne's release, but they soon went beyond that. The series culminated, so far as parliament was concerned, in the so-called 'large' petition of May 20. Here it was affirmed first of all that the end of all government was the welfare and freedom of the governed and that no government could be more just than that of a parliament freely elected by the people. Oppressors had formerly declared the mere mention of a parliament to be a crime, and the people had fought for parliament as for their deliverer. 'But such is our misery. . . . Wee still find the Nation oppressed with grievances of the same destructive nature as formerly, though under other notions.' The lords oppress commoners as formerly Star Chamber did. The ministers persecute those who think contrary to themselves as did the bishops. The Merchant Adventurers monopolize trade as did the old patentees. Laws are still unjust, tithes are still exacted, debtors are still thrown into jail, jailers still demand their fees, the poor still live in beggary. And any who show themselves sensible of these grievances or move to remedy them are reproached as 'Round-heads, Sectaries, Independants, Hereticks, Schismaticks, factious, seditious, Rebellious, disturbers of the publike peace.' And all this, 'after so long a Session of so powerfull, and so free a Parliament . . . made and maintained by the abundant love, and liberall effusion of the blood of the people.'

The 'large' petition, for the framing of which Walwyn was almost certainly responsible, raised no question as to the authority of the present parliament. It did not propose a new election or a change in the mode of representation. Yet the house of commons ordered the petition to be burned by the common hangman, and the reason is not difficult to understand. The party of Lilburne and Walwyn pointed to applications and consequences of the so-far-accepted principles of the Puritan Revolution which went far beyond the expectations and interest of the men who by this time had gained control of parliament and assembly, the little knot of lawyers and gentry still holding place in the one and of ministers in the other.

The petition asked for a number of specific reforms to afford relief and greater scope for the class that Lilburne represented, but the essential demand, without which all the others were meaningless, was for liberty of conscience. Yet the petition itself was evidence that liberty of conscience now meant not only freedom to preach as one chose or to gather with others about a preacher of one's choice but also the right to meet with other men about other matters as well, to speak, write, print, sell books, and above all petition to parliament without interference. What made this demand particularly obnoxious was, of course, that it was or at any rate it was made to seem the inevitable and long-sought outcome of the whole movement of events since the beginning of the present parliament, indeed since the Reformation. In the name of free conscience Puritans had demanded above all else freedom to preach the Word of God to the people, and they had cast the prelatical clergy in the role, long assigned to the papists, of enemies of the Word and the people. The enemy now, according to Lilburne's party, was first of all the Presbyteriàn clergy, who, it was charged, were trying to repress free conscience for their own advantage and prevent the expression of the people's grievances and the relief of their needs. The welfare of the people was now conceived not in abstract or figurative terms but in terms of particular social and economic benefits, and the term people was given a new and disturbing signification. The people to whom Christ was now said to have given sovereignty over his church were not simply those who came within the limits of that term as defined by the assembly, but they included all men, all, that is, who had not yet rejected the grace of Christ's atonement, which was offered to all. The gentlemen and lawyers who sat in parliament were not the people but the people's representatives. So it came to this, that for all practical purposes of state the people comprised those members of the populace, of London and its environs especially, whom Lilburne, Walwyn, and their associates had brought together for common action. They comprised a multitude of common men who had thus been made conscious of their needs and articulate in expressing them, the multitude of the unprosperous and discontented, especially all those who, instead of profiting by parliament's success, had suffered, they believed, in its cause. The petition of May 20, 1647, represented a new force in the community which no one fully understood or knew how to deal with, the power to arouse, control, and direct public opinion, which had been put within reach of men of no recognized standing in the state by the pulpits, conventicles, taverns, shops, law courts, printing presses, and bookstalls of London.

Parliament ordered the large petition burned, and the petitioners might conceivably have responded by calling for a new parliament. But there was no legal way of displacing the existing parliament, and the course chosen by Lilburne and his associates was to appeal to the army. The soldiers had also followed his story and read his pamphlets; they had been indoctrinated with free justification; and parliament itself supplied them with a grievance.

IX

The Agreement of the People
1647-1648

WITH the cessation of fighting, the problem for all parties at the close of 1646 was to reestablish order and peace in the community. Parliament must make good its claim to supreme authority in both state and church and the church's claim under the newly approved Directory of Worship to authority over the spiritual life of the nation. To that end the first thing was to dispose of the army. In March, 1647, parliament undertook to discharge the greater part of the soldiers and reenlist a smaller number for service in Ireland under commanders acceptable to the Presbyterians. The intention was to get rid of Independents and sectaries. Cromwell was definitely to be excluded. These proposals might have succeeded but for the fact that they made no allowance for certain conditions of utmost practical importance. Probably only a minority of the soldiers would have stood out against orders on grounds of conscience alone, but the proposed terms of discharge supplied all alike with hardly less compelling reasons for disobedience. All alike had valid claims for back pay, for various indemnities, and for protection against risks to be expected upon return to civil life. If any were to reenlist, they hoped to serve under commanders, above all Cromwell, in whom they had learned to trust. Yet these claims parliament first ignored, then rejected, and at last conceded only in part, grudgingly and tardily. The outcome was a struggle for mastery of the revolutionary state in which the faction now in control of parliament, the assembly, and the city were outmatched in political competence and address by the men and commanders of the army. Parliament was in effect superseded; presbyterian church government was not put into operation; the army became the decisive factor in the situation and for a time at least the principal arena for revolutionary debate.

i. THE ARMY COUNCIL: LILBURNE, WILDMAN, AND THE AGITATORS

In March, 1647, parliament sent commissioners to apprise the regiments through their commanders of the proposed arrangements for their disbandment. Upon consideration the officers responded with a petition demurring at the terms prescribed, and the soldiers protested in a petition addressed to Fairfax as commander-in-chief.[1] These complaints were promptly condemned by parliament and the petitioners declared enemies of the state and disturbers of the peace. The men of the New Model were not, however, to be easily daunted, nor were they at a loss to know how to proceed in such circumstances. They were accustomed to join together for securing the religious edification they desired. They were familiar with the process of getting up petitions for making their wants known. They had Lilburne and his party to instruct them in the methods of political demonstration. By the beginning of April eight regiments of horse had each elected two representatives, called agitators, for the purpose of presenting their grievances to their officers,[2] and the officers soon after presented a vindication of the army's proceedings to parliament. By the middle of May agitators had been elected throughout the army, and officers and agitators were working together to press the army's claims. Parliament, however, while making some concessions, continued to haggle until May 25 when it issued peremptory orders to the army to disband. At this the officers summoned the regiments from their various quarters to a general rendezvous at Newmarket.

But whoever prompted this course of action realized that the person of the king was too important a pawn to be let fall into unfriendly hands. Charles had found refuge after Naseby among the Scots at Newcastle, but in February, 1647, the Scots settled accounts with parliament and withdrew across the border, leaving the king to the custody of a small English force under the authority of parliament at Holmby House in Northamptonshire. When three months later the call went forth for a rendezvous of the army in defiance of parliament, a troop of horse appeared at Holmby to take the king in charge and, as things turned out, bring him to Newmarket. Charles arrived at that place at the same time as Cromwell. Cromwell at the conclusion of hostilities had resumed his seat in the house of commons, had served on the commission to negotiate with the army concerning its disbandment, and had even assured parliament that the soldiers would lay down their arms upon command. Nevertheless, when the break came, his place was obviously not on the side of the Presbyterians and the Scots. He was in some way privy to the army's seizure of the king, and he probably rode out of London on the very day, June 4, on which Charles left Holmby House.

Cromwell arrived at Newmarket just as officers and men were giving approval to a manifesto entitled *An humble Representation of the Dissatisfactions of the Army . . . Unanimously agreed upon and subscribed by the Officers and Soldiers of the several Regiments* (June 4, 5).[3] This was a detailed statement of the army's claims and grievances with reasons for its refusal to obey parliament's orders. It was immediately followed by *A Solemn Engagement of the Army . . . read, assented unto, and Subscribed by all Officers and Soldiers of the several Regiments.* This was an agreement binding all ranks to stand together until their demands had been satisfied and setting up a general council of the army, composed of the general officers and of two commissioned officers and two private soldiers from each regiment. All were to be persons 'who have concurred and shall concur with us in the Premises, and in this Agreement.'[4]

Confronted thus by open and organized insubordination, the dominant group in parliament had either to give way or find means to enforce its orders. They could count on a general desire in the city to be relieved of the burdens of war as quickly and cheaply as possible. They could count on the backing of all who held that, if order were to be resumed in the state, it would have first to be restored in the church. With such support they might hope, if necessary, to raise an armed force to outmatch the army, they might once more seek the aid of the Scots, and they might try for an understanding with the king and his adherents. But the army, both the leaders and the rank and file, was alive to these possibilities, and as parliament hung back, making concessions but never enough to satisfy expectations and never in time to allay apprehensions, the agitators grew bolder in their demands upon the army council for action, the army moved by stages closer upon London, and its spokesmen at each step issued fresh justifications of its proceedings and of the role it was presuming to play. From Royston on June 10 Fairfax, Cromwell, Ireton, and nine other officers dispatched a letter to the city officials, reassuring them as to the army's intentions while at the same time intimating a warning against any hostile action.[5] From St. Albans on June 14 came a statement entitled *A Declaration, or, Representation from his Excellency, Sir Thomas Fairfax, and the Army under his command, Humbly tendered to the Parliament, Concerning the just and Fundamentall Rights and Liberties of themselves and the Kingdome.*[6] This pronouncement went beyond the army's former plea for redress of particular grievances to demand far-reaching reforms in the constitution of the state itself.

But as parliament and the city continued obdurate, the agitators grew more pressing in their demands. On June 25 the army shifted headquarters to Uxbridge and threatened to impeach the eleven members of the house of commons who led the opposition to its pleas. The eleven members withdrew, and the army withdrew to Reading, but the agitators still urged an immediate advance upon the city and a purge of parliament against the arguments of Cromwell and Ireton for an attempt at settlement by negotiation with parliament and the king. The outcome of this debate was yet another statement, called *The Heads of the Proposals agreed upon by his Excellency Sir Thomas Fairfax and the Council of the Army.*[7] Drafted by Ireton, this was a bolder, more explicit formulation of the program of constitutional reform already set forth in the *Declaration* of June 14. Charles, however, was pinning his hopes on the Scots and the Presbyterians, and the Presbyterians were fomenting riotous demonstrations in the city and Westminster. The result was that the agitators got their way, and on August 6 the army marched into London, restored order, and moved into headquarters near by in Surrey. But seeing that even after this the Presbyterians kept up obstructive tactics in parliament, Cromwell posted troops close by and himself resumed his seat in the house.

The events of the spring and summer of 1647 made plain that parliament would have to take the army into account and that the army leaders would have to take account of the men under their command. The moving spirits among the soldiers, who now stood for Puritan doctrine in its most dynamic form, required little prompting to speak and act for themselves after their own fashion. Probably this would have been the case even if no Lilburne had been at hand to egg them on, but the leader of the Leveller party had many close connections with the army, and the effect of parliament's rejection of the soldiers' appeals for redress of grievances was greatly to enhance the force of his example and the scope of his party's activities. He too had a grievance, the story of which he had told over and over again, presenting himself always as the common man, soldier of Jesus Christ, battling for his rights against the great ones of the world—bishops, lords, parliament men, monopolists, governors, grandees of whatever sort. And naturally he and his friends made certain that his story should be told also to the soldiers of the New Model. When the house of commons in 1646 slighted his petitions for release from the Tower, he set, he says, 'underhand on foot, for Justice and my liberty [and] applied my selfe vagarously unto the honest blades, the private Souldiers, I meane, of the Army.' [8] 'I made,' he says, 'a vigorus and strong attempt upon the private Soldiery . . . not daring to meddle with the Officers.' [9] As late as February, 1647, he was still appealing for himself and Overton to the house of commons as the only authority in the state he could justly acknowledge, 'for what by the wills of the Lords is done to us to day, may be done to any Commoner of England to morrow.' [10] But in March, as soon as he heard 'by an Officer out of the Army, and by another knowing man yesterday, that came a purpose to me out of the Army,' of the army's intended petition to parliament and of the petition's certain rejection, he was ready to make common cause with the disaffected soldiery and to stir them up to make common cause with him in his quarrel with their common superiors.[11]

Lilburne perceived at once that, in any clash between the army and the faction in control at Westminster, the key person was Cromwell, a member of the house of commons but at the same time the military leader most trusted by all ranks in the army. Whichever side Cromwell took in the impending dispute was likely to prevail, and no one, probably not Cromwell himself, could yet be certain which side that would be. Hence Lilburne at once (March 25) addressed Cromwell in a characteristic appeal, which he presently published (July 26) with the heading, 'To the Man whom God hath honoured, and will further honour, if he [Cromwell] continue honouring him [God].' [12] Nothing shows better the kinship of spirit which drew these two together even when Lilburne was busy fomenting a crisis which Cromwell was able to surmount only by repudiating him. Much after Cromwell's own manner when similarly moved Lilburne could on occasion make the language of his time and kind, often so distended and shapeless, resound with piercing clarity. He acknowledged the help Cromwell had given him in 1640. He had in return faithfully discharged his duty and affection. He admitted that Cromwell had since appeared faithful to 'the poore people of God,'

And God hath honoured you sufficiently for it, not only in giving you extraordinary large roome in the affections of thousands, and ten thousands of his chosen ones, *but in hanging upon your back the glory of all their atchievements,* by meanes of which you have been made mighty and great, formidable and dreadfull in the eyes of the great ones of the world, and truly my selfe and all others of my mind that I could speak with, have looked upon you as the most absolute single hearted great man in *England,* untainted or unbiased with ends of your owne.[13]

But Cromwell must not now turn aside from his duty because parliament has lately voted him £2,500 a year. 'Think not with thyselfe, that thou shalt escape in the Parliament House, more then all the rest of the Lambs poore despised ones.' If he holds his peace, if he impedes or undermines the petitions of the soldiers and of Lilburne's friends, 'then shall enlargement and deliverance arise to us poore afflicted ones . . . from another place then from you silken Independents, the broken reeds of Egypt in the House and Army.'[14]

Lilburne was soon sending copies of his pamphlets to the army by the hand of Edward Sexby,[15] a private soldier, formerly in Cromwell's, now in Fairfax's regiment, one of the first and most persistent of the agitators. 'A great part of the mischief,' Baxter tells us, which Saltmarsh and his kind accomplished among the soldiers, was 'by way of Pamphlets, which they abundantly dispersed: such as *R. Overtons, Martin Mar-Priest,* and more of his; and some of *J. Lilburn's* . . . And Soldiers being usually disperst in their Quarters, they had such Books to read when they had none to contradict them.'[16] By April it was being said that Lilburne's books were being quoted by some of the soldiers as statute law,[17] and again that the army was 'one Lilburne throughout.'[18] The army's *Declaration* of June 14 begged that 'all such as are imprisoned, for any pretended misdemeanor' may be speedily given a hearing and a trial, and if they have been unjustly treated, that they may receive reparations 'according to their sufferings and the demerit of their oppressors.' [19] At the meeting of the army council at Reading a month later, thé agitators demanded that all prisoners illegally committed, naming Lilburne and others of his party, be immediately released and recompensed.[20] Lilburne at once responded with a letter, addressed to Fairfax, thanking him and 'my true friends the Adjutators.' He now says that he appealed from parliament to the soldiers because he became convinced that his life could be preserved only 'by men that had swords in their hands and resolution in their spirits.' He might, he says, have been rescued long since 'if I had imbraced their earnest desire to breake prison and goe to them,' [21] and even though he restrained himself from joining the 'honest blades' of the army, he continued to urge them on to violent courses. He assailed Cromwell and Ireton for betraying their followers. He wrote again to Fairfax on August 21 and presently printed both that and his former letter, along with 'Advice to the Private Soldiers,' in a pamphlet which he called *Juglers Discovered*. At the same time, the army having now taken the upper hand in the city, he reissued the pamphlet which had landed him in jail in 1646, *The Just Mans Justification*, 'with divers Additions presented as a necessary Apologie by the Author, to all the Commons of England, but especiallƴ to the Private Soldiers of his Excellency, Sir Thomas Fairfax his Army, August 1647.' The principal addition was a concluding epistle 'To his much honoured Friends the Councell of Adjutators,' once more retelling his familiar story. He might, he is sure, have been hanged for his pains, 'if God had not inabled me fully and effectually to have staited my case with my pen, which I presented in print to the world.' [22]

The soldiers put the example and instruction of Lilburne and his followers to effective use. The election of agitators was a skillful application to an unprecedented situation of devices which Lilburne and his party had developed and exploited beyond anything that had been known earlier. Now the Levellers kept the soldiers informed of the reception and treatment of their cause at Westminster. 'I thinke the Lords are all madd,' wrote one correspondent, 'Tell Mr. Saltmarsh now is the tyme of tryall.' [23] Early in May, Sexby or some other wrote a set of directions for the management of the insurgent movement which might as well have come from Lilburne himself or still more likely Walwyn. Particularly significant was the injunction to 'Keepe a partie of able penn men at Oxford and the Army, where their presses be imployed to satisfie and undeceive the people'; 'Hold correspondence with the Soldiers and well affected friends in the severall Counties of the Kingdome'; 'Present the generall Officers with the heads of your demaunds in writing and subscribed.' [24] Sexby, writing from London, urged that the army should set up a press and hire a printer of its own.[25]

The efforts of both agitators and Levellers centered upon the general council of officers and agitators, which is to say upon the army leaders. Fairfax, Cromwell, and their associates, having possessed themselves of power, were constrained to put it to use with as little delay as possible lest it be taken by other hands and turned against themselves. They held the defeated king in their grasp. They had overridden their opponents in parliament. They were able for the time being to prevent anything that could be prevented and accomplish anything that could be accomplished by force. Yet Charles was still head of the state, the handful of men who clung to their seats at Westminster were all that was left of parliament, and the army leaders themselves were by habit and disposition inclined to do nothing without at least the color of legality. Their problem, therefore, if civil government as they understood it was to be set going again, was to induce parliament and the king to agree to a settlement which the army in its present mood could be induced to accept. Common sense called for an accommodation based upon compromise, but the question was, compromise at whose expense or at the sacrifice of what principle held by whom to be sacred and indefeasible? The Presbyterians could not admit an outcome which would confirm the disruption of Christ's kingdom upon earth. The royal saint, self-centered, opinionated, narrow-minded, and conscientious as any Puritan divine, was ready to die for his principles or pit one faction of his enemies against another but not to understand or allow for the ideas and convictions of men who might think differently from himself. And then there was the army. While the officers endeavored to negotiate a settlement, and while

Charles and the Presbyterians chaffered and hung back, the common soldiers felt their material grievances, not to mention their spiritual aspirations, to be neglected. They grew apprehensive of betrayal by their own leaders, suspicious of counsels of moderation or expediency, insistent upon immediate extreme measures against all whom they regarded as their enemies. In this mood they were more than ready to follow the lead of Lilburne and his party.

Lilburne himself was still in the Tower. The agitators had pressed for his release, but though the army leaders yielded to army opinion so far as to coerce parliament in what they took to be the army's interest, they were not willing to have Lilburne turned loose so that he might stir up the rank and file against their commanders as he had already begun to do. 'I cannot but acquaint the Reader,' he wrote in October, 'that a grand objection against me, wherefore I should not have my liberty and justice, is because, if I were at liberty, it is said I would go down to the Army, and make new hurly burlyes there.' [26] But nothing could stop him from making hurly-burlies before parliamentary committees or from reporting his words and his wrongs to the public in print. On October 20 he made another such appearance and a few days later told the story in *The grand Plea of Lieut. Col. John Lilburne . . . before an open Committee of the House of Commons.*

By this time Lilburne's party had made a move of great strategic significance. The soldiers' apprehension of betrayal and defeat, the dragging out of negotiations with Charles and the rival factions in parliament, a speech of Cromwell in the house seeming to imply a willingness to yield to the claims of the king, these circumstances gave the Levellers occasion to press demands for immediate action, seemingly so just, so consistent with what had been said before in the army's behalf, so arguable in the idiom of the time, that they could be neither ignored nor rejected out of hand. Early in October five regiments of horse chose new representatives to replace those who had been elected in June, and on October 18 these agents, as they were now called, presented a manifesto to Fairfax as commander-in-chief, called *The Case of the Armie Truly stated, together with the mischiefes and dangers that are imminent, and some sutable remedies.*[27] The actual drafting of this document appears to have been the work not of the soldiers who put their names to it on behalf of their regiments but of John Wildman, a young man of about twenty-four, educated at Cambridge and the Inns of Court, one of Lilburne's associates, apparently one of those 'bold, peremptory, pertinacious conceipted Spirits, of fierce, daring, and provoking language' such as Walwyn was accused of stirring up to 'trumpet out matter of discontents, jealousies, and pretended miscarriages of those that are in Authority.' [28]

The Case of the Armie sharply reiterated all of the soldiers' complaints and suspicions. But it also offered as remedy a program of constitutional change which carried the principles of *The Heads of the Proposals* to the extremes foreshadowed in the whole series of petitions, manifestoes, and pamphlets with which Lilburne and his party had been besetting parliament since 1645. The signers of the present paper expressed confidence that their action in stating the army's case—'how declined from its first principles of safety, what mischiefes are threatned thereby, and what remedies are sutable for prevention'—would not be considered strange or refractory. Their excuse was the familiar one that 'God hath given no man a talent to be wrapt up in a Napkin & not improved, but the meanest vassall in the eye of the Lord is equally oblieged and accomptable to God with the greatest Prince or Commander under the Sun, in & for the use of that talent betrusted unto him.' [29] In the face of such urgency, a meeting of the general council of officers and agitators was promptly summoned, and the agents of the five regiments, with Wildman again probably to do the writing, submitted their proposals for the council's consideration in the form of a declaration to which they gave the title *An Agreement of the People for a firme and present Peace, upon grounds of common-right and freedome.* [30] The council met at Putney on October 28 and debated the proposed agreement daily until November 11.

ii. THE PUTNEY DEBATES

Clarendon observed that in 1647 the army set itself up as a rival parliament with the agitators as a house of commons and the officers as peers. [31] It would be more accurate to say that the general council of the army at Putney took upon itself the role of a quasi-constituent assembly in which the common soldiers or their representatives debated the future structure of the state on equal terms with their superiors in rank. Cromwell had drawn into the service men of independent spirit and moral self-assurance. Now he had to deal with these men not simply as soldiers or as saints but, thanks in some measure to Lilburne and his party, as men conscious of being members also of the civil community. 'We were not a meere mercinary Army,' it had been asserted in the *Declaration* of June 14, 'hired to serve any Arbitrary power of a State; but called forth and conjured, by the severall Declarations of Parliament, to the defence of our owne and the peoples just rights, and liberties.' [32] *The Case of the Armie* declared again that the soldiers had been called forth by parliament itself to defend the people's rights.

The report of the debates which now ensued at Putney, unstudied and incomplete as it is, still fascinates us with its suggestion of things to come. The curtain is suddenly drawn back and we see and hear these men as it were in the life, so recognizably that before we know it we have discounted much of the difference that time has put between us and them. We impute greater consistency and clarity of thought to these laboring disputants than could probably have been theirs. We read meaning into their words which we cannot be certain were really intended. We define their differences in terms which derive significance from a later context. The debate at Putney should be studied as the latest phase of one revolution before being scanned for portents of others still unthought of. The differences which came to a head on that occasion were differences among men who had arrived together by the same or parallel routes at the predicament in which they now found themselves. They were men who up to a point on matters they regarded as all-important believed alike, hoped or thought they hoped for the same things, and in spite of differences expected to reach agreement as to both means and ends.

They had all embraced the doctrine of calling and covenant in some form or other. All believed or professed to believe that their lives had been transformed from within by divine grace, that grace was also in process of transforming the life of mankind in general, and that in that process England had an especially important part to play. As children of grace they had nothing to fear which the new man within them lacked power to overcome. Nothing could stand against them so long as the Lord was with them. They might momentarily disagree, but there could be no disagreement which faith could not resolve by the light of scripture. One more struggle, prolonged it might be for chastening and strengthening, and they were certain to triumph over all difficulties. This was in essence the Word as preached to parliament by Marshall, Calamy, and the rest of the brotherhood in the early days of the present crisis and again by Saltmarsh, Dell, Peters and their kind to the New Model. Now at Putney, Rainborowe, Goffe, Cromwell, Ireton, even Wildman, all paused every now and then in the midst of their disputing to reassure each other that, God being with them, they had no reason to doubt the success of their efforts. All still shared the sanguine expectation of Puritan revolutionaries that, if they kept straight on in their spiritual striving, they could not fail to arrive finally at new heaven and new earth.

But the problem now as before was to determine and agree upon the actual configuration of that new earth. The doctrine of calling and covenant at its first onset came to most men with great liberating effect. It sent them to the scriptures looking for a law to shape and guide the human polity, but what they found there was not law but life itself in untrammeled variety. The Word gave them courage and set them free to go their ways, but it left them free to pick their ways in time and circumstance as best they could, and the ways opening before them were not few, nor did they all lead in one direction. The preachers in 1642 had assured the members of parliament that they were bound to obey the Lord though earthly rulers might command otherwise. This was Christian liberty. But what Christian liberty might lead to in positive effect was not so clear. For some it meant that the church should be reduced to order and its authority restored over the whole of society. For others it meant freedom to partake in spiritual communion with like-minded souls in the satisfying seclusion of the congregation. For still others it meant that the saints should take over the entire government of men at once. Besides these there were the many searching souls, undetermined whether to plump for the presbyterian Zion or mount the sectarian ark or get ready for the millennium and the rule of Christ and his saints or, it might be, simply wait upon the Lord a little longer. But meanwhile the concern for liberty could not be limited to the saints and the church. The king's opponents in parliament took advantage of the preachers' contention for freedom to preach the Word in order to forward their own contention for power in the state. Their apologists followed up the preachers' claim to the liberty of Christians under the gospel by laying claim to the liberty due to men simply as men under the law of nature. But to distinguish between one liberty and another was more than most men had time or wish or judgment for. How was any given man to keep in mind the distinction between himself as Christian and himself as man or as Englishman? Surely Christ died to save all men; the laws of England did not contravene the laws of God revealed in his Word and in his works; the rights of Christians, men, and Englishmen were all of a piece.

But this did not answer the question, what had God and nature set men free to make of themselves and the state in the realm of England in 1647? Granted that the authority of rulers rests upon a covenant with and among the people and that the people's good is the supreme end of the state, who should judge whether that covenant was being duly kept or not? Who in particular were the people whose good must be considered? In what did it consist? How should they go about securing it? Who should speak for them? Nineteenth-century historians, writing under the spell of Carlyle's hero-worship of Cromwell, were inclined to judge Lilburne harshly because of the trouble he made for that great man. Full as they were of Burke's conception of the constitution, they deplored the Levellers' unwillingness to wait for freedom to broaden down from precedent to precedent. But Cromwell was not Sir Robert Peel or even Mr. Gladstone, and the state of England in the interval between the first and second civil wars was not what it became after the Reform Bill of 1832. It was on the contrary one of extreme insecurity and constitutional confusion in which the Levellers transposed the doctrine of calling and covenant and the principle of *salus populi* into concrete terms applicable to the immediate situation. If the men in power in the state really intended the people's good, let them liberate John Lilburne from the Tower, give him a hearing and a trial by his peers, pay him the reparations acknowledged to be due, allow him to follow his own conscience and speak his own mind free from interference by the Presbyterian ministers or the Stationers' Company. Let them make it possible for him to earn his living free from tithes, excise, customs, and the monopolistic restrictions of the Merchant Adventurers. Let them consider the needs of the people represented in the series of petitions which culminated in the 'large petition' of May, 1647. Let them care for the needs of the soldiers as set forth in the petitions and manifestoes of the army.

Lilburne and the class he spoke for were as yet less accustomed to make their opinions and desires known by voting at the polls than by riotous demonstrations in the streets and at the doors of parliament. Nevertheless, out of the hullabaloo which he and his followers raised, there emerged a theory of the state, a conception of politics, and a program of political action which went beyond mere riot to substantive constitutional reform, plausibly derived from familiar notions of law and equity, historic tradition, conscience, and right reason. This program, as parliament and the king continued obdurate, the army took over and, notwithstanding the disagreements which presently arose, never wholly abandoned. Thus the debate at Putney over the *Agreement of the People* came in fact as the climax of the campaign which Lilburne and his supporters had been waging against parliament and assembly. His first move when arraigned by the lords in 1646 had been to challenge the authority of that house and appeal to the commons. By entertaining his appeal while delaying decision and by leaving him in the Tower to plead his cause before the public, the house of commons gave him occasion and opportunity to dramatize the idea that the only function of that house under the constitution and the very reason for its being in the nature of things was to represent and serve the people, of whom he was one.

The clearest statement of this position and of its most extreme implications came from Richard Overton, whom the house of lords had sent to Newgate in 1646 for championing Lilburne in the press and then imitating his tactics. Overton proclaimed it as axiomatic that all men are born naturally free and equal, that all authority of state rests upon the people's consent, and that the necessary consequence of these principles is representative government. 'The cause of our choosing you,' he had told parliament in his *Remonstrance of Many Thousand Citizens* in July, 1646, was only to preserve the commonwealth, and the only power parliament could lay claim to was the power granted by the people for that purpose.[33] Kings, lords, lawyers, and clergy had labored ever since the Conquest to enslave and deceive the people through the rites of religion, the forms of the law, the pageant of royalty, and control of the press. But at last the people threw off the tyranny of Charles, Strafford, and Laud and elected a house of commons truly to represent them and restore their natural rights. Some parliament men, to be sure, had only run with the tide in the expectation of erecting a new tyranny out of the house of commons. But although the present house, which should by law have served for only one year, had now gone on for five without accomplishing the purpose for which it was elected, there was still, thanks to the army, opportunity to make popular rights and representative government secure. But the time grew short. 'Yee are not to reckon that yee have any longer time to effect the Great Worke we have entrusted unto you: for wee must not loose our free choice of a Parliament once every yeer, fresh and fresh for a continuall Parliament.' They are to arrange for meetings to be held 'upon one certaine day in *November* yeerly throughout the Land in the Places accustomed,' and the persons chosen to attend those meetings—how selected he does not say—are 'to make choice of whom they think good, according to *Law.*'[34]

Undaunted by the lords, the ministers, or the stationers, Overton in Newgate kept up his pamphleteering while Lilburne was doing the same from the Tower. There may have been some justice in the complaint that the latter seemed to think that parliament should drop all other business until his wrongs were righted. Yet his insistence, seconded by Overton, upon the supposed representative character and function of the house of commons drove home the fact that the existing house no longer represented anybody except the faction in control at the moment. It also made plain the fact that, except in the unlikely event that the men still hanging on at Westminster would remove themselves, there was no way except force by which the present parliament could be brought to an end. Whence Lilburne expected that force to come, he made clear in his letter to Cromwell of March 25, 1647. Parliament, he said, was now tyrannizing worse than the king had ever done, and 'it is ten times easier to prove it lawful for us to take up

Armes against them in the wayes they now go, then it was for them
to take up Arms when they did, against the King . . . For, if, as they
have often said, *That tyranny be resistable,* then it is resistable in a
Parliament as well as a King.' [35]

From this point Lilburne and his party, while giving the army close
support in its campaign for the relieving of soldiers' grievances, went
on to elaborate the proposals for constitutional reform foreshadowed
in Overton's *Remonstrance* the year before. In *The resolved mans
Resolution* at the end of April, Lilburne put into print his charge that
the house of commons with its committees was outdoing the king in
violating the law and oppressing the people and that the only remedy
was to dissolve the present body and elect future parliaments from year
to year. A month later, when parliament had ordered the Leveller
'large petition' burned and the army disbanded, he issued a fifty-six
page pamphlet called *Rash Oaths unwarrantable.* Again he told the
story of his wrongs but followed it now with the story of the rejection
and burning of the Leveller petition and the rejection of the army
petition of the preceding March. He included the texts of both petitions and the declaration of the two houses condemning the army.
Parliament, he said, had become nothing but a conspiracy of lawless
and unbounded men, bent upon destroying the laws and liberties of the
people. There was, consequently, nothing left for the people to do but
appeal to the army 'by force of Armes to root up and destroy these
tyrants' on the same grounds on which they had themselves formerly
levied war against the king.[36] As for the future, let there be annual
parliaments, chosen by a more equitable system of election and representation. The representation of boroughs should be fixed according to
the number of members in each corporation and of counties according
to the number of ratepayers. But Lilburne makes another recommendation, one which reflects the equalitarian ideas which Overton had been
so stridently urging. The purpose should be to make certain that 'all
the people (without confusion or tumult) may meet together in their
severall divisions and [that] every free man of *England,* as well poore
as rich, whose life [,] estate &c. is [liable] to be taken away by the law,
may have a Vote in chusing those that are to make the law, it being a
maxim in nature, that no man justly can be bound without his own
consent.' [37]

Lilburne made these proposals at the end of May, 1647, just as Cromwell was setting out for the army rendezvous at Newmarket. In mid-July, when the agitators were pressing for a march on London and a purge of parliament, Overton issued *An Appeale From the degenerate Representative Body the Commons of England assembled at Westminster: To the Body Represented, The free people . . . of England, . . . And in especiall, To his Excellency, Sir Thomas Fairfax and to all the Officers and Souldiers under his Command.* There are those who object, the writer says, that no precedent can be found for an appeal from parliament to the people, but 'to such I shall returne even the late words of (our now degenerate Parliament) *That Reason hath no president for Reason is the fountaine of all just presidents,*' and he adds the appropriate references to the Parliamentary Book of Declarations. What reason teaches is, of course, that '*Magistracy* in its *nature, institution,* and *administration,* is for such a kinde of *safety* Nationall and generall, as wherein every individuall or particular person, of what sort or society soever, may fully and freely enjoy his liberty, peace and tranquillity, *civill* and *humane.*' It follows that 'the destroyers and subverters of humane society . . . are to be corrected, expulsed, or cut off for preservation of safety, and prevention of ruine both *publike* and *private.*' [38] And it follows too that the army is called to expel the present parliament. Overton concludes with a schedule of proposed reforms, similar to those in the petition which parliament had ordered to be burned. While this appeal was being published, Lilburne, in a pamphlet entitled *Jonahs Cry out of the Whales belly,* was printing the letters in which he had been pleading with Cromwell to lead the army in taking action against the two houses.

The history of the general council of the army, from its setting up at Newmarket in June to the debate at Putney in October, was one of increasing tension between officers and agitators, concluding in an open clash between Cromwell and Ireton on the one hand and the more extreme representatives of the soldiers on the other, the latter, of course, strongly under the influence of the Levellers. This conflict was essentially a struggle for control of the army as such and hence, inevitably, of the state. It did not arise initially from disagreement over the principles and immediate objectives of army policy. As events moved on, the program of reform to which Lilburne and his associates gave explicit statement in their attack upon parliament came to seem to many men of all ranks in the army the remedy for their own predicament and, indeed, the natural outcome of the whole revolutionary movement. All were agreed that the authority of parliament, while lawfully supreme, depended no less than that of the king upon the consent of the people, whose representative it was supposed rightfully to be. But it was also generally agreed that the existing parliament in some measure no longer represented the people and had forfeited their obedience. The army, therefore, presuming to speak and act for the people as well as for itself, felt obliged to recall parliament to its duty by whatever means might be necessary. The obvious conclusion to such reasoning was that the army should expel those it regarded as its enemies from the house of commons. But once begun on that course, there would be no telling where to stop. Necessity might also require the army to repress the existing body altogether and in the name of the people to reconstitute a legal parliament upon a more equitable basis of representation. And if Charles continued to impede such reconstitution of the state, the army might presently find itself proceeding in the people's name against both the office and the person of the king.

Such in its main features was the policy forecast by Lilburne and his associates in the spring of 1647 and such were the ideas which became rife in the army after the rendezvous at Newmarket. Such too were the principles which would be cited in justification of the army's course up to Pride's Purge and the execution of the king. The proposals for parliamentary reform so precisely set forth by Ireton in *The Heads of the Proposals* in August had been foreshadowed in the army's *Declaration* in June and by Lilburne in *Rash Oaths unwarrantable* in May. The agitators, to be sure, under Lilburne's influence, were straining to proceed faster and farther than their leaders were as yet prepared to go, and the leaders were endeavoring to hold them in check. Nevertheless, Cromwell and Ireton went along with the forces under their command which were making for the most extreme action. They expected, no doubt, that parliament and the king would presently give way, but when they did not, there was nothing for the army leaders to do but ride on with the storm to conclusions they had been unable or unwilling to anticipate.

It was assumed that the constitutional changes called for in *The Heads of the Proposals* were to be enacted by parliament itself with the royal assent, and yet, what parliament was expected to enact and the king approve under threat of military compulsion was a large measure of Lilburnian reform, though stopping short of equal suffrage. The present parliament was to terminate within a year. Future parliaments were to be elected at regular intervals for a fixed term. Representatives were to be allotted to localities according to the number of ratepayers or 'according to some other rule of equality of proportion, to render the House of Commons (as near as may be) an equal representative of the whole.' The administration of justice was to be under the jurisdiction of parliament, and commoners were to be judged only by their peers. Excise, rates, and tithes were to be reduced; monopolies and restraints of trade were to be taken off; the administration of law was to be simplified and imprisonment for debt eased. There was to be liberty of conscience and immunity from incriminating questions and ensnaring oaths. Soldiers were to receive their arrears of pay.[39] Nor were the army leaders forgetful of the uses of publicity. At the end of September the whole series of petitions and manifestoes which had so far been issued in the army's behalf, from the first petition in March down to the latest remonstrance put out in September, were gathered together and published in a single volume, usually referred to as 'The Book of Army Declarations.' It bore a frontispiece showing 'The manner of his Excellency Sir *Thomas Fairfax*, and the Officers of His Armie sitting in Councill.' [40]

To the modern mind it has seemed obvious that, if Charles and the Presbyterians had been willing to settle with the army on some such terms, all parties might have had peace at once and England could have started promptly forth on what was to be her future course of constitutional development. But for Charles in 1647 a settlement on such terms would have meant to surrender most of the things he would rather die than give up. For the Presbyterians it would have meant giving way to the Antichrist of disruption in the church. Consequently all that the army leaders gained by endeavoring to negotiate a settlement on the basis of *The Heads of the Proposals* was, if anything, to delay the resort to arms which came in the ensuing spring, and that delay gave agitators and Levellers the more occasion to foment the apprehensions and suspicions of the soldiers. *The Case of the Armie* merely restated with sharper emphasis the arguments and proposals which had just been brought together in the so-called 'Book of Army Declarations.' *The Agreement of the People* merely stated in more extreme terms the program for constitutional reform set forth in *The Heads of the Proposals.*

The Levellers' purpose was to force the army leaders to immediate action under threat of attack as the latest betrayers of the army's and the people's interests. Wildman, author of *The Case of the Armie,* and Maximillian Petty, apparently another member of the party, were admitted to the debate at Putney. The soldiers were directly represented by Lilburne's friend Sexby and by others of their own number. Their cause was also championed by Colonel Thomas Rainborowe, a regimental commander with a record of gallantry in the field. Other partisans of the Levellers were at hand, and Lilburne was kept informed of the course of debate from day to day. The discussion was opened by Sexby, supported by Wildman, with the accusation that Cromwell and Ireton were betraying the army by seeking an agreement with the king and parliament which would be to their own personal advantage. Wildman and the agitators insisted that no agreement, covenant, or promise should bind the army contrary to what the army might deem just and reasonable at the time. This contention led to a broader argument, pursued by Wildman, Rainborowe, and others, for the substantive reforms proposed in the *Agreement.* If soldiers' grievances were to be remedied and people's rights preserved, the existing parliament must be dissolved; succeeding parliaments must be elected at regular intervals for limited terms; representation must be equitably distributed according to population; every free man must have the privilege of voting; peers and commoners must be equal before the law; the enactments of the house of commons must be free from the veto of crown or lords; and the only limitation on the people's representative must be the formal recognition of fundamental and inalienable rights, especially liberty of conscience, inherent in the people themselves. The new system was to be instituted by popular consent, though how this was to be managed, unless the army took upon itself an interim but plenary function of representation, the Levellers were unable to say.

Cromwell and Ireton defended themselves against the attack of Sexby and Wildman by declaring that the army must be faithful to its engagements and commitments. But they questioned the implications of the newly proposed constitutional scheme and of the arguments urged in its support. When Rainborowe and Wildman insisted that reason and justice required its immediate adoption regardless of scruples and difficulties, Cromwell's rejoinder was that the 'pretensions' of the *Agreement* were plausible enough, 'if we could leap out of one condition into another.' But how, he asked, 'do we know if, while we are disputing these things, another company of men shall [not] gather together, and put out a paper as plausible perhaps as this?' [41] Events, which more than any other he had himself helped to bring about, were now forcing Cromwell into an equivocal position. He had insisted above all upon complete victory in the field against the king. No one had done so much as he to shape the spirit of the army. He had not shrunk from using military force to compel parliament to do the army's will. Nevertheless he still clung to the idea that the army's purpose must be to restore government by king, lords, and commons and to induce all three to act in the present circumstances to that end. The only possible alternative to a settlement in line with the ancient accustomed order seemed to him at this stage to be not government by agreement of the people but anarchy and confusion. After all that had happened and that he had caused to happen, he still seemed to believe that the army could do nothing except through parliament. 'Either they are a Parliament or no Parliament. If they be no Parliament they are nothing, and we are nothing likewise.' The king's party say, 'if they give us rope enough we will hang ourselves.' The army must not let go its status as an army commissioned by parliament. We are like a drowning man, he said; 'if it be but an hare swimming over the Thames, he will take hold of it rather than let it go.' [42]

By turns a mystic and an opportunist, in politics as in war, Cromwell was a consistent character but not a consistent thinker. He was capable of taking the position he did at Putney and yet, when circumstances changed and the Lord dispensed other light, of overriding both king and parliament with what seemed, for all that anyone could tell, as little compunction as might have been expected from a Wildman or a Rainborowe. At Putney it was Ireton who penetrated with a keener, clearer, more analytical mind to the true dividing issue between the class to which he and his father-in-law instinctively adhered and the party which had sprung up about Lilburne. This is not to say that Cromwell and Lilburne and their respective followers were at odds at every point. Ireton agreed that government rested in some fashion upon consent of the people and that the people's obedience lapsed when rulers sought not their subjects' safety but their destruction. For that reason, he also agreed, parliament had been justified in resisting the king and the army in disobeying parliament. But the purpose of such actions was not to break the covenant which binds subjects and rulers to their duty but to enforce and maintain it. The covenant, according to Ireton's reasoning, still held firm. It had been denied and violated by the actions first of Charles and then of parliament but not revoked. The army's business was to restore it, that is to say, to reestablish, not to destroy or displace, the government by king, lords, and commons in its ancient place and function. From this point on, Ireton went straight to what seemed to him the real danger in his opponents' proposals and arguments. If men in general were free to break covenant whenever they deemed it just and reasonable to do so, then every man must be supposed to possess a natural right to decide for himself at any time whether any given law of state was to be obeyed or not. But if that were so, no man could call anything his own, because property rests not upon natural right but upon the law of the state, which rests upon covenant.

The crux of the dispute came over the question of parliamentary representation. *The Heads of the Proposals*, drafted by Ireton himself, provided that this be apportioned to localities according to the number of ratepayers. *The Agreement of the People* provided that it be apportioned according to population, and Wildman and Rainborowe urged that the right to vote, then limited to forty-shilling freeholders and members of borough corporations, should be extended to all free men. Since all men, they said, are bound by the law of nature to preserve their own lives and to that end are endowed by the creator with reason, so every man possesses a natural right to a voice in choosing those who make the laws he is required to obey in the state. 'For really,' said Rainborowe, 'I think that the poorest he that is in England hath a life to live, as the greatest he; and therefore . . . that every man that is to live under a government ought first by his own consent to put himself under that government.' 'I do hear nothing at all that can convince me, why any man that is born in England ought not to have his voice in election of burgesses.' Nothing, he said, in the law of God, of nature, or of nations requires 'that a lord shall choose twenty burgesses, and a gentleman but two, or a poor man shall choose none.' But to all such reasoning Ireton replied that, if all men are by right of nature entitled to vote, then 'you must deny all property too.' The rule which would give 'one man . . . an equal right with another to the choosing of him that shall govern him' would give every man an equal right to anything he sees, meat, drink, clothes, land, 'anything that any one doth account himself to have any propriety in.' But to deny property is to deny the state itself. 'For here is the case of the most fundamental part of the constitution of the kingdom, which if you take away, you take away all by that.' Hence the right to elect members of parliament, granted a somewhat more equitable distribution of seats, must still be reserved to those whom Ireton describes as making up the 'permanent' and 'local' interest of the kingdom.[43]

The dispute between Ireton and Rainborowe over liberty and equality in relation to property and the state, however significant it may seem in the history of political theory, had no great practical bearing on the immediate situation in November, 1647. By the permanent and local interest of the kingdom Ireton meant the interest of the landed gentry with their connections in town and country, who since Tudor times had been steadily advancing toward control of parliament and who had now, through their control of parliament, seemingly stripped the crown of its powers. But the handful of men who actually controlled what was left of parliament owed their ascendancy no longer to their position as gentry but to the support of the army they had evoked in their contention with Charles, and the men who commanded the army could not hope to maintain their own ascendancy, let alone that of parliament, if they permitted that command to be taken from them. They were in no real danger of having their property voted away from them. But if they allowed the influence of Lilburne and his party among the soldiers to go unchecked, they were in very great and imminent danger of losing control of the army, the army was in danger of losing its effectiveness as an instrument of power, and both the army and its commanders were in danger of losing everything they had or had hope to get.

The strength of the Levellers' influence was not due, however, merely or primarily to their advocacy of equality of suffrage in parliamentary elections. It was due much more to the skill and address with which, in the confusion and distress of the moment, they pressed forward with what seemed positive remedies and reforms deduced from principles and justified by sanctions which no one on their side of the national struggle was able to deny or refute. Either rulers were bound by the laws of God and in the nature of things to put the people's interest above their own or parliament and the army had no warrant for anything that had been done against the king. Parliament, Lilburne and his party insisted, was not the people but only the people's representative. We, they said, are the people, we and those for whom we speak, and finally, of course, the men who had fought parliament's battles in the field. When parliament turned against the people as embodied in the army, it broke the compact which was the essence of the state and so justified the army in demanding a new agreement which should reconstitute the state by reconstituting parliament as the people's representative in the state. Only thus could the just grievances of the army and the people find their remedy. If the present parliament would not accede to these demands, it must be made to yield. If the king continued to stand in the way, he must be called to account as the chief and original offender. To such declarations the army commanders, certainly Cromwell and Ireton, were prepared to offer no denial in principle. They might not wish to proceed as fast or as far as the most extreme of the agitators and Levellers. But they were at least becoming convinced that, if order was to be restored in the state, it would have to be by the army and that, when restored, it would have to be based upon a newly constituted house of commons.

Why then, if officers and agitators, even with the Levellers at hand, were so nearly at one in their principles and objectives, did the debate at Putney turn out as it did? The reason is clear. Agitators and

Levellers, in their zeal for representative government, would have transformed the army itself into a representative body, setting aside military authority and superseding parliament. The army, according to Lilburne, had ceased to be an army when the war came to an end and officers and men had, he said, 'associated themselves only as a company of free Commons of *England*' for the recovery of their own and the people's rights and liberties. He recalled how at that time officers who refused to join in that agreement had been cashiered and hooted from the field and a new council of the army set up 'not by the Gen[eral]s wil or according to the degrees or offices of men in the Army, but in a Parliamentary way by the Soldiers free election.' [44] It was one thing, however, for the army commanders to stand together with the common soldiers against the ruling faction at Westminster, and quite another to let the agitators with Lilburne and his party behind them disrupt military discipline on the pretext of reforming the state. The power of the army to control the state in the present crisis depended not upon its becoming a democratic representative assembly or an arena for free discussion but upon its continuing to function effectively as a military force.

iii. THE ARMY, PARLIAMENT, AND THE LEVELLERS

The army commanders brought the debate at Putney to an abrupt conclusion by a brusque reassertion of their authority. They ordered the participants, officers and agitators alike, back to their regiments and the regiments to several separate places of rendezvous. On November 15 Cromwell repressed as mutiny the attempt of certain regiments to continue their agitation for what they called their rights, and the commanders at the same time put forth *A Remonstrance from his Excellency Sir Thomas Fairfax, and his Councell of War*.[45] This was in effect an ultimatum to the whole body of the army, probably penned by Ireton, and a skillfully calculated move to circumvent the Levellers by allaying insubordination without seeming to repudiate the substantive proposals which had just been put forward in the army council with their support. The officers claimed to have fulfilled the army's engagements, and if any had been neglected, they were ready, they said, 'to amend the Default, and to hearken to what any Man would soberly offer for that Purpose, or to lead them to anything better.' So much for free conscience and free speech. But some members of the army, 'assuming the Name of Agents for several Regiments,' and joined by 'private Persons that are not of the Army,' had acted as 'a divided Party,' drawing the soldiers away from the officers and the officers from one another.

If these divisions continued, the general threatened to lay down his command. If they ceased, he would endeavor to secure relief of soldiers' grievances, bring the present parliament to a close, and provide for a new one with 'Freedom and Equality of Elections thereto; to render the House of Commons (as near as may be) an equal Representative of the People that are to elect.' Decisive though the officers' *Remonstrance* was in its effect, a few agitators and their partisans still continued their activities. John Saltmarsh, delirious with fever and on the point of death, journeyed from Essex to Windsor to warn Fairfax and Cromwell that the Lord had forsaken the army because of their treatment of the saints within its ranks.[46] But the commanders had little trouble in recovering their control. Soldiers demanding their supposed rights too insistently were put down as mutineers. Parliament and the city were pressed for settlement of army grievances. On December 21 the officers met at Windsor to seek the Lord's favor and exhort each other to 'Unity and Affinity.' The next day they spent as a fast, and Cromwell, Ireton, Peters, and others prayed 'very fervently and pathetically' from nine in the morning until seven at night. All recent offenses, even Rainborowe's, were confessed and forgiven among them.[47]

Meanwhile events moved rapidly to fix the army in its recovered unity. On November 11 the king had fled from Hampton Court, where he had been held since September in the army's custody, to the Isle of Wight. There, still under surveillance, he embarked upon a new series of negotiations with the various incompatible factions among his enemies. The army leaders wished for a settlement which should have the color of legality, allow for tender consciences, and leave the essentials of power in their own hands. The city wished for relief from present burdens and anxieties. The Presbyterians and the Scots wished for the enforcement of the Directory of Worship. Charles, though seemingly ready to negotiate with all parties, would yield nothing of significance to any of them. The outcome was that, just as the army was reconciling its own internal differences, the king finally rejected the proposals of parliament and entered into an uneasy engagement with the Scots. When on January 3 word of these decisions reached Westminster, Cromwell and Ireton were in their seats, fresh from the prayer meeting at Windsor. They declared that the time had come for the members to decide whether they would submit to the obstinate man whose heart God had hardened against them or stand by those who had shed their blood in parliament's defense. 'Teach them not,' Cromwell said, 'to think themselves betrayed . . . lest despair teach them to seek their safety by some other means then adhering to you, who will not stick to your selves.' At this point, it was noted, the speaker laid his hand upon his sword.[48] After that, parliament voted to send no more addresses to the king and in place of the old Committee of Both Kingdoms set up a new Committee of Both Houses, commonly called the Derby House Committee, to serve as the agent of its authority. But to make certain that parliament would not again get out of hand, the army leaders posted two regiments at Westminster.

Lilburne and the Levellers, though rebuffed in the army, were not ready to desist from their activities in the city. On Novembr 9, just as the debate at Putney was being brought to so summary a close, the house of commons voted to release Lilburne from the Tower from day to day, apparently in order to enable him to argue his personal case more freely before a newly appointed committee.[49] He used his freedom also to issue a new series of manifestoes on behalf of the agitators, now being reduced to obedience by Cromwell in the army.[50] There seemed to the Levellers only one explanation, which Wildman set forth in *Putney Projects* on December 30, for the course which Cromwell and Ireton were taking. This was that, in spite of all pretenses, these two were still seeking to strike a bargain with the king which should make them masters of the state. Hence Lilburne and his associates, defeated in their endeavor to turn the army into an instrument of political reform, reverted to their former tactics and strategy. The appeal from parliament to the army having failed, they set about organizing an appeal from the army back to the house of commons. A petition was drafted and printed for circulation in the city and surrounding communities. Directions were sent out for holding local meetings, collecting signatures and funds, and sending representatives to a central committee in London.[51] A broadside was published, entitled *The mournful Cryes of many thousand poor Tradesmen, who are ready to famish through decay of Trade. Or, The warning Tears of the Oppressed.*[52] And on January 17, a meeting was held in 'Well-Yard, in, or neer Wapping, at the house of one Williams a Gardiner,' at which Lilburne and Wildman explained the proposed petition and the reasons for their shift in policy in appealing once more to parliament. 'We must,' they were reported to have said, 'own some visible Authority for the present, or else we shall be brought to Ruine and Confusion: but when we have raised the spirits of the people. . . . We shall force them to grant us those things we desire.'[53]

Parliament, however, now again in the grip of the army leaders and the Independents, did not take lightly the threat poised by Lilburne and his party. An informer at once reported (January 18) what had been said at the meeting in Well Yard,[54] and Lilburne and Wildman were the next day brought to the bar of the house and confronted with their accuser. Lilburne, according to his own account, made a long speech in defense of himself, his party, and their projected petition, but the house remanded him to the Tower and sent Wildman to the Fleet. The next day it ordered the Derby House Committee to prepare a declaration 'to undeceive the People, and satisfy them with the Dangers and Inconveniences' likely to ensue from the activities of Lilburne and his party. The result of this order was the publication about the middle of February of *A Declaration of some Proceedings of Lt. Col. Iohn Lilburn, And his Associates,* giving a vivid account of the doings of Lilburne and his party, a vigorous rebuttal of their arguments and demands, the informer's report of the Well Yard meeting, and the text of the offending petition and of the manifesto called *The mournfull Cryes.* Lilburne's assailants had learned much from him concerning both the art and the usefulness of publicity. Nothing could have testified more eloquently to the nature and extent of his accomplishment or to the importance of the position he had created for himself as a popular leader. But there was still no silencing him. He from the Tower and Wildman from the Fleet at once took to print in self-defense. In *The peoples Prerogative and Privileges, asserted and vindicated . . . for the instruction, information and benefit of all true hearted Englishmen,* with a proem dated February 17, 1648, Lilburne told his own story of the recent dealings of the army leaders with himself, his partisans, and the soldiers, and with it he published his own gathering of relevant documents. At about the same time he replied directly to *A Declaration of some Proceedings* and resumed his long quarrel with the lords in *A Whip for the present House of Lords.* In *An Impeachment of High Treason* in 1649, resuming his attack on Cromwell and Ireton, he told the story of his speech at the bar of the house of commons on January 19 of the year before, including the text of the petition which occasioned his appearance.

The reason for the prompt action taken against that petition is clear. It reiterated in brief terms the demands for constitutional reform made in the *Agreement of the People* and reflected in the officers' own *Remonstrance* of November 14. It reiterated the controversial proposal to extend the right to vote to all free men. In these proposals, however, there was nothing new. What made them so obnoxious in January, 1648, was the circumstances in which they were put forth and the kind of support Lilburne and his party understood but too well how to evoke for them. The army leaders had taken steps for the relief of army grievances, promised constitutional reform, and so regained military control. But after ten years of revolution and war there were many men outside the army with grievances and anxieties more difficult to put off or allay. There was a literate, articulate, opinionated populace, alive to its own woes and needs, full of yeasty notions derived from sermons and pamphlets and much talk, adept at gathering in conventicles and committees, prone in moments of excitement to take to the streets and go swarming out to Westminster. And there was Lilburne, expert at the trick of putting inflammatory words into their mouths and explosive ideas into their heads.

'Oh that the cravings of our Stomacks could be heard by the Parliament and City!' began *The mournfull Cryes of many thousand poor Tradesmen.* 'O you Members of Parliament, and rich men in the City, that are at ease. . . . Is there none to pity? . . . . and are our Rulers become cruell like the Ostrich in the Wildernesse. Lament. 4.3.' 'Parliament-men, Committee-men, Customers, Excise-men, Treasurers, Governors of Towns and Castles, or Commanders in the Army,

Officers in those Dens of Robbery, the Courts of Law'—these are no different from the people's old oppressors. 'O ye Parliament-men hear our dying cry, Settle a Peace, settle a Peace . . . settle the just common Freedomes of the Nation, so that all Parties may equally receive Justice, and injoy their Right . . . Carry our cries in the large Petition to the Parliament, and tell them, if they still be deaf, the Teares of the oppressed will wash away the foundations of their houses. Amen, Amen, so be it.' [55]

The petition itself gave a precise and revealing catalogue of the hardships and confusions of peace at the close of a war which appeared to have settled nothing. Parliament had promised freedom to the people and justice upon their oppressors. But the people's petitions had been burned, and the king was still unpunished. Faithful men were being interrogated, vexed, and imprisoned without just cause or legal warrant by parliamentary committees. Old abuses continued worse than ever—laws in French, bribery and corruption in the courts, imprisonment without trial, monopolies and other restrictions upon trade, failure of public officials to account for public funds, limitations upon the right to vote, ensnaring oaths, neglect of the poor, neglect of fishing and manufactures, inequitable taxes, delay of reparations to the victims of former tyranny, postponement and evasion of promises and engagements by parliament. 'Oh dissolve not all Government into the Prime laws of nature, and compell us to take the naturall remedy to preserve our selves, which you have declared no people can bee deprived of.' And after a marginal reference to parliament's own declarations of 1642 against the king and to the well-known manifesto of that year, *A Question Answered*, the petition draws to a close with the first four verses of the Eighty-second Psalm: 'Oh remember that the righteous God standeth in the congregation of the mighty . . . deliver the poor and needy, and rid them out of the hands of the wicked.' ' 'Tis indeed called a Petition,' was the comment in *A Declaration of some Proceedings*, 'but the whole frame and matter of it is nothing else but a Calumnie against those they seem to petition, charging upon their account all those Evills that are upon the Kingdome.' [56] Lilburne in his speech before the house of commons acknowledged his part in this petition, including the marginall notes, and reiterated its main points.

'The people,' he now defiantly asserted, 'are more for the King then the Parliament' because, notwithstanding all the blood and treasure which have been spent in their behalf, their burdens are greater than before. They were engaged by parliament to fight for their liberties but never told what their liberties were. The glory and splendor of them was never held forth, 'to make them in love with them, and to study how to preserve them.' [57]

X

The Dispensations of Providence
1648-1649

THE king's engagement with the Scots at the close of 1647 brought
the house of commons once more under the domination of Cromwell
and Ireton, but there was now no time for that reconstitution of parliament which the army commanders had promised. The king's adherents
were presently up in arms, and the Scots were making ready to invade
England in his behalf. The army, however, knew well how to deal with
such a contingency. Fairfax moved skillfully against the uprisings in
Kent and Essex and by the end of August had brought the royalists
at Colchester to surrender. By that time too the uprising in Wales had
been put down, and Cromwell had shattered the Scots and their English auxiliaries in Lancashire and was proceeding north to make the
Scots at home yield to the dispensations of providence. By the end of
October he was back in Yorkshire, directing the siege of Pontefract,
the last royalist stronghold.

These successes made the problem of making peace more difficult
than ever. Once danger abated, the only support the army leaders could
count on in parliament and the city was that of the Independents
and their sectarian followers. The city authorities and a majority in
both houses resented domination by the army and were certain to re-
act against it at the first opportunity. Though the army was the Presbyterians' only protection against full recovery of power by the king and
the bishops, it was also the greatest bar to the kind of unity they believed essential to the peace and order of the nation. The irony of their
predicament was that the unity they hoped for was not now to be had
except by the use of force, and the only sufficient force was in the hands
of men who owed their power to their willingness to grant a measure
of free play to those dynamic elements in the Puritan movement which

the Presbyterians had helped to evoke and were now endeavoring to bring under restraint.

Egged on by the Presbyterian preachers and their adherents, parliament soon began taking steps to guard against the effects of another victory by the army in the field. In May both houses approved the long-pending ordinance against heresy and blasphemy so offensive to dissenters of all sorts. In June the house of commons reinstated the surviving ten out of the eleven members who had been expelled at the army's insistence the year before. At the beginning of August the house set Lilburne free and the lords revoked their sentence against him in the expectation that he would stir up fresh trouble for the army commanders. Major Huntington of Cromwell's regiment was induced to accuse his superior of treason. At the end of August the commons rescinded their vote of no more addresses to the king and, in September, with news arriving of victory in Essex and the north, commissioners were sent to treat for peace with Charles at Newport. Negotiations began September 18 and dragged on for over two months until the army was ready once more to march on London. The intention was to confront the army leaders with a settlement, approved by the king and conforming as nearly as possible to presbyterian principles of church government. Four members of the Westminster Assembly, headed by Stephen Marshall, were sent along to deal with the bishops and future bishops who made up the king's clerical advisers. The two groups argued over the same issues which Smectymnuus and Milton had debated with Bishop Hall seven years before, and with much the same result. The royal saint would concede nothing his conscience could not approve, and although the Presbyterians seemed willing at the last moment to risk almost anything rather than yield to the army, none of their concessions was of any avail.[1] The net effect of their endeavor to make peace without the army was to fix the hold of the most uncompromising of the army leaders upon the forces under their command and to set in motion the chain of events which presently brought the Puritan Revolution to its irretrievable climax.

i. THE ARMY AND THE LEVELLERS ONCE MORE: THE WHITEHALL DEBATES

The attempt of the Presbyterians to make peace with the king brought the army and the Levellers once more into line with one another. The imperative need to maintain military discipline, which had compelled the army commanders to repress the agitators, had caused them also to suppress the Levellers' petition of January 19, 1648, and send Lilburne back to the Tower. But the expectation of the Presbyterian faction in parliament that, if given his freedom, he would again foment insubordination among the soldiers was doomed to disappointment. Lilburne perceived that he and his party must still look to the army if they wished to see their principles put into practical effect, and he also perceived that those principles offered the army the most plausible grounds for justifying the course upon which it was now venturing. On August 3, two days after his release, he wrote to Cromwell in the north, 'I am no stagerer from my first principles that I engaged my life upon, nor from you, if you are what you ought to be, and what you are strongly reported to be.' [2] His partisans were soon ready with a pamphlet, probably by Walwyn and in Thomason's hands by August 21, called *The Bloudy Project, Or a discovery of the New Designe, in the present War*. A petition to the house of commons followed on September 11. Petition and pamphlet made clear that Lilburne's party stood with the army in opposition to the schemes of the Presbyterians for peace with the king. The petition recapitulated once more the whole case for constitutional reform as it had been developed through successive stages by parliament, the army, and the Levellers since 1642. [3] The people were to be acknowledged supreme; the house of commons was to be acknowledged as their supreme representative; representation was to be extended and made more equitable; fundamental rights were to be reserved by common agreement; reforms were to be undertaken for relief of the people's grievances.

It is easy to say that such a program was one for three hundred years and not for the moment, but that does not account for its impact upon the men actually involved in the crisis of 1648. The ancient structure of the state had been demolished, and the institutions which were to arise in the future out of that situation were as yet but half-formed, untested notions in men's minds. The movement for reform of the church had arrived at deadlock between parliament—which is to say, the faction in control of the quasi-permanent body which parliament had become; the royal saint who had managed to lose everything except his sense of right and the devotion of a great body of his subjects; and the army with its assurance of grace confirmed by success in war. This impasse Lilburne and his party proposed to overcome by a deliberate reorganization of civil government according to principles which, it was not unreasonably presumed, neither parliament nor army could consistently deny. The idea of an agreement of the people as the basis of the state seemed the logical necessary fulfillment of everything that had been said by the supporters of parliament since the beginning of the struggle, by parliament's own apologists, by preachers in countless sermons, by the army in its recent declarations and remonstrances, as well as by the Levellers in their petitions, pamphlets, and public demonstrations. Here was the way, the Levellers said in effect, to ground the liberty which had now been won for the people upon English law, to obviate the intractable problem of the church, and to allay popular discontent. If the former tyranny was not to be readmitted and if military domination was ever to be brought to an end in the state, what other plan was there upon which to constitute a government?

Among the things the people now expected of parliament, according to the petition of September 11, was that 'you would have done Justice upon the Capitall Authors and Promoters of the former and late Wars.' Parliament, it was said, should have laid to heart the blood that had been spilled and the havoc wrought 'by express Commissions from the King.' The council of officers at Windsor the preceding April had resolved 'that it was our duty, if ever the Lord brought us back again in peace, to call *Charles Stuart*, that man of blood, to an account.' [4] After the fall of Colchester, with Cromwell still in the north, the real leadership of the army fell to Ireton, and the men of his and other regiments took up the cry for justice without respect of persons upon the promoters of the recent uprising. By the middle of November the council of officers at St. Albans was drafting a remonstrance to parliament against negotiating with the king. On November 15 a number of officers and ministers met with Lilburne and other members of his party at a tavern in the city. At this meeting, according to Lilburne, the army men were for proceeding at once to extreme measures, while the Levellers were for calling together representatives of the army and of 'the well-affected people in every County' to draw up 'the foundations of a just Government' [5] as proposed in the petition of September 11. The next day at St. Albans the officers approved the *Remonstrance,* drafted by Ireton and submitted to parliament on November 20. This document reflects the attitudes of both groups at the tavern meeting reported by Lilburne. The danger now, both realized, was that the army should be held responsible for all the burdens of war and revolution while Charles became the symbol of all the lost blessings and comforts of peace. It seemed obvious that, if he were allowed to continue on the throne under any conditions, he would presently recover all the power that had been taken from him through the army's efforts. He must, therefore, be called promptly to account as the prime offender against the public interest. But that was not all. The house of commons must be recognized as the supreme authority in the state, and yet, as the Levellers had demanded, a date must be set for its dissolution and arrangements made for the periodic election and meeting of parliaments in future, providing always that no parliament be allowed to 'render up, or give, or take away any of the foundations of common Right, Liberty or Safety contained in this settlement and Agreement.' [6]

The Levellers believed that their proposal for summoning a representative assembly to draft an agreement as a basis for a new government was, as Lilburne said, 'very well accepted and approved by the great ones' at St. Albans, and he and his friends followed the officers' council to Windsor in order to press for its adoption.[7] The king was a tyrant and the present parliament little better, but the Levellers had been cozened before by the army leaders, and they feared lest all power now devolve unchecked into their hands. The army leaders for their part felt a need to put forth a statement of principles and a program of reform to counteract the anticipated treaty of peace with the king. But time was running out, and there was danger that the army would not or could not wait for the proposed constituent assembly. At Windsor, therefore, the Levellers moved that, in place of the larger body, a joint committee, consisting of four army men, four parliament men of the 'honest' party, four Independents, and four of their own group, be called together at once to draft the proposed agreement without further delay. Again Lilburne believed that he had the consent of all concerned, and with three of his associates and Henry Marten immediately went to work.[8] Meanwhile, however, the house of commons, disregarding the army's *Remonstrance*, continued its endeavor to deal with Charles. The result was that the council of officers on November 30 issued a *Declaration* in which they expressed disinclination to interfere with parliament but went on to say, nevertheless, that 'we apprehend our selves obliged in duty to God, this Kingdom and good Men therein, to improve our utmost abilities in all honest ways, for the avoiding of these great Evils we have remonstrated, and for the prosecution of the good things we have propounded.' In conclusion they gave notice that 'we are now drawing up with the Army to *London* there to follow Providence as God shall clear our way.'[9] Two days later the army was in the city. Yet still the house, after a speech by Prynne, voted to continue treating with the king, and the outcome was that, when the members came on December 6 to take their seats as usual, they encountered Colonel Pride and his troopers at the doors barring the entrance to all who had opposed the army's will.

The joint committee for drawing up an agreement of the people met at Whitehall after Pride's Purge. 'And a long and tedious tug we had,' Lilburne wrote, 'with Commissary Generall Ireton, yea sometimes whole nights together, Principally about Liberty of Conscience, and the Parliaments punishing where no law provides.' The fruit of these discussions was the draft of an agreement which Lilburne expected the council of officers to subscribe without more ado. 'But alas poor fools we were meerly cheated and cozened.' When the proposed draft was brought before the council, 'there came the Generall, Crumwell, and the whole gang of creature Colonels and other Officers, and spent many dayes in taking it all in pieces.' Lilburne lost patience and on December 15, without waiting for the officers to conclude, published the draft which he understood had been approved by the joint committee with the title *Foundations of Freedom; or an Agreement of the People.*[10] He added a letter of protest to the reader, and with a number of his associates he protested directly to the council on December 28 in *A Plea for Common Right and Freedom.*[11]

Comparison of Lilburne's version of the much-discussed agreement with that presently submitted by the officers to parliament shows how far the army leaders had in fact come toward avowing the principles and aims which he and his party had been so effectively publicizing. No alternative to a Presbyterian settlement by treaty with Charles seemed now so appealing as the kind of program to which the Levellers had given the name Agreement of the People. In the minds of those who looked to Cromwell and Ireton for leadership, there seemed no question now but that a company of men by taking thought might indeed 'make Way for the Settlement of a Peace and Government of the Kingdom upon Grounds of common Freedom and Safety.' [12] No one denied that the people were supreme and that a house elected by the people at regular intervals for a limited term was the necessary instrument of the people's will in the state. Though the Levellers would have reapportioned parliamentary seats more drastically than the army leaders, both parties now agreed on the extension of the suffrage to all ratepayers. Ireton was apparently no longer concerned for the 'permanent and local' interest of the country, and the Levellers were at pains to forbid parliament to 'levell mens Estates, destroy Propriety, or make all things common.' [13] Officers and Levellers alike sought redress of substantially the same grievances and reform of the same abuses. Both were for equality before the law and for the punishment of offenders without respect of persons. Both were for reserving fundamental rights to the people, and in the main the same rights. The crucial difference between the disputants at Whitehall arose over religion, and even on that point their respective proposals seem now not far apart. The Levellers would have had the civil government maintain public worship, instruction, and discipline out of public funds, though not by tithes. They would at the same time have had no one compelled to conform to the state religion or, barring popery, restrained from following his own. The officers' proposals were more exact and detailed rather than essentially different. They too would have had the state support public worship—that is, Christian worship—

without compulsion, without tithes, and, barring prelacy as well as popery, without restraint of peaceful persons—Christians, that is—from worshiping as and where they chose.[14]

Nevertheless, the question how far the proposed agreement should go in limiting the authority of the magistrate in matters affecting conscience was the question which finally broke up the association of the Levellers with the army leaders. The dispute came to a head in a meeting of the council on December 15 at which Ireton found himself pitted against John Goodwin and Philip Nye, representing the Independent ministers, and Lilburne, Wildman, and Overton, speaking for the Levellers. Long practice had prepared the ministers to demonstrate the invincibility of conscience and the incompetence of any single person, whoever he might be, to overrule its dictates in another. The Levellers, while ready with the same argument, had learned by experience that power of no sort could safely be entrusted to any man in the state unless it were securely hedged in against the corruption certain to beset its possessors. But, Ireton objected, 'there are many things that men may own and practise under pretense of religion' in which they ought to be restrained. Was the liberty allowed to conscience to be such 'as shall necessarily debar any kind of restraint on anything that any will call religion?' That was the question, he said, but Lilburne interrupted, 'It is *not* the question.' The question was, he insisted, not whether the conscience of the individual should be limited but the power of the ruler. In the prefatory letter to *Foundations of Freedom*, Lilburne declared that no man would ask for unlimited authority in the state 'but he that intends to be a Tyrant' and that no man would yield to such authority in another 'but he that resolves to be a slave.' But surely, Ireton argued, the end and purpose of the state is not the preservation of liberty—'for then I am most free when I have nobody to mind me'—but 'the preserving of human society in peace.' If there were no such thing as power in the state, the 'contrary wills, lusts, and passions of men'—and he might have added consciences—'would lead every one to the destruction of another, and to seek all the ways of fencing himself against the jealousies of another.' [15]

Thus Ireton, commanding the unanswerable but unconstitutional argument of armed force, pled for an agreement to restrict liberty in the interest of peace. Lilburne, commanding only the weapons of political agitation, sought to impose constitutional limitations upon the free exercise of power by anyone in the state. The issue was fundamentally the same which first or last divided every party to the Puritan Revolution, and the meeting at Whitehall in December, 1648, came no nearer to an answer acceptable to all than the Westminster divines had done. All were caught in the same predicament. The Puritan movement had begun with the preachers' endeavor to free themselves from the restraints imposed by prelacy. It had led step by step to the denial and disruption of one constituted authority after another—church, crown, and parliament. And yet, though men had never before been actually so free to preach and print, no one thought of contending for a liberty that should be absolutely without bounds of any sort. True liberty, all agreed, was but obedience to higher law. All were at pains at every stage of the movement to call upon scripture and history, conscience and reason, to justify everything they did or undertook. And still the question rose, how, having attained the liberty they sought, were men to be restrained from pressing the demand for liberty even farther by an appeal to the same sanctions? How, by the methods of free discussion, was agreement ever to be reached about anything in time for effective action? Free discussion seemed merely to breed more discussion, liberty for some to produce still more liberty for others, until the only body left in the state with any real power to decide and to act was the army.

ii. GODLINESS IN ACTION: CROMWELL, JOHN OWEN

Yet though this was the fact, it was not a fact that could be admitted in its pure anomalous simplicity. Hobbes might reason that power of state needed no justification beyond itself. Hugh Peters, when asked by what authority members of parliament were being excluded from their seats, might in a perhaps unguarded moment reply, the power of the sword. And as time went on and the army leaders solidified their hold upon the state, the pretense that any other power really counted might grow difficult to keep up. Nevertheless, at every stage on the way to absolute control, the army leaders had to give assurance, not least to themselves, that all they were doing or were about to do squared with the principles which had guided them from the beginning of the revolution.

The ascendancy of the army brought with it the ascendancy of Cromwell, and Cromwell was possessed by the gift of inspiring in others but first of all in himself the conviction that he had been called to be the instrument of a purpose the Lord would not allow to fail. Yet though dedicated to a purpose, Cromwell was never quick to commit himself to a program. He was at any rate always more intent on getting the Lord's work done than on thinking it through, and he hated frustration more than he cared for consistency. His endeavor in the deadlock of interests and parties was to surmount immediate and pressing difficulties rather than to seek solutions of fundamental issues. In 1647 he assured parliament of the soldiers' loyalty and then joined officers and men in defying parliament's orders. He went along with the soldiers in their seizure of the king and their demand for constitutional change and then attempted to effect a settlement with the king and parliament by compromise. He thwarted the agitators' attempt to democratize the army and subvert discipline and then joined with his fellow commanders in a promise to seek reforms of the sort proposed in *The Agreement of the People*. Balked by the intransigence of men with more consistent minds, he moved steadily away from the position he had taken at Putney and nearer to that defined in the Leveller petitions of January and September, 1648, even while repudiating the Levellers themselves. In the end he was driven to the most extreme conclusions not by logic but by faith in himself and by the momentum of events.

Though outraged by Charles's refusal to accept defeat as the judgment of providence on his cause, Cromwell probably welcomed the relief from indecision which came with renewal of war in the spring of 1648. The campaign in Wales, the west midlands, the north, and finally Scotland was the first in which he enjoyed sole command, and the record of his doings is that of a man exulting in the exercise of a special seasoned gift for military leadership. He takes command in a stirring speech to his men at Gloucester, lays siege to Pembroke, marches north into Yorkshire, and all along the way looks energetically after the needs of an army in action. He directs Lambert's advance operations and then at the right moment himself strikes across the hills to take the enemy by surprise and shatter him completely. After that we see him rounding up prisoners, summoning Berwick and Carlisle, enforcing discipline, bringing the Scots to terms in their own capital, and in the intervals between these exploits sending reports of victory to Westminster. Cromwell's enemies from that day to this have usually said that in all his doings he was always secretly contriving the king's destruction to make way for his own advancement. Others have at least assumed that his thoughts were much occupied in 1648 with the question, what fate should be meted out to a man who had now a second time defied God's judgment upon the field of battle. But power accrued to Cromwell through the impact of character upon men and circumstances in a revolutionary crisis rather than by calculation. While his letters and speeches betray a steady hardening of his attitude toward Charles and all who joined with him to renew the war, they reveal not a speculative, far-seeing, contriving intelligence but a saint after the Puritan fashion, seeking and striving, a twice-born soul, for outward confirmation of the grace of which he feels assured from within.

'The Lord is with you, while ye be with him; and if ye seek him, he will be found of you' was a text which had often been used in the pulpit since Stephen Marshall had chosen it for the theme of his sermon to the house of commons on that first fast day in November, 1640. Cromwell was one who had taken such teachings to heart with results not altogether to the liking of many preachers. 'You see how God hath honoured and blessed every resolute action of these for Him,' he wrote to Robert Hammond in December, 1647; 'doubt not but He will do so still,' and a few days later he wrote, "Go on in the strength of the Lord; and the Lord be still with thee.' 'I pray God teach this Nation,' he wrote to Fairfax in June from before Pembroke, 'what the mind of God may be in all this, and what our duty is . . . for these things that have lately come to pass have been the wonderful works of God; breaking the rod of the oppressor, as in the day of Midian.' Starting north against the Scots, he told the citizens of Bristol, 'our joy is that God hath cleared up our way by the appearance of his providence in his former assistances,' and all members of the army, he declared, are ready to die 'in owning of that only, which God and reason allows.' And after Preston he wrote to the committee at Manchester, 'It hath pleased God, this day, to show His great power by making the Army successful against the common Enemy.' At the close of his long report of the battle to Speaker Lenthall, he wrote, 'Surely, Sir, this is nothing but the hand of God, and wherever anything in this world is exalted, or exalts itself, God will pull it down.' He was in the dangerous mood of a man possessed by the imagery of the eighth chapter of Isaiah, convinced that God is a sanctuary to the faithful, a stone of stumbling and a rock of offense to those who conspire against Him and them. He told Oliver St. John at the same time that neither too little nor too much should be made of 'outward dispensations. . . . They shall,' whatever men make of them, 'fulfil the good pleasure of God, and so shall serve our generations.' The next day he wrote to Lord Wharton, 'I think, through these outward mercies (as we call them), faith, patience, love, hope, all are exercised and perfected, yea, Christ formed, and grows to a perfect man within us.' [16]

Full of such notions, Cromwell advanced upon Scotland itself after overwhelming the Scottish army, 'The witness that God hath borne against your army,' he told the garrison at Berwick, 'doth at once manifest His dislike of the injury done to a nation that meant you no harm.' If they deny the recent dispensation shown against them, 'we must make a second appeal to God, putting ourselves upon Him in endeavouring to obtain our rights, and let Him be judge between us.' This was to turn back upon the Scots with a vengeance an argument their own preachers had often made free with. But with Cromwell and his notorious army bearing down upon them, they could offer no reply for the time being but submission. He for his part showed a surprising and rather ingenuous moderation in dealing with them from this point. The engagement with Charles and the invasion of England had been the work of Hamilton and his faction, and their defeat gave the more extreme Presbyterian party of Argyle, backed now by Cromwell, opportunity to recover control. Cromwell felt a kinship of spirit with these people more significant to him than differences of church or doctrine. 'I desire from my heart,' he wrote to Hammond in November, after his return to England, 'I have prayed for it, I have waited for the day to see union and right understanding between the godly people (Scots, English, Jews, Gentiles, Presbyterians, Independents, Anabaptists, and all.)' The Scots had, to be sure, been enemies, 'really Presbyterians,' but, he said, 'God hath justified us in their sight. . . . It is an high conviction upon them.' They are therefore henceforth to be loved and trusted; they are of the godly, and godliness is everything.

Needless to say, the Scots, though willing to take advantage of Cromwell's sudden access of confidence, were by no means ready to adopt his way of thinking. But we are not to conclude that his way of thinking had arrived at something later generations would have recognized as toleration or democracy. By the providence of God, he said, opposing parties had been brought into 'balance' in Scotland and so peace had been secured. 'If there be any dangerous disproportion it is that the honest party . . . in my apprehension are the weaker.' But—Cromwell's syntax is sometimes badly raveled—he feels justified for his part in all this, seeing 'that a lesser party of a Parliament hath made it lawful to declare the greater part a faction, and made the Parliament null, and call a new one, and to do this by force, and this by the same mouths that condemned it in others.' The Puritan saint was grasping after freedom and power, but only for the 'honest' party, though it might be the lesser and the weaker; that is to say, for the godly, the sign of godliness being belief in an in-dwelling but emergent and active power which was expected to be fulfilled and confirmed by providence in the event.[17]

Arrived at Pontefract at the end of October, Cromwell had time to brood over what was going on at Newport. Parliament's negotiation with Charles, now in full swing, augured a settlement which might mean the dissolution of the army, the reorganization of the church under Presbyterian auspices, the eventual return of the king to power, and the suppression of Independents and sectaries. To oppose such a settlement might require action against parliament and king more drastic and extreme than anything that had been found necessary so far. To submit might be to repudiate at last all that the godly believed in and the army had fought for. Cromwell's reflections on this hard choice appear in a letter of November 25 to his intimate friend Robert Hammond. The latter had been allowed to withdraw from active service in the army to wrestle with his conscience in the quiet of the governorship of the Isle of Wight. There, however, he suddenly found himself saddled with responsibility for the person of the king and torn anew by conflicting loyalties. Conscience required obedience to lawful authority, but where did lawful authority reside, and what if obedience to lawful authority in one direction demanded disobedience in another?

The point of Cromwell's advice to his friend is clear enough, though his expression is, as it often was, clouded by the intensity of his feelings. He wrote out of the heart of his religious experience, rationalized by the axioms of Puritan revolutionary theory. True, 'Authorities and powers are the ordinance of God,' but since they are also human institutions, they are subject to various limitations. 'All agree there are cases in which it is lawful to resist,' and the question is, 'Whether ours be such a case?' Is the treaty with the king likely to serve the safety of the people? Or is not 'the whole fruit of the war like to be frustrated, and all most like to turn to what it was, and worse?' But is not the army itself 'a lawful power, called by God to oppose and fight against the king upon some stated grounds?' For the people's sake, Cromwell seems to be trying to say, the army may lawfully oppose one authority as well as another, even the authority of parliament, by which it had itself been called into being. The quarrel was not made lawful by decree of the power which began it; it was lawful in itself. 'But truly,' he says, 'these kinds of reasonings may be but fleshly . . . My dear friend, let us look into providences; surely they mean somewhat. They hang so together; have been so constant, so clear and unclouded.' [18]

So now as before it came to this with Cromwell, that the one authority which could overrule every other was that which spoke in the breast of the godly and was evinced in action. By dispensations and providences, by success, God makes good in the event the commands he puts upon the saints whom he has covenanted to sustain against their enemies, no matter who they may be. 'We wait upon the Lord,' Cromwell had said in his former letter, 'who will teach us and lead us whether to doing or suffering.' Now he wrote:

I can tell thee: I am such a one as thou didst formerly know, having a body of sin and death, but I thank God, through Jesus Christ our Lord there is no condemnation, though much infirmity, and I wait for the redemption. And in this poor condition I obtain mercy, and sweet consolation through the Spirit, and find abundant cause every day to exalt the Lord, and abase flesh, and herein I have some exercise.

As to outward dispensations, if we may so call them, we have not been without our share of beholding some remarkable providences, and appearances of the Lord. His presence hath been amongst us, and by the light of His countenance we have prevailed. We are sure, the good-will of Him who dwelt in the bush has shined upon us, and we can humbly say, We know in whom we have believed, who is able and will perfect what remaineth, and us also in doing what is well-pleasing in His eyesight.

There is no telling whether the author of these words foresaw exactly where such ideas were leading him in the crisis before him. He was now, however, in favor of imposing the sternest punishment on the contrivers of what he could regard only as rebellion against the dispensations of providence. 'I find a very great sense in the officers of the regiments,' he wrote Fairfax, 'of the sufferings and the ruin of this poor kingdom, and in them all a very great zeal to have impartial justice done upon Offenders . . . and I verily think and am persuaded they are things which God puts into our hearts.' [19] A few days after writing to Hammond, Cromwell received a summons from Fairfax to report at headquarters. He arrived in London toward the end of the day on December 6, a few hours after Pride's Purge, and according to all accounts took the leading part in the events which immediately followed.

It was now apparent that no settlement by agreement between the king and the Presbyterians was possible unless the army leaders were prepared to risk the loss of all the power to control events which, Cromwell believed, providence had put into their hands. It was also apparent that, if the proposed Agreement of the People, whether in Ireton's version or Lilburne's, were actually put into effect, the decisive voices in choosing and directing a new house of commons would not be those favorable to the army. There might still be liberty of a sort, but hardly peace, and the army leaders had already all the liberty they needed to quell disorder and make themselves secure.

Parliament was not dissolved. The purged house of commons, with the 'honest' party in control, was retained as the quasi-constitutional implement of the army commanders, who now became the virtual masters of the state. On December 23 the king was brought by their orders to Windsor. On December 28 an ordinance was introduced in the house, calling for his trial and punishment. On January 4 the house

voted 'that the People are, under God, the Original of all just Power:
That the Commons of *England*, in Parliament assembled, being
chosen by, and representing the People, have the supreme Power in
this Nation: . . . That whatsoever is enacted, or declared for Law,
by the Commons, in Parliament assembled, hath the force of Law;
and all the People of this Nation are concluded thereby, although the
Consent and Concurrence of King or House of Peers be not had thereunto.' [20] On January 6 the house voted to set up a High Court of
Justice 'for the hearing, trying, and adjudging of the said Charles
Stuart' under a charge of treason against the people of England.[21] So
far the most extreme of the Levellers could have asked for little more.
But as to the rest of the program laid down in the *Agreement of the
People* and the various petitions and manifestoes which had attended
that document, the case was different. The officers' council concluded
its discussions at Whitehall on January 15 and on January 20 submitted
its version of the Agreement to the purged house of commons, which
received it with thanks. But on that day the king's trial began, and on
January 30 the crisis initiated by the Scots ten years before was brought
to its climax by an act of power committed by the army under Cromwell's leadership. Parliament did nothing more about any Agreement
of the People.

The collapse of monarchical and ecclesiastical authority and the
triumph of the army set all godly souls at last completely free to heed
whatever call or revelation they believed had come to them, to com-
mune with one group or another as the spirit moved them or with none
at all, a law to themselves in what seemed to many a lawless world.
Some, clinging even in dissent to the idea of the true church made
visible, might cohere into more or less closely organized bodies, withdrawn from the unregenerates about them, but the sect was not the
only, the terminal, or the most significant outcome of the Puritan im-
petus. All who remained true to their faith in the Word as originally
preached in the Puritan pulpit knew that the primary, decisive, essential element in spiritual experience lay not in communion but in vocation, not in being gathered with others but in being chosen and called
by and for something within oneself. Grace which might come to anyone must come to each severally, and grace was all a man needed to
be saved. Justified by grace within, one could afford to wait as long

as necessary for grace to manifest itself as it would in a visible church. Yet one might also at the same time look for regenerate souls to turn up in any company of men not certainly of Antichrist. And for the sake of all such, the state was bound to protect the freedom of every peaceable communion while regarding all, whether papists, prelatists, or presbyterians, who sought to persecute the saints, as enemies of Christ. The spirit of godliness in a man, not his adherence to this or that doctrine or communion, was all that really mattered.

Puritans who moved on to such conclusions were frequently assailed by other Puritans as seekers, antinomians, anabaptists, and what not, as churchless, lawless men, bent upon impeding the reparation of Zion. They were in fact representatives of a way of thinking about the issues of the Puritan Revolution to which many sorts of men were coming by various approaches from different points of view, men ready enough to agree upon the essential importance of faith while asserting the fewness of things necessary to be believed, or at any rate to be insisted upon by the aid of the temporal sword. The way to salvation, they said, should not be made to seem more intricate than charity or common sense or civil prudence would allow. Such notions had already, to go no farther back, been voiced on behalf of the traditional church by Henry Hammond and Jeremy Taylor. Similar considerations had turned Walwyn from contemplating the dissidence of the sects to organizing a political movement for democratic government and humanitarian reform. They had been held forth in various terms by army preachers, and they had been turned to practical advantage by Cromwell in shaping the army for victory in the field. Now at the final crisis of revolution, they were made to justify the army in overriding moral and theoretical objections to the use of power to meet the responsibilities which the possession of power made inescapable.

The work of presenting the army's case in the pulpit was naturally not for the London divines who had been urging parliament to make peace with the king. Fast days continued to be held, though not every preacher at St. Margaret's during these critical weeks was invited to publish his sermon or chose to do so. What Stephen Marshall found to say to the remnant of the house of commons after Pride's Purge is not known. What Hugh Peters may perhaps have said about the same time was alleged by a witness against him at his trial in 1660. This person testified that Peters, preaching at St. Margaret's in December, 1648, had exclaimed how sad a thing it would be if London citizens, like the Jews of old, allowed Christ to be crucified, meaning the army, and Barabbas to go free, meaning Charles.[22] The sermons of Thomas Brooks and Thomas Watson on December 27 were both published, the one by invitation of the house, the other not. Brooks, an Independent, said to his hearers that, if they failed to do justice to malefactors, they would 'provoke God to throw all your religious services as dung in your faces.' Watson, a Presbyterian, warned them that all things were naked to the eye of God.[23] On January 31, the day after the execution of the king, the preachers who addressed the house of commons by invitation given the month before were John Cardell and John Owen. The former was a person of slight importance about whom little is known. Owen, we learn from Anthony Wood, was one of the two 'Atlasses and patriarchs of independency,'[24] the other being Thomas Goodwin.

Goodwin, with the other Independents, had, as we have seen, withdrawn from the assembly in April, 1645 to devote himself to preaching and to wait for his opponents to be checkmated by the success of the New Model. He was soon to be made president of Magdalen College, Oxford. Owen was now to become the leading voice in determining the policy concerning the church to be followed under the Commonwealth. A brilliant and rising young man of thirty-three, a graduate of Oxford, and at this time the Puritan incumbent of an Essex vicarage, he came forward to expound in the idiom and tone of high intellectual authority that conception of spiritual life which possessed the minds of Cromwell and other army leaders and to define with precision a suitable attitude and policy in regard to the disorder into which the church had fallen. He did not speak the usual language of the seeker or the antinomian. He was no visionary or demagogue, no Saltmarsh, Dell, or Peters. He was a great pundit in the manner of his age and his party, erudite in the scriptures, the fathers, and the classics, a competent disputant as well as an eloquent speaker. He could open and divide a text, expound a doctrine, solve an objection, and expatiate on uses and applications with the best of his cloth. After the Restoration he went on preaching and arguing for liberty as he conceived it until his death in 1683, and not even Clarendon could induce him to conform. Anthony Wood said of him, 'His personage was proper and comely, and he had a very graceful behaviour in the pulpit, an eloquent elocution, a winning and insinuating deportment, and could by the persuasion of his oratory, in conjunction with some other outward advantages, move and wind the affections of his admiring auditory almost as he pleased.' In dress and manner he was hardly what a Puritan divine is commonly supposed to have been. As vice-chancellor of Oxford, if Wood is to be trusted, he went cloakless in order to show off his figure, powdered his hair, and wore large tassels on his bandstrings, pointed ribbons at his knees, Spanish leather boots with large lawn tops, and 'his hat mostly cock'd.' [25]

In several tracts and sermons before January, 1649, Owen had already advanced the ideas which the army leaders found so appropriate to their situation after that date.[26] On April 29, 1646, he had preached before the house of commons a sermon called *A Vision of Unchangeable free mercy* and appended to it, when he came to publish, 'A short defensative about Church-government . . . Toleration and Petitions about these things.' On August 28, 1648, he preached by invitation before Fairfax at Colchester and at about the same time before another audience at Romford. The two sermons were published shortly afterward with the title, *Eben-ezer. A Memoriall of the Deliverance of Essex County.* Next came *A Sermon Preached to the Honourable House of Commons, in Parliament Assembled: On January 31* (1649), and to this Owen added 'A Discourse about Toleration, and the Duty of the Civill Magistrate about Religion.' He preached again to the house of commons on April 19 and published the sermon with the title ΟΥΡΑΝΩΝ ΟΥΡΑΝΙΑ. *The Shaking and Translating of Heaven and Earth.*

In the first of these sermons the preacher began, as so many of his predecessors in that pulpit had done, with the legend of England's special place in the history of the world and of the church. His hearers heard again that God sends his gospel to certain peoples at certain times but first of all to his Englishmen. The familiar notion of England's primacy in divine favor was now, however, made to support that conception of the workings of grace which had prevailed with such effect in the army. 'The Reformation of *England*,' the preacher said, 'shall be more *glorious* then of any Nation in the world, being carried on neither by *might* nor *power*, but onely by the spirit of the Lord of Hosts.' Once more England has been delivered from tyranny and superstition by the gospel alone, and her people kept from turning back to Egypt. 'And let none seek to *extenuate* this mercy, by *Catalogues* of errours still amongst us.' 'I would to God . . . we were all of *one* minde, even in the most *minutulous* differences that are now amongst us.' But there is more danger, he says, 'in one *Babylonish* Errour, owned by men, pretending to *power* and *jurisdiction* over others, then in five hundred, *scattered* amongst inconsiderable disunited *Individuals*.' [27]

This sermon of April 29, 1646, was in idea and intention obviously in line with Hugh Peters' sermon earlier in the same month at the thanksgiving for the army's victory in the west. Owen's two sermons after the victory at Colchester, dedicated to Fairfax with a laudatory allusion to Cromwell, gave eloquent expression to that sense of God's immediate presence in the army's actions and achievements with which Cromwell's letters at this time were so full. God walks with his people, Owen said, showering mercies upon them, and still newer mercies according as they remember thankfully that he is with them. 'God came from Naseby, and the holy one from the West . . . He went forth in the North, and in the East he did not withhold his hand.' The people are not, however, to forget that these mercies have come to them not because of their deservings but out of God's love. The man who serves providence without discovering the hand of God in the things that befall him 'travailes in the wildernesse, without a directing cloud.' 'If God appears not in light, who can expect he should appear in operation?' 'Cleare shining from God must be at the bottome of deepe labouring with God.' 'If you have no great discoveries,' that is to say, of God's presence within you and in the events of which you are a part and an agent, 'you will wex vaine in great undertakings.' And in conclusion these ideas are applied more boldly than ever to the immediate and pressing problem of the church. 'Is it for any of you, O ye sons of men, to measure out Gods childrens portion. . . . ? If in taking what God hath measured out for them, they should not all comply with you . . . do them no harm, impoverish not their families, banish them not, slay them not.' To run when you are not sent is never safe. Those you pursue may prove to have been following 'divine Directions.' [28]

In his sermon to the house of commons the day after the execution of the king, Owen made no explicit allusion to that event. In his appended 'Discourse about Toleration, and the Duty of the Civill magistrate about Religion,' however, he directed his hearers' attention to the responsibility which they had brought upon themselves. No longer were they in the position of men who have reason to fear persecution or to plead for toleration. They had themselves become the temporal sword, beset by the problem which had bedeviled rulers since before the Puritan Revolution. Committed to the principle of Christian liberty, they were bound to reject any scheme, presbyterian or other, for a comprehensive church order to be imposed by force. But the practical question still remained, how far religious differences might be allowed to jeopardize their authority as rulers to protect themselves and defend the liberty of others. What restraints might properly be imposed upon the free play of conscience among the people, especially of that which enemies might choose to call conscience? This was the question which Ireton had raised only shortly before in the debate at Whitehall, and Owen was now in effect endeavoring to formulate an acceptable answer. The result was a professedly dispassionate but vigorous elaboration of the position which had been outlined in the Agreement of the People, whether in Ireton's or Lilburne's version.

It was the duty, the reader was told, of individuals, magistrates, and churches alike to maintain truth and oppose error, but nothing, certainly not the prison or the halter, can really serve to that end but 'Gospel conviction.' 'No spirituall *Remedy* can be too sharpe for a spirituall *disease*,' but 'Are the *Hammer* of the Word, and the *Sword* of the Spirit . . . now quite uselesse?' Let the sword of spiritual discipline be sheathed in the blood of heresies, but no sword whatever in the blood of heretics. The gospel has been persecuted in all ages by the worst of men sitting at the upper end of the world and making the repression of error an excuse for suppressing the truth. Yet it does not follow that the magistrate has no responsibility whatever for religion. He must himself be sure to know the truth while yet keeping a humble spirit lest pride of knowledge and of place betray him into error. He must see that truth is made known to the people, that public places are provided for that purpose and ministers maintained. And though no man can grasp truth in its entirety this side the grave, yet truth sufficient for salvation is comprehensible by all in the few essential fundamental tenets common to all communions, presbyterian or independent. The magistrate should not trouble himself or his people over differences springing up among the godly. He should permit no kind of public worship which he knows to be an abomination unto the Lord. Heresy and schism, however, he should ignore unless and until they threaten positive harm or breach of the peace. At the same time he should reduce to order: false believers who cause disturbances —'but actuall disturbances indeed'; persons who propagate singular opinions in extravagant ways, causing 'horror of mind' to true believers; vagabond preachers—'abiding in no place, taking care of no families . . . uncommanded, undesired . . . [going] up and down, from place to place, creeping into houses'; 'all who by pretense of religion draw others into the practise of vice (but not every foul story about Brownists and Puritans is to be believed).' [29]

What then is to be done in such cases, and who shall decide? The minister is able to determine what is error but has no authority to punish the erring except by the spiritual lash. The magistrate has no authority in spiritual matters but is bound to punish offenses against the peace of the state. So it comes to this, that error may be left to the church so long as it is directed only against truth, the church being recognized as the communion of the godly. But error which makes itself felt as an attack upon the civil peace must of necessity be proceeded against by the magistrate. Owen was not unaware of the equivocal position in which such a rule might seem to leave the particular men to whom he was addressing himself, and he has the suitable qualification ready. 'If *Opinions* in their owne natures tend to the disturbance of the *publike peace*, either that *publike Tranquillitie* is not of God, or God alloweth a penall restraint of those Opinions.' Proof, however, must be looked for not through disputation but 'in the things themselves, *Actum est*, let who will plead for them.' 'And I am the more inclin'd to assert a *restraint* to all *such* as these, because it may be established to the *height*, without the least prejudice unto the *truth*, though *persons erring* should injoy the place of authority.' [30] Here was a statement of principle and policy, couched in the most impressive terms of the Puritan pulpit but keyed to the temper and the interest of the men now in power. Preaching again at St. Margaret's on April 19, 1649, Owen told his audience.

You may be apt to think, that if you can carry on, and compasse your purposes, then all your Enemies will be assuredly disappointed: do but embrace the Lord Jesus in his kingly power in your bosomes, and *ipso facto* all your Enemies are everlastingly disappointed: you are the *grains,* which in the sifting of the Nation, have been kept from falling to the ground. Are you not the residue of all the Chariots of *England?* Oh that in you might appear the reality of the kingdom of the Lord Jesus, which hath been so long pretended by others.[31]

The speaker was directly afterward invited to join the expedition for the subjugation of Ireland as Cromwell's chaplain.

iii. THE TENURE OF KINGS: THE LONDON MINISTERS, JOHN GOODWIN, JOHN MILTON, AND JOHN LILBURNE

Cromwell was the great representative in action of the doctrine of vocation by the in-dwelling Christ. Writing to one of his daughters in October, 1646, he said of another, 'she seeks after . . . that which will satisfy. And thus to be a seeker is to be of the best sect next to a finder; and such an one shall every faithful humble seeker be at the end. Happy seeker, happy finder,' and he concludes by saying, 'that which is best worthy of love in thy husband is that image of Christ he bears. Look on that, and love it best, and all the rest for that.'[32] The husband in question was Henry Ireton. But to expect a band of well-placed clergymen to look for the image of Christ in an army of seekers and sectaries rather than in a visible church framed according to the Directory of Worship, drafted with so much agony of debate, was asking too much. The advance of the army under Cromwell's leadership meant the final defeat of the work of the Westminster Assembly. With parliament and the city under control, the Presbyterians might order the army to disband, decree the setting up of presbyteries, forbid unlicensed preaching and printing, and threaten heretics with direst penalties, but they were helpless to enforce any of these commands. For Cromwell and the army leaders had done what the brotherhood of preachers and their supporters had failed to do. While the brotherhood was breaking up in dissidence and parliament was letting the realities of power slip from its grasp, Cromwell and his associates in the army were forging the spiritual energies aroused by Puritanism into an instrument of decisive action in the state, and their power to control events had been confirmed in the debates at Putney, the abortive mutiny which followed, and the prayer meeting at Windsor which preluded the second civil war.

The effect of these developments on the preachers and their flocks was at first merely to increase dissension and intensify the feeling of frustration. The truth was that the Presbyterian preachers, though entrenched in their pulpits, were losing their hold upon the people at large with the result that a change, natural but unlooked for, was coming about in their own position and attitude. As the work of putting presbyteries into effect went only haltingly on and the clamor of dissent rose louder and louder, the Presbyterians were driven more and more to assume the role of a minority on the defensive and themselves to take on the characteristics of a Puritan sect. ' 'Tis now many years,' Peter Sterry told the house of commons in October, 1647, 'since our *Fasts* and our *Fights* have been mutually interwoven. Yet, what Profit have we of the One? What Peace from the Other? what end of either? Still we *fast*, still we *fight*, if not in Camps, yet more dangerously in Counsailes?' [33] They had, Marshall declared in July, 1648, made plain the rule God had prescribed for the church in his Word, but the people would have none of it, though it 'bee only to make them holy.' 'Wee have our monethly Fasts,' he said, 'but alas, they are brought to a meere formality.' [34] William Gouge complained that on fast days people now went about their own affairs, 'yea their pleasures and pastimes, in a kinde of dislike, if not a detestation of these duties.' [35]

In March, 1647, as the soldiers were making ready to resist disbandment, parliament decreed a special day of fasting, prayer, and preaching for the suppression of heresy. Richard Vines and Thomas Hodges in the pulpit at St. Margaret's harped upon what was now becoming the constant theme of their party in that place. If the church were allowed still to go unreformed, if strife and confusion still prevailed, it was because sin and error had not yet been beaten down, and the mystery of that iniquity was that the faithful should be found contending with one another while their enemies lay in the dust. At the close of 1647, when it appeared that the army had checked its opponents in parliament and the city, the London ministers turned once more to the press in defense of their cause. *A Testimony to the Truth of Jesus Christ . . . Subscribed by the Ministers of Christ within the Province of London* appeared early in January, 1648. It bore the names of fifty-two ministers, including thirteen members of the assembly. It was presently seconded by a number of similar testimonies, subscribed and published by the ministers of various outlying districts. It opened with the charge that the authority of scripture, the life of godliness, and the reformation of the church were being borne down by heresy, blasphemy, looseness, profaneness, and 'contempt of the Authority and Government of our Lord Jesus Christ.' This assertion was supported by a list of current errors, illustrated by quotations or paraphrased passages from various writers who were named in the margin. Without resorting to personal abuse in the fashion of Thomas Edwards, the writers offered a temperate but forceful statement of that conception of the church which a short time before few opponents of prelacy would have questioned. 'A well-ordered Church Government,' they declared, was 'necessary and effectuall' for the preservation of faith and piety. '*Presbyteries* and *Synods,* in a due line of subordination of the lesser to the greater,' as set down in scripture and practiced by the best reformed churches, were such a government, to establish which had been the expectation of all good men when the present parliament began. But now 'we are torn in pieces with destructive schismes, Separations, Divisions and subdivisions.' 'Multitudes are not ashamed to presse and plead for a publike, formall and universall Toleration' of the errors and corruptions which the church was designed by its founder to subdue and destroy.[36]

The stage to which religious opinion had arrived after seven years of Puritan preaching under the stress of revolution is well illustrated by the London ministers' *Testimony.* Wishing to discredit as well as refute their opponents, they do not fail to cite the four tracts which had so often been held up for condemnation, Overton's *Mans Mortallitie,* Milton's *Doctrine and Discipline of Divorce,* Walwyn's *Compassionate Samaritane,* and Williams' *Bloudy Tenent.* For the same reason they cited the recent arguments of Paul Best [37] and John Biddle [38] against the doctrine of the trinity and a notorious work by Laurence Clarkson [39] known as *The Pilgrimage of Saints*. John Saltmarsh and other exponents of free justification were also condemned along with a number of writers lumped under the term Anabaptists. But the offender to whom the ministers accorded most attention was the author of *Hagiomastix* and *The Divine Authority of the Scriptures*.

That the immortality of the soul is contingent upon the use men choose to make of their powers, that men may divorce their wives, that magistrates have no responsibility for the spiritual condition of their subjects, that ministers have no special calling denied to other men, that the Son and the Holy Ghost are not one with the Father, these were notions which, it might be assumed, needed only to be named to be damned. John Goodwin was the grand expositor of the all-too-plausible heresy which accounted for all such particular errors and which yet seemed to spread the more widely the more the orthodox doctrine of election was set forth. Once men were persuaded that any one of them might hope to be absolved by grace from the fault imputed to all by the first man and so lay hold of the hidden strength made available to the elect through Christ the new man, they consequently found it all too easy to conclude that every man might be saved if he wished. For if God offered his grace to anyone, why not to everyone, and if men were called, why should they be denied the power or the will to heed the call, and if the call were heeded, why should it fail? In *Hagiomastix* and *The Divine Authority of the Scriptures*, Goodwin had argued at great length that, having been granted the ability to believe, men also possessed the power to discover and understand what they were required to believe. Truth is revealed in God's Word and in his works, and faith lights the way for reason to find it out. Men were under no necessity to depend upon any authority outside themselves to mediate between them and whatever they took to be revealed to their own inquiring discoursing minds. And by that reckoning the ministers of the province of London could lay claim to no authority peculiar to themselves, their order, or the church as they conceived it for explicating the Word and applying it to the lives of men.[40]

The dispute with Goodwin exposed the weakness of the position into which the Presbyterians were being forced by the failure of their cause. To them as to others an ordered society was inconceivable except as comprehended within a church organized according to the principle of natural subordination. They were bound, however, to demonstrate that their particular system of subordination was prescribed by God's Word and that every deviation was contrary. And as one deviation after another was proposed, also in the name of scripture, the defenders of presbyterianism were obliged to define the truths they found revealed in scripture more and more precisely and minutely. More than that, they were moved to stigmatize every disagreement as rebellion against Christ and his church, clear sign of irremediable reprobation. Disagreements which might in other circumstances have been ignored as venial differences of opinion on this or that fine point better left undetermined were treated as evidence of moral obliquity, and on the other hand the common sins that all flesh is heir to were taken as sure signs of intellectual error and spiritual corruption. It followed that the spokesmen for the central Brahmin caste of preachers, as they approached the final collapse of their hopes, found less and less to say in their pulpits about calling and covenant and more and more about the sins of those who did not think as they did. In this they were falling into the pattern which would be followed by other Puritan groups as each in turn was compelled to give up the hope of making over the church and the world according to its own notion of divine intention. Puritanism everywhere, when put on the defensive by forces it had itself helped to set moving, was to become at last puritanical.

The ruin which the ministers saw impending in January, 1648, they saw actually upon them a year later, and on January 18, 1649, some forty-seven of them addressed the army leaders in *A serious and faithfull Representation . . . of Ministers of the Gospell Within the Province of London*. This was a last desperate protest against the seizure and imprisonment of the king, the purging of parliament, the proposed Agreement of the People, the betrayal of the covenant with the Scots and of the Directory of Worship. Religion, they declared, had been made to stink, the golden cord of government broken, magistracy laid in the dust, parliament made contemptible. They supported these charges with the usual citations of scripture against breach of covenants and disobedience of higher powers, but they did something more. They went on to a penetrating analysis of the motives and attitudes to which the army leaders appealed in justification of their proceedings. 'Put case,' the ministers said, that 'some other Party of men . . . Whose Principles had not been concurrent with yours, should have attempted acts of such a nature, as those that you have performed.' That which the army leaders now account a virtue in themselves they have often condemned as a crime in others. Success signifies nothing as to right or wrong; 'it is one of the greatest Judgements, when God suffers men to prosper in sinfull courses.' It is not safe for any men to assume that providence has marked out the way for them; 'God doth not approve the practice of whatsoever his Providence doth permit.' Nor is it safe to follow 'Impulses of Spirit, or pretended impressions on your hearts, without or against the rule of Gods written Word.' This may be to put Satan on equal footing with the Holy Spirit. Does history, the ministers demand, show any example of 'an impulse of spirit falling upon Multitudes of Persons at the same time, putting them all at once upon performances contrary to morall Precepts?' And in any case, can it be that one person, under the impulse of the spirit, may command others to do that to which they are not themselves spiritually impelled? To the plea of necessity—'least what you pretend as a glorious worke, might else miscarry'—there was the obvious rejoinder that God 'stands not in need of our sinne to carry on his owne worke.' The necessity in any case must be 'Absolute, Present, and Clear; not Doubtfull, Uncertain, and Conjectural.' [41]

To such assertions there could truly be no reply, but not so to the argument that the army was bound to obey parliament as the higher power contrary to what might conscientiously be claimed to be the people's and the army's interest. On that point John Goodwin, some two weeks earlier, had already published the counterargument to which all Puritan theorizing about sovereignty up to that moment clearly led. The ministers' *Serious and faithful Representation* was probably directed not only against the army's recent manifestoes but also against Goodwin's *Right and Might well met, or, A briefe and unpartiali enquiry into the late and present proceedings of the Army.* This was a cogent reassertion of the by-now familiar doctrine of a law imposed by God upon all his creatures, transcending the laws of church and state and justifying in case of need the most extreme action against constituted authority in any form. Natural necessity, it was said again, requires that men defend themselves from all attacks from any quarter upon life and liberty. Offenses against civil and ceremonial laws may be absolved but not those against the natural and moral laws written in the breast. On that ground parliament had contravened the constitution and called the army into being to resist the king. Should the army now deny the reason for its existence because commanded by the same body of men seeking to contravene the law which had alone justified its own and the army's former action? Goodwin does not blink the question, how the army is to determine what the need may be which it is compelled to serve or how it may go about justifying its claim to the right of decision. He appropriates Prynne's comparison of the state to a ship imperiled by a drunken captain. That which was lawful for parliament when threatened by the king is lawful for the army when threatened by parliament acting in collusion with that same king, and the army has the same right as parliament to judge of the people's necessity. To say that the army may not lawfully act in the people's behalf for the reason that the people have not regularly called it to do so is absurd, 'especially at such a time, when there is no possibility of obtaining, of receiving a formall call from the people, without running an eminent hazard of losing the opportunity for doing that excellent service unto them, which the providence of God in a peculiar juncture of circumstances, exhibits for the present unto us.' [42] Need argues consent. This is the law of nature, which is the law of God and therefore in truth also the law of the land. Thus, with intricate logic and many interwoven allusions to the scriptures and the classics, Goodwin carries Puritan doctrine to its final extreme conclusions.

But he was not the only one to do so. As the army leaders were bringing the king to trial, Milton wrote *The Tenure of Kings and Magistrates: Proving, That it is Lawfull, and hath been held so through all Ages, for any, who have the Power, to call to account a Tyrant, or wicked King, and after due conviction, to depose, and put him to death; if the ordinary Magistrate have neglected, or deny'd to doe it. And that they, who of late, so much blame Deposing, are the*

Men that did it themselves. A copy of this work was in Thomason's hands on February 13, and a second edition, with added matter, appeared a year later. Milton's immediate purpose was to refute the ministers' *Serious and faithfull Representation* of January 18 and the Scottish commissioners' *Letter* of January 22 to the speaker of the house. His larger purpose was to defend the action against Charles as the fulfillment of principles to which parliament, the army, and the ministers themselves were long since committed and as the necessary next step toward that reformation which was the avowed object of all their striving.

The question whether Charles had violated his trust as king, Milton said, was one to be decided by his judges according to law. The question raised by the ministers was whether or not any ruler whatever might be held accountable for crimes against his people, and to that Milton's reply is clear: 'If such a one there be . . . the Sword of Justice is above him,' and it is to be wielded by anyone who is able to do so. 'For if all human power to execute, not accidentally but intendedly, the wrath of God upon evil doers without exception, be of God; then that power . . . so executing that intent of God, is lawfull, and not to be resisted.' [43] After his usual fashion Milton was pushing a general principle to an extreme practical conclusion, and this conclusion he now supported by a lucid exposition of the doctrine of the covenant as the basis of the state, deduced from the scriptural account of the fall of man and its supposed consequences. No one can deny, he said, that man is to begin with free. But his continued enjoyment of freedom is contingent upon his obedience to the laws of his being as apprehended by reason. By disobeying reason and law, man surrenders his freedom and incurs death. This is justice. Yet the laws of being, notwithstanding the fall, are still within the power of reason to apprehend and of conscience to heed. Men are in some measure able to renew obedience, recover liberty, and live. The law of life within them prompts them to agree among themselves to entrust to one or more of their number authority to require obedience of everyone and to execute judgment upon any who refuse. And all goes well with the state so long and so far as the people and their chosen rulers keep faith with one another and with the Lord, for the Lord can be trusted always to keep faith with them.

But kings and magistrates are but men like other men and in violation of their trust may aspire to be tyrants even as their people may submit to be slaves. The people consequently, except when they have given up their freedom, have invented laws 'either fram'd, or consented to by all,' in order to 'confine and limit the authority of whom they chose to govern them: that so man, of whose failing they had proof, might no more rule over them, but law and reason abstracted as much as might be from personal errors and frailties.' As in the beginning rulers had been set above the people for the people's good, so was law set above rulers for the same purpose, and it follows that parliaments have the duty both of making laws and of seeing that they are obeyed and offenders punished, whoever they may be. The only qualification Milton admits to this rule is that 'none can love freedom heartilie, but good men' or, more particularly, that the work of altering laws and subverting unfaithful princes is, when the time comes, not for everybody but only for 'those Worthies which are the soule of that enterprize, to be swett and labour'd out amidst the throng and noises of Vulgar and irrational men.' 'Who in particular is a Tyrant,' he would leave, he says, 'to Magistrates, at least to the uprighter sort of them, and of the people, though in number less by many, in whom faction least hath prevaild above the Law of nature and right reason.' [44]

The idea that the basis of the state is a covenant binding upon both rulers and ruled but terminable by either was one which all parties to the revolutionary movement had had a share in elaborating. Henry Parker had spoken for parliament, Stephen Marshall for the brotherhood of preachers, Samuel Rutherford for the kirk, Lilburne and Overton for the populace, Wildman and the agitators for the soldiery, Ireton for the army commanders. Bradshaw, who presided over the king's trial, and Cook who was appointed to conduct the prosecution, both had the idea at tongue's end.[45] And Milton, who had appealed to it as the basis of marriage, now in the most cogently written statement of the idea which had yet appeared in England, put it into print in the nick of time to justify the men who were making Charles pay the extreme penalty if not for his crimes certainly for his mistakes. But timely effective rhetorical statement was not all that Milton brought to the support of his cause. 'A Tyrant,' he said, 'whether by wrong or by right comming to the Crown, is he who regarding neither Law

nor the common good, reigns onely for himself and his faction.' What
the people may lawfully do against such a one, 'I suppose no man
of cleare judgement need goe furder to be guided then by the very
principles of nature in him.' Nevertheless the vulgar folly of men
requires the assurance of other men's reason, and so Milton gives it
in plenty out of the best authorities—'and no prohibited Authors, nor
many Heathen, but Mosaical, Christian, Orthodoxal, and which must
needs be more convincing to our Adversaries, Presbyterial.' [46] The
chronicles of the chosen people in the Old Testament supplied him,
as they had done many before him, with abundant instances of faithless
rulers brought to book. But Milton did not spare citations as well from
historians, philosophers, reformers, and poets, English, Scottish, continental, and ancient, all the way back to Justinian, Seneca, Euripides,
and Aristotle. He made great play with the Scottish reformers, Knox,
and Buchanan, and with their English sympathizer, Goodman. Jesuit
writers, for obvious reasons, he omitted, but in his second edition he
added an array of Protestant reformers.

His announced objective was to show 'that they, who of late, so
much blame Deposing, are the Men that did it themselves.' The task
was not a difficult one. He had but to confront the preachers and the
Scots with the record of their own doings and sayings from the beginning of the crisis to the latest negotiations with Charles at Newport.
'And whether the Presbyterians have not don all this and much more',
they will not put mee, I suppose, to reck'n up a seven years story fresh
in the memory of all men.' But he does not refrain from taunting his
opponents with the reminder that they had once called upon everyone
in the name of God to curse—'as bitterly as *Meroz* was to be curs'd,
that went not out against a Canaanitish King' [47]—all those who would
not join with them in making war against Charles. Stephen Marshall,
a member of Smectymnuus, who had preached the notorious sermon
on 'Curse ye, Meroz' in February, 1642, was, as Milton doubtless
knew, one of the ministers who took part in the effort to make peace
with the king in 1648. Milton also doubtless knew that the great
preacher held his lucrative lectureship at St. Margaret's while hanging on to his living at Finchingfield over the protests of his parishioners
and that Thomas Young, who had just gone from his preaching post

in the city to the headship of a Cambridge college, had not relinquished the emoluments of his vicarage at Stowmarket.

Milton had said nothing in print about his former friends and associates since replying in *Tetrachordon* and *Colasterion* to the critics of his divorce tract. But he had been far from oblivious of the claims and pretensions of the Presbyterian ministers during their brief prosperity and precarious success, and he had suffered in pride and pocket at the hands of their supporters in parliament. It was not surprising in the circumstances that his projected exemplary history of heroic Britons and Saxons had turned under his hand into a chronicle of doltish rulers conspiring with venal churchmen as always to mislead and barbarize the people. The ancient British clergy, 'Pastors in Name, but indeed Wolves,' [48] were the same 'blind mouths' who had preyed upon the church in all ages and were now again at work. *The History of Britain* became for its author a kind of private outlet for the ethical disdain and disgust which he had come to feel for the Puritan clergy, and in his pamphlet on the tenure of kings he poured out in print the disillusion and indignation he had not been able to keep out of his history. His bitter flyting of his former associates was the more effective for being aimed at a whole class of men and not, in spite of the resentment he must have felt toward Thomas Young and perhaps other Smectymnuans, against any single individual. Again he accused them of going back on their own principles. These were the men who had first themselves 'disannointed' the king, 'nay curs'd him all over in thir Pulpits and thir Pamphlets,' and then, having thus led others more sincere than themselves into an enterprise they are too honest to retreat from, the ministers turn about and charge disloyalty. Let no one be deluded, Milton says, by 'our dancing Divines, who . . . come with Scripture in thir mouthes, gloss'd and fitted for thir turnes with a double contradictory sense . . . and with the same quotations to charge others, which in the same case they made serve to justifie themselves.' Beware of 'prevaricating Divines,' who 'with a ridling Covenant in thir mouths' swear 'almost in the same breath Allegeance and no Allegeance.' They are 'Ministers of sedition, not of the Gospel'; 'Mercenary noisemakers, of whose fury, and fals prophecies we have anough experience'; 'pragmatical Sidesmen of every popular tumult and Sedition'; 'Ministers of Mammon in stead of Christ'; 'Pulpit-firebrands.' 'For Divines,' he concludes in his second edition,

> have thir postures, and thir motions no less expertly and with no less variety
> then they that practise feats in the Artillery-ground. Sometimes they seem
> furiously to march on, and presently march counter; by and by they stand,
> and then retreat; or if need be can face about, or wheele in a whole body,
> with that cunning and dexterity as is almost unperceavable; to winde them-
> selves by shifting ground into places of more advantage. And Providence
> onely must be the drum, Providence the word of command, that calls them
> from above, but always to som larger Benefice. . . . But if there come
> a truth to be defended . . . strait these nimble motionists can finde no
> eev'n leggs to stand upon: and are of no more use to reformation throughly
> performed, and not superficially, or to the advancement of truth (which
> among mortal men is alwaies in her progress) then if on a sudden they were
> strook maime, and crippl'd.[49]

There was something in this indictment of the Puritan clergy more significant than mere personal disillusion and chagrin. For ages the church had claimed liberty to speak to and for all men in the name of God and had often spoken more freely than rulers liked or would willingly endure. But the temptation of churchmen in every age had been to assume that the authority to speak claimed for the church was the special privilege of its ministers, a privilege they could not always resist turning to their own advantage. The overthrow of prelacy had not rendered Puritan churchmen immune to the temptations common to men of their cloth. Still thinking of the church as the unique organ of spiritual life on earth, they clung to the belief that a great new age of the world would begin as soon as church government and discipline had been refashioned according to their understanding of God's Word set down in scripture. And if the headstrong central corps of ministers could have had their way, the result might have been to reduce all thought and expression to their control. This was not to be. The outcome of all their striving in pulpit and press was to be the triumph of their teaching and the disappointment of their expectation. Liberty, they should have learned, is, as Milton said, a two-edged sword. They had taught men to think that, if they wished to be counted among the elect, they must feel in their hearts a command to put every ability and every occasion to the service of the Lord, assured that he would not let that service come to nothing. They had taught men to seek confirmation of such teachings for themselves in the Bible, assured, as Milton said, that 'truth among mortal men is alwaies in her progress.' They had promised that, if men obeyed the truth thus revealed, reformation might be accomplished in England in their own time and 'throughly performed' bring new heaven and new earth. Thus they aroused not in the humble and poor in spirit only but in men of many conditions in an expanding world and a changing society a quickened consciousness of life and power within themselves, a sense of participating in the designs of providence, an expectancy of great things to come.

The result was not reformation but the emergence of an articulate vernacular public, free from many of the inhibitions and impediments of customary attitudes and sanctions. This insurgency, giving unforeseen application and force to the doctrine of calling and covenant, made possible the seizure of initiative in the state first by parliament and then by the army. The theory of the social contract might be of dubious validity as law or history, but its acceptance by the public which came forward in the Puritan Revolution pointed to the inescapable condition of all government in the age to come. Kings and magistrates would henceforth in fact be compelled to exercise their authority under the constant impact of complaint and criticism by all who could command the means to evoke and direct the opinions and passions of men for their own purposes, means which could only with difficulty be denied to anybody. This condition gave peculiar significance as time went on to the role which Milton had chosen to play. There were other men with the same overweening confidence in the power of discourse. There were others who urged similar ideas with greater immediate effect than he. Most of these would in a few years have become names which meant little, while the name of the great poet meant more and more to men of all persuasions. Milton, who to most of his contemporaries in 1649 was merely one of many pamphleteers, became for later generations a kind of herald and prototype of that oncoming fourth estate of publicists of all sorts, poets, and pamphleteers, journalists and men of letters, with whom governments in future would have to reckon. His pamphlets, their influence sustained and enhanced by the poems which grew out of his revolutionary experience, would become one of the main channels by which Puritan revolutionary ideas in their most dynamic form would reach the age of John Locke.

The enduring significance of *The Tenure of Kings and Magistrates* and the later tracts written in defense of the Commonwealth lies in the ideal of national life which in the midst of all their fume and fury they set forth. Their author was holding fast to that idea of England as a nation of worthies and sages, the humanist New Jerusalem, the godly republic, which he had urged upon parliament in *Areopagitica* in 1644 and which he now at last expected to be realized under the Commonwealth. God, he says, having turned the people away from the false prophets of the Presbyterian faction, will 'incline them to hearken rather with erected minds to the voice of our Supreme Magistracy, calling us to liberty and the flourishing deeds of a reformed Common-wealth.' God will bless the people if they make him alone their 'leader and supreme governour'—'if we have at least but so much worth in us to entertaine the sense of our future happiness, and the courage to receave what God voutsafes us: wherein we have the honour to precede other Nations who are now labouring to be our followers.' [50] To the prospect held forth by the ministers of a society enclosed in a visible church under strict clerical control, here was the answer of the Puritan of humanistic learning, believing in the power of reason and discourse to bring about the redemption of mankind. Milton was no less certain than the ministers that, as some were called to rule, others were called to teach, and that some were especially called to seek out and make known 'what is infallibly good and happy in the state of man's life, what in it selfe evil and miserable.' [51] But for Milton this ministry was one to which any were called who had the gift, and it required no ordination or laying on of hands save that signified by the gift itself. Let the tyrant now be brought to justice, let the wise give counsel and the virtuous command, and nothing more would be requisite to speed the nation toward the coming of the perfect image and embodiment of truth but to speed the processes of public enlightenment. For truth could be known; being known it could be taught; being taught, it could be heeded; and being heeded, it would conclude in the good of man. The best instructed nation requires the least government; the least government is the best. Therefore let rulers keep free all the ways to knowledge. Let those who profess to teach know whereof they speak, let them speak well whereof they know, and it will follow that rulers will govern wisely, people will obey freely, and in the end men will govern and be governed only by the truth within them.

But meanwhile the free proliferation of the Word in all its protean manifestations led not to the New Jerusalem as conceived either by Milton or by the ministers but to confusion worse confounded among its own promoters. The historic visible church was not reformed but disrupted, and that disruption was attended finally by the complete disruption of the state itself. The question which the authors of that irretrievable act of power had then to face was not simply how to get civil government going again. To reconstitute the state without the church as the organ and symbol of spiritual unity within the nation was for them as for most men still inconceivable, and yet to reconstitute or replace the church was beyond their power. Toleration was not a solution of that problem but merely a way of evading for a time the difficulties arising from failure to find a solution. For the failure of the Commonwealth in both aspects of the problem, spiritual and temporal, proved in the event utter and decisive. The English people were never again to be united in a visible church of any sort. Wherever they went in the world, and they were about to go everywhere, their religious alignments and affiliations would reflect not their oneness as a people but their internal differences of rearing, education, class, and nationality. They would not lose their common characteristic outlook and way of feeling—quite the contrary—but such unity as would be theirs in future would have to transcend the church and all its disparate manifestations and maintain itself by other means and another kind of ministry.

The English people were destined to draw apart into separate communions, classes, and nationalities, but they would still, in England, New England, Virginia, or wherever, be joint heirs of the intermingled traditions of Reformation and Renaissance. They would still speak the same language and acknowledge the same laws. They would read the same books, the scriptures first of all but also the classics and, with the scriptures and the classics to go on, the abounding literature they were creating for themselves in their own vernacular. They might give up the expectation of coming together again in one visible church and, through such a church, of redeeming mankind at large, but they would not give up their sense of being a people called to lead mankind into a great new age. Herein lay Milton's significance as a revolutionary pamphleteer. More than any other writer of his time, he expressed the more far-reaching implications and broader developments of the movement in which he chose to play so intimate and active a part. He was both the most Puritan and the most English of pamphleteers and also, as things turned out, of poets. He was the propagandist of revolution whom the adherents of royalism and of what in time came to be called Anglicanism have found it hardest to accept. He was at the same time the imaginative genius and literary artist who expressed most compellingly those positive and enduring ideals which sprang from Puritanism and, notwithstanding the rejection of the Puritan commonwealth, came to permeate English life and give it much of its distinctive character and momentum.

Meanwhile the final episode in Lilburne's long contention for liberty and reformation on his own terms may illustrate for us in conclusion the dilemma and the impasse at which revolution had arrived in 1649. The Council of State convened on February 17 and a month later appointed the author of *The Tenure of Kings and Magistrates* to be its 'Secretary for Foreign Tongues.' The secretary's primary duty was to transpose the communications of the new government to foreign states into Latin, but Milton was also called upon to write in its defense against enemies and critics at home and abroad. One of the earliest if not the first of his assignments was to reply to Lilburne's declaration of war against the regime. Lilburne said that he would have been content if parliament, after the rejection of his own constitutional scheme, had gone on to summon that 'new, equal, and just representative' called for in the officers' version of *The Agreement of the People*, but that proposal was laid aside and quickly forgotten. Constitutional government was not restored. Economic grievances were not abated. Tithes, taxes, monopolies, and the exactions of committees, lawyers, and officials continued as before. Hence on February 26 Lilburne appeared once more at the bar of the house with a petition in his hand and a crowd at his heels. The petition was immediately printed and circulated with the title *Englands New Chains*

Discovered. This was followed by *The Second Part of Englands New-Chaines Discovered*, by several other tracts and petitions by Lilburne and his friends, and finally by mutiny in the army. Cromwell, however, was not at this late date inclined to temporize with his old associate. The mutiny in the army was promptly crushed, the leading Levellers were arrested and on Cromwell's insistence sent to the Tower under a charge of treason. This was for Lilburne in effect the end. No jury could ever be got to convict him, but Cromwell kept him in prison or exile until 1657 and released him only in time for him to join the Quakers and die.

Milton was probably close at hand on March 28 when Cromwell, thumping the table, told the Council of State, 'you have no other way to deale with these men, but to breake them in pieces.' The newly appointed secretary wrote, however, no observations, as he had been directed, 'on a Paper lately printed, called Old and New Chains,' and his neglect may possibly have been not without meaning or motive. Lilburne in his own way was a hardly less significant exponent of the most pregnant implications of revolutionary Puritanism. More concretely and realistically than Milton he saw what liberty of thought and expression must lead to in the life of the state. Both men saw that the belief that the state rests necessarily upon agreement and covenant required that provision be made within the body politic itself for the free play of discussion, criticism, complaint, opposition, and adaptation to change. They differed in their notions of the particular provision that must be made, and on that point the champion of *The Agreement of the People* was clearer and more practical in his thinking than the author of *Areopagitica* and *The Tenure of Kings and Magistrates*. Milton expected the rulers of the Commonwealth to maintain liberty by repressing disorder and providing that all who had the gifts of knowledge and discourse should be free to impart whatever they had learned of good and evil to governors and people alike. Lilburne, more mindful of the political consequences of Adam's fall, suffered no illusion that men in power, if left free from any control except their own consciences and the instruction of the learned and the wise, could be long trusted to respect the liberty of others. Milton's recourse against tyranny was that of the high-minded intellectual and man of letters, secure in his own position, remote from the hurly-burly of politics, confident in the good intentions of enlightened responsible individuals of his own class. Lilburne's was that of the Protestant martyr in his latest embodiment, the English folk-hero risen out of the London mob, the popular leader suspicious of the motives of the rich and the powerful and burning to slake the needs and wants of common men. For him the people's only certain protection from the encroachments of rulers upon their rights was law, known law resting upon their consent and set down in English for everyone to read and obey. The only sure implement of law and guardian of liberty under law was a representative house of commons. And always the recourse of free men against tyranny was the appeal to the judgment and conscience of their fellows.

But the question in 1649 was how to reconcile the judgment and conscience of John Lilburne and the judgment and conscience of Oliver Cromwell. The only way by which Lilburne and his party could keep up their contention for what they believed to be their constitutional rights was by open rebellion against the only power left in the state to enforce any kind of order at all. And the only way Cromwell could think of to put an end to war and anarchy was by repressing the self-appointed champions of liberty and constitutional rights as mutineers and traitors. The truth was that liberty was not itself the solution of the problems it brought to men's apprehension and perhaps created but only the condition which made progress toward solution possible. It was not salvation but only the hope of salvation still to come. Men learned by being free that the world was all before them. 'Many there be,' Milton wrote in *Areopagitica*, 'that complain of divine Providence for suffering Adam to transgresse, foolish tongues! When God gave him reason, he gave him freedom to choose, for reason is but choosing.'

Notes

I: A GODLY PREACHING MINISTRY

1. For the role of the church in the development of Scottish society, see especially J. G. MacGregor, *Scottish Presbyterian Polity*, 1926; A. F. Scott Pearson, *Church and State, Political Aspects of Sixteenth Century Puritanism*, 1928; and F. W. Maitland, 'The Anglican Settlement and the Scottish Reformation,' *Cambridge Modern History*, 1902–12, Vol. II, Chap. XVI.

2. John Knox, *Historie of the Reformation*, 2d edition, 1644, p. 317; first edition, 1587.

3. S. R. Gardiner, *Constitutional Documents of the Puritan Revolution 1625–1660*, 1906, pp. 124–134.

4. Andrew Stevenson, *History of the Church and State of Scotland*, Edinburgh, 1844, p. 308.

5. John Milton, *Second Defence of the People of England* in *The Works of John Milton*, Columbia edition, 1931–40, VIII, 127.

6. Much of this material is reprinted in Stevenson, *History*.

7. Clarendon, *History of the Rebellion and Civil Wars in England*, ed. W. D. Macray, Oxford, 1888, I, 147–148. Clarendon says that about the end of 1638: "They [Covenanters] published bitter invectives against the bishops and the whole government of the Church, which they were not contented to send only into England to kindle the same fire there, but, with their letters, sent them to all the Reformed Churches, by which they raised so great a prejudice to the King that too many of them believed that the King had a real design to change religion and to introduce Popery."

8. John Rushworth, *Historical Collections*, 1721–22, II, 830–833.

9. *Tenure of Kings*, in Milton, *Works*, V, 29.

10. *Of Reformation*, in Milton, *Works*, III, 60–61.

11. Richard Montagu, *Articles of Enquiry and Direction for the Diocese of Norwich*, 1638, 'Titulus 4. Concerning Lecturers, and Lectures.' See also William Prynne, *Canterburies Doome*, 1646, pp. 368–380.

12. Selden, *Table-Talk*, 1689, p. 31; another edition, ed. by Sir Frederick Pollock, 1927.

13. Peter Heylyn, *Cyprianus Anglicus*, 1671, pp. 403–406.

14. S. R. Gardiner, *History of England 1603–1642*, 1884, X, 10, 12.

15. Robert Baillie, *Letters and Journals of Robert Baillie*, ed. David Laing, 1841–42, I, 273–274.

16. Sir Simonds D'Ewes, *Journal of Sir Simonds D'Ewes from the beginning of the Long Parliament to the opening of the trial of the Earl of Strafford*, ed. Wallace Notestein, New Haven, 1923, pp. 277, 313; Baillie, *Letters and Journals*, I, 286, 291–292; *Commons Journal*, January 23, 1641.

17. Burges, *A Sermon Preached to the Honourable House of Commons Assembled in Parliament at their Publique Fast, Novem. 17. 1640*, 1641; Marshall, *A Sermon Preached before the Honourable House of Commons, now assembled in Parliament, at their publike Fast, November 17. 1640*, 1641.

18. Milton, 'Outlines for Tragedies,' in *Works*, XVIII, 239, noted the same text as a possible subject for a tragedy.

19. See Haller, 'John Foxe and the Puritan Revolution' in *The Seventeenth Century: Studies in the History of English Thought and Literature from Bacon to Pope*, by Richard Foster Jones and others writing in his honor, 1951, pp. 209–224.

20. Marshall, *Sermon*, p. 19.

21. Burges, *Sermon*, p. 57.

22. Marshall, *Sermon*, pp. 33, 49.

23. *First and Large Petition of the City of London*, 1641. See also Rushworth, *Historical Collections*, IV, 93–96, and S. R. Gardiner, *Constitutional Documents*, 1906, pp. 137–144, in which the petition appears with the heading, *The Humble Petition of many of his Majesty's Subjects in and about the City of London*.

24. Baillie, *The Unlawfulnesse and danger of Limited Episcopacie*, 1641; *Letters and Journals*, I, 303; Alexander Henderson, *The Unlawfulnes and Danger of Limited Prelacie*, 1641.

25. Digby, *The Third Speech of the Lord George Digby, to the House of Commons, concerning Bishops, and the Citie Petition, the 9th. of Febr: 1640*, 1640[1], p. 7; Rushworth, *Historical Collections*, IV, 171.

26. Digby, *Third Speech*, p. 17; Rushworth, *Historical Collections*, IV, 174.

27. Rushworth, *Historical Collections*, IV, 437; Gardiner, *Constitutional Documents*, pp. 202–232.

28. Rushworth, *Historical Collections*, IV, 456–457; Gardiner, *Constitutional Documents*, pp. 232–233.

29. Sir Simonds D'Ewes, *Journal of Sir Simonds D'Ewes From the first recess of the Long Parliament to the withdrawal of King Charles from London*, ed. W. H. Coates, New Haven, 1942, pp. 271–273; John Nalson, *An Impartial Collection*, 1682–83, II, 733–735.

30. Nalson, *Impartial Collection*, II, 764–766.

31. *Commons Journal*, September 8, 1641. According to D'Ewes the motion was made by Cromwell, in The Journal of Sir Simonds D'Ewes from . . . July 5, 1641 to . . . September 9, 1641, ed. H. B. Barber, 1927, II, p. D660 (Unpublished dissertation in library of Cornell University).

32. D'Ewes, *Journal*, ed. Coates, pp. 337–338.

33. Rushworth, *Historical Collections*, IV, 462.

34. Clarendon, *History*, I, 451–452; D'Ewes, *Journal*, ed. Coates, pp. 337–338.

35. *Apology*, in Milton, *Works*, III, 339–340.

36. D'Ewes, *Journal*, ed. Coates, p. 358 and note; Lilburne, *Legall Fundamentall Liberties*, 1649, in Haller and Davies, *Leveller Tracts*, 1944, p. 406.

37. Fairclough, *Troublers Troubled*, p. 29.

38. Marshall, *Peace-Offering*, pp. 45, 50.

39. Burroughs, *Sions Joy*, p. 19.

40. Calamy, *Englands Looking-Glasse*, Sig. A and p. 23.

41. Marshall, *Reformation and Desolation*, pp. 18, 10, 6, 7.

42. Ashe, *Support for the sinking Heart*, p. 32.

II: REFORMATION IN ENGLAND

1. Lilburne, *Jonahs Cry out of the Whales belly*, 1647, pp. 1–2.

2. Hall, *An Humble Remonstrance*, pp. 1, 2, 40, is probably referring to A Short View of the *Praelaticall Church*, 1641, dated by Thomason as January and usually attributed to Richard Barnard.

3. Dated by Thomason as February; *Stationers' Register*, March 20, 1641.

4. *Calendar of State Papers, Domestic Series, of the Reign of Charles I*, X, 1867, p. 545. Report by Sir Nathaniel Brent, Vicar General, of his visitation of the diocese of London, 1637–38.

5. Fuller, *History of the Worthies of England, Endeavoured by Thomas Fuller*, 1662, Huntington-shire, pp. 52–53

6. Clarendon, *History*, I, 401.

7. Fuller, *Worthies, loc cit.*

8. *Life & Death of Stephen Marshall*, 1680, pp. 22–23; Richard Baxter, *Reliquiae Baxterianae*, 1696, I, 42.

9. Baillie, *Letters and Journals*, II, 89, 97, 235–237.

10. Baxter, *Reliquiae*, I, 62; *Life & Death of Stephen Marshall*, p. 20.

11. Ashe, *Gray Hayres crowned with Grace*, 1655. The writer also includes a 'M. *Goodal* Minister at *Horton* by *Colebrook*' in the list, whom Masson identifies as Edward Goodal who in 1631 became rector of the parish at Horton, site of Milton's father's country home. Masson, *Life*, I, 559.

12. Arthur Barker, 'Milton's Schoolmasters,' *Modern Language Review*, XXXII, No. 4 (Oct. 1937), 517, note 2.

13. Letter to Thomas Young, in Milton, *Works*, XII, 12; David Laing, *Biographical Notices of Thomas Young*, Edinburgh, 1870.

14. Young, *Lords Day*, pp. 277–279.

15. That Young had the principal hand in compiling Smectymnuus' *Answer*, which is little more than a brief summary of the main argument of *Dies Dominica*, to Hall's *Humble Remonstrance* is a likely inference, for which there is no definite proof. (Masson, *Life*, II, 219) Baillie tells us that Henderson, addressing the Gen-

eral Assembly at Edinburgh on July 29, 1641, alluded to Young as the author of 'the Synctymnias for the most part,' but Henderson may have exaggerated the importance of the fellow-Scot he had found in the front rank of London preachers. The point of view and the kind and extent of learning displayed in the reply to Hall were not exceptional and could have been supplied by any of the five members of Smectymnuus. It is impossible to say certainly that Milton had any direct hand in their *Answer*. Hall had stigmatized the 'Postscript' to their pamphlet, which consists of illustrations of the venality of prelates drawn from the English chronicles, as 'a goodly Pasquin' borrowed from Leighton's *Sions Plea* (1628) and Prynne's *Breviate* (1637). The Smectymnuans in their *Vindication* asked why they should be thought to have taken their information from an author 'whom we durst not for feare of the Prelates keepe in our studies, rather then from the Chronicles themselves?' Milton presently declared that the matter contained in the Postscript was drawn 'from as authentique authors in this kinde, as any in a Bishops library,' adding that 'the collector of it sayes' that, should he need more of the same sort, he will not need to go to Prynne or Leighton for it. Masson inferred from this (*Life*, II, 260–261) that Milton must have supplied the Smectymnuans at least with rough notes for their Postscript, and a ring of something like anticlericalism in these pages supports the inference. But there can be no certainty about the matter. The information in question was accessible and well known; the use made of it was thoroughly conventional; any of the Smectymnuans could have supplied it as well as he.

16. *Stationers' Register*, April 12, 1641; Masson, *Life*, II, 253.

17. *Stationers' Register*, June 26, 1641; Masson, *Life*, II, 255.

18. Thomason entered a copy in his collection with the notation, 'By Mr. John Milton. Ex Dono Authoris,' on the title page; Masson, *Life*, II, 248.

19. Thomason entered the date as July, and the words 'By John Milton' on the title page of his copy.

20. Dated by Thomason as September.

21. *Stationers' Register*, July 28, 1641; dated by Thomason as September with the note 'By Bisp: Hall & his Sonn.'

22. Dated by Thomason as January.

23. Dated by Thomason, 'Ex dono Authoris,' May, 1642.

24. *Letter Lately sent by a Reverend Bishop from the Tower to a private Friend: and by him thought fit to be published*, 1642, dated by the author January 24, 1641[2], appears as 'Letter sent from the Tower,' in Hall, *Works*, 1863, I, xlix–lii; 'Bishop Hall's Hard Measure,' in Hall, *Works*, 1863, I, lvii–lxix.

25. *Reason of Church-government*, in Milton, *Works*, III, 242.

26. *Of Education*, in Milton, *Works*, IV, 273–291.

27. *Ibidem*, III, 246; *Of Reformation*, in Milton, *Works*, III, 35; *Of Prelatical Episcopacy*, in Milton, *Works*, III, 104.

28. *Of Reformation*, in Milton, *Works*, III, 32–33.

29. *Reason of Church-government*, in Milton, *Works*, III, 183–184.

30. *Animadversions*, in Milton, *Works*, III, 139–140.

Notes

31. *Of Reformation*, in Milton, *Works*, III, 33.

32. John Aylmer, *An Harborowe for Faithfull and Trewe Subjectes*, 1559 [Sig. P 4ᵛ, margin; Sig. Rᵛ].

33. Haller, 'John Foxe and the Puritan Revolution,' in R. F. Jones and others, *The Seventeenth Century*, pp. 209–224.

34. Leighton, *An Appeal to the Parliament; Or Sions Plea against the Prelacie*, 1628.

35. Prynne, *Looking-Glasse*, pp. 31–32. In addition to Foxe, the writer is probably referring here to *The Ancient Ecclesiasticall Histories of the First Six Hundred Yeares after Christ, Written in the Greek Tongue by three learned Historiographers, Eusebius, Socrates, and Evagrius. . . . All which Authours are faithfully translated out of the Greek Tongue, by Meredith Hanmer. . . . The fourth Edition corrected and revised*, 1636–37. First edition, 1579. Other issues dated 1585, 1607, 1619. Hanmer (1543–1604) was an active Elizabethan Puritan divine and dedicated his work to the Earl of Leicester. Probably many of the numerous references in tracts and sermons after 1640 to Eusebius, Socrates, and Evagrius are to Hanmer's translation.

36. 'Life,' in Mede, *Works*, 1664, I, vii.

37. *Ibidem*, I, x.

38. *Of Reformation*, in Milton, *Works*, III, 5.

39. *Animadversions*, in Milton, *Works*, III, 145, 78, 79.

40. *Apology*, in Milton, *Works*, III, 357–358.

41. *Of Prelatical Episcopacy*, in Milton, *Works*, III, 101; *Animadversions*, in Milton, *Works*, III, 139.

42. *Of Reformation*, in Milton, *Works*, III, 10.

43. *Of Prelatical Episcopacy*, in Milton, *Works*, III, 82.

44. *Of Reformation*, in Milton, *Works*, III, 23–28.

45. *Ibidem*, III, 40–41.

46. *Reason of Church-government*, in Milton, *Works*, III, 256–262.

47. *Animadversions*, in Milton, *Works*, III, 163.

48. *Apology*, in Milton, *Works*, III, 346.

49. *Animadversions*, in Milton, *Works*, III, 163–164.

50. *Reason of Church-government*, in Milton, *Works*, III, 217, 274–275.

51. *Ibidem*, III, 219–227. See above, p. 18.

52. *Apology*, in Milton, *Works*, III, 313, 343.

53. *Animadversions*, in Milton, *Works*, III, 148.

54. Marshall, *Meroz Cursed, or, A Sermon Preached to the Honourable House of Commons . . . Febr. 23. 1641*, 1641, pp. 1–2.

55. *Reason of Church-government*, in Milton, *Works*, III, 238.

56. *Ibidem*, III, 236–238.

57. J. H. Hanford, 'Chronology of Milton's Private Studies,' *PMLA*, XXXVI (1921), pp. 264–265; *Commonplace Book*, in Milton, *Works*, XVIII, 207.

58. *Reason of Church-government*, in Milton, *Works*, III, 239–240.

59. 'Outlines for Tragedies,' in Milton, *Works*, XVIII, 228–245.

60. *Reason of Church-government*, in Milton, *Works*, III, 231.
61. *Apology*, in Milton, *Works*, III, 314.
62. *Apology*, in Milton, *Works*, III, 335–339.
63. *Ibidem*, III, 339–340.

III: THE CONSENT OF THE GOVERNED

1. Rushworth, *Historical Collections*, IV, 543.
2. *An Exact Collection of all Remonstrances, Declarations . . . betweene the Kings . . . Majesty, and . . . Parliament . . . December 1641 . . . untill March . . . 1642, Printed for Edward Husbands*, 1643, p. 556.
3. Clarendon, *History*, II, 319–321.
4. *Charles I in 1646*, John Bruce, ed., Camden Society, 1856, p. 79.
5. James I, 'Basilikon Doron' in *Political Works of James I*, C. H. McIlwain, ed., Cambridge, Mass., 1918, p. 14.
6. *Commons Journal*, December 24, 1641.
7. *Lords Journal*, August 24, 1642.
8. *Commons Journal*, February 11, 14, 15, 1643; *Lords Journal*, February 15, 1643.
9. Rushworth, *Historical Collections*, V, 364.
10. On February 21, 1642, the house ordered that the fast ordered to be held on February 23 be solemnized by the house in Lincoln's Inn Chapel. On the next day the house voted to change the place of its observance to St. Margaret's, Westminster. D'Ewes reports that he spoke in favor of the change on the ground 'that in St. Margarets Church 3000 persons may heare as well as 300 in Lincolns Inne.' D'Ewes, *Diary*, f.398b, transcription furnished by W. H. Coates.
11. *Commons Journal*, February 18, March 25, 1642.
12. *Commons Journal*, August 21, 1643.
13. *Commons Journal*, February 28, 1644; A. P. Stanley, *Historical Memorials of Westminster Abbey*, 1924 (reprint of 8th edition), pp. 429–430.
14. *Commons Journal*, September 24, 1642.
15. See for example the list, which runs from November 17, 1640, to May 31, 1643, appended to John Strickland's sermon, *Gods Work of Mercy*, delivered December 27, 1643, and published early in 1644.
16. See especially Edward Symmons, *Scripture Vindicated, From the Misapprehensions Misinterpretations and Misapplications of Mr Stephen Marshall*, Oxford, 1644. Clarendon condemns Marshall's sermon and mentions several texts besides 'Curse ye Meroz' which, he says, were perverted by the preachers at this time in the endeavor to root out all who opposed parliament in defense of the king. Clarendon, *History*, II, 320–321. Kurt Weber, who is making a special study of Marshall, tells me that *Meroz Cursed* was probably preached on more than one occasion and is extant in several versions.
17. *Calendar of State Papers, Domestic Series*, January 24, 1631; July 26, 1634.

18. *Commons Journal*, March 15, 1642.

19. *Commons Journal*, March 16, 1642.

20. *An Exact Collection*, Husbands, pp. 250–251.

21. *A Question answered*, dated by Thomason April 21, 1642; *An Exact Collection*, Husbands, pp. 150–151; Rushworth, *Historical Collections*, IV, 542–543.

22. Oliver St. John, *Speech or Declaration . . . Concerning Ship–Money*, 1641, dated by Thomason January 7.

23. Dated by Thomason October 16.

24. Parker, *Jus Populi*, p. 3.

25. *Ibidem*, p. 57.

26. S. R. Gardiner, *History of the Great Civil War*, 1904, I, 21; Baxter, *Reliquiae*, p. 42; Gardiner, quoting Nehemiah Wharton, *History of the Great Civil War*, I, 27; John Vicars, *Jehovah-Jireh*, 1644, p. 200.

27. Cheynell, *Sions Memento*, 1643. See especially the epistle to the house of commons.

28. Perne, *Gospell Courage*, 1643, p. 15.

29. Dated by Thomason October 21.

30. Dated by Thomason November 4.

31. Goodwin, *Anti-Cavalierisme*, p. 3.

32. *Second Defence*, in Milton, *Works*, VIII, 129, 131.

33. B. A. Wright, 'Milton's First Marriage,' *Modern Language Review*, XXVI, 383–400, and XXVII, 6–23, has argued convincingly that Milton's marriage to Mary Powell must have occurred in 1642, and not, as was supposed by Masson, one year later.

34. For the laws relating to marriage, see C. L. Powell, *English Domestic Relations, 1487–1653*, 1917. For Puritan teaching on the subject of marriage, see William and Malleville Haller, 'The Puritan Art of Love,' *Huntington Library Quarterly*, V, 235–272.

35. *Apology*, in Milton, *Works*, III, 302–306.

36. *Ibidem*, III, 306.

37. *Doctrine and Discipline of Divorce*, in Milton, *Works*, III, 400; *Tetrachordon*, in Milton, *Works*, IV, 205; *Doctrine and Discipline of Divorce*, in Milton, *Works*, III, 492, 394–395.

38. *Tetrachordon*, in Milton, *Works*, IV, 90; *Doctrine and Discipline of Divorce*, in Milton, *Works*, III, 390, 374.

39. *Doctrine and Discipline of Divorce*, in Milton, *Works*, III, 388; *Tetrachordon*, in Milton, *Works*, IV, 77.

40. *Judgment of Martin Bucer*, in Milton, *Works*, IV, 11.

41. *Tetrachordon*, in Milton, *Works*, IV, 105, 101; *Doctrine and Discipline of Divorce*, in Milton, *Works*, III, 382, 391, 396–397.

42. *Doctrine and Discipline of Divorce*, in Milton, *Works*, III, 398, 400–402; *Tetrachordon*, in Milton, *Works*, IV, 85, 86.

43. *Paradise Lost*, in Milton, *Works*, II, 123; *Tetrachordon*, in Milton, *Works*,

IV, 85, 82–83, 97, 98; *Doctrine and Discipline of Divorce*, in Milton, *Works*, III, 391.

44. *Tetrachordon*, in Milton, *Works*, IV, 84, 87; *Doctrine and Discipline of Divorce*, in Milton, *Works*, III, 422–423.

45. *Doctrine and Discipline of Divorce*, in Milton, *Works*, III, 402, 485.

46. *Ibidem*, III, 440, 445; *Tetrachordon*, in Milton, *Works*, IV, 135–137.

47. *Doctrine and Discipline of Divorce*, in Milton, *Works*, III, 374, 375, 419, 481–482.

48. *Tetrachordon*, in Milton, *Works*, IV, 104, 82, 84.

49. *Doctrine and Discipline of Divorce*, in Milton, *Works*, III, 418–419, 469, 466.

IV: AN ASSEMBLY OF DIVINES

1. Obadiah Sedgwick, *Hamans. Vanity, or, a Sermon Displaying the birthlesse Issues of Church-destroying Adversaries*, 1643; Charles Herle, *Davids Song of Three Parts*, 1643; Edmund Calamy, *The Noble-Mans Patterne of true and reall Thankfulnesse*, 1643; Stephen Marshall, *The Song of Moses*, 1643.

2. W. A. Shaw, *History of the English Church*, 1900, I, 124–127 note.

3. W. M. Clyde, *Struggle for the Freedom of the Press*, 1934, pp. 66–76.

4. Joseph Mede, *Clavis Apocalyptica*, 1627, 1632; translated by Richard More as *The Key of the Revelation*, 1643, with preface by William Twisse.

5. Baillie, *Letters and Journals*, II, 186, May 31, 1644.

6. *Ibidem*, II, 83, 81, 89, 90.

7. *The Covenant: with A Narrative of The Proceedings and Solemn Manner of Taking it by the Honourable House of Commons, and Reverent Assembly of Divines the 25th day of September, at Saint Margarets in Westminster. Also, Two Speeches Delivered at the same time; The one By Mr. Philip Nye, the other By Mr. Alexander Hendersam. Published by speciall Order of the House*, 1643, pp. 3–4, 14, 30.

8. *Commons Journal*, July 5, 1643; *Lords Journal*, June 29, 1643.

9. The most direct and explicit witnesses to the disagreements and delays of the Westminster divines are Robert Baillie, to whom reference has already been made, and John Lightfoot. The latter kept a private journal of the proceedings from July 1, 1643, to December 31, 1644, which was published in *The Whole Works of the Rev. John Lightfoot*, edited by J. R. Pitman, 1824, Vol. XIII. (The Journal is described on the title page of this edition as 'from January 1, 1643' but this is obviously a mistake.) The impression created by these observers is further sustained by the evidence of the minutes of the assembly itself. The assembly appointed two scribes, Henry Roborough and Adoniram Byfield, to keep a record of its proceedings. The manuscript of the minutes of the sessions from August 4, 1643, to August 16, 1647, with further brief reports down to March 25, 1652, mostly in the hand of Byfield, is preserved in Dr. Williams' Library, London. The entire manuscript was transcribed by E. Maunde Thompson and a

portion of the minutes, November 18, 1644–February 22, 1649, was published for the Church of Scotland in 1874, edited by A. F. Mitchell and J. Struthers: *Minutes of the Sessions of the Westminster Assembly of Divines.* Through the courtesy of Dr. Williams' Library and of the General Assembly Library of the Church of Scotland, microfilms of the original manuscript and of the transcript in their entirety are available in the Folger Shakespeare Library, Washington. The original is in a hurried and indistinct hand with occasional lapses into shorthand. It consists of hasty and incomplete jottings of debates and speeches rather than of formal and extended minutes. The portion of the manuscript, August 4, 1643– November 15, 1644, which is not included in the edition by Mitchell and Struthers, is that which especially deals with the contention between the Presbyterians and Independents and gives evidence of the frustration and delays during that decisive period. For additional information concerning the proceedings of the assembly, see S. W. Carruthers, *The Everyday Work of the Westminster Assembly,* Philadelphia, 1943.

10. Lightfoot, 'Journal,' *Whole Works,* XIII, 10–11.

11. Baillie, *Letters and Journals,* II, 107–110, 120, 164, 177.

12. *Ibidem,* II, 256.

13. Gardiner, *Constitutional Documents,* pp. 267–271.

14. Thomas Hutchinson, *The History of the Colony of Massachusetts-Bay . . . 1628 . . . 1691,* Boston, New England, 1764, I, 115–117 and note.

15. Thomas Goodwin, *Zerubbabels Encouragement,* 1642, pp. 35, [43]–44.

16. Baillie, *Letters and Journals,* II, 123.

17. *Ibidem,* II, 123, 228, 164.

18. Baillie, *Letters and Journals,* II, 129.

19. Gardiner, *History of the Great Civil War,* I, 264.

20. *Certaine Considerations to Dis-swade Men From Further Gathering of Churches in this present juncture of Time,* 1643; Baillie, *Letters and Journals,* II, 118, 121.

21. Baillie, *Letters and Journals,* II, 129–130.

22. Henderson, *Reformation of Church-Government in Scotland,* 1644, pp. 13, 14, 17, 7. Copies of this book were distributed to members of the assembly on January 24, and the Scots Commissioners were formally thanked by the assembly January 26. Lightfoot, 'Journal of the Proceedings,' *Works,* XIII, 121–122.

23. Lightfoot records the distribution of printed copies of parliamentary sermons to members of the assembly on the following dates: Cawdry, February 22, 1644; Rutherford, March 8; Young, March 18; Baillie, March 20; Gillespie, April 18; Caryl, May 16; Vines and Woodcock, November 21. Lightfoot, 'Journal of the Proceedings,' in *Works,* XIII.

24. Marshall, Θρηνωδια. *The Churches Lamentation for the Good Man his losse,* 1644, p. 42. 'Mr. Marshal's sermon, preached at the funeral of Mr. *Pym,* was delivered to every one of us.' Lightfoot, 'Journal of the Proceedings,' in *Works,* XIII, 98, January 1, 1644.

25. Marshall, *A Sacred Panegyrick,* 1644.

26. Baillie, *Letters and Journals*, II, 135.

27. *Ibidem*, II, 220.

28. Alexander Henderson, *A Sermon Preached to the Honourable House of Commons*, . . . *December 27 1643*, 1644, p. 21.

29. Samuel Rutherford, *A Sermon Preached to the Honorable House of Commons* . . . *Janu. 31. 1643*, 1644.

30. Baillie, *Satan the Leader*, 1644, pp. 2, 3.

31. Young, *Hopes Incouragement*, 1644, pp. 4, 26.

32. *Ibidem*, pp. 20, 31, 32.

33. *Commonplace Book*, in Milton, *Works*, XVIII, 150. The translation in the Columbia edition is incorrect. What Milton read in his source was that Valentinian legalized marriage to a second wife during the lifetime, not after the death of the first. Migne, *Patrologiae Cursus Completus* . . . *Series Graeca*, 1864, Vol. 67, pp. 546–547, Bk. IV, Ch. 31 (not as in Milton's note, Ch. 30). Hanford, 'Chronology of Milton's Private Studies,' *PMLA*, XXXVI (1921), p. 261, dates the entry in the *Commonplace Book* before 1639.

34. Baillie, *Letters and Journals*, II, 220, 221.

35. Vines, *Impostures*, 1644, p. 32.

36. Palmer, *Glasse of Gods Providence*, 1644, pp. 55, 56, 57.

37. Prynne, *Twelve Considerable Serious Questions*, 1644, p. 7.

38. Gardiner, *History of the Great Civil War*, II, 72.

39. *Colasterion*, in Milton, *Works*, IV, 233.

40. *An Answer* is reprinted in facsimile in W. R. Parker, *Milton's Contemporary Reputation*, Columbus, 1940, which also reprints the incidental attacks on Milton's divorce tract which appeared in various publications in 1645 and later.

41. Oliver Cromwell, *Writings and Speeches of Oliver Cromwell*, W. C. Abbott, ed., Cambridge, Mass., 1937, I, 287.

42. Baillie, *Letters and Journals*, II, 229.

43. *Ibidem*, II, 191.

44. Henderson, *A Sermon Preached before the* . . . *Lords and Commons*, 1644, p. 7; Richard Vines, *Magnalia Dei ab Aquilone* . . . *A Sermon Preached Before* . . . *the Lords and Commons* . . . *July 18*, 1644.

45. Baillie, *Letters and Journals*, II, 211–212.

46. *Commons Journal*, August 9, 1644.

47. Baillie, *Letters and Journals*, II, 228; Lightfoot, 'Journal of the Proceedings,' in *Works*, XIII, 309–310; *Minutes of the Sessions of the Assembly of Divines*, manuscript transcript made in 1868, September 9 and 10, 1644; George Gillespie, *Notes of Debates and Proceedings of the Assembly of Divines*, Edinburgh, 1846, pp. 67–70. 'Mr Calamy said, There are false causes suggested in the city, as, that this blow was given at the very time when the Assembly was upon a way of suppressing the Anabaptists and Antinomians, and the like.' Gillespie, *Notes*, p. 67.

48. Newcomen, *A Sermon, Tending to Set Forth the Right Use of the Disasters that Befall our Armies. Preached Before* . . . *Parliament* . . . *Sept. 12. Anno 1644*, 1644, pp. 31–38.

49. Reprinted in *Narragansett Club Publications*, 1866–1874, Vol. III.

50. Reprinted in William Haller, *Tracts on Liberty in the Puritan Revolution*, 1934, Vol. III. See also Vol. I, 64–74.

51. *Ibidem*, I, 56–63, 121–127; Vol. III.

52. Calamy, *Englands Antidote*, 1645, pp. 26–27.

53. Spurstowe, *Englands Eminent Judgments*, 1644, p. 28.

54. *Commons Journal*, September 13, 1644.

55. Clyde, *Struggle for the Freedom of the Press*, p. 56.

56. *Commons Journal*, August 24, 26, 1644.

57. Milton, *Areopagitica*, *Works*, IV, 353.

58. *Lords Journal*, December 9, 1644. The lords' displeasure was probably caused by a single printed sheet beginning 'Alas pore Parliament,' attacking Essex and Manchester, dated by Thomason, 'Decemb: 9th being Monday 1644,' with the note, 'written by some Independant against Ld. Gen. Essex and Ld. Manchester, and scaterd about ye Streets in the night.'

59. *Lords Journal*, December 28, 1644.

60. *Tetrachordon*, in Milton, *Works*, IV, 64.

61. Hezekiah Woodward, *Inquiries Into the causes of our miseries*, December 23, 1644, p. 3, title page, p. 1; *Soft Answers unto Hard Censures Relating . . . To a Book printed without Licence*, February 5, 1645.

62. *Apologeticall Narration*, 1643, Imprimatur, in Haller, *Tracts on Liberty*, Vol. II.

63. Thomas Edwards, *Gangraena*, 1646, I, 97; III, 105.

64. Haller, *Tracts on Liberty*, I, 136–138.

V: THE HONEST LIBERTY OF FREE SPEECH

1. *Commons Journal*, October 5, 1642.

2. *Ibidem*, May 3, 1641.

3. Burton, *Protestation Protested*, 1641, Sigs. B3, C2; see also Burton, *Vindication of Churches, Commonly Called Independent*, 1644.

4. Burton, *Truth Shut out of doores*, 1645; *Truth, still Truth*, 1645; Calamy, *Door of Truth*, 1645; A. G. Matthews, *Calamy Revised*, 1934, under Calamy.

5. John Vicars, *To his Reverend and Much Respected Good Friend, Mr. John Goodwin*, February 11, 1645, published with a reply by Daniel Taylor, Goodwin's colleague and successor at St. Stephen's; Goodwin, *Innocencies Triumph*, October 26, 1644, *Calumny Arraign'd*, January 31, 1645, *Anapologesiates*, August 27, 1646. See also, Edwin Freshfield, *Discourse on some Unpublished Records of the City of London*, 1887; W. A. Shaw, *History of the English Church*, 1900, II, 134–136; A. G. Matthews, *Calamy Revised*, p. 227.

6. See above, p. 13.

7. Goodwin, *Imputatio Fidei*, 1642.

8. Goodwin dedicated Ἀπολύτρωσις Ἀπολυτρώσεως, *Or, Redemption Redeemed*, 1651, to Whichcote.

9. Goodwin, *Certain briefe Observations and Antiquaeries: on Master Prin's Twelve Questions about Church-government*, October 4, 1644, p. 1.

10. Goodwin, *Hagiomastix*, February 5, 1647, 'Epistle.'

11. Goodwin appears generally to have used not the Authorized Version but the earlier Geneva translation.

12. Goodwin, *Theomachia*, 1644, pp. 17–19. There is a facsimile in Haller, *Tracts on Liberty*, Vol. III.

13. Prynne, *Independency Examined*, September 26, 1644, pp. 5–6.

14. Prynne, *Twelve Considerable Serious Questions*, September 16, 1644, p. 7.

15. Edwards, *Gangraena*, III, 126.

16. Cotton, 'A Reply to Mr. Williams,' p. 8, in *The Bloudy Tenent, Washed, and made white in the bloud of the Lambe*, 1647. The 'Reply' is reprinted in *Publications of the Narragansett Club*, Vol. II.

17. *Ibidem*, pp. 27–28.

18. Williams, *A Key into the Language of America*, p. 53.

19. The full title continues: *Or, An help to the Language of the Natives in that part of America, called New-England. Together, with briefe Observations of the Customes, Manners and Worships, &c. of the aforesaid Natives, in Peace and Warre, in Life and Death. On all which are added Spirituall Observations, Generall and Particular by the Authour, of chiefe and speciall use (upon all occasions,) to all the English Inhabiting those parts; yet pleasant and profitable to the view of all men*, 1643. Reprinted in *Publications of the Narragansett Club*, Vol. I.

20. Nathaniel Ward, *Simple Cobler of Aggawam*, 1647, p. 3.

21. Published anonymously; dated by Thomason, February 9, 1644; attributed to Williams by Cotton in 'Reply' in *Bloudy Tenent, Washed*. Reprinted in *Publications of the Narragansett Club*, Vol. II.

22. Cotton, *A Letter of Mr. John Cottons Teacher of the Church in Boston, in New-England, to Mr. Williams a Preacher there. Wherein is shewed, That those ought to be received into the Church who are Godly, though they doe not see, nor expressely bewaile all the pollutions in Church-fellowship, Ministery, Worship, Government.* Published in London, 1643, without Cotton's knowledge, perhaps from a copy somehow procured from Williams. Reprinted in *Publications of the Narragansett Club*, Vol. II.

23. Williams, *Bloudy Tenent*, p. 105.

24. Williams, *Queries of highest Consideration*, 1644, p. 20.

25. Williams, *Bloudy Tenent*, pp. 16–17.

26. Cotton supplied the Independents of the assembly with two statements of the Massachusetts plan of church organization: *The Keyes of the Kingdom of Heaven . . . Published by Thos. Goodwin* [and] *Philip Nye* September 7, 1644; and *The Way of the Churches of Christ in New-England*, April 4, 1645. In the meantime Thomas Welde, one of the commissioners sent by Massachusetts to secure an extension of its patent to include the Narragansett country, published an account of the affair of Mrs. Hutchinson, emanating from Governor Winthrop, namely *A Short Story of the Rise, reign, and ruin of the Antinomians*, February 19,

1644. This publication was obviously intended to help discredit Williams' attempts to get a charter from parliament, and perhaps to serve as an offset to his *Key into the Language of America*. Baillie, however, in his *Dissausive*, argued that the excesses there described were the inevitable result of Independency.

27. W. K. Jordan, *Men of Substance*, 1942; Haller, *Tracts on Liberty*, I, 64–73.

28. Robinson, *Answer to Mr. William Prynn's Twelve Questions*, November 1, 1644; *Short Answer to A. S.*, February 3, 1645; *Falsehood of Mr. William Pryn's Truth Triumphing*, May 8, 1645; 'To the Reverend and much honoured, Mr. John Dury,' dated November 5, 1644, in *Some Few Considerations Propounded*, July 18, 1646. *Short Answer* is also attributed to John Goodwin. See Haller, *Tracts on Liberty*, I, p. 67 note 56, p. 68 note 58.

29. Robinson, *Liberty of Conscience*, 1644, p. 39. There is a facsimile in Haller, *Tracts on Liberty*, Vol. III.

30. *Ibidem*, p. 6; Robinson, *Answer to . . . Prynn's Twelve Questions*, p. 17.

31. Robinson, *Liberty of Conscience*, p. 8.

32. Robinson, *Answer to . . . Prynn's Twelve Questions*, pp. 20–21.

33. Robinson, *John the Baptist*, 1644, p. 39.

34. Newcomen, *A Sermon . . . Sept. 12 . . . 1644*, p. 38; Walwyn, *The Compassionate Samaritane*, 1644, pp. 23–24. There is a facsimile in Haller, *Tracts on Liberty*, Vol. III.

35. Walwyn, *A Whisper in the Eare of Mr. Thomas Edwards*, 1646, p. 3. There is a facsimile in Haller, *Tracts on Liberty*, Vol. III.

36. *Ibidem*, p. 6.

37. Walwyn, *Walwyns Just Defence*, 1649, p. 8. Reprinted in William Haller and Godfrey Davies, *Leveller Tracts*, 1944.

38. Vines, *Impostures*, p. 11.

39. Edwards, *Gangraena*, I, 96.

40. *Walwins Wiles*, 1649, pp. 4–6. Reprinted in Haller and Davies, *Leveller Tracts*.

41. *Ibidem*, p. 7.

42. Humphrey Brooke, *Charity of Church-men*, 1649, p. 4. Reprinted in Haller and Davies, *Leveller Tracts*.

43. Walwyn, *Whisper*, p. 5.

44. Walwyn, *Walwyns Just Defence*, p. 10.

45. *Ibidem*, p. 9.

46. Fuller, *Abel Redevivus*, 1651, p. 434.

47. The authorship and date of this work are somewhat uncertain. It was published anonymously with an address to the reader by John Downame but without date.

48. *A Learned Discourse of Justification* had appeared separately in 1612 and 1613. It was one of the 'Certayne Divine Tractates' appended to the 1617 edition, and to later editions of the *Ecclesiastical Polity*.

49. Walwyn, *Walwyns Just Defence*, pp. 9–12.

50. Montaigne, *Essayes . . . done into English by J. Florio*, 1603, 1613, 1632; Seneca, *Workes*, tr. T. Lodge, 1614, 1620. Joseph Hall, *Meditations and Vowes*, 1605, 1606 and later eds.; Hall, *Heaven upon Earth*, 1606, 1607, 1609; Pierre Charron, *Of Wisdome*, tr. S. Lennard, [1612?] and later eds.

51. Seneca, *Workes*, 1620, pp. 236, 282, 286, 315.

52. Walwyn, *Walwyns Just Defence*, p. 11.

53. *Walwins Wiles*, pp. 10, 27.

54. Walwyn, *Power of Love*, 1643, pp. 2–3, 7, 8, 43. There is a facsimile in Haller, *Tracts on Liberty*, Vol. II.

55. Walwyn, *Compassionate Samaritane*, p. 5.

56. *Ibidem*, pp. 8, 11, 14, 15, 39.

57. *Commons Journal*, August 24, 26, 1644.

58. Ambroise Paré, *Workes*, tr. T. Johnson, 1634.

59. Overton, *Mans Mortallitie*, 1644, p. 4.

60. *The Doctrine and Discipline of Divorce*, in Milton, *Works*, III, 370; *Judgement of Martin Bucer*, in Milton, *Works*, IV, 12.

61. *Tetrachordon*, in Milton, *Works*, IV, 70.

62. *Of Education*, in Milton, *Works*, IV, 279, 286–287.

63. *Areopagitica*, in Milton, *Works*, IV, 346.

64. *Ibidem*, IV, 344, 343, 345.

65. *Ibidem*, IV, 341, 329, 352, 329, 345, 340.

66. *Ibidem*, IV, 339, 341, 343, 340, 341.

67. *Reason of Church-government*, in Milton, *Works*, III, 229.

68. *Areopagitica*, in Milton, *Works*, IV, 340, 311.

69. *Ibidem*, IV, 311, 324.

70. *Ibidem*, IV, 293, 354.

VI: THE WORD OF GOD IN THE NEW MODEL ARMY

1. See above, p. 75.

2. Baxter, *Reliquiae Baxterianae*, p. 51. See also W. G., *A Just Apologie for an Abused Armie*, January 29, 1647.

3. Baxter, *Reliquiae Baxterianae*, p. 51.

4. Baillie, *Letters and Journals*, II, 170, 185, 209, 229.

5. Baxter, *Reliquiae Baxterianae*, pp. 53, 51.

6. *The cleere Sense*, 1645, pp. 3, 10.

7. Baxter, *The Saints Everlasting Rest*, 1650, Dedication.

8. Baxter, *Reliquiae Baxterianae*, 'Breviate of the Contents' and Part I.

9. Edwards, *Gangraena*, III, 45–46; Baxter, *Reliquiae Baxterianae*, p. 56.

10. Baxter, *Reliquiae Baxterianae*, p. 53.

11. Baxter, *Saints Everlasting Rest*, pp. 21, 31.

12. *Ibidem*, pp. 66, 65.

13. Baxter, *Aphorismes of Justification*, 1649, 'To the Reader.'

14. Baxter, *Rich: Baxter's Confession*, 1655, Preface, p. 4.

Notes

15. Thomas Fuller, *The History of the Worthies of England*, York-shire, p. 212.

16. For fuller account of the antinomian sects and preachers in England before 1643, see Haller, *Rise of Puritanism*, 1938, Chap. V.

17. Saltmarsh, *Free-Grace*, 1645, title page, 'To the Reader.'

18. Saltmarsh, *Sparkles*, 1647, pp. 314–316.

19. Saltmarsh, *The Smoke in the Temple*, January 16, 1646.

20. Dell, *Power from on High*, 1645, pp. 5–6.

21. Dell, *The Building and Glory*, 1646, 'To the Reader,' pp. 15–16.

22. Dell, *Right Reformation: or, The Reformation of the Church of the New Testament, Represented in Gospel-Light . . . Together with a Reply to the chief Contradictions of Master Love's Sermon, preached the same day*, 1646. The quotations are from the Epistle.

23. Love, *Short and plaine Animadversions On some Passages in Mr. Dels Sermon . . . Imprimatur Ja. Cranford. Decemb. 17. 1646*, 1646.

24. See Edwards, *Gangraena*, II, 13–14.

25. Haller, *Rise of Puritanism*, pp. 270–271; A. S. P. Woodhouse reprints a large part of *A Glimpse of Sions Glory* in *Puritanism and Liberty*, 1938, pp. 233–241.

26. Edwards, *Gangraena*, I, 76–77.

27. *Ibidem*, III, 98.

28. Baxter, *Reliquiae*, p. 111; Edwards, *Gangraena*, I, 89–91; C. H. Firth and Godfrey Davies, *Regimental History of Cromwell's Army*, 1940, pp. 456–457.

29. Noteworthy among the Baptist preachers who became active after the triumph of the army in 1646 were Samuel Richardson, author of *Fifty Questions propounded to the Assembly . . . whether Corporal Punishment may be inflicted upon such as hold different Opinions on Religion*, 1647, and later tracts, and Thomas Collier, author of *The Exaltation of Christ*, 1646, and many later tracts and sermons.

30. Hugh Peters, *A Dying Fathers last legacy to an Onely Child*, 1660, p. 100.

31. *Commons Journal*, March 8, April 25, June 27, 1644.

32. Joshua Sprigge, *Anglia Rediviva; . . . being the History of . . . the Army under . . . Fairfax*, 1647, p. 70.

33. *Commons Journal*, July 26, 1645.

34. Cromwell, *Writings and Speeches*, ed. Abbott, I, 382.

35. Baillie, *Letters and Journals*, II, 165, April 12, 1644.

36. Edwards, *Gangraena*, I, 98–100; II, 61; III, 76. See also William Coddington, *Collections of the Massachusetts Historical Society*, Vol. VII, Fourth Series, 1865, p. 281.

37. Lilburne, *Discourse Betwixt . . . Lilburn . . . and . . . Peter . . . May 25, 1649*, 1649, pp. 2, 5; *Legall Fundamentall Liberties*, 1649, p. 31, reprinted in Haller and Davies, *Leveller Tracts*.

38. Peters, *Dying Fathers Last Legacy*, 1660, pp. 104, 106.

39. *Ibidem*, p. 6.

40. Peters, *Gods Doings*, 1646, pp. 18, 19, 24.

41. *Ibidem*, Epistle, p. 43.

42. Peters, *Mr. Peters Last Report*, 1646, pp. 7, 12.

43. Peters is quoting I Corinthians 7: 31 in the Geneva translation.

44. Cromwell, *Writings and Speeches*, ed. Abbott, I, 97.

45. Baxter, *Reliquiae Baxterianae*, pp. 98--99.

46. Cromwell, Speech, April 13, 1657, in Cromwell, *Writings and Speeches*, ed. Abbott, IV, 471.

47. Cromwell, letter to Bridget Cromwell, *ibidem*, I, 416.

48. *Ibidem*, I, 292, 340, 360.

49. *Ibidem*, I, 256.

50. *Ibidem*, I, 278.

51. *Ibidem*, I, 360, 365.

52. *Ibidem*, I, 377.

53. Baillie, *Letters and Journals*, II, 247.

54. *Ibidem*, II, 280.

55. Baxter, *Reliquiae*, pp. 53, 57.

VII: THE DISSIDENCE OF DISSENT

1. The arguments of the Independents as presented to the assembly finally at the close of 1644 were submitted by the assembly with its replies to the house of commons on December 23. The house ordered three hundred copies of this document and no more to be printed under the supervision of the scribe of the assembly. It was published with the title, *The Reasons of the Dissenting Brethren against the Third Proposition concerning Presbyteriall Government*, 1645. Gardiner's statement that the house authorized the printing of only three hundred reasons instead of three hundred copies is a mistake based upon misunderstanding of the entry in *Commons Journal*. *Commons Journal*, December 23, 1644; Gardiner, *Great Civil War*, II, 108.

2. Cromwell, *The Conclusion of Lieuten. General Cromwells Letter*, 1645. Thomason reports, 'Sept. 22. This was printed by the Independent party and scatrd up and downe the streets last night, but expresly omitted by order of the House.' *Thomason Catalogue*, I, 395, 397. See also Cromwell, *Writings and Speeches*, ed. Abbott, I, 378 note.

3. *A Copy of a Remonstrance Lately Delivered in to the Assembly. By Thomas Goodwin. Jerem: Burroughs. William Greenhill. William Bridge. Philip Nie. Sidrach Simson. and William Carter. Declaring the Grounds and Reasons of their declining to bring in to the Assembly, their Modell of Church-Government*, 1645; *Minutes of the . . . Westminster Assembly*, ed. A. F. Mitchell and John Struthers, 1874, p. 148. For a statement of the facts relating to the controversy between Presbyterians and Independents concerning toleration in these years, see Shaw, *History of the English Church*, II, 35–70.

4. *Of Reformation,* in Milton, *Works,* III, 6.

5. Alexander Henderson, *A Sermon Preached before the Right Honourable House of Lords,* 1645, 'To the Christian Reader.'

6. Baillie, *Letters and Journals,* II, 256, 265.

7. *Ibidem,* II, 273, 304–305.

8. *Ibidem,* II, 314, 317, 321.

9. *Ibidem,* II, 362.

10. Stephen Marshall, *Gods Master-Piece,* 1645; Herbert Palmer, *The Duty & Honour of Church-Restorers: . . . Septemb. 30. 1646,* 1646.

11. Marshall, *A Sermon Preached before the Honourable House of Commons . . . November 17. 1640,* p. 33.

12. Marshall, *Gods Master-Piece,* p. 6.

13. Marshall, *A Two-edged Sword out of the Mouth of Babes,* October 28, 1646.

14. Thomas Goodwin, *The Great Interest of States & Kingdomes,* 1646, p. 51.

15. Case, *Deliverance-Obstruction: Or, The Set-backs of Reformation . . . a Sermon Before the . . . Peers . . . March 25,* 1646, p. 10.

16. Wilkinson, *Miranda, Stupenda,* July 21, 1646, p. 24.

17. Vines, *The Authours, Nature, and Danger of Haeresie,* March 10, 1647, Epistle.

18. Lightfoot, *A Sermon Preached before the Honorable House of Commons,* February 24, 1647, p. 30.

19. Newcomen, *Duty of Such as would Walke Worthy of the Gospel,* February 8, 1647, pp. 34–35; *The All-Seeing Unseen Eye of God,* December 30, 1646, pp. 47–48.

20. Edwards, *Gangraena,* I, Epistle.

21. Baillie, *Letters and Journals,* II, 215–216, August 7, 1644.

22. *Ibidem,* II, 352, February 20, 1646, Baillie writes, 'Some late books have done them good; especiallie Mr. Edwards's Gangraena.' Thomason entered a copy, apparently of the second edition, in his collection with the date, February 26.

23. Edwards, *Gangraena,* II, 'To the Christian Reader.'

24. *Ibidem,* II, 10–11.

25. *Ibidem,* I, Epistle.

26. *Ibidem,* I, 69–70.

27. *Ibidem,* I, 60, margin.

28. *Ibidem,* I, 135–136.

29. *Biographia Britannica,* 1778–93, V, 543.

30. Coleman, *Hopes Deferred,* 1645, Epistle.

31. *Commons Journal,* August 9, 1645.

32. Gillespie, *Sermon . . . 27th of August 1645 . . . Whereunto is added A Brotherly Examination,* 1645; Coleman, *Brotherly Examination Re-Examined,* November 1, 1645 (title page 1646); Gillespie, *Nihil Respondes,* November 13, 1645; William Hussey, *Plea for Christian Magistracie,* December 20, 1645

(title page 1646); Coleman, *Male dicis Maledicis*, January 9, 1646; Gillespie, *Male Audis*, January 24, 1646.

33. Coleman, *Hopes Deferred*, Epistle, pp. 24–27.

34. Hussey, *Plea for Christian Magistracie*, 'To the Reverend Commissioner of Scotland, Mr. George Gillespie.'

35. Bulstrode Whitelocke, *Memorials*, 1732, p. 71.

36. John Aubrey, '*Brief Lives*,' ed. Andrew Clarke, 1898, II, 220.

37. Baillie, *Letters and Journals*, II, 265–266.

38. Selden, *Joannis Seldeni Jurisconsulti Opera Omnia*, 1726, Vol. III, Part II, pp. 1370–1395, 1452–1457.

39. Selden, *History of Tythes*, 1618, Preface.

40. *Ibidem*, Preface, p. VI.

41. Richard Tillesly, *Animadversions upon M. Seldens History of Tythes*, 1619, Animadversions upon the Preface.

42. Selden, *History of Tythes*, Preface, pp. xix–xx.

43. Wallace Notestein and F. H. Relf, *Commons Debates for 1629*, 1921, pp. 58–59.

44. Heylyn, *Cyprianus Anglicus*, 1671, p. 303.

45. In 1642 Selden published a Latin translation from the Arabic of Eutychius' *Ecclesiae suae Origines*, including a commentary of his own in which, Heylyn points out, 'he made it his chief business to prove, that Bishops did no otherwise differ from the rest of the Presbyters then doth a Master of a Colledge from the rest of the Fellows.' Heylyn, *Cyprianus Anglicus*, pp. 303–304.

46. Clarendon, *History*, II, 114.

47. Selden, *Table Talk*, ed. Sir Frederick Pollock, 1927, pp. 117, 119 and note, 12, 11, 38, 30, 32, 20, 100, 61, 69.

48. *Doctrine and Discipline of Divorce*, in Milton, *Works*, III, 376.

49. *Second Defence*, in Milton, *Works*, VIII, 137.

50. *History of Britain*, in Milton, *Works*, X, 32.

51. *Ibidem*, X, 3.

52. *Ibidem*, X, 68, 69, 60, 51, 101.

53. *Ibidem*, X, 102, 104, 134–135, 179.

54. *Ibidem*, X, 3.

55. *Ibidem*, X, 323, 317, 324.

56. Thomas Case, *Deliverance-Obstruction*, Epistle.

57. Thomas Goodwin, *The Great Interest of States & Kingdomes*, pp. 51, 52, 53.

58. Dated by Thomason October 24, 1645.

59. Jeremiah Burroughes, *A Sermon Preached before the Honorable House of Commons . . . August 26, 1646*, 1646, p. 33.

60. Jeremiah Burroughes, *A Sermon Preached before the Right Honourable the House of Peeres . . . the 26. of Novemb. 1645*, 1646, pp. 44–46.

61. John Owen, *A Vision of Unchangeable free mercy . . . in A Sermon Preached before the Honourable House of Commons, April 29 . . . Whereunto*

is annexed, A short defensative about Church-Government, . . . Toleration and Petitions about these things, 1646; William Bridge, *The Saints Hiding-Place in the time of Gods Anger. Presented in a Sermon to the Right Honorable the House of Lords . . . October 28. 1646,* 1647.

62. Ralph Cudworth, *A Sermon Preached before the Honourable House of Commons,* March 31, 1647, pp. 13–14.

63. Jeremy Taylor, θεολογία Ἐκλεκτικὴ *A Discourse of the Liberty of Prophesying,* 1647, Epistle, p. 6.

64. See above, pp. 236–37. Thomason entered Prynne's tract on January 2, 1645, and Goodwin's on January 8.

65. Matthews, *Calamy Revised,* p. 227. See above, pp. 145–46.

66. Goodwin, *Innocency and Truth Triumphing together,* 1645, Epistle.

67. Goodwin, *Divine Authority of the Scriptures Asserted,* 1648, p. 58.

68. Walwyn, *Walwyns Just Defence,* p. 29.

69. Goodwin, *Twelve considerable serious Cautions,* 1646, p. 3.

70. Goodwin, *Divine Authority of the Scriptures,* p. [17].

VIII: THE RISE OF THE LEVELLER PARTY

1. The principal source of information concerning Lilburne's character and career is his own tracts, supplemented by other tracts relating to the Leveller movement. An extensive manuscript bibliography of this material is to be found in the Huntington Library. The most authoritative account of the Leveller movement is still that of T. C. Pease, *The Leveller Movement,* 1916, and the most exact outline of Lilburne's career, with indication of sources, is still C. H. Firth's article in the *Dictionary of National Biography.* Additional information appears in M. A. Gibb, *John Lilburne,* 1947.

2. Sir Philip Warwick, quoted in Cromwell, *Writings and Speeches,* Abbott, I, 121.

3. Lilburne, *A Worke of the Beast,* in Haller, *Tracts on Liberty,* II; see also *Rise of Puritanism,* p. 434.

4. Lilburne, *Answer to Nine Arguments,* 1645, p. 43.

5. Lilburne, *Innocency and Truth Justified . . . Unto which is annext a Coppy of a Letter,* 1645; 'a Coppy of a Letter' is dated from the Fleet, November 11, 1638.

6. Lilburne, *A Copie of a Letter . . . to Mr. William Prinne,* 1645, p. 5.

7. *Ibidem,* pp. 2–4.

8. *Ibidem,* p. 6.

9. In *The Reasons of Lieu. Col. Lilbournes sending his Letter to Mr. Prin, humbly presented to the Honorable Committee of Examinations* (June 13, 1645), Lilburne followed up his quarrel with Prynne. In July, Prynne issued a counterblast to Lilburne and other assailants in *A Fresh Discovery of some Prodigious New Wandring-Blasing-Stars, & Firebrands,* and Lilburne defended himself in *The Copy of a Letter to a Friend* early in August. In October in *The Lyar Confounded,*

Prynne again reviewed Lilburne's iniquities, and in January the latter once more poured forth his story in print in *Innocency and Truth Justified*.

10. Prynne, *Lyar Confounded*, 'To the Impartiall Reader.'

11. Lilburne, *Just Mans Justification* (dated by the author June 6, 1646; reissued August, 1647).

12. Lilburne, *Free-mans Freedome*, 1646; *Legall Fundamentall Liberties*, p. 25; *Lords Journal*, June 11, 1646.

13. Lilburne, *Legall Fundamentall Liberties*, pp. 25, 26; *Lords Journal*, June 22, 23.

14. Lilburne, *Anatomy of the Lords Tyranny*, 1646, pp. 2–5, 12–15; *Londons Liberty In Chains discovered*, 1646, pp. 23–26; Walwyn, *Just Man in Bonds*, 1646; *Lords Journal*, July 11, 15, 1646.

15. Lilburne, *Anatomy of the Lords Tyranny*, p. 6; *Londons Liberty In Chains*, pp. 26–27.

16. *Lords Journal*, July 11, 1646; *Vox Plebis*, 1646, pp. 46–47.

17. *Vox Plebis*, pp. 46–47; Lilburne, *Anatomy of the Lords Tyranny*, p. 17.

18. *Commons Journal*, July 3, 1646.

19. Lilburne, *Londons Liberty In Chains*, pp. 65–70, 32. The text of the petition is given without date. The chronology of these episodes as reported by Lilburne is somewhat confused.

20. *Lords Journal*, September 16, 1646; *Vox Plebis*, p. 36.

21. *Vox Plebis*, pp. 45–58; Lilburne, *Liberty Vindicated against Slavery*, 1646; *Oppressed Mans Oppressions* [1646].

22. Lilburne, *Innocency and Truth Justified*, pp. 46–47.

23. Lilburne, *Londons Liberty In Chains*, pp. 8, 21, 13, 22, 72.

24. Andrew Horn, *Mirroir des Justices*, brought to light for the first time by Coke in the second part of the *Institutes*, was put into print in 1642 and translated into English in 1646; *The Mirror of Justices*, edited by W. J. Whittaker with an introduction by F. W. Maitland, 1895; Haller and Davies, *Leveller Tracts*, pp. 46–47.

25. *An Exact Collection*, 1645, p. 150.

26. Lilburne, *Englands Birth-Right*, 1645, pp. 1, 2, 36, in Haller, *Tracts on Liberty*.

27. *Vox Plebis*, pp. 2–3.

28. *Regall Tyrannie*, 1646, pp. 40–41.

29. John Goodwin, *Calumny Arraign'd and Cast* (January 31), 1645; Walwyn (anonymous), *Helpe to the right understanding of a Discourse Concerning Independency* (February 6); Henry Robinson, *The falsehood of Mr. William Pryn's Truth Triumphing* (May 8); Overton (anonymous), *The Araignement of Mr. Persecution* (April 8), *A sacred Decretall* (May 31), *Martins Eccho* (June 27), *The Nativity of Sir John Presbyter* (July 2), *The Ordinance for Tythes dismounted* (December 29).

30. Prynne, *Fresh Discovery*, p. 17; Lilburne, *Innocency and Truth*, pp. 4–5; Edwards, *Gangraena*, I, 67; *Commons Journal*, June 4, 1645.

31. Lilburne, *Innocency and Truth*, p. 29; *Commons Journal*, August 26, October 14, 1645.

32. *A Letter of the Ministers of the City of London . . . to the Reverend Assembly of Divines . . . Against Toleration* (January 29), 1646; Overton, *Divine Observations upon the London Ministers Letter* (January 24); [Walwyn], *Tolleration Justified* (January 29).

33. *To The Honourable The House of Commons Assembled in . . . Parliament: The humble Remonstrance and Petition of the Lord Major, Aldermen and Commons of the City of London in Common Council Assembled* (May 26) 1646.

34. Walwyn, *Walwyns Just Defence*, 1649, p. 31, in Haller and Davies, *Leveller Tracts*.

35. Lilburne, Letter to John Goodwin, February 13, 1646, in *Jonahs Cry out of the Whales belly* (July 26) 1647.

36. H. R. Plomer, 'Secret Printing During the Civil War,' *The Library*, 2d series, V (1904), 374–403.

37. Edwards, *Gangraena*, I, 96.

38. *A true Relation of all the remarkable Passages, and Illegal Proceedings . . . against William Larner . . . for selling eight printed sheets of paper . . . intituled, Londons last Warning*, 1646.

39. Reprinted in Haller, *Tracts on Liberty*, III.

40. Dated by Thomason, November 9, 1646.

41. Dated by the author, February 1, by Thomason, February 10; reprinted in Haller, *Tracts on Liberty*, III; *Lords Journal*, January 5, 6, 1647.

42. Overton, *Remonstrance*, p. 3.

43. Overton, *Arrow against all Tyrants*, pp. 3–5.

44. Walwyn, *Englands Lamentable Slaverie*, p. 8.

45. Bastwick, *A Just Defence of John Bastwick*, 1645, p. 17.

46. Edwards, *Gangraena*, I, 96.

47. Walwyn, *A Word More to Mr Thomas Edwards* (March 19); *An Antidote against Master Edwards* (June 10); *A Prediction of Mr. Edwards his Conversion* (August 11); *A Parable, or Consultation of Physitians* (October 29), 1646.

48. Walwyn, *A Demurre to the Bill for Preventing the Growth and Spreading of Heresie* [1646]; *Walwyns Just Defence*, 1649, p. 3.

49. Walwyn, *Pearle in a Dounghill*, p. 4.

50. *Walwins Wiles*, p. 18, reprinted in Haller and Davies, *Leveller Tracts*.

IX: THE AGREEMENT OF THE PEOPLE

1. *The Clarke Papers. Selections from the Papers of William Clarke, Secretary to the Council of the Army, 1647–1649*, 1891–1901, edited by C. H. Firth in Camden Society Publications, New Series, Nos. 49, 54, 61, 62, Vol. I, x–xi; *Puritanism and Liberty, Being the Army Debates (1647–9) from the Clarke*

Manuscripts with Supplementary Documents, edited by A. S. P. Woodhouse, 1938, p. [21]. See also Gardiner, *History of the Great Civil War*, III, 223–226.

2. *An Apollogie of the Souldiers to all their Commission Officers*, 1647 (dated by Thomason March 26); Woodhouse, *Puritanism and Liberty*, 396–398; Firth, *Clarke Papers*, I, xii; Cromwell, *Writings and Speeches*, Abbott, ed., I, 439–440.

3. Rushworth, *Historical Collections*, VI, 505; Gardiner, *History of the Great Civil War*, III, 279–280.

4. *Leveller Manifestoes of the Puritan Revolution*, edited by D. M. Wolfe, 1944, pp. 146–151; Rushworth, *Historical Collections*, VI, 510; Woodhouse, *Puritanism and Liberty*, pp. 401–403; Gardiner, *History of the Great Civil War*, 280–281.

5. Gardiner, *History of the Great Civil War*, III, 287–288; Cromwell, *Writings and Speeches*, ed. Abbott, I, 459–461; *Lords Journal*, June 11, 1647; Rushworth, *Historical Collections*, VI, 554.

6. Gardiner, *History of the Great Civil War*, III, 293–295; Haller and Davies, *Leveller Tracts*, pp. 51–63; Woodhouse, *Puritanism and Liberty*, pp. 403–409.

7. Gardiner, *Constitutional Documents*, pp. 316–326; Firth, *Clarke Papers*, I, 176–217; Cromwell, *Writings and Speeches*, ed. Abbott, I, 476–490; Woodhouse, *Puritanism and Liberty*, pp. 422–426.

8. Lilburne, Letter to Cromwell, July 1, 1647, in *Jonahs Cry out of the Whales belly*, p. [9].

9. Lilburne, Letter to Sir Thomas Fairfax, July 22, 1647, in *Juglers Discovered*, p. 3.

10. Lilburne, *Oppressed Mans Oppressions*, 1647; *Outcryes of Oppressed Commons*, 1647, pp. 3–4.

11. Lilburne, Letter to Cromwell, March 25, 1647, in *Jonahs Cry*, p. [3].

12. *Ibidem*, p. [1].

13. *Ibidem*, p. [2].

14. *Ibidem*, p. [3].

15. Lilburne, *Juglers Discovered*, p. 1.

16. Baxter, *Reliquiae*, p. 53.

17. Gardiner, *History of the Great Civil War*, III, 237.

18. *Ibidem*, III, 245.

19. Haller and Davies, *Leveller Tracts*, p. 61.

20. Firth, *Clarke Papers*, I, 170–173.

21. Lilburne, Letter to Fairfax, July 22, 1647, in *Juglers Discovered*, pp. 1, 3.

22. Lilburne, *Just Mans Justification*, pp. 1, 24, 25.

23. Firth, *Clarke Papers*, I, 2.

24. *Ibidem*, I, 22–23.

25. *Ibidem*, I, 82–83, 85–86.

26. Lilburne, *Grand Plea*, 1647, p. 22.

27. Haller and Davies, *Leveller Tracts*, pp. 64–87; Wolfe, *Leveller Manifestoes*, pp. 196–222.

28. *Walwins Wiles*, in Haller and Davies, *Leveller Tracts*, p. 85.

29. Wildman, *Case of the Armie*, 1647, in Haller and Davies, *Leveller Tracts*, p. 85.

30. Gardiner, *Constitutional Documents*, pp. 333–335; Woodhouse, *Puritanism and Liberty*, pp. 443–449; Wolfe, *Leveller Manifestoes*, pp. 223–234. For an account of the *Agreement* in its successive forms and texts, see J. W. Gough, 'The Agreements of the People,' *History*, New Series, Vol. XV, 1930–1931, pp. 334–341.

31. Clarendon, *History*, IV, 219–220.

32. Haller and Davies, *Leveller Tracts*, p. 55.

33. Haller, *Tracts on Liberty*, III, 353.

34. *Ibidem*, III, 369–370.

35. Lilburne, *Jonahs Cry*, p. [4].

36. Lilburne, *Rash Oaths*, p. 47.

37. *Ibidem*, p. 50.

38. Overton, *Appeale*, pp. 2, [24].

39. *The Heads of the Proposalls*, in Woodhouse, *Puritanism and Liberty*, p. 422.

40. *A Declaration of the Engagements, Remonstrances, Representations, Proposals, Desires and Resolutions from His Excellencey Sir Thomas Fairfax, and the generall Councel of the Army. For setling of His Majesty in His just Rights, the Parliament in their just Priviledges, and the Subjects in their Liberties and Freedomes*, 1647.

41. Woodhouse, *Puritanism and Liberty*, p. 7.

42. *Ibidem*, pp. 97, 98.

43. *Ibidem*, pp. 53, 55–58.

44. Lilburne, 'Defence for the honest Nownsubstantive Soldiers,' written in November, 1647, directly after the breakup of the meeting at Putney, in *Peoples Prerogative* (February), 1648, pp. 42–44; reprinted in Wolfe, *Leveller Manifestoes*, pp. 243–247.

45. Cromwell, *Writings and Speeches*, ed. Abbott, I, 557–560.

46. *Wonderfull Predictions*, 1648, with imprimatur dated December 29, 1647.

47. Rushworth, *Historical Collections*, VII, 943; Cromwell, *Writings and Speeches*, ed. Abbott, I, 571–572.

48. *Ibidem*, I, 575–576; Clement Walker, *Compleat History of Independency*, 1661, I, 71–72.

49. *Commons Journal*, November 9, 1647.

50. On October 15, 1647, Henry Marten as chairman of the committee of the house of commons which had been considering Lilburne's case finally made report to the house, and the report was referred to a new committee, headed by Sir John Maynard (*Commons Journal*, October 15, 1647). On October 20 Lilburne appeared before this committee and shortly afterward published *The grand Plea of Lieut. Col. John Lilburne, Prerogative Prisoner in the Tower of London, against the present tyrannicall House of Lords, which he delivered before an open Committee of the House of Commons, the twentieth day of October, 1647* (re-

corded by Thomason, November 1, 1647). Lilburne at once issued a brief summary of his argument, *For every Individuall Member of the Honourable House
of Commons,* dated November 11 (recorded by Thomason, November 13). On
November 14, the night before the demonstration at Corkbush Field, repressed
as mutiny by Cromwell, Lilburne is reported to have been near by at Ware (William Clarke, 'A full Relation of the Proceedings,' in Maseres, *Select Tracts,*
I, lvi–lviii). He also probably had some part in the Petition, *To the Supream
Authority of England, The Commons in Parliament assembled,* which was submitted to parliament on November 23 (*Commons Journal,* November 23, 1647;
recorded by Thomason, November 25). At the same time he submitted another
brief statement of his personal case, *A new complaint of an old grievance,* which
he dated November 23. About the same time, also, he prepared 'A Defence for
the honest Nownsubstantive Soldiers, against the proceedings of the Gen. Officers
to punish them by Martiall Law.' He again attacked the army leaders in *Englands Freedome, Souldiers Rights,* 1647, dated by the author December 14. He
wrote a defense of the petitioners of November 23 and another of certain London citizens who had refused to pay tithes and presently published the two together in *A Defiance to Tyrants* (recorded by Thomason, January 28, 1648).
He published all the manifestoes just mentioned, except *The grand Plea, The
Additionall Plea,* and the petition of November 23, in *The Peoples Prerogative,*
which appeared in February, 1648, after Lilburne had been remanded to the
Tower.

51. See Lilburne's epistle to the men of Hertfordshire, dated January 8, 1648,
and published in *Peoples Prerogative,* and the letter to the people of Kent, signed
by Lilburne, Wildman, and two associates and printed in *A Declaration of Some
Proceedings,* 1648, pp. 20–23; reprinted in Haller and Davies, *Leveller Tracts.*

52. Thomason recorded a copy, January 22, 1648; *Declaration of Some Proceedings,* pp. 51–57.

53. *Declaration of Some Proceedings,* p. 13. The petition is not known to
exist in separate printed form but appears in *Declaration of Some Proceedings,* pp.
26–34, and in Lilburne, *Impeachment of High Treason,* 1649, pp. 45–53.

54. Wildman, *Truths Triumph,* February 1, 1648; George Masterson, *The
Triumph stain'd,* licensed February 9, 1648; Jah. Norris, *A Lash for a Lyar,*
February 22, 1648.

55. *Declaration of Some Proceedings,* pp. 55–56.

56. *Declaration of Some Proceedings,* p. 35.

57. Lilburne, *Impeachment of High Treason,* pp. 24–25.

X: THE DISPENSATIONS OF PROVIDENCE

1. *His Maiesties Reason Why He cannot in Conscience consent to abolish
Episcopal Government,* 1660; *The Kings Majesties Answer to the Paper Delivered*

in by the Reverend Divines Attending the Honourable Commissioners, 1660; *The humble Answer of the Divines*, 1660; *His Majesties Finall Answer Concerning Episcopacie*, 1660, with note on the title page, 'Printed 1648. . . . Reprinted 1660.' See also Sir Edward Walker, 'Perfect Copies of all the Votes, Letters, Proposals and Answers, Relating unto . . . the Treaty Held at Newport' in *Historical Discourses*, 1705.

2. Lilburne, *Legall Fundamentall Liberties*, p. 28.

3. *To the right Honorable, The Commons of England In Parliament Assembled, The humble Petition*, 1648, in Haller and Davies, *Leveller Tracts*, pp. 146–155.

4. William Allen, *A faithful Memorial*, 1659, p. 5; *Somers Tracts*, VI, 501.

5. Lilburne, *Legall Fundamentall Liberties*, p. 30.

6. *A Remonstrance of His Excellency Thomas Lord Fairfax . . . and of the Generall Councell of Officers*, 1648, p. 67.

7. Lilburne, *Legall Fundamentall Liberties*, pp. 30–31.

8. *Ibidem*, pp. 33–34.

9. *The Declaration of his Excellency the Lord Fairfax and his General Council* [1648]; Rushworth, *Historical Collections*, VII, 1341.

10. Lilburne, *Foundations of Freedom*, 1648, reprinted in Wolfe, *Leveller Manifestoes*, pp. 291–303; *Legall Fundamentall Liberties*, pp. 34–36.

11. Woodhouse, *Puritanism and Liberty*, pp. 472–474; Firth, *Clarke Papers*, II, xvii–xix.

12. 'Humble Petition' prefixed to '*An Agreement of the People*' presented to parliament by the officers, January 20, 1649, reprinted in *Parliamentary or Constitutional History of England*, 1763, XVIII, 517.

13. Lilburne, *Foundations of Freedom*, p. 4.

14. Gardiner, *Constitutional Documents*, pp. 359–371.

15. Woodhouse, *Puritanism and Liberty*, 'The Whitehall Debates,' pp. 143–144, 130.

16. Cromwell, *Writings and Speeches*, Abbott, I, 574–575, 577, 619, 629, 632, 638, 644, 646.

17. *Ibidem*, I, 650, 677, 678.

18. *Ibidem*, I, 697.

19. *Ibidem*, I, 677, 696, 690.

20. *Commons Journal*, January 4, 1649.

21. *Cobbett's Complete Collection of State Trials*, 1809–1826, IV, 1052.

22. According to *Parliamentary History*, XVIII, 463, 477, Peters preached before parliament on December 8 and 22. The story given here is from *Cobbett's State Trials*, V, 1129–1130, and probably refers to December 22, since the witness says the incident occurred a few days before the act for the king's trial.

23. Thomas Brooks, *Gods Delight*, 1649, pp. 14–15; Thomas Watson, *Gods Anatomy upon Mans Heart*, 1649. An erasure is indicated in *Commons Journal*, December 30, 1648, at the point where thanks to Watson and an invitation to print would ordinarily appear.

24. Anthony Wood, *Athenae Oxoniensis,* ed. Bliss, IV, 98.
25. *Ibidem*, pp. 102, 98.
26. John Owen, *Certaine Treatises,* 1649.
27. Owen, *A Vision of Unchangeable free mercy,* 1646, pp. 27, 25.
28. Owen, *Eben-ezer,* pp. 13, 15, 22, 23.
29. Owen, *Sermon Preached to the . . . Commons,* 1649. pp. 48, 49, 64, 83.
30. *Ibidem*, pp. 41, 83.
31. ΟΥΡΑΝΩΝ ΟΥΡΑΝΙΑ. *The Shaking and Translating of Heaven and Earth,* 1649, p. 39.
32. Cromwell, *Writings and Speeches,* Abbott, I, 416.
33. Peter Sterry, *The Clouds In Which Christ Comes,* 1647, p. 29.
34. Stephen Marshall, *The Sinne of Hardnesse of Heart,* 1648, p. 25.
35. William Gouge, *The Right Way,* 1648, p. 27.
36. *A Testimony to the Truth of Jesus Christ,* pp. 24–25, 30, 31.
37. Paul Best was imprisoned February 14, 1645, upon the betrayal of his private papers to the authorities. His published writings were: *A Letter of Advice unto the Ministers assembled at Westminster,* 1646; *To certaine honourable persons of the House of Commons,* 1646, dated by Thomason August 13 with a manuscript note, 'He denied the Sacred Trinitie'; *Mysteries Discovered,* 1647.
38. John Biddle was imprisoned upon the betrayal to the authorities of a private statement of his opinions. His *Twelve Arguments Drawn out of the Scriptures, Wherein the commonly received Opinion touching the Deity of the Holy Spirit, is clearly and fully refuted,* 1647, was burned by order of the house of commons. *Commons Journal,* September 6, 1647.
39. Laurence Clarkson, who had a long career in various sects, was first prosecuted as a Baptist in 1645. His *Pilgrimage of Saints* was condemned by Thomas Edwards in *Gangraena I* and frequently by other writers but is not now extant, so far as I know.
40. For Goodwin's *Hagiomastix* and *Divine Authority of Scriptures,* see pp. 249–250. Goodwin animadverted on the London ministers' *Testimony* in *Sion-Colledg visited* (February 1) 1648, to which John Vicars responded in *Coleman-street Conclave Visited* (March 21), including a portrait of Goodwin with a windmill above his head blown upon by pride and error. William Jenkyn followed up the attack with Ἀλλοτριοεπίσκοπος. *The Busie Bishop* (March 30), Goodwin replied in Νεοφυτοπρεσβυτερος, *or, The Yongling Elder* (June 15), and Jenkyn countered with Ὁδηγος Τυφλος *The Blinde Guide, or the Doting Doctor* (November 23, 1648.
41. *A Serious and faithfull Representation,* 1649, pp. 11–15.
42. Goodwin, *Might and Right,* p. 14.
43. Milton, *Tenure, Works,* V, 7.
44. *Ibidem*, pp. 9, 1, 3, 6–7.
45. *Cobbett's Complete Collection of State Trials,* IV, 1069–1070; John Cook, *King Charls his Case,* 1649, pp. 6–7, 22–23.
46. Milton, *Tenure, Works,* V, 18, 19, 7–8.

47. *Ibidem*, pp. 32, 38.
48. Milton, *History of Britain, Works*, X, 134–135.
49. Milton, *Tenure, Works*, V, 2, 5, 35, 36, 39, 44, 45, 46, 56–57.
50. *Ibidem*, pp. 39–40.
51. Milton, *Reason of Church-government, Works*, III, 229.

Index

Index

391

Rogers, Richard, 35, 49

Rutherford, Samuel, 104, 118, 221; sermon, 121; idea of basis of state, 349; *Due Right of Presbyteries*, 118

St. German, Christopher, *Dialogue in English . . . betweene a Doctor . . . and a Student*, 70, 72, 272, 274

St. John, Oliver, 36, 73, 114, 124, 132, 133, 330

St. Margaret's, Westminster, parliamentary sermons at, 16, 18, 26, 29, 66, 67-68, 100, 103, 203, 246, 335, 336, 364; Covenant subscribed at, 103

St. Paul's Church, ministers engaged to preach at, 68

Sallust, 241, 244

Saltmarsh, John, 141, 195, 208, 293, 344; antinomianism, 198; attacked by Edwards: reply, 226, 227; spreading ideas alarming to Presbyterians, 255; encouragement to soldiers, 299; warning to Fairfax and Cromwell, 313; *Dawnings of Light*, 141, 198; *Free-Grace . . .* , 198; *Groanes for Liberty*, 226; *Holy Discoveries and Flames*, 198; *Reasohs for Unitie, Peace, and Love*, 226; *Smoke in the Temple*, 198; *Sparkles of Glory*, 198; excerpts, 199 f.

Salvation, elect bound to work for, 18; by faith, 29, 82, 83, 164, 247; essence of, 152; by God's grace, 199

Saxons, exaltation of, 273

Schism, Milton charged with promoting, 56; rise of, 128-34

Scotland, conditions before 1638: contention with Charles I, 3-9; National Covenant, 7; commissioners sent to English parliament, 21; Solemn League and Covenant, commissioners sent to Westminster Assembly, 103-9; Second Civil War, invasion of England, defeat by Cromwell, 319; Church of, kirk and covenant, 3-9; leaders' conception of responsibility of rulers, 5; general assembly's attack on bishops: rejection of prayer book and prelacy:

ordered to dissolve, 7; need to secure freedom and solidarity of, 8; resistance to royal authority in, 10; government of, 104-5; influence on people, 105-6, 112; General Assembly, 1581, 6; at Perth, 1616, 6; at Glasgow, 1638, 7, 10, 105; at Edinburgh, 1645, 222; *see also* Presbyterianism *and* Westminster Assembly

Scottish commissioners, bafflement at Westminster, 109, 111; effort to induce parliament to take sterner measures with dissenters, 121; purpose in coming to Westminster, 221; final reliance on Scottish army, ultimate frustration, 222

Scriptures, *see* Bible

Sectaries, in command of army, 222; attacked by Edwards, 227, 228; centralized control over spiritual life rejected by, 238; disbandment of army to get rid of, 288

Sects, Milton charged with promoting multiplication of, 56; leaders of out-and-out, 107; multiplication of: separatist character, 203; differences and peculiarities: leaders, 204

Sedgwick, Obadiah, 100

Selden, John, 113, 222; quoted, 12, 234 f.; against clerical pretension, 220; most formidable critic of Westminster divines, 230 ff.; on tithes, 231; called before Star Chamber, 232; sponsor of Petition of Right, 233, 234; in prison: argument against Grotius, 233; *History of Tythes*, 231 f.; *Table-Talk . . . Discourses of John Selden Esq. . . .* , 234

Seneca, 170, 172; quoted, 171

Separatists, 11, 167; Walwyn's defense of, 173; *see also* Sectaries

Serious and faithfull Representation of Ministers . . . London, A, 345-48

Sermons, importance as propaganda, 16; preached in London and Westminster, 26; epic of spiritual war set forth in, 28; preached under official auspices, 67; usually published, 68; parliamen-